Humana Festival 2004
The Complete Plays

Humana Inc. is one of the nation's largest
managed health care companies
with approximately 6 million members in its health care plans.

The Humana Foundation was established in 1981
to support the educational, social, medical and cultural development
of communities in ways that reflect
Humana's commitment to social responsibility
and an improved quality of life.

SMITH AND KRAUS PUBLISHERS
Contemporary Playwrights / Collections

Humana Festival: 20 One-Acts Plays 1976–1996
Humana Festival '93: The Complete Plays
Humana Festival '94: The Complete Plays
Humana Festival '95: The Complete Plays
Humana Festival '96: The Complete Plays
Humana Festival '97: The Complete Plays
Humana Festival '98: The Complete Plays
Humana Festival '99: The Complete Plays
Humana Festival 2000: The Complete Plays
Humana Festival 2001: The Complete Plays
Humana Festival 2002: The Complete Plays
Humana Festival 2003: The Complete Plays

New Playwrights: The Best Plays of 1998
New Playwrights: The Best Plays of 1999
New Playwrights: The Best Plays of 2000
New Playwrights: The Best Plays of 2001
New Playwrights: The Best Plays of 2002
New Playwrights: The Best Plays of 2003
New Playwrights: The Best Plays of 2004

Women Playwrights: The Best Plays of 1992
Women Playwrights: The Best Plays of 1993
Women Playwrights: The Best Plays of 1994
Women Playwrights: The Best Plays of 1995
Women Playwrights: The Best Plays of 1996
Women Playwrights: The Best Plays of 1997
Women Playwrights: The Best Plays of 1998
Women Playwrights: The Best Plays of 1999
Women Playwrights: The Best Plays of 2000
Women Playwrights: The Best Plays of 2001
Women Playwrights: The Best Plays of 2002
Women Playwrights: The Best Plays of 2003

If you require pre-publication information about upcoming Smith and Kraus books, you may receive our semi-annual catalogue free of charge, by sending your name and address to *Smith and Kraus Catalogue, PO Box 127, Lyme NH 03768. Or call us at (603) 643-6431, fax (603) 643-1831. www.smithandkraus.com.*

Humana Festival 2004
The Complete Plays

Edited by
Tanya Palmer and Adrien-Alice Hansel

Contemporary Playwrights Series

SK
A Smith and Kraus Book

A Smith and Kraus Book
Published by Smith and Kraus, Inc.
177 Lyme Road, Hanover, New Hampshire 03755
www.SmithKraus.com

Manufactured in the United States of America

Cover and Text Design by Julia Hill Gignoux
Layout by Jennifer McMaster
Cover artwork © Istvan Orosz

First Edition: March 2005
10 9 8 7 6 5 4 3 2 1

Library of Congress Cataloguing-in-Publication Data
Contemporary Playwrights Series
ISSN 1067-9510
ISBN 1-57525-385-2

Contents

Acknowledgments

The editors wish to thank the following persons for their invaluable assistance in compiling this volume:

David Clark
Erin Detrick
Trish Pugh Jones
Dan LeFranc
Marc Masterson
Jennifer McMaster
Cathy Mellen
Steve Moulds
Jeff Rodgers
James Seacat
Kyle J. Schmidt
Kyle Shepherd
Wanda Snyder
Alexander Speer
JoSelle Vanderhooft
John Zalewski

Beth Blickers
John Buzzetti
Michael Cardonick
Val Day
Morgan Jenness
Sarah Jane Leigh
Bruce Ostler

Foreword

Plays that stand the test of time. Plays that are of the moment. Plays that are universal. Plays that spring from a strong sense of place. Plays that look outward to the world. Plays that celebrate an inward poetic journey. Plays of language. Plays of ideas. Plays by young artists. Plays by women...

If 2004 was considered by many to be one of the most successful Humana Festivals in recent memory, it is because all of this (and more) is represented in the plays contained in this volume. Here is a vibrant testament to the vitality of the contemporary American playwright. The many facets and styles of expression in this collection are unified by a heightened sense of theatricality and an implicit understanding that great plays are made in three-dimensional space with fine actors, strong design and an audience to receive them.

For the twenty-sixth consecutive year, the festival was made possible by a grant from The Humana Foundation. This remarkable support represents one of the longest continual corporate contributions to an American performing arts group. We are extremely proud of this long association as well as the abundant legacy of new plays that their generosity has made possible. With the addition of these fascinating works from 2004, we continue to celebrate and support great writing for the stage.

Marc Masterson
Artistic Director
Actors Theatre of Louisville

Editors' Note

Critics, theatre practitioners and lovers of theatre often struggle to describe the experience of delving into the world of a new play. Dramaturg and teacher Elinor Fuchs evocatively describes the experience of reading a play as taking a "visit to a small planet." Sometimes that planet seems familiar: its rules, assumptions, values—its topography—all closely resemble our own. Other times that world is wildly unfamiliar: landing there feels akin to arriving in a country where one doesn't speak the language or understand the culture, and even those rules we assume we'll share—the laws of gravity, the forward movement of time—cannot to be taken for granted.

The sheer inventiveness required to craft a play is stunning. Playwrights create not only a compelling narrative and engaging characters, but a distinct universe for them to inhabit. That spirit of inventiveness was evident in abundance at the 2004 Humana Festival of New American Plays. In *Sans-culottes in the Promised Land*, Kirsten Greenidge's lush, lyrical and surprising new play about an upper-middle class Black family, metaphor supplants the laws of nature, causing a forest to grow through the floorboards of their McMansion. Naomi Iizuka's *At the Vanishing Point* is a stunning portrait of a Louisville community developed through interviews and research and performed site-specifically in the neighborhood that inspired its creation. The play ruptures the boundary between the living and the dead, reminding us of the continued presence of the past in our lives and our landscape. Playwright Melanie Marnich redefines a world first created in the seventeenth century by Jacobean dramatists Thomas Middleton and Walter Raleigh. In *Tallgrass Gothic*, the decidedly dark story of *The Changeling* is transported to the contemporary Midwest, with similarly shocking and bloody results. Gina Gionfriddo's biting satire *After Ashley* pits her young hero and his dedication to the hard truth against a society increasingly seduced by media spin. And in two plays, *Kid-Simple* by Jordan Harrison and *The Ruby Sunrise* by Rinne Groff, invention itself takes centre stage, introducing us to two fiery and determined young inventresses whose vision for a changed world transforms their own lives in the process.

As playwrights push to match the stories they tell to the form of the world that contains them, so Actors Theatre has a tradition of challenging playwrights to respond to new structures. This year's festival featured the ethical round robin *Fast and Loose*, in which four writers responded to four ethical questions and each wrote part of the resultant four storylines. The ten-minute plays—developed by Actors Theatre and now a standard feature of the Humana Festival—featured sharp and distinct takes on the form: *A Bone Close to My Brain*, Dan Dietz's meditation on brotherly love and responsibility; Stephen Dietz's abrasive media satire *The Spot*; *Kuwait*, Vincent Delaney's interrogation of journalistic freedom and accountability under the fire of the first Iraqi war and Craig Wright's *Foul Territory*, which finds in the absurd curve of foul balls two drastically different views of fate and human will.

This spirit of inventiveness—of pioneering impulses, grand dreams and wild ambitions—is an ideal subject for the Humana Festival, an event built on grand ideas. Since 1979, when Jon Jory first conceived the idea of creating a home for American playwrights in Louisville, Actors Theatre has had the joy and privilege of working with an ever-increasing cadre of talented, passionate playwrights. We hope we have succeeded in doing justice to these worlds, created in private by playwrights, brought briefly to life through the generous support of the Humana Foundation and the energy and commitment of the countless artists who work tirelessly each spring, and offered here to you, as a blueprint to these luminous and distinct small planets.

Tanya Palmer and Adrien-Alice Hansel

Kuwait
by Vincent Delaney

BIOGRAPHY

Vincent Delaney's play include *The Robeson Tapes*, *Perpetua*, *MLK and the FBI*, and *Kuwait*, which shared the 2004 Heideman Award. A full-length version of *Kuwait* won the New Play Award at the Sonoma County Rep, and was featured at Fresh Ink at Illusion Theatre. His work has been developed at the Alabama Shakespeare Festival, Woolly Mammoth, the Empty Space, the Jungle, and PlayLabs. Commissions include A Contemporary Theatre, the Cleveland Playhouse, the Drilling Company, and a Jerome Commission from Commonweal Theatre Company. His short play *Acceleration Red* won the Lamia Ink! playwriting contest. He is the recipient of a Bush Foundation Fellowship, a McKnight Fellowship, and an Artist Grant from the Seattle Arts Commission. Mr. Delaney is a Core Member of the Playwrights Center, and a graduate of the UC Davis M.F.A. Playwriting program.

HUMANA FESTIVAL PRODUCTION

Kuwait premiered at the Humana Festival of New American Plays in April 2004. It was directed by Meredith McDonough with the following cast:

Rachel . . . . Julie Jesneck
Kelsey . . . . Asa Somers
Miles . . . . Stephen Thorne

and the following production staff:

Scenic Designer . . . . Paul Owen
Costume Designer . . . . John P. White
Lighting Designer . . . . Paul Werner
Sound Designer . . . . Benjamin Marcum
Properties Designer . . . . Doc Manning
Stage Manager . . . . Debra A. Freeman
Assistant Stage Managers . . . . Michael Domue
Brady Ellen Poole
Dramaturg . . . . Steve Moulds
Assistant Dramaturg . . . . Dan LeFranc

CHARACTERS

RACHEL, a journalist
KELSEY, a soldier
MILES, an escort

SETTING

A hotel room in the Middle East

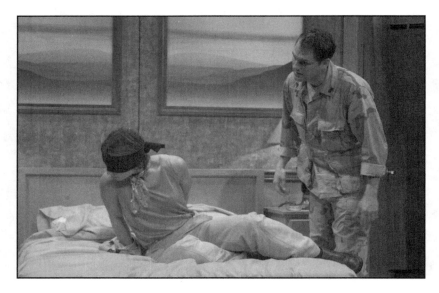

Julie Jesneck and Asa Somers
in *Kuwait*

28th Annual Humana Festival of New American Plays
Actors Theatre of Louisville, 2004
photo by Harlan Taylor

Kuwait

A hotel room in the Middle East. A single bed, table and chair, bathroom to the side, a window downstage which looks out over a city. Several bland desert prints on the wall.

The door bursts open. RACHEL stumbles in, blindfolded and handcuffed. She's followed by KELSEY, in uniform, who stands in the door, holding her travel bag.

RACHEL: I'm suing, I'm suing, you are so sued. You personally, whoever you are, and I know you hear me, you have got legal bills like you can't imagine. Go ask for a raise, because you owe by the minute.
(She collides with the bed.)
Is this a bed? All right. My driver knows I left this morning, because he was with me. He is aware, do you hear me, he is most certainly aware that I've been kidnapped and he will be looking, I said he will be looking for me!
(KELSEY shuts the door. It clicks softly. She hears it.)
My name is Rachel Cayman, I'm a correspondent for the *Times* and an American citizen. Hello? If anyone else is here please say something. My paper will offer a reward, in dollars.
(KELSEY unpacks RACHEL's bag. He lays out her equipment: camera, tape recorder, notebooks, purse.)
Is that my bag? Are you in my bag? Son of a bitch. I know we're back in Saudi, okay? I timed it. Ten thousand five hundred seconds. One hundred eighty minutes. Three God damn hours in the back of your non-air conditioned Jeep. Do you know who I am? I am going to own you, soldier.

KELSEY: Unescorted pool reporters are not allowed in the combat zone.

RACHEL: It speaks. They must have raised the bar for recruits.
(KELSEY unsnaps her camera case.)
Don't touch that. Don't. All right, I snuck into the zone. I admit it. I broke the rules. I took pictures of dirt. I interviewed a camel. There's nothing on my film but sand dunes. Wait. Asshole!
(He pulls the film out of her camera, unravels it.)
They teach you this at boot camp? You're very good at it.

KELSEY: Per the standing orders regarding breach of the combat zone, you will be detained here for twenty-four hours.

RACHEL: What the fuck are you talking about? The war will be over in twenty-four hours.

KELSEY: At the end of that time, you will be released to the custody of your
military escort.

RACHEL: Hey asshole, did you hear me?

(She lurches toward him.)

KELSEY: Please desist. I don't wish to use restraints.

RACHEL: Oh, but they'd be so much fun.

(She sits. He reads through her journals.)

So you pulled guard duty. Poor kid. If I were you I'd be pissed. Maybe
you'd like to talk about it. I've got time.

(He tears pages out of her journals, sets them aside.)

That's my notebook, isn't it? Well done. You've arrived, soldier. All those
push-ups paid off. Here you are, on the front line, taking on a journalist.
Fair warning, I know yoga. Isn't the blindfold kind of melodramatic? Or
is this bedspread classified?

KELSEY: The rules of engagement provide for the use of necessary correctives.

RACHEL: Could you say that again?

KELSEY: The rules of engagement provide for the use of necessary correctives.

RACHEL: Thank you. Now tell me what the fuck it means.

KELSEY: You were issued the directives regarding press access. You are advised
to read them.

RACHEL: Okay, hand me my copy.

(He dumps her purse out.)

Help yourself. You smoke? That sounds like a yes. Pack of Marlboros in
my purse. Go ahead.

KELSEY: I don't smoke.

RACHEL: Come on soldier, got to do better than that. I hear nicotine in your
voice. What you gonna do, you get captured? *(Accent.)* American
Yankee, when marches the Great Satan on our cities? *(Mimics KELSEY.)* I
don't know. But I swear I don't smoke. *(Herself.)* Just trying to improve
your mood.

(He pulls out a mini-tape recorder, pops out the cassette.)

These cuffs should be tighter. I'm not even getting chafed here.

KELSEY: What's on this cassette?

RACHEL: Motley Crüe. Serious, I'm a metal freak. Play it if you don't believe
me. Play it!

(He sets the tape down.)

Do you even care that I'll be fired for this?

KELSEY: Sorry if the war is inconveniencing you.

RACHEL: Could that have been irony? Did I just hear sharp, caustic sarcasm from the mouth of my military keeper? Do that again.

(KELSEY *looks at her cigarettes.*)

Go ahead, light up.

(*Startled, he goes to her and checks her blindfold.*)

Don't worry, it's pitch black in here. I just smelt the craving.

KELSEY: If you require any special considerations please make a request to the duty officer.

RACHEL: I have a request.

KELSEY: Sanitary facilities are provided. Upon request, a female officer will escort you to them.

RACHEL: I have a request.

KELSEY: Special dietary needs may not be met.

RACHEL: I have a request.

KELSEY: What is your request?

RACHEL: Tell me your name, rank and serial number.

(*Silence.*)

In that case I'll just sit here and picture you. I'm guessing five foot six. That's below minimum. Let's say five six and a half. Five seven in boots. Extremely broad. Squat body. Arms won't fully extend. All that muscle mass. Completely bald on top. Sort of a Bruce Willis, Sylvester Stallone, Wallace Shawn hybrid. Am I close?

(*He lights a cigarette.*)

Guess I nailed it. Make yourself at home, soldier.

(*He watches her, smoking.*)

So how big's your gun? You mean you don't have one? I am so sorry. If you did have one, I'm sure it would be a big one. What you do to get stuck with me? Must have been bad. Let me guess. Panic under fire? Oops, shouldn't have said that.

(*He smokes.*)

Where's mine?

KELSEY: Smoking is not permitted.

RACHEL: Won't tell if you don't. Give me a drink. Piece of shit.

KELSEY: That's not how we ask.

RACHEL: Do you know who I am? Do you know how much I make? Do you know how utterly insignificant you are, right here, right now? Do you?

(*Beat.*)

May I have a drink, please?

(KELSEY takes a cup to the sink.)

No, a drink. It's been a bitch of a day. I want a beer.

KELSEY: A beer.

RACHEL: Don't tell me there's no beer.

KELSEY: There's no beer.

RACHEL: Oh come on. You are old enough. Aren't you?

(Beat.)

This could be your first beer. Ever. A beautiful thing.

KELSEY: The consumption of beer is not permitted.

RACHEL: Okay, how about a martini? You don't have a sense of humor, do you?

KELSEY: If you need anything, please ring the bell.

RACHEL: What bell? Wait, that was humor. That was very nice.

KELSEY: This isn't Motley Crüe. Is it?

RACHEL: Would I lie to you?

(KELSEY turns the tape on. Motley Crüe roars forth. RACHEL busts out laughing.)

I got him! I got him! I love it.

(He puts the cigarette out, paces.)

Sorry. Motley Crüe just really gets me off. That heavy metal beat, sounds like a Scud missile. BOOM da da BOOM da da BOOM BOOM BOOM, primal, like gutting the enemy with a brick. Maybe that's what you lack, soldier. Little more AC/DC in your life. Get your hormone level up. Make those little jewels finally drop down. Let's pick a band for you. Slayer? Too masculine. Prong? Doesn't really fit, does it? I know: Anthrax. That wasn't funny. Social gaffe, social gaffe. Open a window, I'm hot.

KELSEY: There's no window.

RACHEL: No window?

KELSEY: We're underground.

RACHEL: We're in a hotel room.

KELSEY: It's a bunker.

RACHEL: A what?

KELSEY: This is an interrogation facility.

RACHEL: Interrogation? What, torture?

KELSEY: We wouldn't do that, would we?

RACHEL: Oh my God, I got the one with a sense of humor.

(KELSEY goes in the bathroom, breathes deep, washes his hands.)

What are the chances of getting this thing off my face?

KELSEY: Not good.

RACHEL: National security?

KELSEY: No. I just don't feel like it.

RACHEL: We are getting familiar, aren't we? Hey! Asshole! Even prisoners of war have rights!

(He returns, holding his towel.)

KELSEY: You're not a prisoner of war.

RACHEL: What do you expect me to do in here?

KELSEY: Enjoy the view.

RACHEL: You chicken-shit babysitter. Just cause they don't want your ass holding a rifle, don't keep me down! I'll take fire! I won't cower on guard duty! I know you hear me, you coward! I have a story to file, you piece-of-shit underage no-balls babysitter!

(She leaps up. He comes to her, graceful, swift, and takes her back to the bed. He straddles her, whispers his speech right in her ear.)

KELSEY: It's brick in here. Floor to ceiling. So dark you can't hardly see. Scratches on the wall. Long ones, from fingers, broken nails. Stains, blotches all over. One just by your head. Up on the ceiling, that's a blood spatter. Big one, spreading out, dried up. Here, feel it.

(He takes her hand, brushes the wall.)

That's a Polaroid. Taped on the wall. All around you, on the walls, pictures, couple hundred. Souvenirs, leftovers. Guys bleeding, guys dead, guys getting shocked. Guys getting drowned. We use a basin. Just a little one, maybe half-gallon. Take a long while, drown a guy that way. Shove his face in, thirty seconds, let him breathe. Shove him back in, sixty seconds…let him breathe. Make him hope. Think he might live. Then we start talking to you. How's it feel? What you think about, in the water? You see death in there? You see him looking up at you, going for your eyes? Shove your face in…in…and maybe…you don't…get to breathe any more.

(KELSEY flicks his towel at her.)

RACHEL: Why are you doing this to me?

(KELSEY recovers, gets away from her, takes his gun out, breaks it down.)

I want the female escort.

KELSEY: You don't have to go.

RACHEL: Yes I do, I have to go.

KELSEY: No you don't.

RACHEL: I have to go.

KELSEY: You're faking.

RACHEL: I know my own bodily functions!

KELSEY: No.

RACHEL: How can you tell?

KELSEY: You learn.

RACHEL: Is it a tone of voice thing?

KELSEY: You learn.

RACHEL: My driver is looking for me.

KELSEY: Your driver is dead.

RACHEL: Dead.

KELSEY: Land mine. On the way back.

RACHEL: He's dead?

KELSEY: Things happen.

RACHEL: No.

KELSEY: How much information do you really want?

(Silence.)

RACHEL: So you do have a gun.

(He steps to her, holding his gun.)

KELSEY: Not everybody gets interrogated. Maybe you're sound asleep. In the dark, in a trench. Can't hear a thing. Like a tomb in there. Air is warm, heavy, desert air. And we bring a bulldozer, right over you, and do we wake you first? Do we say, get out, leave your weapon, just get out and walk away, we don't want you, we know you didn't choose this, we know you're a person? No, we bury you. Under all that sand. Not crushed, buried.

(He pulls a blanket up and drapes it over her.)

Still alive. Maybe you hear it, for a second, that trembling, and then we punch through the berm, we move the sand and you're under it. Press on your chest, press on your face, all that sand, like an avalanche, but warm, trickling, sliding like snakes, can't even open your eyes and if you did what could you see? What could you see? On your head, on your eyes. So quiet now. Twenty feet of sand, trickling in your ears, still breathing, so quiet. What can you see? You're going to live a few more seconds, you can hope, no reason not to hope, and what do you hope for? What do you want now? Tell me what you want now!

(RACHEL screams. MILES enters.)

MILES: Okay, this looks cozy. Let me guess, charades. She too cold? Ma'am, are you too cold? You want to take that off her, please, Kelsey?

(KELSEY pulls the blanket off RACHEL.)

Blindfolded? Whose bright idea was that? I guess the bedspread's classified. How you doing in there?

RACHEL: Okay.

MILES: Is there a reason you're all tied up?

RACHEL: I've been a bad girl.

MILES: Damn right you have, Rachel. Sure gave me the slip. Wraps her face like a Bedouin and saunters right past me in the lobby. Right out into the desert. Takes a driver, and off she goes. Without me. Really fucked me over with my C.O. Guess what my punishment is?

RACHEL: More time with me.

MILES: You ought to enlist, you're sharp.

RACHEL: Where am I?

MILES: Where do you think you are? Let's get this shit off you.

(MILES pulls off her blindfold. She takes him in, the room, the walls, and finally KELSEY, who stands to the side, looking away. Silence.)

Am I missing something here?

RACHEL: When we went in, did we bury any Iraqis?

MILES: Bury Iraqis?

RACHEL: In the sand. With bulldozers. Did we bury any of them alive?

MILES: I'd say the cuffs are a tad melodramatic, wouldn't you?

RACHEL: I asked you a question.

MILES: Let's get you decent. Key, please.

(MILES holds out his hand, but KELSEY ignores him, goes and uncuffs RACHEL. He steps back. They stare at each other.)

Somebody want to tell me what's going on here? Has this soldier behaved in an inappropriate manner?

RACHEL: Not at all.

MILES: So, good news is, your paper pitched a holy diva, and now you're back down in the lobby, full credential. Bad news is, I'm down there with you. With my career fucked. So let's go.

RACHEL: No.

MILES: No?

RACHEL: Go on back, Miles. Kelsey will bring me to the lobby.

MILES: I'm your escort. It's my job.

RACHEL: He'll bring me.

(MILES stares at them both, starts to speak, then gives up and exits. A beat.)

Do you want to talk about it?

(KELSEY looks away, then at her. He sits. Blackout.)

END OF PLAY

A Bone Close to My Brain
by Dan Dietz

BIOGRAPHY

Dan Dietz's plays include *Tilt Angel, tempOdyssey, Dirigible* and *Blind Horses*, and have been seen in New York, Los Angeles, Seattle, Austin and elsewhere. His short play *Trash Anthem* received the 2003 Heideman Award from Actors Theatre and was produced in that year's Humana Festival of New American Plays. Other honors include a James A. Michener Playwriting Fellowship, a Josephine Bay Paul Fellowship and the Austin Critics Table Award for Best New Play. He was a finalist for the 2001 and 2002 Princess Grace Awards and a nominee for the 2004 American Theatre Critics/Steinberg Award. Mr. Dietz is a resident company member of Salvage Vanguard Theater.

HUMANA FESTIVAL PRODUCTION

A Bone Close to My Brain premiered at the Humana Festival of New American Plays in April 2004. It was directed by Meredith McDonough with the following cast:

Man . . . . Michael A. Newcomer

and the following production staff:

Scenic Designer . . . . Paul Owen
Costume Designer. . . . . Shana Lincoln
Lighting Designer . . . . Paul Werner
Sound Designer . . . . Benjamin Marcum
Properties Designer . . . . Doc Manning
Stage Manager . . . . Debra A. Freeman
Assistant Stage Managers . . . . Michael Domue
Brady Ellen Poole
Dramaturg . . . . Steve Moulds
Assistant Dramaturg . . . . Erin Detrick

Michael A. Newcomer
in *A Bone Close to My Brain*

28th Annual Humana Festival of New American Plays
Actors Theatre of Louisville, 2004
photo by Harlan Taylor

A Bone Close to My Brain

A MAN stands beside an easel with a large white pad on it;
he uncaps a marker and draws a big tooth on the paper.

MAN: today my brother is a dentist
    he knows all about these little bones
    huddling tight inside your mouth
    incisors, bicuspids, wisdoms way in the back
    he knows them all
    their shapes and contours
    their uses and misuses
    the damage they can reasonably take
    from impact or decay
    my brother is a dentist today

    i don't mean he just got certified
    i don't mean he opened a practice
    i mean that today my brother is a dentist
    just like yesterday he was a radiologist
    and last month he was a reporter for the *new york times*
    only two things about him stay the same
    day in, day out
    his address, this tidy little house in new jersey
    which we've shared for the nine years
    since our parents passed away
    and the fact that i am his big brother
    no matter what else he erases and remakes
    inside his mind
    these two facts sit solid and bonehard
    within his head

    he can't feed himself
    he doesn't grasp the need to fuel his body
    he can't bathe himself
    left on his own, he'll either starve or stink himself to death
    he doesn't live in his skin, his stomach, his fingernails
    he lives here

in the bulbous gray organ
just above and behind
the roof of his mouth
that's his house

(MAN *draws a roof and windows on the tooth, maybe even a chimney with a curlicue of smoke.*)

the rest of him
skin, stomach, fingernails
is like a yard

(*He draws a yard by the house.*)

a yard that needs a full time, round the clock landscaper
to keep from going to hell
that's me
i tend him
he trusts me
anyone else comes near the yard
(skin, stomach, fingernails)
he screams, hits, bites
gets arrested, gets bailed out, forgets, etc.
but not me
he would never hurt me

except for today
today he will hurt me
in about ten minutes
he will walk in here
lay me down on this chair
and tear out of my head
a single, white, completely healthy
tooth

(*He flips to a new sheet, draws a new tooth.*)

and i will let him

i can't get used to the way teeth look
strange
spiny
like they belong on the outside
of some prehistoric fish
not sprouting from my face
maybe i should smile more
but i was always that way
even as a kid
i can't find one picture of me
smiling showing my teeth
always just a twist of the lips
to indicate a grin

gerald always smiled with teeth
he's smiling right now
in the kitchen, sterilizing his instruments
which consist of a penlight
and a pair of pliers

he's brilliant
he learns this stuff in just hours
pores over textbooks
random ones i pick up
from the public library
to keep his house

(He draws a roof on the tooth, draws a yard.)

occupied

(Draws a happy stick figure waving from the house.)

he dives into the volumes
(the only medication he'll accept)
and the next time i see him
he's completely reborn
he's memorized it all

he's a dentist
(radiologist, reporter)
and he can't remember a day
when he wasn't a dentist
(radiologist, reporter)

he was reading tolstoy at age eight
studying fractals at eleven
those huge numbers
blooming out infinite all over the place
numbers that want to be pictures
he called them

what does a number do
if it wants to be a picture

he grew into adolescence
his head devouring everything
like his eyes were mouths
awards, acclaim
the "g" word tossed about
(and i don't mean "gerald")
by people important enough to believe
he was slated to graduate high school
before his sixteenth birthday

then mom and dad died
when our house
got broken into

(Draws a hole on the house and an arrow pointing into the hole.)

attempted robbery
became
attempted rape
became

i was away at college
i didn't have to come downstairs
didn't have to try to stop it
try to save
but gerald

he was fifteen
the same age as the boy
they caught and convicted
after finding his skin cells
beneath my mother's

i moved back home
took a break from school
gerald however refused to take a break
so close to graduation
less than a year
but the things he started saying
and doing

it was like his mind had twisted
to indicate a person

(Points to the person waving from the house.)

a person
that wants to be a picture
and he'll erase and try again
until he gets the picture
right

he's beautiful at night
he sits in his room
soft light
pages blurring by

he was expelled
for tearing open a substitute's blouse

he insisted she was in danger
her beat was irregular
he could hear it across the room
he had to press his stethoscope
to her bare chest
to be sure

silly
tragic moments are always
so fucking silly

like this one
today

(Flips to a new sheet, draws a new tooth.)

today my little brother
will remove my tooth
which he is convinced
upon examination with his penlight
is rife with decay

(Draws holes on the tooth.)

little holes
in a bone close to my brain

he will administer anesthetic
a rag steeped in ether
(which he got from god knows where)
and pluck out my tooth
("pluck" is probably not
the right word)
and smile
believing
he has saved me from danger
i will give him this belief
today

and tomorrow
i will take him to a place
where they will administer
a more sophisticated anesthetic
one which will
maybe
combined with other treatments
over the course of years
help

tomorrow
i will turn him over to people
who will break into his house

(Draws a roof on the tooth, draws a yard, draws arrows pointing into the holes in the tooth.)

and do their best
as he flails and screams
to clean the damn thing up

i will leave him there
i will erase him and

because i can't i

you wake up one day
and the decay

i can't find myself
in this picture

i will leave him there
and return here

(Turns to a fresh blank page.)

to my house

and gerald
i know
will hold onto my tooth
forever
a bone close to my brain
perhaps it will reside
beneath his pillow
as he sleeps
giving him dreams
of his big brother
crying "don't hate me"

don't hate me

and perhaps
somewhere in the back of my mouth
i will feel the head
of my little brother shift
in the night
every night
after
tonight.

END OF PLAY

The Spot
by Steven Dietz

BIOGRAPHY

Steven Dietz is a Seattle-based playwright and director. Since 1981, his twenty-plus plays and adaptations have been widely produced regionally as well as Off-Broadway. International productions of his work have been seen in England, France, Germany, Japan, Russia, Sweden, Australia, Argentina, Peru, Singapore, Slovenia and South Africa. Recent work includes *Fiction, Inventing van Gogh* and *Over the Moon*.

HUMANA FESTIVAL PRODUCTION

The Spot was produced at the Humana Festival of New American Plays in April 2004. It was directed by William McNulty with the following cast:

Chumley . . . . Mary Tuomanen
Wagner . . . . Mauro Hantman
Roger . . . . Fred Sullivan, Jr.
Nelson . . . . Tom Kelley
Gloria . . . . Jody Christopherson
Betsy . . . . Emily Ruddock

and the following production staff:

Scenic Designer . . . . Paul Owen
Costume Designer . . . . John P. White
Lighting Designer . . . . Paul Werner
Sound Designer . . . . Benjamin Marcum
Properties Designer . . . . Doc Manning
Stage Manager . . . . Debra A. Freeman
Assistant Stage Managers . . . . Michael Domue
                                                              Brady Ellen Poole
Dramaturg . . . . Steve Moulds
Assistant Dramaturg . . . . Dan LeFranc

CHARACTERS

CHUMLEY, woman or man. The Communications Director. Well-dressed. Nervous.

WAGNER, man. Director of "The Spot." Khaki pants, black turtleneck. Fashionable glasses. An *auteur*.

NELSON, woman or man. The Pollster. Disheveled. Always working at a laptop computer which is strapped to her/his body. Often sipping from a diet soda.

ROGER, man. The Senior Advisor to the Candidate. Three-piece power suit. Expensive cowboy boots. Cell phone headset attached to his ear at all times.

BETSY, woman. A young mother. Dressed casually—a cardigan sweater, slacks.

GLORIA, woman. A production assistant. Jeans. Headset.

TIME AND PLACE
The present. A sound stage.

SETTING
An open area with one simple chair and side table, center.

NOTE ON STYLE
Fast. Fun. Fierce.

The Spot premiered at The University of Washington in February, 2004.

Cast
in *The Spot*

28th Annual Humana Festival of New American Plays
Actors Theatre of Louisville, 2004
photo by Harlan Taylor

The Spot

At center: a chair and a small side table. On the table, a cup of tea.

Surrounding this—four people, all staring at the chair: WAGNER, NELSON, CHUMLEY and ROGER.

CHUMLEY: —so, Roger, what we've envisioned—and Wagner just jump right on in here if I miss something—what we envision for "The Spot" is a sort of solid, homespun, no-nonsense, eyes-right-into-the-camera kind of thing—

WAGNER: Something that cries out: *"Here-we-are-in-her-livingroom-and-she's-gonna-be-straight-with-us-so-help-her-god."*

CHUMLEY: The young mother we've found—and Wagner correct me if I'm off-base here—this young mother is really just a *perfect choice* for—

ROGER: She really a mother?

CHUMLEY: Pardon me?

ROGER: She really have kids?

CHUMLEY: Well, as far as—

ROGER: People *want in*, Chumley. Everyone wants to be *in* "The Spot."

CHUMLEY: Yes, I know—

ROGER: They'll *lie through their teeth* to be in "The Spot."

WAGNER: She has kids.

ROGER: Real kids?

WAGNER: Yes.

ROGER: You've seen 'em?

WAGNER: Yes, I have.

ROGER: What are their names?

CHUMLEY: Roger—just to be clear, just to be what I like to call *"crystal"*: this woman's kids are *not in* "The Spot." It's just her.

ROGER: I see.

CHUMLEY: No kids in "The Spot." No kids at all.

ROGER: Got it.

CHUMLEY: Thank you, sir.

ROGER: *(Immediately, to WAGNER.)* What are their names?

WAGNER: Joey and Gretchen.

ROGER: *(Immediately, to NELSON.)* I want those names *polled*.

NELSON: Right away, sir. *(Begins typing on her/his laptop.)*

CHUMLEY: Shall we bring her in and get started? Her name is—

ROGER: I don't give a turd in a taco what her *name is*—WE'RE ON THE *CLOCK*, CHUMLEY—*GET HER BUTT IN HERE.*

CHUMLEY: Yes, sir.

WAGNER: *(Calls off.)* GLORIA—

ROGER: *(Stops, suddenly.)* You a *religious person*, Wagner?

WAGNER: Not as a rule.

ROGER: Then why the HOSANNA? Why the sudden *speaking in tongues?*

WAGNER: I was just calling my assistant—

   (GLORIA appears—friendly and efficient.)

GLORIA: *(To WAGNER.)* Yes—what can I do for you?

ROGER: Is this the little mother?

WAGNER: No—

GLORIA: I'm Gloria.

WAGNER: She's my assistant.

ROGER: *This one* I like! This one's got spunk. Moxie! Great heaps of chutzpah! Look at her—she's not one of those punky, pierced-up, tattoo-on-her-titties troublemakers! This one's got VIM AND VIGOR. This one EATS MEAT. Don't you, Gloria?

   (GLORIA nods, polite, confused.)

   Atta girl! GLORIA HALLELUJAH!

WAGNER: *(To GLORIA.)* We're ready for the talent.

   (GLORIA nods and is gone.)

NELSON: Roger.

ROGER: What?

NELSON: The name "Joey" polled at 78.

ROGER: Good. What about "Gretchen"?

NELSON: *31.*

ROGER: Toss it out.

NELSON: Right.

ROGER: How 'bout "Sally"? Run the numbers on "Sally."

NELSON: Will do. *(Back to her/his laptop.)*

ROGER: "Sally" always *packs a punch.*

   (GLORIA enters with BETSY.)

GLORIA: Everyone: this is Betsy Taylor.

BETSY: Hello.

CHUMLEY: We're so glad you're doing this.

WAGNER: I've been *dying* to work with you.

CHUMLEY: Betsy, I'd like you to meet Roger—he's the Senior Advisor to the Candidate.

BETSY: *(Extends her hand.)* A pleasure.

ROGER: *(Suddenly.)* YOUR HAND?

BETSY: Pardon?

ROGER: YOU WANT TO OFFER ME YOUR *HAND?*

BETSY: I just wanted to—

ROGER: WELL, YOU CAN TAKE THAT HAND AND CHOP IT OFF WITH A STEAK KNIFE AND FEED IT TO THE BEAR THAT'S GONNA *CRAP ALL OVER YOUR FACE!* HOW *DARE* YOU TRY TO PULL A STUNT LIKE THIS? WHO DO YOU THINK YOU'RE *DEALING WITH?*

(It becomes clear that he is talking into his phone.)

THE DAY MY CANDIDATE SHAKES THE HAND OF SOMEONE FROM YOUR PARTY—YOUR *TRIBE*—YOUR *GANG,* YOUR *SECT,* YOUR *CABAL*—THE DAY I LET MY CANDIDATE GET IN BED WITH THE LIKES OF YOU IS THE DAY *PIGS WILL PLAY HOCKEY IN HELL!!!*

(He clicks the call off. Turns pleasantly to BETSY. Extends his hand.)

Hi, there. I'm Roger. Did you meet Gloria? Isn't she something? Don't you just want to download that face and make it your screen saver?! *(Before she can respond.)* I'm told you're a mother. Joey and Sally.

BETSY: Gretchen.

ROGER: Huh?

BETSY: My daughter—Gretchen.

ROGER: Sorry. It didn't poll. Rhymes with "Chechen." On the other hand—

NELSON: Sally's at 83.

ROGER: —"Sally" polled like a champ. Rhymes with "rally"—good times ahead! You've got a daughter named Sally. You must be very happy. Mint? *(Offers her one.)*

BETSY: No, thank you.

CHUMLEY: *(Jumping in, nervous.)* Okay—let's get you in place, Betsy.

(BETSY sits in the chair. WAGNER approaches her.)

WAGNER: Now, the *aesthetic* I'm—are you with me?—the *paradigm* I'm working with in "The Spot" might well be called a "post-ironic, reality-infused, Mom-at-home" kind of thing—

CHUMLEY: Something I like to call: *"honesty."* Are you with me?

BETSY: Sure.

WAGNER: And you're clear on the text?

CHUMLEY: What I call "the lines."

BETSY: Yes, I am.

WAGNER: Okay, then, people: let's shoot one.

GLORIA: *(Calling out.)* QUIET ON THE SET.

ROGER: *(Re: GLORIA.)* Isn't she a *pistol?!*

GLORIA: *(Calling out.)* ROLL SOUND.

WAGNER: And... ACTION.

(BETSY looks straight ahead and speaks. Calm. Honest. Very good at this.)

BETSY: Just the other day, my daughter— *(Slight pause.)* Sally— *(ROGER smiles.)* —asked me who I was going to vote for. And I told her that there are three things I look for in a candidate: *trust, honor,* and *integrity.*
(She lifts her tea.)
And this year, only *one* candidate has all of—

ROGER: STOP RIGHT THERE!

BETSY: What is it?

CHUMLEY: WAGNER:

Roger, what on earth—   CUT.

ROGER: Set. The teacup. *Down.*
(She does.)
What are you *doing,* Betsy? Are you trying to *kill me?* Are you trying to *butcher my candidate?*

BETSY: *(Worried, confused.)* I'm not sure I—

ROGER: Do you know the *numbers* on TEA? They are *abysmal.* Tell her the numbers on tea, Nelson—

NELSON: *(Helpfully.)* 17.

ROGER: Seventeen! The TEA is polling at SEVENTEEN and there you are in your little sweater and your little chair and you're LIFTING THE TEA TO YOUR LIPS. Why don't you just DO SOME CRACK?! Why don't you just *MAKE OUT* WITH O.J. and DANGLE A BABY OVER A BALCONY?!

CHUMLEY: WAGNER:

Roger, please, we're on a deadline—   *(To BETSY.)* What I think Roger's looking for—

ROGER: What we call an *"election,"* Betsy—this quaint little practice of people *"going out to vote"*—that is nothing but a *nostalgic formality*—just a *symbolic narcotic* to placate the populace. *(Grandly, to NELSON.)* THE *REAL*

VOTES ARE NOT CAST *AT THE POLLS*—BUT WITH THE *POLL-STERS*—with great Americans like Nelson here.

(*NELSON lifts her/his diet soda.*)

And has the Carefully Polled Public voted for TEA, Betsy?—*I think not.*

CHUMLEY:	WAGNER:
Roger, let me explain—	Perhaps we can rethink it—

ROGER: Tell them, Nelson. Tell them who America wants Betsy to be.

(*As NELSON fires the data very quickly off her/his laptop—
Gloria instantly produces the necessary items and places them on the side table, transforming it as directed.*)

NELSON: Well, in addition to Joey and Sally—

BETSY: Her name is not—

NELSON: You have a husband named Bill and a dog named Buster.

(*GLORIA adds photographs of each to the side table.*)

(*Quickly consults new data on laptop.*) Correction! No husband—you're a single mom.

ROGER: Get Bill out of there!

(*GLORIA does.*)

NELSON: You work at Wal-Mart.

BETSY: No, I—

(*GLORIA affixes a bright "Welcome to Wal-Mart" nametag to BETSY's chest.*)

NELSON: And your Joey's all grown up—

BETSY: He's only nine!

NELSON: Sorry, ma'am: he's a soldier now, gone to rid the world of evil.

(*New photo of Joey the soldier.*)

ROGER: Atta boy, Joey!

NELSON: And you're not sipping tea—

ROGER: I told you!

NELSON: (*Overlapping.*) No, Betsy, you're sipping a Starbucks extra-hot low-fat double-tall mocha with *extra whipped cream.*

BETSY: But, I—

(*GLORIA immediately puts the coffee in BETSY's hand and tops it off with a major swirl of whipped cream. Takes the tea away.*)

ROGER: (*Buoyantly.*) *THAT* IS THE WOMAN THEY WANT, Betsy—and, hey, don't look at me, *I* didn't invent her—she is the Love Child of Entitlement and Complacency—the voice of the American vox populi— she is the PEOPLE'S CHOICE!

(*He places a small American flag on the side table.*)

ROGER: (Cont'd.) NOW: LET'S SHOOT HER!

GLORIA: (Calling off.) QUIET ON THE SET.

ROGER: You tell 'em, Gloria!

GLORIA: ROLL SOUND.

WAGNER: And... ACTION.

> (BETSY takes her place, about to begin, then—)

BETSY: (Stands, suddenly.) I won't do it.

EVERYONE: *WHAT?!*

BETSY: I just won't do it.

ROGER: You *won't do it?*—what's *that* mean?

BETSY: It's not true—it's all a lie.

ROGER: Just what the hell kind of actress *are you*, anyway?

BETSY: I'm not an actress.

ROGER: Oh, you can say THAT again.

BETSY: (Genuine, with passion.) I'm a wife and a mother. I was chosen for "The Spot" because I really *believe in it.* I believe in your candidate. I want to give him my vote. When I look into the camera, I am speaking from my *heart.*

> (Silence.
>
> ROGER *turns to* CHUMLEY, *then* WAGNER, *then* NELSON, *as if to say:* CAN THIS BE TRUE?
>
> CHUMLEY, WAGNER, *and* NELSON *all shrug and reluctantly nod:* YES.
>
> ROGER *turns back to* BETSY. *Approaches her, slowly.*)

ROGER: Take off your sweater.

BETSY: What?

ROGER: You heard me. Take it off.

BETSY: But, didn't you hear what I said? I really—

ROGER: Here's the thing about people who speak from their heart: I don't trust 'em. Hearts are *fickle*, Betsy. *Hearts change.* And when the future of the free world is on the line, I can't be taking a chance on what *people believe in their hearts.*

> (Beat. He stares at her, hard.)

Take. It. Off.

> (BETSY, *staring right at* ROGER, *takes off her sweater.*
>
> Underneath, attached with a strap over her shoulder, is a tape recorder.)

See there.

CHUMLEY:	WAGNER:
Betsy—?	Oh, my...

ROGER: Hand me the tape recorder.

> *(She does.)*

This another one of your TRICKS?!

BETSY: I'd like a chance to explain—

ROGER: *(Overlapping.)* ANOTHER WAY TO TRY TO "SHAKE MY HAND"?—GET IN BED WITH OUR CAMPAIGN?—SELL US OUT TO THE JACKALS AT THE NETWORKS?!—IS THAT WHAT THIS IS?!

BETSY: No, not at all—

> *(We realize that, once again, he is speaking into his phone.)*

ROGER: YOU LISTEN TO ME: WE'RE GONNA WIPE THE FLOOR WITH *YOU* AND *YOUR CANDIDATE* AND YOUR *DONORS* AND YOUR *PARTY*—AND THEN IN THE TRUE SPIRIT OF AMERI-CAN POLITICS: WE ARE GOING TO GLOAT LIKE HYENAS AND BEHAVE VERY VERY BADLY! *(Quickly, a smile.)* Bye-bye.

> *(Turns immediately to BETSY.)*

What did they pay you?

> *(BETSY does not answer.)*

Fess up, SuperMom—I know how they work—what did it cost them?

BETSY: I didn't want their money. I did it—

ROGER: Because of your *beliefs,* I suppose.

BETSY: Yes.

ROGER: What you *feel in your heart.*

BETSY: Yes.

ROGER: You disgust me.

> *(He tosses the tape recorder to GLORIA, who catches it.)*

Get her out of here.

> *(Chumley walks BETSY away, as—*
>
> *ROGER's cell phone rings.)*
>
> *(Instantly, into phone.)* Yes? Mr. Candidate—great to hear from you, sir!—it's going extremely well—couldn't be better! Yes, we'll send you a rough cut before the day is out. Thank you, sir. Goodbye.

> *(He ends the call.*
>
> *CHUMLEY rushes back in—)*

CHUMLEY: *(In a panic.)* Oh my god, Roger, we are just—I mean, Wagner, cor-rect me if I'm wrong here—but it seems to me that we are now what I like to call *"completely screwed."*

ROGER: *(Calmly.)* Nelson.

NELSON: Yes, sir?

ROGER: Run the numbers on "Gloria."

NELSON: Right away. *(Back to her/his laptop.)*

CHUMLEY: Roger, no—

> *(ROGER turns to GLORIA.)*

ROGER: Gloria—do you know the feeling we're going for?

GLORIA: Well, yes, but—

ROGER: And you're clear on the lines?

GLORIA: Yes, but I'm not really a—

ROGER: And do you *believe in them,* Gloria—do you believe in them *deep in your heart?*

> *(Beat.)*

GLORIA: *(Simple, direct.)* Not at all.

ROGER: *THIS ONE's* got *MOXIE.*

CHUMLEY: *(Really worried.)* Roger, listen to me—

ROGER: *THIS ONE* we can *SHOOT.*

CHUMLEY: Roger, *please*—

ROGER: *(Exultant.)* PUT ON THE SWEATER!

> *(WAGNER leads GLORIA to the chair and helps her into the sweater and her microphone, powders her face, etc.)*
>
> *(Firing questions.)* Gloria, I want you to finish this sentence: my candidate is—

GLORIA: *(Firing back, enjoying herself.)* —dumb as a box of hammers.

ROGER: You bet he is! And people like me are—

GLORIA: —the scum of the earth.

ROGER: You bet we are! Have a mint.

> *(She does.)*

NELSON: "Gloria" is polling at 93—

ROGER: You bet she is! "Gloria"—

WAGNER: QUIET ON THE SET.

ROGER: —rhymes with "euphoria"!

WAGNER: ROLL SOUND.

ROGER: And... ACTION!

> *(Fast blackout.)*

END OF PLAY

After Ashley
by Gina Gionfriddo

BIOGRAPHY

Gina Gionfriddo has received the Susan Smith Blackburn Prize, the Helen Merrill Award for Emerging Playwrights, a Lucille Lortel Fellowship and a Rhode Island State Council on the Arts Fellowship. In addition to *After Ashley* (Vineyard Theatre, NY in 2005 and Humana Festival, 2004), her work includes *Safe* (*Trepidation Nation*, Humana Festival Anthology 2003); *U.S. Drag* (Connecticut Repertory Company; Clubbed Thumb, NY; published by Smith and Kraus in *Women Playwrights: The Best Plays of 2002*); and *Guinevere* (Eugene O'Neill Playwrights Conference). Her plays have received development support from Denver Center Theatre Company, Trinity Repertory Company, ACT (A Contemporary Theatre), Philadelphia Theatre Company, Basic Grammar, and Chicago Films. She has held residencies at the MacDowell Colony, Yaddo and Hedgebrook. She is a graduate of Brown University's M.F.A. Playwriting Program.

HUMANA FESTIVAL PRODUCTION

After Ashley premiered at the Humana Festival of New American Plays in March 2004. It was directed by Marc Masterson with the following cast:

Justin Hammond . . . . Jesse Hooker
Ashley Hammond . . . . Carla Harting
Alden Hammond. . . . . Stephen Barker Turner
David Gavin. . . . . Frank X
Julie Bell. . . . . Sabrina Veroczi
Roderick Lord . . . . Jason Pugatch

and the following production staff:

Scenic Designer . . . . Paul Owen
Costume Designer . . . . Connie Furr-Soloman
Lighting Designer. . . . . Tony Penna
Sound Designer . . . . Vincent Olivieri
Properties Designer. . . . . Mark Walston
Stage Manager . . . . Andrew Scheer
Dramaturg. . . . . Liz Engelman
Assistant Dramaturg . . . . Dan LeFranc
Directing Assistant. . . . . Brad DePlanche
Rap Music . . . . SHUV
Casting . . . . Jerry Ellis Beaver

CHARACTERS

JUSTIN HAMMOND, 17
ASHLEY HAMMOND, 35
ALDEN HAMMOND, 40
DAVID GAVIN, 52
JULIE BELL, 19
RODERICK LORD, 30-35

SETTING

Bethesda, Maryland; New York City and Central Florida

.

TIME

1999 and 2002.

This play was originally commissioned by Philadelphia Theatre Company and was supported by a residency and public staged reading at the 2003 Eugene O'Neill Playwrights Conference.

After Ashley is for Jennifer Izzo.

Jesse Hooker
in *After Ashley*

28th Annual Humana Festival of New American Plays
Actors Theatre of Louisville, 2004
photo by Harlan Taylor

After Ashley

ACT ONE

In darkness, we hear the voice of DR. BOB, *a talk show psychologist. He has a loud authoritative voice and speaks to his audience slowly, gently, and deliberately as if anticipating they won't understand him.*

DR. BOB: *(Voice-over.)* ... and I will say to you... what I say to patients in my private practice. There are five things you need to know to get yourself a life license. You ignore these rules and you are living without a license and you will be pulled over, you will find yourself stalled on the expressway while the other drivers speed ahead. There are five rules and number one is your eyes are open or your eyes are closed but they can't be both and if they're closed, you are getting ready to drive right into a wall... You're gonna hurt yourself and maybe somebody else. And number two, you can drive without a map, but you will get lost and you will reach your destination either too late for dinner or not at all. Number three, if you do not focus, you will miss your exit... and you can go back and correct your error, but you're gonna lose time and you're gonna be late for dinner and that's rule number four.... If you do not show up in time for dinner, there is no guarantee of leftovers. And what do we know about leftovers? They are often cold, they are not fresh—

(A suburb of Washington, D.C., summer of 1999. Lights up on ASHLEY, *35, and* JUSTIN, *14, mother and son.* JUSTIN *is home sick from school and the two are watching television together. A bed and a bedside chair? A living room sofa? Whatever works for ease of set transformation.* JUSTIN *aims a remote control and mutes the sound of the TV.)*

JUSTIN: I'm sorry—I can't listen to this. This man is an idiot.

ASHLEY: I want to hear what he tells the couple with the incompatible sex drives. I want to see if he tells them to split up.

JUSTIN: I can't believe you watch this. He's a moron. The people who talk to him are morons.

ASHLEY: Morons with incompatible sex drives. What do you think they should do?

JUSTIN: I don't care.

ASHLEY: That's not helpful, Justin. These people have incompatible sex drives and they are asking for help. What should they do?

JUSTIN: They should stay home. They should have some dignity.

ASHLEY: You think sexual dysfunction is shameful?

JUSTIN: I think it's private.

ASHLEY: So they should stay home and be sexually incompatible and not tell anyone—

JUSTIN: No. They should go to a... a doctor or something. His degree is in sociology, you know. He's not even licensed—

ASHLEY: I'm not converted. I haven't bought his book yet.

JUSTIN: Mom, you cannot buy his book.

ASHLEY: I know—

JUSTIN: He named his book after an Eagles song. He is beyond ridiculous.

ASHLEY: Sometimes I think I want that, though. "Life in the Fast Lane." Don't you?

JUSTIN: What?

ASHLEY: Life in the fast lane. Doesn't that sound sort of great?

JUSTIN: It sounds like an Eagles song.

ASHLEY: You're no fun. Listen to you... dignity, privacy, "he's not licensed." Whose child are you?

JUSTIN: I just think he's a fraud. I could give better advice than that.

ASHLEY: Really? Can I tell you my problems?

JUSTIN: I guess. Is it time for me take more Advil?

ASHLEY: I don't know.

JUSTIN: You were supposed to write it down.

ASHLEY: Oh. Fuck. I'm a bad mother. Are you hot?

JUSTIN: Yeah...

ASHLEY: So take more. It's not going to kill you. (She doles out the pills.) So, let's talk about how you got this. Is she cute?

JUSTIN: What do you mean?

ASHLEY: Mono's the kissing disease, right? I want to know who you're kissing.

JUSTIN: I'm not kissing anyone.

ASHLEY: So how'd you get it?

JUSTIN: I just.... Teenagers get it. They just... I might have drunk out of someone's soda. I don't know.

ASHLEY: OK, fine. If you're not opening up to me, I'm not opening up to you.

JUSTIN: You can ask at school. I'm the only one in my class who has it.

ASHLEY: So you're messing around with someone you don't go to school with. Intriguing. Can I guess?

JUSTIN: I'm not messing around.

ASHLEY: The girl who babysits for the Stollers.

JUSTIN: No.

ASHLEY: She's cute though, isn't she?

JUSTIN: She's fine.

ASHLEY: The Stollers' maid.

JUSTIN: You're insane. She's like forty years old.

ASHLEY: So she's not sexy? I'm almost forty. *(No answer.)* If you're kissing, we should have a sex talk.

JUSTIN: I'm not kissing.

ASHLEY: Well, let's have it anyway. You're here, I'm here. Let's have a sex talk.

JUSTIN: No.

ASHLEY: How about a drug talk? Should we have a drug talk?

JUSTIN: I'm not... *(Pause.)* You really think you should do the drug talk?

ASHLEY: I know about.... What do you mean by that?

JUSTIN: Nothing. I feel like shit. I don't want to have any talks.

ASHLEY: Why do you think I shouldn't do the drug talk? I know about drugs.

JUSTIN: No kidding.

> *(Pause.)*

ASHLEY: Speak.

JUSTIN: You know what I... I'm not completely stupid, you know. I know you smoke pot.

> *(Pause.)*

ASHLEY: Is that a problem?

JUSTIN: Normally, no. When it's ninety-five degrees and I have mono, it makes me sort of nauseous.

ASHLEY: How—

JUSTIN: I can smell it. I'm not nine anymore.

> *(Pause.)*

ASHLEY: You know what I want to tell you about pot?

JUSTIN: No.

ASHLEY: I'm a very unusual smoker. I smoke it now and then, but I'm not addicted. It doesn't interfere with my life.

JUSTIN: OK.

ASHLEY: So, if you're thinking of experimenting, just keep that in mind. You might really like it and there's no guarantee you could control it like I do. I'm an occasional smoker and not everyone can do that.

JUSTIN: Does smoking every day make you an occasional smoker?

ASHLEY: I don't smoke every day.

JUSTIN: Yeah, you do.

(Pause.)

ASHLEY: OK, I do. I do and I'm glad we're talking about this.

JUSTIN: So does that mean I can try it or not?

ASHLEY: You can try it with me. If you're going to try it anyway. We should do that. Do you want to do that?

JUSTIN: Maybe.

ASHLEY: I think we should. I think we should do that. I have some. Do you want to try it now?

JUSTIN: Yeah. Yeah, definitely, Mom. I have a hundred and two degree fever and I'm, like, colonized by virus, I should probably try pot now.

ASHLEY: I'm sorry. I didn't think.

JUSTIN: You're acting really weird.

ASHLEY: I'm not stoned.

JUSTIN: I know. You're mellow when you're stoned.

ASHLEY: I'm not mellow now?

JUSTIN: No. You're all, like… agitated.

ASHLEY: I know. (Pause.) Why don't we have the sex talk?

JUSTIN: No! Mom! Jesus. What the fuck?!

ASHLEY: I'm sorry. You know… I just need to talk. I just do and—

JUSTIN: So talk! Go ahead. I just don't want to have a sex talk.

ASHLEY: OK, but what if I do?

(Pause.)

JUSTIN: About me or about you?

(Pause.)

ASHLEY: About you… by way of me.

(Pause.)

JUSTIN: I'm not sure what that means.

ASHLEY: It's not a sex talk. It's more a life talk. I'm just… I just have been feeling like something's got to change, you know? OK, I know you hate Dr. Bob, but he talks about, you know, traveling without a map and I feel like that's exactly what I did. I—I didn't use a map and now here I am and it's all wrong and the choice is keep going or exit and—

JUSTIN: Can you talk about this without road metaphors?

ASHLEY: Don't get married young. I got married young and I fucked up my life.

JUSTIN: OK…

ASHLEY: Don't get married until you're thirty. Thirty-five. You don't know who you are in your twenties. Try not to get a girl pregnant, but if you do, have an abortion. It's not the end of the world. You'll be traumatized for like two days but then you'll get over it.

JUSTIN: Did you have an abortion?

ASHLEY: No, but I could have and.... Look, I love you more than anything. You're the only good thing in my life. But I was twenty-one and I didn't know myself and I didn't know your dad at all; we'd been dating like a couple of months—a little longer…

JUSTIN: So I'm an accident?

ASHLEY: Yeah. Should I not have told you that?

JUSTIN: I'm not sure.

ASHLEY: Am I screwing you up by telling you this?

JUSTIN: I don't know yet.

ASHLEY: I was just way too young. I was twenty-one which I know sounds really old to you, but oh my God… Sometimes I look at you and I think you should be demented. I can't believe you're not totally demented.

JUSTIN: Why—because you got stoned when you were pregnant?

ASHLEY: No. I mean, I did once or twice, but I mean.... We bought a house and your dad went to work and there I was. With you. I'm twenty-one and I'm a housewife and it was OK when you were a baby and I just sorta strapped you on and took you places but when you started to walk JESUS CHRIST. My whole life was chasing after you making sure you didn't kill yourself and I got so depressed. Really… psycho depressed. I used to stick you in your crib and go smoke and then you'd cry and I'd go back in cuz I felt guilty and I'd just sit in front of your crib. I'd sit on the floor and just hang onto the bars on the crib like I was in jail and I would cry. And then you'd cry because I was crying and I'd cry more because what kind of horrible mother makes her baby cry, you know?

JUSTIN: Yeah… I don't know if you should be telling me this.

ASHLEY: But it's OK, see? Because you're great. You're amazing. You survived me. But that's you and you're extraordinary. Don't do what I did. Don't be irresponsible and wreck your life and fuck up your kid and have a wife who hates you.

JUSTIN: You hate dad?

ASHLEY: He's fine. He's a fine… person. We just have nothing in common. If we'd dated even a month longer I think we'd have figured that out. Do not marry someone you don't know well. *(Pause.)* Sorry. I know he's your father but he drives you crazy, too. I can see it.

JUSTIN: He's.... He's fine.

ASHLEY: Right. He's fine. For someone else he's fine. He's just not like us.

JUSTIN: He's just sorta straight.

ASHLEY: Straight-laced you mean? No kidding. He's rigid is what you're saying.

JUSTIN: I'm not saying anything.

ASHLEY: And a hypocrite. He's a huge fucking hypocrite.

JUSTIN: Why?

ASHLEY: His big liberal heart bleeds for the downtrodden masses. He's losing sleep over people he doesn't know while his own house goes to shit.

JUSTIN: You think I'm going to shit?

ASHLEY: No. No, I don't. I was being vague and inclusive so it wouldn't seem like I was complaining about my marriage which, of course, I am. I probably shouldn't be telling you this, but... I don't have anyone else to talk to.

JUSTIN: You need friends. Like maybe one of the other moms...

ASHLEY: They're all too old. I went to a PTA meeting. I felt like a freak. I need a job, but I have no skills.

JUSTIN: You teach art. That's a job.

ASHLEY: Not really. It's a play job. It's part-time. And I'm not good at it. I don't like children and I'm not a good artist.

JUSTIN: You're a really good artist.

ASHLEY: You're sweet, but you know—I'm not. That's what I would have figured out if I hadn't gotten married so young. I would have tried to get my art into shows and stuff and I would have failed but it would have been OK cuz I would have been young enough to switch careers.

JUSTIN: You can switch careers now.

ASHLEY: Yeah, but what would I do? I have no idea what I would do. That's the problem with Dr. Bob. He says it's OK to change lanes, but he doesn't... he's never specific—

JUSTIN: Right. He's an idiot. Did you just say you hate children?

ASHLEY: Yeah. Yeah, I do. I always have. I mean, you can't say that. It's like being a racist or a fascist or something. You just can't say it, but... I don't think they're cute. I don't think their artwork, their little clay animals, are cute. I'm a fucking fraud as a teacher.

JUSTIN: Did something happen?

ASHLEY: What do you mean?

JUSTIN: Why is this happening now?

ASHLEY: Why is what happening?

JUSTIN: You freaking out.

ASHLEY: I'm not freaking out, I'm just... I don't know. Mid-life crisis. Maybe.

JUSTIN: Thirty-five isn't mid-life anymore.

ASHLEY: I know. I know, I just... I'm not happy.

JUSTIN: Maybe you should go to therapy or something.

ASHLEY: We went to marriage counseling. It didn't work. Remember when you had that babysitter so we could go take a cooking class? That was a lie. We were in therapy. It didn't work.

JUSTIN: Then you should get a divorce.

ASHLEY: We can't do that, but if we did who would you want to live with?

JUSTIN: You. Probably.

ASHLEY: See?! He's impossible, right?

JUSTIN: He's.... He's fine. He tries. He's not... I would choose you. Let's leave it at that. Why can't you get a divorce?

ASHLEY: We talked about it. We don't have enough money for two households and you have to go to college.

JUSTIN: I can go to a state school. You shouldn't stay together because of that.

ASHLEY: I feel like I screwed up my life, like... like I took the wrong exit, you know? I got off early. I didn't read the map...

JUSTIN: Not to... prolong the bad highway metaphor, but maybe you should take a trip. Seriously like... go to Europe for a month. A couple months. Bum around.

(Pause.)

ASHLEY: I think a lot of this is about sex, you know.

JUSTIN: OK, no. You can't—

ASHLEY: I'm thirty-five and I've never had like... movie sex, like swept away—

JUSTIN: OK, Mom—you need to phone a friend or like write in a journal or just... I don't know, but if you're gonna talk about sex, you know, about YOU and sex, I just can't...

ASHLEY: It's not just about me, though. I was gonna tell you about me and then there would be a moral. Not a moral—a message. Fuck. I just want to encourage you to sleep with a lot of people before you get married. Safely, you know, and respectfully. God. We should talk about that, too, you know about not being a dick. Because that song, you know, Joe Jackson? "It's Different for Girls?" It is. Different for girls. Young girls anyway. Right now I could fuck someone who didn't care about me. I could do that. Right now I could fuck like nine people who don't care about me—

JUSTIN: No. No. Stop. I can't... And that song is meant ironically. He actually doesn't think it's different for girls.

(Pause.)

ASHLEY: Are you sure?

JUSTIN: Positive. This girl keeps telling him it's different for girls and then she dumps him and the song is like… It's angry. He's saying it's not different for girls. Guys get hurt, too.

ASHLEY: Wow. See? You're so much smarter than me. That's the other thing. I'm not that bright. I mean, I get by—I'm not retarded, but… your dad is super smart and so are you. I'm really average. But back to sex and respect…. You need to be really respectful because when you're young sex is serious for girls and guys, with the possible exception of Joe Jackson, just see it as getting off. So don't be a dick.

JUSTIN: Sleep with lots of women but don't be a dick?

ASHLEY: You're right. I should clarify that. What I mean is that your father is the second person I ever slept with and the first person I only did it with once and…. You can't learn all there is to know about sex from one person especially if you're not sexually compatible with that person which in my case I'm not.

JUSTIN: Holy fuck—I better wake up tomorrow and this all better be a dream.

ASHLEY: Why?

JUSTIN: Because you're telling me my father is…. You just can't do that! You can't…. You can't talk to me like this.

ASHLEY: I know. I wish you were a girl sometimes.

JUSTIN: You can't talk to a daughter like this either! Are you nuts?

ASHLEY: Yes. Yeah, there's something really wrong with me.

JUSTIN: You're fine. You just…. You lack a fucking peer group is the problem…. What about that woman you went to galleries with?

ASHLEY: Marcy. She had a baby. She's boring now. Something did happen.

JUSTIN: What do you mean?

ASHLEY: I didn't do it.

JUSTIN: Do what?

ASHLEY: A guy. One of the dads. At school. He hit on me.

JUSTIN: OK.

ASHLEY: The first few times I didn't even get it. I'm so…out of touch. But he kept it up.

JUSTIN: Do I know him?

ASHLEY: No. His kid is five. You wouldn't…. He kept it up and I just never took the hint so finally he gave me his number and said call me, let's get a drink. And I felt so shitty, you know. He must think I'm so stupid, so dense. It was like weeks and weeks of really obvious sexual innuendo like.... Like when I had clay on my face he'd like wipe it off and say something like "Oh, your teacher is very dirty."

JUSTIN: Oh, Jesus.

ASHLEY: Obvious, right?

JUSTIN: Cheesy.

ASHLEY: You think?

JUSTIN: Yeah.

ASHLEY: So I have his number and I just... Part of me really wants to call.

JUSTIN: What do you want me to say?

ASHLEY: I want someone to tell me what to do.

JUSTIN: You're talking about my dad...

ASHLEY: I know. I know. Forget it. I'll get a therapist or something. A licensed one. Are you pissed at me now?

JUSTIN: No. I just... I can't really be your girlfriend. You know?

ASHLEY: I know. *(Pause.)* Marriage is hard. People used to die at thirty-five, you know. We weren't meant to be together this long. Can I give you advice if it's nonsexual?

JUSTIN: OK.

ASHLEY: When you fall in love with a girl, think really hard about her exceptional qualities. Like maybe she's really supportive of your work or maybe she tells you you're gorgeous when you're having sex with her. Think good and hard about these things because ten years down the road these are the things that are going to drive you fucking ape shit—

JUSTIN: So you're telling me my marriage is doomed? I'm gonna wind up hating my wife?

ASHLEY: No. No, that wasn't my point. I believe in love.

JUSTIN: It doesn't sound like it.

ASHLEY: No, I do. I guess what I'm saying is get to know her. Wait until you're a little bit sick of her and then decide if you want to marry her.

JUSTIN: Marry a girl I'm sick of?

ASHLEY: Yeah. If you're sick of her and you still want to be with her it will probably last.

JUSTIN: You have no idea what you're talking about, do you? You are making this shit up as you go along.

ASHLEY: The last part, yeah. I don't know anything about successful relationships. So I am sort of pulling that out of my ass as the kids say.

JUSTIN: What did you like about dad when you liked him?

ASHLEY: The exact same stuff that pisses me off now. His sensitivity. When I was twenty I thought it was just amazing that a guy could be so passionate about the pro-choice movement. He would say things like, "Your body is your own" and I got weak. I remember there was a series of rapes on our campus and he cried. I swooned over that, you know?

JUSTIN: And now you think these are bad things?

ASHLEY: Not bad. Phony. Or something. I mean, he can read about a massacre in Africa and just… he feels their pain, you know? But when it's people he knows, well… Real people aren't pure innocents. You know?

JUSTIN: No.

ASHLEY: It's no great feat to pity strangers. The test of… of humanity is to feel sorry for people you know well enough not to like.

(ALDEN HAMMOND enters.)

ALDEN: How's the patient?

JUSTIN: Hey.

ALDEN: Is your fever down?

JUSTIN: I'm not sure.

ALDEN: *(To ASHLEY.)* You should probably check his temperature.

ASHLEY: He's taking Advil. It'll go down when it goes down.

ALDEN: What are we watching?

JUSTIN: Dr. Bob.

ALDEN: Why is the sound off?

JUSTIN: Because he's a moron.

ALDEN: Why are we watching him if he's a moron?

ASHLEY: Turn it off.

(JUSTIN uses the remote to turn off the television.)

ALDEN: So, what's up?

ASHLEY: Where have you been?

ALDEN: I have been at a school board meeting… Starbucks and… Borders. *(To JUSTIN.)* I bought you an audio book. I was thinking now that you're feeling a little bit better we should work on making better use of this downtime. Find some entertainment options besides the TV. Maybe audio books.

JUSTIN: OK.

ASHLEY: If you had a school board meeting that means you're writing tonight?

ALDEN: I am writing, yes. Small piece…. This was a very interesting meeting concerning the foreign language curriculum at the high school level. *(To JUSTIN.)* Did you take Latin?

JUSTIN: No. Spanish.

ALDEN: OK. Was Latin an option or did you choose—

JUSTIN: It wasn't an option.

ASHLEY: Do you really not know this stuff?

ALDEN: Excuse me?

ASHLEY: Do you read his report cards?

ALDEN: I read them, yes. I don't memorize them. Do you?

ASHLEY: No, but I'm not an education reporter for a major newspaper. This is stuff you maybe oughtta know.

ALDEN: Well. The question they're grappling with is this idea that in an increasingly multicultural society, is it perhaps... irresponsible to allow a... dead language to fulfill a foreign language requirement. Which I think is a valid question.

ASHLEY: Yeah. This country is becoming so... French, I don't know what I would do without all the French I took.

ALDEN: Well, French is still a living language. It's still—

ASHLEY: In any of your travels, did you happen to pick up milk?

ALDEN: I'm sorry. I completely forgot. I'll go.

ASHLEY: No. I'll go.

(*ASHLEY starts to get up.*)

ALDEN: (*To ASHLEY.*) I want you to call this number tomorrow.

ASHLEY: What is this?

ALDEN: I met someone who is willing to do the yard work for a very reasonable amount of money.

ASHLEY: I'll do it for a very reasonable amount of money.

ALDEN: Well, you haven't in the last several months, so... I think this is a very good option.

ASHLEY: Why does this say "pay phone?"

ALDEN: He lives in a shelter.

ASHLEY: He's homeless?

ALDEN: He is homeless.

ASHLEY: You're not serious.

ALDEN: I spoke with him for nearly an hour. He's a very interesting guy... highly motivated... and he's trying to get on his feet.

ASHLEY: Why is he homeless if he's so highly motivated?

ALDEN: I'm not.... You're smarter than that.

ASHLEY: Smarter than what? Why is he homeless?

ALDEN: Well... that's an ignorant—

ASHLEY: It's not ignorant. People are homeless for a reason.

ALDEN: Not because they're lazy.

ASHLEY: I'm sure some people are homeless because they're lazy.

ALDEN: Just call him.

ASHLEY: Some people are homeless because they're lazy. Some people are homeless because they're stupid.

ALDEN: I'm not going to dignify—

ASHLEY: What? Am I wrong? You can't make these blanket statements. "No one is homeless because they're lazy." "All battered women are victims."

ALDEN: I'm not going to engage you in a discussion—

ASHLEY: Yeah, because you can't win.

ALDEN: No, because you're being… provocative.

ASHLEY: Some homeless people are lazy; some battered women are fucking pains in the ass.

ALDEN: Well, that's a good… theory to advance in front of your son.

ASHLEY: He watches *Springer*. We watch it together. There are women on there who I would beat the shit out of if I had to see them every day of my life.

ALDEN: That's enough.

ASHLEY: Justin agrees with me. Speaking of…. Does he get to weigh in on turning our home into a work camp for indigents?

ALDEN: Give me the number. I'll call him.

ASHLEY: No, I'll call him. But tell me what's wrong with him.

ALDEN: He is mentally handicapped.

ASHLEY: He's retarded?

ALDEN: He has an affective disorder.

ASHLEY: Which one?

ALDEN: He is a medicated schizophrenic.

ASHLEY: *(Not confrontational.)* You're an asshole.

ALDEN: I'm not going to talk to you when you're like this and I'm not going to listen to the language in front of him—

ASHLEY: I apologize, Justin.

ALDEN: It's unacceptable.

ASHLEY: It's definitely not a good use of his downtime.

ALDEN: I'm going to make myself something to eat unless you…

ASHLEY: Unless I cooked? It's a hundred fucking degrees, Alden.

   (ALDEN leaves the room.)

JUSTIN: You should maybe rethink that divorce.

ASHLEY: He's ridiculous. He's out at Starbucks introducing himself to street people.

JUSTIN: OK, but.... You provoke him.

ASHLEY: That's true.

(Pause.)

JUSTIN: Why don't you go out?

ASHLEY: Out where?

JUSTIN: I don't know. Go somewhere. Air-conditioned. Chill out. Go to, like, a bar or something.

ASHLEY: Alone?

JUSTIN: Look in the *City Paper*. Find, like, a poetry reading or something.

ASHLEY: Maybe...

JUSTIN: You need to do something. You need to leave the house.

ASHLEY: You might be right. I should think about that.

JUSTIN: You shouldn't think about it, you should do it. You need to find, like, outside activities.

ASHLEY: I know. It's hard, though. You know?

JUSTIN: A lot of things are hard. You just have to suck it up and do them, you know? Because when you leave here, I know you're either gonna go pick a fight with him or get stoned in your bathroom and... and... I think there are better options, you know?

ASHLEY: Better uses of my downtime?

JUSTIN: Basically. Yeah.

ASHLEY: OK. OK. *City Paper*.

(ASHLEY kisses JUSTIN.)

ASHLEY: I love you so much. I'm sorry I'm being a dick. I don't know what's wrong with me.

JUSTIN: It's hot. You need a change. It's not a big deal. Just.... Go out, OK?

ASHLEY: OK. Out. Mom is getting out.

(ASHLEY leaves. JUSTIN stares after her. Lights dim slowly. The stage gets very dark. We hear the following 911 call.)

OPERATOR: *(V.O.)* 911. What is your emergency?

JUSTIN: *(V.O.)* My mother *(Some inaudible words.)*... in the basement.

OPERATOR : *(V.O.)* I'm sorry—you said your mother—

JUSTIN: *(V.O.)* She's in the basement.

OPERATOR : *(V.O.)* Is she hurt?

JUSTIN: *(V.O.)* Yes. You have to come. Right now.

OPERATOR : *(V.O.)* Do you know the nature of—

JUSTIN: *(V.O.)* He did something to her. There is blood everywhere—

OPERATOR : *(V.O.)* OK, when you say he, do you know who—

JUSTIN: *(V.O.)* Do you have my address?

OPERATOR : *(V.O.)* Is this person in the house with you—

JUSTIN: *(V.O.)* Do you know my address?

OPERATOR : (V.O.) I have you on the screen as Shellburne Place. Is that—

JUSTIN: *(V.O.)* Yes. How soon—

OPERATOR : *(V.O.)* OK, if you believe this person may still be in the house, you need to leave—

JUSTIN: *(V.O.)* I'm not leaving her! She's my mother!

OPERATOR : *(V.O.)* Sir, are you near an exit?

JUSTIN: *(V.O.)* I'm not leaving her! Jesus Christ! She's my mother!

> *(Actors/stagehands enter and transform the set.*
> *It's 2002 and we're in New York City. The lights get very bright as we transition into the set of a cable television talk show called "Profiles in Justice."*
> *In the transition, we hear the theme to "Profiles in Justice" as follows:*
> *Dramatic theme music and military-esque drums, then…*
> *A police siren.)*

WOMAN: *(V.O.)* My daughter is missing! She's not in her room!

A NEWSCASTER: *(V.O.)* …Guilty of all counts…

A SHERIFF: *(V.O.)* Don't eat. Don't sleep. We're coming after you.

JUSTIN: *(V.O.)* I'm not leaving her! She's my mother!

> *(Dramatic theme music swells, as DAVID GAVIN enters and addresses the audience.)*

DAVID: The people of this country have had enough. America's crime victims are not going to be silenced. They will not be told that justice is none of their business. Justice is my business and your business.… You don't need a badge or a law degree to make justice happen; you only need a voice…

> *(Lights rise on the set of DAVID GAVIN's television talk show. ALDEN and JUSTIN are his guests.)*

DAVID: I'm David Gavin. Tonight on *Profiles in Justice*, I am joined by Alden Hammond and his son, Justin. Alden Hammond is formerly an education reporter for *The Washington Post*. He is, more recently, the author of the critically-acclaimed book, *After Ashley*. The book chronicles the 1999 murder of his wife, Ashley Hammond, and traces the crime's profound impact, not only on a family but on a nation. I want to say first, to both of you, how sorry I am for your loss. As the parent of a murdered child, I know how fierce a pain and how enduring a sorrow familial loss is.

DAVID: *(Cont'd.) (Pause.)* Justin, we used a portion of your 911 call in the opening of our show. That's three years ago now, but I'll bet it seems like yesterday.

JUSTIN: Actually, it seems like three years ago.

DAVID: That 911 call affected a lot of people very, very deeply. That voice… of that boy… who wouldn't leave his mother, even while he knew the killer might still be in the house… I want our audience to hear a piece of that call.

JUSTIN: *(V.O.)* I'm not leaving her! She's my mother!

OPERATOR: *(V.O.)* Sir, are you near an exit?

JUSTIN: *(V.O.)* I'm not leaving her! Jesus Christ! She's my mother!

DAVID: The courage… of that child. Justin, *People* magazine called you The 911 Kid. How do you feel hearing that tape again?
(Pause.)

JUSTIN: Well… your decision to use my voice in your opening credits was very helpful to me.

DAVID: Terrific. Helpful in what way?

JUSTIN: Financially. Helpful. *(Pause.)* I'm not using drugs anymore but when I was, the royalty checks I received from your show helped cover costs—

ALDEN: Can we stop?

DAVID: We don't stop, but we edit.

ALDEN: We have discussed this. You either participate in a constructive, adult fashion or you do not participate. I am fully prepared to do this alone.

JUSTIN: What did I say? Did I lie?

ALDEN: Listen to me—

JUSTIN: I can't talk?! The 911 Kid isn't allowed to talk?!

DAVID: Justin, I think it's a focus issue. The people want to hear about the book. They want to hear about the good work your dad is doing. Now, I don't believe in sugarcoating the truth. We can allude to the problems you've had, but I gotta be goal-oriented here and the goal is to inspire. You got that?

JUSTIN: To inspire.

DAVID: Yes. I survived a violent loss and so did you two and that's why we're on TV instead of the ones who fell apart and gave up. We're providing an example here, OK?

JUSTIN: Got it. I'm sorry.

DAVID: No problem at all. Now let's go back. *(Pause.)* Alden, you've written a simply fantastic book.

ALDEN: Thank you, David. I appreciate that more than I can say. Your book, *A Crime Against Hope,* was an essential book for me when I began finding my voice.

DAVID: I'm glad it could help you. Let's go back, for those people who are not familiar with this story, to the summer of 1999. You're living in Washington, D.C.

ALDEN: In Bethesda, actually.

JUSTIN: Excuse me. Sorry. What is a crime against hope?

ALDEN: It's the title of.... We've actually spoken about this. He knows—

DAVID: No, no. I'm happy to elaborate, for Justin and for any new viewers who may not know... I lost my daughter, Rachel, ten years ago. She was murdered at seventeen. And I want to say to you, Justin, that even though not a day goes by that I don't think of her, the character of the pain has changed over time. It has evolved... to something that I can endure.

JUSTIN: That's interesting. I mean, that actually wasn't my question, but... it's interesting.

DAVID: I'm sorry. Did you have a different question that I could—

JUSTIN: You hadn't seen her in like... a bunch of years, right? You split when she was—what—seven or eight, so...

ALDEN: That's not relevant—

DAVID: No-No, I'll address that. Justin, you're right. I was not in my daughter's life for the last ten years she was alive and I regret that terribly. I let the acrimony of my divorce, affect my parenting—

JUSTIN: Well, it didn't affect it as much as it, you know, ended it. Right?

DAVID: And that haunts me. If I can send any message to the viewers at home, that would be it.

JUSTIN: Don't ditch your kids?

ALDEN: Justin—

DAVID: No. The message is that time is precious and the future uncertain. Don't postpone love. *(Pause.)* Now, Alden, take us back. You hired a homeless man by the name of Glenn Wise to do some yard work at your home—

ALDEN: Yes.

DAVID: How did this come about?

ALDEN: I met him in a Starbucks, in Washington. He noticed that I was writing and he asked about it. I was working on a piece about student loan... issues, I believe, and he was interested. We had a somewhat lengthy discussion—

DAVID: And you were struck—

ALDEN: I was completely, um…. This is a man who completed three years of college. This is a highly educated and intelligent individual who is living on the streets because of mental illness—

DAVID: But how did this evolve into a situation where he is working in your home?

ALDEN: I'm asked this all the time, David. We are originally from the West Coast. We had lived in communities with large homeless populations. We regarded these people as neighbors, as members of our community—

DAVID: Had you ever employed one before?

ALDEN: No.

DAVID: And whose idea—

ALDEN: It was mine, but my wife just immediately rose to the occasion to help—

JUSTIN: I have a different memory!

ALDEN: This is a learned man, David.

DAVID: A learned man and a man in need.

ALDEN: Absolutely. It was a crisis situation, really desperate poverty. And we needed to hire someone to do yard work and we thought, OK here's something we can…. You know, David, again—we're coming from a place where we've seen so many strategies for helping these people. We know what doesn't work and we thought this makes sense, let's try this.

JUSTIN: I have to voice my objection to the continued use of the pronoun "we."

ALDEN: Ashley shared my concerns about this man's situation.

DAVID: She wanted to make a difference.

ALDEN: Yes, she did. And we both understood that it was a… progressive choice.

JUSTIN: Progressive and economical.

DAVID: How long did he work for you?

ALDEN: About two months.

DAVID: What happened? I'm assuming this was two months without incident.

ALDEN: It was terrific. He worked very hard and boundaries were respected. I mean you torture yourself, you go back and you comb that time for any indication. I know now that he was off his medication during this time, that he was hallucinating—

DAVID: But no indication.

ALDEN: No.

JUSTIN: David, I'm with my dad on this one. We didn't observe anything that couldn't be written off as… benign eccentricity. A lot of perfectly healthy people talk to themselves, perhaps not as... extensively or enthusiastically as Glenn did, but we didn't want to judge.

DAVID: In any case... this arrangement went terribly wrong. This man raped and murdered Ashley Hammond. *(Pause.)* Alden, you were at work; Justin you were asleep upstairs.

ALDEN: Yes.

DAVID: Mr. Wise is quickly apprehended. The case is solved immediately and he pleads guilty so there is no trial.

ALDEN: We were very lucky in that regard.

DAVID: But it isn't over.

ALDEN: Not remotely.

DAVID: Talk about that. Talk about after... After Ashley.

ALDEN: David, I wrote a series of articles for *The Washington Post* which became the basis for the book. The mail we received and the coverage in other papers.... It became apparent very quickly that this crime was taking on a sociological significance that I was not prepared for.

DAVID: Talk about that significance.

ALDEN: What I saw was people in the District and in other states—we got mail from all over—drawing a sort of moral from our story.

DAVID: Which was?

ALDEN: Which was don't help. It was here's what you get if you cross the class line, if you try to make a difference with underprivileged populations in any kind of hands-on way. And it was offensive to me, frankly, that this was my wife's legacy. That people who, let's be honest, were already doing nothing to help this population, were latching onto my wife's death as a justification for their apathy and inaction.

DAVID: You speak in the book about your wife becoming the poster girl for right-wing, conservative—

ALDEN: Oh, absolutely. Rush Limbaugh spoke about this crime on his radio show and his message was basically this is what you get. It became fodder for his anti-welfare agenda, this notion that underprivileged persons are underprivileged because they're amoral and lazy. He's been arguing for years that America owes nothing to its underclass and he seized on this as fuel for his argument.

JUSTIN: Just to sort of paraphrase, if I could, David. Our story, like yours, is not without a message, but we want to be very clear on what that message is.

ALDEN: Justin, I couldn't have said that better—

JUSTIN: David, you said your message was don't postpone love. Ours is don't hire healthy, skilled persons for jobs a homeless person can perform for a fraction of the cost. The fact that the man we hired *killed my mother* should not deter anyone from bringing the homeless home. And that's our message at its most pithy: Bring the homeless home.

ALDEN: Can we stop taping?

DAVID: We can edit. Justin, you have a lot of anger and that's completely valid.

ALDEN: These are not constructive expressions! We have discussed this and you understand that there is a constructive way to express your feelings which is not—

DAVID: Alden, we'll fix it. Let's move on, let's talk about the book. This is a big book, an epic book… The *New York Times* described it as American epic tragedy. I'd like to read a few of the reviewer's comments…

"Once upon a time in America, before September Eleventh exploded America's sense of security and hope, a young family on the outskirts of America's capitol city hired a mentally challenged man to work in their home. It seems an action from another era now, a time before fear fractured the American psyche."

Alden, this was 1999, but there's a way in which this tragedy almost prefigures September Eleventh.

ALDEN: David, I resisted that linkage for a long time, but I think there's a strange truth in it. This crime was an act that destroyed our sense of safety. Not just my family's but across the country—

JUSTIN: I'm sorry. You're gonna have to help me out. I don't understand how terrorists crashing airplanes into the World Trade Center has anything to do with my mother—

DAVID: Both events shattered a sense of safety in this country. They are both violent acts that ended an era of comfort.

JUSTIN: What era was that? In what era was it OK to give a psychotic stranger the key to your house? This is a totally ludicrous discussion.

DAVID: OK, let's confront the mental illness question. It obviously weighs heavily on Justin's mind. Alden, you interviewed your wife's killer extensively. You interviewed his family and you tracked his journey through the American medical landscape. Your book is a critique, a very damning critique, of the deinstitutionalization movement in America. Would you agree with that?

ALDEN: Absolutely.

DAVID: You interviewed the killer. You spent a week at his family's summer home in Maine.

ALDEN: Yes, I did.

DAVID: Justin, I'm guessing that that must have been hard on you, seeing your father make contact with the killer's family.

JUSTIN: David, I'm not gonna lie to you. Seeing my father go to the prison was hard for me to take. By the time he went on vacation with the killer's family, I was under the influence of too many drugs to feel much of anything. So that impacted me in a lesser way.

DAVID: Alden, you dedicate the book to Arlene Wise, the killer's mother. Why is that?

ALDEN: She is, like Ashley, a wife and a mother... a person of tremendous strength and character whose life is a casualty of Glenn Wise and, I would argue, the mental health system in this country that failed him.

DAVID: Another mother, another victim.

JUSTIN: The similarities are startling except that she's, you know, still alive.

DAVID: Does that make you angry Justin? Did you feel, perhaps, that the book should have been dedicated to you?

JUSTIN: Not at all, David. I understand that my drug and alcohol abuse and, of course, my hospitalization and arrests impeded the completion of the book. Arlene, on the other hand, contributed childhood stories about the man who hammered my mother's head in. Arlene provided that extra special something that elevated the book from true crime pulp to American epic. So, in answer to your question about the dedication, I'm fine with it.

(Stunned silence.)

DAVID: From enormous pain, a book of great beauty and power. Alden and Justin Hammond, I thank you very much.

Please join us next week on *Profiles in Justice* when Jon and Holly Poltscheck will discuss the murder of their six-year-old daughter, Kylie, and their campaign to take fingerprints, blood, and hair samples from every American child. I'm David Gavin. Thank you for being with us. Join us again and don't postpone love.

ALDEN: I want to apologize.

DAVID: Alden, there's no need.

ALDEN: *(To JUSTIN.)* Are you under the influence?

JUSTIN: Not right now.

ALDEN: You were deliberately confrontational and we have discussed that, we have talked with Dr. Shaw about appropriate expressions of anger... I'm sorry. This is between us. But I would like you to apologize to David.

DAVID: It's not necessary.

ALDEN: No—we have an understanding in our family that there are consequences for inappropriate behaviors. I want you to apologize.

JUSTIN: I apologize.

ALDEN: I want you to drop the snide demeanor right now and apologize genuinely.

(Pause.)

JUSTIN: I apologize for being confrontational and critical. I understand that this was a celebration of my father's book and my mother's life. I'm sorry that my feelings of exclusion were inappropriately expressed.

(ALDEN stares. Not satisfied.)

DAVID: I want to say to both of you what I have said to my former wife, my daughter's mother. We each travel our own road through the dark woods that confront us in the aftermath of violence. There is a clearing at the end of those woods and we will all make it there, but we will each travel at our own pace. We need to be tolerant and respectful of our different journeys. That means patience with the one who walks more slowly through those woods and acceptance of the one who more swiftly finds his way. I want you both to think about that.

(Pause.)

JUSTIN: And did she buy that?

DAVID: Excuse me?

JUSTIN: Your ex-wife. She's suing you for like... eight years of back child support, right?

ALDEN: That's it. Wait for me outside. David, I will call you tomorrow to thank you properly—

DAVID: Tomorrow's no good; I'm going to Los Angeles. I need a word with you before you go.

ALDEN: *(To JUSTIN.)* Go get a soda and wait in the car.

JUSTIN: Yes, sir.

(JUSTIN exits.)

DAVID: He'll make it. He's one whipsmart kid.

ALDEN: I'm tremendously embarrassed. I would not have included him if I had any idea that—

DAVID: The interview was fine. We need to talk about you and your future with this network.

ALDEN: What do you mean?

DAVID: I'm going to Los Angeles tomorrow and I may be gone for a while. I'm going to be covering the Shannon Smith trial for Court TV.

ALDEN: Shannon Smith…

DAVID: Soap opera actress. Murdered by a co-star. It's an awful story. The judge won't allow cameras in the courtroom, so I'm going out there. I'm going to cover the trial for Court TV and I'm writing a trial log for *Esquire*. So I'm gonna be swamped. Meanwhile, I've had a promotion from the network. They've made me a producer.

ALDEN: Congratulations.

DAVID: Thank you. They've made me the producer in charge of crime programming. I'm looking at a series of crime-based programs down the road, but first thing I want to do is overhaul this show. It's not working.

ALDEN: I don't know that I'd agree—

DAVID: Alden, I'm on the women's channel. I'm here doing Charlie Rose and that's not what the viewers want. They want emotion. So, we change the format. We continue talking to victims, but we add color. We do re-enactments of the crimes. The current thinking—because it's a women's network, and because NBC is doing incredibly well with this, uh, *Law and Order the Special Victims Unit*… the idea is to shift the focus to sex crimes. Lot of interest in sex crimes right now. Now, I'm all for it, but I can't do it. I've got this gig in L.A. and I'm producing. So. I spoke with the network about you and they're very interested in you taking over as host.

ALDEN: Wow. My background, you know, is print journalism.

DAVID: Sure. They know, but they've seen you. On Charlie Rose, on Oprah. We've seen your approach, your demeanor and we feel very good about it. You are a man making peace. And that's the energy we want.

So new format: keep the victim interviews, limit the show to sex crimes, add re-enactments…

ALDEN: You're going to re-enact the… sex crimes?

DAVID: Tastefully. Also, one of the execs is interested in a crime prevention element. Safety tips, self-defense…

ALDEN: I think that's an excellent idea.

DAVID: Yeah. You re-enact, you bring on Officer Friendly to demonstrate the choke hold. I'm being flip, of course—

ALDEN: You are.

DAVID: The prevention angle is important to you?

ALDEN: The notion of serving victims is important. I think—

DAVID: Got it. We're on the same page. So this interests you?

ALDEN: It's unexpected but not unwelcome by any means, um…

DAVID: They're gonna ask to use the title.

ALDEN: The title?

DAVID: *After Ashley.* They like the title very much for a woman-focused show.

ALDEN: OK…

DAVID: That one you can think about. Room for negotiation on all of this, but one thing which may be a deal breaker. They want to move production to Florida.

ALDEN: Wow.

DAVID: It's just too expensive here and they have a studio there. It's nice, weather's beautiful. My concern, quite frankly, is Justin.

ALDEN: Today was an unusually bad… episode.

DAVID: There's some… anxiety at the network about his behavior problems. They want to really push this show and that means a commitment on your part. If your kid is in trouble, I have to ask you if that's a commitment you feel you can make.

ALDEN: He has made extraordinary progress. Today, obviously, was unpleasant. But I have to tell you, today also represents an enormous leap. Since Ashley's death, we've been through drugs and alcohol and petty criminal sort of acting out stuff and that is in the past. We made an enormous leap with his therapist in teaching him to use words to address the discomfort instead of acting destructively.

DAVID: Right… using words is good. I'm gonna be blunt here. Your credibility goes out the window if you've got a messed-up kid. Especially on a woman's show.

ALDEN: I completely understand. I can assure you that Justin is out of the woods. He's angry, but he's… bright and he's strong. His destructive phase was just that. A phase. It's over.

(*DAVID looks at his watch.*)

DAVID: My flight's at eight. Can you do a drink at the hotel in, say, an hour?

ALDEN: Absolutely.

DAVID: Good man.

(*DAVID exits. JUSTIN enters. He's heard the end of the conversation.*)

JUSTIN: Are we moving to Florida?

ALDEN: I've been presented with an exceptional opportunity.

JUSTIN: I heard. Are we moving to Florida?

ALDEN: I'd like to talk to you about it. I'd like us to sit down and brainstorm ways in which you can be a part of this. You have terrific ideas and you could really help me.

JUSTIN: Let's bottom line this. You're going to take the job no matter what I say, right? *(Pause.)* Remember that little pact we made with Dr. Shaw? I don't bullshit you, you don't bullshit me?

(Pause.)

ALDEN: I am going to take the job. And I need your commitment to supporting—

JUSTIN: I'll keep a low profile. I'm gonna need my own place, an ample allowance, and a reliable fake ID.

ALDEN: That's not... I'm not doing anything illegal.

JUSTIN: Fine. I'm going to need a five hundred dollar advance for... oh, let's call it... resort wear. Plus the allowance, the apartment, and the car.

ALDEN: Car?

JUSTIN: Used car. Just has to run.

(Pause.)

ALDEN: Fine. I think that's all fine.

(JUSTIN turns to the audience and addresses them.)

JUSTIN: Once upon a time in America.

(Music. A maudlin, syrupy song we associate with tributes to the dead. For example, Eric Clapton's "Tears in Heaven" or U2's "Walk On" (performed at post-9/11 U2 concerts while names of the dead were scrolled on a big screen.)

(JUSTIN leaves the stage. DAVID and ALDEN separate, move to opposite sides downstage. Make-up artists (tech crew?) rush on stage and apply make-up. Lights on DAVID.)

DAVID: In opening statements today, we heard a story of talent, turmoil, and fatal obsession in the dream capitol of the world, Hollywood. Shannon Smith loved children, horses, and the ocean. She used her soap opera earnings to send her little sister to college. And she loved a man named Ryan Bogart who prosecutors say took first her heart, and then her life. I stand today in a Hollywood darkened by the theft of one bright star. I'm reminded today of my own daughter whose death, like Shannon Smith's, I refer to as a crime against hope.

ALDEN: *(This is new to him; he's not as comfortable as DAVID.)* In the landscape of American violence, sexual crimes are a most dastardly violation. I lost my wife in just such an attack. Her name was Ashley and I can think of no better tribute to her memory than a program that gives victims a voice and concerned women a forum in which to address their fears. I'm Alden Hammond. Please join me weekdays at four o'clock as I try to make America After Ashley a better place for women.

(Music begins: Eminem's "Stan.")

(A bar in Central Florida. JUSTIN leans against the bar and drinks a beer. He looks self-conscious. A girl, JULIE, dances to the song, "Stan," Eminem's tale of a violent fan. JUSTIN watches for a bit. The girl notices him watching and joins him at the bar.)

JULIE: Hi.

(JUSTIN waves.)

JULIE: Is it ok if I sit here?

JUSTIN: Go for it.

JULIE: *(Sitting.)* I'm Julie.

JUSTIN: Justin.

JULIE: It's nice to meet you. Are you by yourself?

JUSTIN: Am I by myself? Uh.... No. No, I'm not.

JULIE: *(Getting up.)* OK—

JUSTIN: I walk with Christ, so... I'm never alone.

JULIE: Wow. Wow, that's amazing. *(Pause.)* It must be so... comforting to have that.

JUSTIN: Him. I have him. J.C.

JULIE: Wow. I'd love to know what that feels like. If it isn't too personal. I mean, I'm not religious, but it seems like we're living in such a lonely time. All the structures that traditionally connected us have eroded and it's like...

JUSTIN: Yeah... I was actually fucking with you.

JULIE: Sorry?

JUSTIN: It was a joke.

JULIE: Oh. OK. A lot of people here are really religious so it didn't seem that far out. *(Pause.)* Do you believe in God?

JUSTIN: Umm.... Wow. You are just determined to have a bonding moment.

JULIE: I'm sorry. I just wanted to talk to you. If you don't want to—

JUSTIN: We can talk. There's just usually this whole flirting/drinking step that precedes the, uh, revelation of metaphysical belief systems.

JULIE: That seemed invasive?

JUSTIN: Not invasive, just… bizarre. One minute you're grinding to violent, misogynist rap, the next minute you're, like, in my lap lamenting the collapse of the family. Who are you?

JULIE: I'm… Julie.

(Pause.)

JUSTIN: OK, Julie. Let's do this old school. What's your sign?

JULIE: Pisces.

JUSTIN: How's this weather treating you?

JULIE: I don't really like the sun.

JUSTIN: And you live in Florida. Neato. And what do you do, Julie, when you're not writhing provocatively to gangsta rap?

JULIE: I go to school. Eminem isn't gangsta rap.

JUSTIN: And in school, you study…

JULIE: English. Literature.

JUSTIN: OK. Now I know you. Buy me a whiskey and let's talk about God.

JULIE: Um… my purse is at the table. You think you know me now?

JUSTIN: I totally know you. The rap music is throwing me a little. Other than that you're very clear.

JULIE: Really?

JUSTIN: Really.

JULIE: OK, who am I?

JUSTIN: You are… the sad little Goth girl who won't play kickball.

JULIE: Excuse me?

JUSTIN: You… cut gym class to smoke cigarettes and read… Sylvia Plath. The lesbian gym teacher—we'll call her Jean—she's like, "Julie put down *The Bell Jar* and go play kickball." So you go. You get out there in your little black shorts and your Nine Inch Nails babydoll tee and you… you wince as boy after boy kicks the ball at you. You stand… still, but not indifferent, pummeled by the kickball…. taunted and jeered at… too alienated and lethargic to just kick the fucking ball—

JULIE: Wow.

JUSTIN: I'm dead on. Right?

JULIE: No.

JUSTIN: Did you cut gym to smoke?

JULIE: Yeah, but—

JUSTIN: BINGO.

JULIE: No bingo. I'm not…. You just totally judged me and made me into this gross caricature based on nothing—

JUSTIN: Hey, you come over here all dressed in black asking if I believe in God—

JULIE: But you started it being all Jesus is my co-pilot. I wasn't the one—

JUSTIN: Fine. New topic. Violent gangsta rap and the women who love it. Discuss.

JULIE: I said Eminem isn't gangsta rap.

JUSTIN: Yeah, but the man sings almost exclusively about hurting women. Bitches. Is this a masochism thing? Is he... sexy in the way that say... you and your Goth friends find Dracula sexy?

JULIE: I'm not a Goth!

JUSTIN: Fine. Eminem wants to cut your throat and throw you in a river. And that makes you dance. I don't get it.

JULIE: I don't feel like he hates women as a whole as much as he hates...

JUSTIN: Every woman he's ever met?

JULIE: He's been through a lot, you know. He had a really terrible life.

JUSTIN: Please—

JULIE: All the women in his life betrayed him.

JUSTIN: So they should die?

JULIE: No. Of course not. But he's entitled to be angry and to express that anger, you know? Sylvia Plath compared her father and her husband to Hitler. Nobody's pulling her books off shelves.

JUSTIN: Fair. Fair point. *(Pause.)* Cool.

JULIE: What?

JUSTIN: Ummm... this. This is cool.

JULIE: What part of this?

JUSTIN: Uh... I don't know. A... really cute girl approaches me in a bar and she turns out to have, like, a functioning brain in her head. And my birthday's not 'til next week.

JULIE: Thank you.

JUSTIN: I'm sorry I was suspicious.

JULIE: That's OK. I'm suspicious when guys come on to me.

JUSTIN: Oh, so you were coming on to me?

JULIE: Well—

JUSTIN: Can we clarify that you were in fact coming on to me?

JULIE: Maybe...

JUSTIN: Awesome. In that case, I will buy *you* a whiskey.

(*JUSTIN fishes through his pockets. A beat.*)

JULIE: This is not an easy place to be... thoughtful.

JUSTIN: Dollar Margarita night at The Sandbar? No, it isn't.

JULIE: Central Florida. I'm not saying everyone's dumb, but... I do think that temperate climates maybe attract a sort of non-reflective personality type.

JUSTIN: Very diplomatic.

JULIE: I'm from New Hampshire.

JUSTIN: Really?

JULIE: Yeah.

JUSTIN: D.C.

JULIE: OK. I've thought about this and I think... I think winter is important. It's a part of the life cycle and to not have it or to choose not to have it, it's like... it perverts your vision of the world. You never see your world shrivel up and die, you know, so you begin to feel... immortal.

JUSTIN: Definitely. Yeah. It's also about... obstacles, you know, impediments. Too fucking hot. Too fucking cold. Getting kicked in the ass by nature eight months out of the year is just plain character building.

JULIE: Exactly! And in a weird way that sorta brings us back to Eminem.

JUSTIN: How so?

JULIE: Eminem, Sylvia Plath. These people have been through things. Awful things. But it made them... who they are. You know? The pain. It enabled them to see things... in a way that most of us can't.

JUSTIN: Sylvia Plath is, you know, rolling in her grave at this comparison...

JULIE: Have you ever read *Man's Search for Meaning* by Viktor Frankel?

JUSTIN: No.

JULIE: Oh, you should. He's this man who survived the Holocaust and became a psychotherapist. He talks about the acquisition of meaning from profound suffering. It's just amazing. I mean... nothing really bad has ever happened to me and in some ways I feel like there's this whole dimension of experience that I've... I don't want to say missed, but—

JUSTIN: Mmm hmm.

JULIE: I haven't been confronted—spiritually—in the way that—

JUSTIN: Well, I'm no Hitler, but I'd be happy to... torture and dehumanize you if it would help you write a poem.

JULIE: That's not what I meant.

JUSTIN: I'm not strong, but I can be extremely insensitive.

JULIE: This seems ridiculous to you?

JUSTIN: It's veering perilously in that direction. But hey—it's important to stay in touch with all that was really good about the death camps. Now let's talk about the weather again...

JULIE: *(Inching closer to him.)* I can't even imagine being in your head...

JUSTIN: And there's no need for you to do that. So it's all good.

JULIE: Have you ever written about it?

JUSTIN: Written about what?

(Pause.)

JULIE: You know... what happened. How it felt...

JUSTIN: Uh.... Growing up in a city built on a swamp? No. Here's an idea for you: All great Southern literature precedes the invention of the air conditioner. What do you think about that?

(JULIE reaches out a hand and touches him.)

JULIE: I so understand if you don't want to talk about it, but I would be here for you if you did. I could never understand, but I could... be here.

(Pause.)

JUSTIN: You know what I think, Julie?

JULIE: What?

JUSTIN: I use the "c" word very, very sparingly and I think you, Julie, are a cunt.

JULIE: What—Why would say that?

JUSTIN: What do you want? What was your objective in talking to me?

JULIE: Just to... I mean, you're alone and you're new here. I just wanted to be nice—

JUSTIN: Right. And there's a guy right outside that door, half-dead from AIDS trying to round up enough change for a meal. But you didn't shake your ass in his face, now did you?

JULIE: No, but that's.... My friend recognized you. She said, "There's The 911 Kid"—

JUSTIN: I am not The 911 Kid! I have a name!

JULIE: I know. I just... I...

JUSTIN: Let's do this, Julie. You're very articulate when you're not lying, so pull it together. Why did you talk to me?

JULIE: You just looked lonely, I thought—

JUSTIN: Bull-shit.

JULIE: I wanted to maybe get to know you—

JUSTIN: Why?

JULIE: Why.... Do I have to have a reason?

JUSTIN: No, but you do. (Pause.) Let's go.

(JUSTIN stands.)

JUSTIN: Come on.

JULIE: What do you mean—"Come on"?

JUSTIN: Come home with me. You can tell all your friends you fucked The
    911 Kid. If you want, I'll slap you around, you can write a haiku.

JULIE: That's your invitation? You think I'm gonna go for that?

JUSTIN: Yeah, I do. You're a Goth in Central Florida. You have nothing better
    to do.

    (Pause. JUSTIN weighs his hands like scales.)

    Creepy guy with murdered mother, rum punch and frat boys at The
    Sandbar. Hmmmm.... What's a sad little Goth girl to do?

    (JUSTIN walks out of the bar, confident she'll follow. After a beat, she does.)

END OF ACT ONE

ACT TWO

*Music: Syndrome Z's "Down to Mother." This is a fictional rap song which
contains a sample of JUSTIN's 911 tape. (*See lyrics at end of script.)*

*We're in JUSTIN's apartment. There is no furniture except for one tattered
armchair and a TV/VCR on the floor. Unpacked boxes here and there.
JUSTIN is asleep on the floor in a sleeping bag. JULIE, partly dressed, tiptoes
around picking up the rest of her clothes.*

JUSTIN: What time is it?

JULIE: Eight-thirty.

JUSTIN: Why are you up?

JULIE: Because you made me sleep in a chair and it was really uncomfortable.

JUSTIN: You said you didn't mind.

JULIE: I lied. Do you know where my purse is?

JUSTIN: Uh.... You left it with your friends.

JULIE: Shit.

    (Silence.)

JUSTIN: Do you want a Coke or something?

JULIE: No, I don't want a Coke.

    (JULIE walks offstage and returns with a glass of water.)

JUSTIN: Sorry about the chair... thing. You should show me that used furni-
    ture place you were talking about—

JULIE: It's not hard to find. It's on Kalmia past the mall.

    (Pause.)

JUSTIN: Are you not a morning person or is this some sort of passive-aggressive snubbing thing…

JULIE: Look. I didn't do anything I didn't want to do, but…. In the light of day I feel like maybe I don't need this.

JUSTIN: Need what?

JULIE: I had too much to drink and I probably sounded like an idiot, but that doesn't give you the right to talk to me like you talked to me last night.

JUSTIN: Hey. Making you sleep in the chair was caddish and I apologize. Very uncool. The rest… I just call it as I see it. If the truth hurts—

JULIE: No. Fuck you, Justin. I knew you were in a hard place and I—

JUSTIN: You don't *know* anything about me.

JULIE: I just mean I know what happened and I thought—

JUSTIN: No—What happened to my mom is none of *your* business. It's not an opportunity for you to… to… take a walk on the dark side or whatever—

JULIE: That's not what I was doing.

JUSTIN: Yes, it is! You hit on me because my mom was murdered. Which in and of itself is repellent, but you didn't even have the decency to be up front about it. You pretended to be attracted to me.

JULIE: You were alone. I made some small talk. Is that a crime?

JUSTIN: You hit on me. You made my day, Julie. You made my year. Then you showed your hand. If you think I'm going to apologize…. You play, you pay, Julie. If you're gonna starfuck—

JULIE: Starfuck? Please. Just because your 911 call is sampled into a rap song—

JUSTIN: Girls coming onto me because of what happened to my mother is disgusting to me, OK? You girls are bottom feeders. I will apologize for making you sleep in the chair but I am not gonna tell you that what you did last night is OK.

JULIE: You're full of shit. You know?

JUSTIN: How's that?

JULIE: You didn't throw a drink in my face and leave. Did you? You got laid. It would seem to me that you lost your opportunity to be morally superior when you brought me home and—

JUSTIN: Hey—You use me, I use you.

JULIE: So drop the superior act. You got to fuck me and tell me off. Now we both feel like garbage. I'm gonna go.

JUSTIN: Can I ask you one question?

JULIE: It depends.

JUSTIN: (*Genuinely curious.*) How does it work—being a… a… victim groupie?

I mean, I got mail from girls for years. I still do. *(Pause.)* Now... I had a variety of reactions to September Eleventh but none of them was, like, wow I'm gonna write to some of the widows and see if I can score.

JULIE: That's different.

JUSTIN: How?

(Pause.)

JULIE: It's the 911 call. You seemed like a really good person.

JUSTIN: Because I called 911?

JULIE: Because you wouldn't leave. The house. I think a lot of people—girls— were... impressed that you were so upset.

JUSTIN: She was my mother.

JULIE: I know. But still... I think a lot of guys would have left. I don't know. I think that's probably why you get mail.

(The phone rings. JUSTIN picks it up.)

JUSTIN: Yeah. *(Pause.)* Not really. I have a friend here. *(Pause.)* A friend. Try not to seem so shocked. *(Pause.)* Fine. Come over. But in the future, I want more notice. And pick up coffee on the way. *(Pause.)* I don't know. I'll ask. *(To JULIE.)* Do you want a... a cross bun or a sunshine cake or whatever the fuck they eat here?

JULIE: No, thanks.

JUSTIN: *(Into the phone.)* Just the coffee. How do you take it?

JULIE: Um... half and half. Light.

JUSTIN: Put a lot of cream in hers. Bye. What?! *(Pause.)* You don't know her. Bye. *(To JULIE.)* My Dad.

JULIE: Is he pissed that I'm here?

JUSTIN: No. How old are you?

JULIE: I'll be twenty in February.

JUSTIN: I knew this was statutory rape. My dad is loosely connected to law enforcement. If I tell him what happened, they'll arrest you. They'll arrest you and then they'll do a show about it. Would you like that?

JULIE: I don't think so.

JUSTIN: The show will feature a tawdry re-enactment of what occurred here. It will be full of dialogue like I'll say, "I don't think I'm ready for this" and you'll say, "Be a man! I didn't come here to talk, babyface!"

JULIE: Is the show really going to be like that?

JUSTIN: The show *is* really like that.

JULIE: It hasn't started yet.

JUSTIN: It hasn't aired yet. They've taped a bunch.

JULIE: You saw them?

JUSTIN: They're over there.

JULIE: Can I see?

JUSTIN: I thought you had to go.

JULIE: I don't have to. You were just being really… aggressive, but if you've calmed down now—

JUSTIN: You want to hit on my dad.

JULIE: No, I don't. Can I see one of the tapes?

JUSTIN: They're horrible.

JULIE: Just a few minutes, get the idea.

(JUSTIN fishes a videotape out of a box beside the chair.)

JUSTIN: Go for it.

(JULIE puts the tape into the machine and presses play. The After ASHLEY theme music plays.

A re-made ALDEN enters. He's definitely been styled and coached for television.)

ALDEN: In the landscape of American violence, sexual crimes are a most dastardly violation…

JUSTIN: No, Dad, you think?

ALDEN: When my wife, Ashley, was murdered, I was completely unprepared for the range of emotions I would experience from anger to guilt to a depth of grief I felt I might never emerge from. But I did emerge and I did survive. I believe that communication heals—

JUSTIN: Jesus Christ.

ALDEN: Today you'll meet a woman who survived a brutal assault at a Milwaukee tavern. She'll share her story and her journey with us in our first half hour. In our second, a veteran law enforcement officer will offer safety tips to keep you from becoming a victim. I'm Alden Hammond. I'm glad you're with me today to help make America a safer place for women… After Ashley.

JUSTIN: Mute it!

JULIE: Wait—can I just watch the re-enactment?

(ALDEN moves back and two re-enactment actors enter. The actress who played ASHLEY plays the RE-ENACTMENT VICTIM. The actor who will play RODERICK plays the RE-ENACTMENT RAPIST. He wears all black including, inexplicably, a cape. The woman applies lipstick in an imaginary mirror. The man grabs her from behind. She screams. They struggle in slow motion. The effect is more voluptuous passion than assault. They freeze in a pose reminiscent of a Gothic romance.… Think Dracula, Dark Shadows. Stylized melodrama.)

JUSTIN: Julie, mute it! Mute the death porn!

(She mutes the volume and ALDEN and the actors freeze.)

JUSTIN: Turn it off. I'm gonna be sick.

(JULIE turns the television off.)

JULIE: I think it was rendered really tastefully.

JUSTIN: Well, it must have been one of those tasteful rapes.

(ALDEN and the RE-ENACTMENT ACTORS exit.)

JULIE: They can't, like, show it.

JUSTIN: Why not?

JULIE: You think they should show... it?

JUSTIN: I don't think they should be re-enacting it at all, but... yeah, if they have to re-enact it, yes, I think they should show it.

JULIE: Why?

JUSTIN: OK. Why do they do re-enactments?

JULIE: To show—

JUSTIN: Why? Show why? Why do they have to show re-enactments of the crimes?

(Pause.)

JULIE: Because television is a visual medium?

JUSTIN: Nonsense. Watch *Meet the Press*. Nobody's re-enacting congression-al... committee meetings.

JULIE: That's completely different. That's not an entertainment—

JUSTIN: Exactly! The re-enactments are purely for entertainment. America likes sex crimes. They find them entertaining and they find them arous-ing. Now. They can have a cable channel devoted to nothing but rape for all I care. I have no objection as long as they show it. None of this *Dark Shadows* Goth romance crap. America wants sex crimes, give them sex crimes.

JULIE: It did look like *Dark Shadows*. You're right. *(Pause.)* And I don't really understand why he was wearing a cape. It was some dive bar in Milwaukee.

JUSTIN: Re-enacted sex crimes are all about ravishing.

JULIE: What do you mean—"ravishing"?

JUSTIN: You're the Goth English major. You tell me. Define ravishing.

JULIE: Well... I guess it's like... kind of a romance novel word, like... a euphemism for sex or.... It's like saying passed away instead of died, it's like a softer way of saying—

JUSTIN: Fucked?

JULIE: I was gonna say had sex, but… yeah. *(Pause.)* Ravishing is kinda like what Dracula did. It's like getting taken, you know, in an overwhelming way. It kind of implies, like, a lack of participation on the woman's part. But it also implies that she enjoys it…

JUSTIN: OK. A+, Julie. Gold star. We're not writing a thesis.

JULIE: Sorry.

JUSTIN: Ravishing. All across America, Julie, housewives will be putting babies in cribs so that their hands may be free to masturbate. And if I weren't here, you would, too.

JULIE: No, I wouldn't.

JUSTIN: You find Eminem sensual. You are this program's target audience.

JULIE: I'm sorry I turned it on.

JUSTIN: I'm sorry it turned you on.

(Pause.)

JULIE: But what would be wrong… I mean, maybe they are lending the crimes a certain tragic beauty in the re-telling. Is that so bad?

JUSTIN: It's appalling and unholy.

JULIE: I don't know. I think maybe that's the only way you heal, you know? To re-imagine your… sorrows as gifts.

JUSTIN: Stop!

JULIE: What's the alternative?

JUSTIN: The truth. The alternative is the truth. There's nothing beautiful about being raped in a bathroom, Julie—

JULIE: So you want to… re-enact it authentically and—

JUSTIN: No! Re-enacting it authentically is second choice. First choice is shutting the fuck up about it.

JULIE: "Shutting up" sounds like you want people to go back to being ashamed—

JUSTIN: Oh, I am ready and willing to lead the return to shame movement. People are on TV eating bugs, trying to marry millionaires. Shame is an idea whose time has come. Back. *(Pause.)* Now, you take September Eleventh.

JULIE: What about it?

JUSTIN: People in this country don't know how to grieve. They're so… estranged from silence and… reverence. Lisa Beamer—my God. That woman makes my father look restrained.

JULIE: Lisa Beamer… the one whose husband said "let's roll"?

JUSTIN: Exactly. That woman fucking trademarked her husband's last words. She's on Oprah within a month, she's got a book out to coincide with the one-year anniversary. Who ARE these people? When my mother died I was like… I could barely fucking dress myself. And we had all these offers to go on TV and stuff and I thought well of course we won't do that because that would be *insane*, but my dad…. *(Pause.)* Do you know who Christopher Collins is?

JULIE: No.

JUSTIN: He writes really long books and sort of superimposes his neuroses on, like, social issues. After my mom died, he started contacting me.

JULIE: Right.

JUSTIN: My dad tried to buddy up to him, but he didn't want Dad. He wanted me to, like, go stay at his house in Iowa so he could "get to know me" and write an article for a magazine.

JULIE: Are you gonna tell me he molested you?

JUSTIN: No. I didn't want to go. It was maybe six months after my mom died and I was still… I was like barely a human, you know. But I went cuz that's what my dad wanted me to do and…. It was actually great. We played video games and ate pizza. We went to theme restaurants with his girlfriend. I needed a friend really badly then because the friends I had were treating me like Quasimoto. No one could deal. So I start feeling good, like, I have a friend who can deal with this, with me. And then it turned. It was like all the good stuff was just fattening me up for the kill. All of a sudden we can't just hang out anymore, it's all creepy conversations like "Did you ever want to fuck your mother, Justin? You can tell me." And I'd be like, "No way, man. Not my thing. Want to go to Denny's again?" And he's all, "I have rape fantasies about my mother, Justin. Nothing you can say would shock me." Finally, I go to bed at, like, nine o'clock just to get the fuck away from him. End of the story? His girlfriend crawled into bed with me and we had sex. I lost my virginity. Guy stopped speaking to me. I charged a seven-hundred-dollar flight home on my dad's credit card, kicked in a window in my house and just stayed… by myself 'til my dad came back from New York.

JULIE: That's so horrible. I'm so sorry.

JUSTIN: It's fine. It's not, like, Bosnia or anything. But it's fucked up! The point is just…. My mother was murdered. I don't know what the aftermath of that is supposed to be, but I don't think it's supposed to be… a book and a TV show and a rap song and a girl in my room. It's like we've lost the truth of it, we've buried it under all this… junk.

JULIE: So your solution is silence? Just don't ever speak of it?

JUSTIN: I don't have a solution. But shutting the fuck up would be a start.
(Pause.)

JULIE: I did hit on you because of your mom. I'm sorry.

JUSTIN: I just don't get it. I haven't read Viktor Frankel, though, so... fuck if I know.

JULIE: I talked to you about Viktor Frankel? Shit. I was really drunk. I'm so sorry.

JUSTIN: It's alright.

JULIE: No, it isn't. *(Pause.)* I wanted to be a writer for a while. I tried. I wasn't good at making things up and I didn't have anything in my life worth writing about—

JUSTIN: Well, that's just lazy.

JULIE: No, it isn't! I mean look at all of Shakespeare.... It's all blood, war, struggle, death, tragic love. I don't have any of that and I don't know how to fake it because.... Anyway. I guess I did think... I do think I'd be deeper if I'd experienced more... darkness. I'm embarrassed. I'm gonna shut up.

JUSTIN: Well.... As far as the writing goes, I still say you're lazy. And reading the wrong books. You should read, like, books by Victorian women on bed rest—

JULIE: What?

JUSTIN: You're the English major. You know what I mean. There's a long proud tradition of bored women going ape shit. From the Brontës to the Carpenters, women with no life experience have held us spellbound—

JULIE: No, you're right. I'm not a writer. I just have to figure out what I am. *(Awkward pause.)* I should probably take off before your dad gets here. But I totally meant that about going furniture shopping.

JUSTIN: *(A little too enthusiastically.)* OK.

JULIE: You can't pick up girls like this.

JUSTIN: I... apologize for the chair.

JULIE: So, you want my number?

JUSTIN: You should stay and get your coffee. You can take it to go.

JULIE: I don't want to make things uncomfortable.

JUSTIN: Actually, my hope was that you'd serve a... buffer-like function.

JULIE: You want me to stay?

JUSTIN: Would you? Just for—

JULIE: Absolutely.

(JULIE settles back in to stay a while. A bit of an awkward silence.)

JUSTIN: So... Julie. Tell me a little bit about yourself.

JULIE: What do you want to know?

JUSTIN: You're from New Hampshire?

JULIE: Yes.

JUSTIN: Why are you here?

JULIE: I'm in school.

JUSTIN: Right. But why… I mean isn't there a mediocre state school a little closer to home, you could—

JULIE: My mother moved here and I— That was a shitty thing to say.

JUSTIN: What?

JULIE: Uh…. Yeah. There is a University of New Hampshire, but at the time my mom was here and I had this boyfriend, so…. It's actually a decent school for what I do, so—

(There's a knock at the door. ALDEN enters with coffee for all.)

ALDEN: Hello… *(Noting JULIE.)* Hi, I'm Alden Hammond.

JULIE: Hi. I'm Julie. Wow. It's incredible to meet you.

JUSTIN: Incredible? Did you just say "incredible"?

JULIE: Well—

JUSTIN: Wow. Go, Dad. I think the best I got was "interesting." What did he do to merit "incredible"?

JULIE: I don't know. I just—

JUSTIN: Do you mean incredible as in… so superior as to defy belief or as in… lacking credibility?

ALDEN: Justin—

JUSTIN: Julie is an English major. She's prepared for the hard questions.

JULIE: Not at 9 A.M. before my coffee.

ALDEN: Fair enough. I'm a java junkie myself. I think this one is yours.

(ALDEN hands JULIE her coffee, then gives JUSTIN his.)

JULIE: Thank you.

JUSTIN: I showed Julie the tape of the show.

ALDEN: Oh, I gather you liked it, then. That's terrific.

JUSTIN: Yeah, we both agreed that it's "incredible."

ALDEN: Oh, good. Good. That means a lot to me. You know this has been an amazing journey. When the smoke clears and I get a couple minutes to myself, there's an essay I want to write about this.

JUSTIN: No kidding.

ALDEN: Yeah. The things I've learned, the women I've met—

JUSTIN: I don't want to hear about the women you've met.

ALDEN: The women we've featured on the program. Their stories are just remarkable. I have found myself… speechless on occasion.

JULIE: It must be kind of inspiring.

ALDEN: You know, it's really been a bizarre mix of emotions. It's inspiring and it's infuriating. Many of these women have had very negative experiences with law enforcement.

JULIE: Wow.

ALDEN: And it's a terrific feeling for me—

JUSTIN: What is? Their degradation?

ALDEN: No. The sense of empowerment they feel from being able to tell their stories. This is where television can really be very powerful. We can send a message with this program that that kind of treatment is unacceptable.

JULIE: It's so true, you know, I worked on a rape crisis line.

JUSTIN: You did?

JULIE: Yeah. And I heard stuff. Like that. You know? I mean if the girl's, say, been drinking or even been to a bar…

ALDEN: The victim is immediately suspect. And I admit my own ignorance. I did not know that attitude was as prevalent as apparently it is.

JUSTIN: And the re-enactments?

ALDEN: What about them?

JUSTIN: Do the women feel empowered by seeing the worst moment of their life re-enacted as soft core?

ALDEN: I don't agree with you, Justin. We've had this conversation.

JUSTIN: You're packaging sickness as entertainment. People are gonna jerk off to it.

ALDEN: Justin. This is one of those areas in which we will agree to disagree and in that agreement honor each other's opinions.

JUSTIN: *(To JULIE.)* We've been in therapy together. In case that sounded a little rehearsed. *(Pause.)* If anyone ever tries to re-enact what happened to mom I will… they'll have to fucking get past me.

ALDEN: We change the topic… now.

(Silence.)

JULIE: It must be very grueling work. Being on television.

JUSTIN: That's the same topic.

JULIE: No, it isn't. I'm talking about the hours and stuff. I mean it must be hard work.

ALDEN: It's unlike anything I've ever done. I have a new-found respect for people who work in television. It is an unbelievably rigorous, exacting medium.

JULIE: Yeah, you look a little tired.

ALDEN: Well.... There's actually an interesting, um, humorous story... I was taken to task for the, um, circles under my eyes which are a product, you know, of these long shoots, early mornings.... In any event, the make-up person on the program put something under my eyes which was absolutely miraculous and I asked her what it was and it was actually Preparation H. The, um, hemorrhoid—

JUSTIN: Ass cream.

JULIE: Wow.

ALDEN: It's apparently a trick of the trade.

JULIE: I never knew that.

ALDEN: I didn't either.

JULIE: It makes sense, I guess.

ALDEN: It must constrict tissue in some way...

JULIE: It shrinks swelling... yeah. I put toothpaste on pimples. Sometimes. That works, too.

ALDEN: Does it?

JULIE: Yeah.

(Silence.)

JUSTIN: OK. Where did this interaction go wrong? Dad, this hot chick called you incredible and then took your side in every one of our arguments. The way to work that to your advantage is not to bring up ass cream.

JULIE: It was interesting.

JUSTIN: It was incredible.

ALDEN: I'm going to get a glass of water. Can I bring anyone—

JUSTIN: That water filter you bought me?

ALDEN: Yes?

JUSTIN: I haven't assembled it.

ALDEN: OK. Well, I'll do that now then. It should just take a minute.

(ALDEN goes to the kitchen.)

JULIE: What the fuck is wrong with you?

JUSTIN: What?

JULIE: Why do you talk to him like that?

JUSTIN: Uh.... Long answer or short answer?

JULIE: If I talked to my parents like that, they would kick my ass.

JUSTIN: One of the perks of having hippie parents. That's never going to happen.

JULIE: You're making me uncomfortable. Stop it.

JUSTIN: If you want to go for it, I won't stand in your way.

JULIE: Why are you doing this? I thought we worked this out.

(ALDEN returns.)

ALDEN: The filter needs to soak for fifteen minutes.

JUSTIN: You should probably keep an eye on it.

ALDEN: Why?

JULIE: Sit down. Chill out. Drink your coffee.

ALDEN: Thank you. Julie, what do you study?

JULIE: English. Literature.

ALDEN: That's great! Do you have an area of interest?

JULIE: I study Romanticism.

ALDEN: Oh! The poets? Byron, Shelley—

JULIE: Right. Some novels, too. I'm actually trying to narrow it.

ALDEN: Sure. Now will you include the Americans?

JULIE: That gets complicated.

ALDEN: I would imagine. Thoreau can be construed—

JUSTIN: We should all get comfortable if he's gonna talk about Thoreau—

JULIE: Justin!

ALDEN: That's fair. Thoreau is a… a passion of mine. I would go on. My only point being that the agendas are similar in many respects, but finally very different. And that ultimately has to do with the American myth, the myth of self-invention. The European writers don't—they can't—embrace self-determinism the way their American counterparts do…. I'll stop.

JULIE: No, I know exactly what you mean. That's so true.

(Pause.)

ALDEN: David Gavin, my producer, is going to be arriving shortly. He has some things he'd like to talk to you about, Justin, so I think it's fair to warn Julie—

JUSTIN: He's a pig.

ALDEN: He's not a pig. He's wearing a producer's hat these days and can come across as rather abrupt. It occurs to me this may not be Julie's idea of how to spend a Saturday morning.

JULIE: I'll go.

JUSTIN: You can stay.

JULIE: No, if you guys are going to talk business…

JUSTIN: I said you can stay. Don't ask my friend to leave. I mean, just because you're done talking ass cream and Thoreau, doesn't mean—

ALDEN: You're right. You're right. That wasn't appropriate. That was your decision to make. I'm sorry. Julie you're more than welcome to stay.

JUSTIN: Hey!! She stays if I say she stays. You don't decide who is welcome in my house!

ALDEN: You're right. I'm sorry. I apologize. I was completely out of line.

(*Pause.*)

JUSTIN: I have a very bad feeling right now. You're doing that thing you do, you know, when you get really, really, uh, I'm gonna use a five-dollar SAT word here—obsequious with me.

ALDEN: I think what I'm doing is acknowledging my error and—

JUSTIN: So when David arrives.... Would I be incorrect in thinking David is coming here to say something that's really gonna piss me off?

ALDEN: I don't know how you're going to feel about what David has to say.

(*DAVID knocks on the door and enters.*)

DAVID: Hello?

ALDEN: Hello. David. Hi. Come in.

DAVID: Hello. Justin, nice to see you again. What's the story here? Where's the furniture?

ALDEN: I've told him. Anytime he wants to—

DAVID: This is unacceptable. Why didn't I know about this? Justin, we're gonna get right on this. A man needs a home. This is not a home.

JUSTIN: David, I couldn't agree more.

DAVID: Yeah? So what gives? You're here over a month. Didn't your father tell you we'd pick up the tab to furnish this place?

ALDEN: I did tell him. I've encouraged him to—

DAVID: Are you in a depression?

ALDEN: He's doing great. It's, you know, trying to get a teenage boy to go shopping, that's just—

DAVID: You're not squatting here, son. This is your home.

JUSTIN: Yes it is. And I am on it, David. I am on it and Julie is on it.

DAVID: Who's Julie?

JULIE: I'm Julie.

JUSTIN: Julie has been showing me swatches for going on two weeks now. And just this morning I was telling her... I was telling her pretty much exactly what you're saying which is that this is my home and I'm a man and I need furniture. It's been all swatches no action, coming on two weeks now.

DAVID: (*To JULIE.*) No, that's not right. What's the hold up?

JUSTIN: The hold up is too many fucking swatches. Too many swatches, too many paint chips, too many design… concepts. She thinks she's an artist…. She's trying to sell me on this whole fucking nautical theme… wallpaper with little anchors and sailor boys…

DAVID: No, no, no, no—

JUSTIN: She tried to sell me a cast-iron globe and a bed shaped like a canoe and that's when I said enough.

DAVID: I don't like the sound of that at all.

ALDEN: Justin—

JUSTIN: I set her straight. Didn't I?

JULIE: You did.

DAVID: If you're not up to the job, someone else is.

ALDEN: Where did you meet… Julie?

JUSTIN: I met her… on my morning run.

ALDEN: Your morning—

JUSTIN: Run. My run. I'm a runner now. A morning runner. *(Pause.)* I run around the… reservoir. I would say have a seat, but…

DAVID: That's fine. I can stand. I can't stay long. Justin, your father and I want to share with you some very exciting news. The show premieres one week from today—

JUSTIN: That's not news. I know that.

DAVID: That's not the news. The news is that we have… I have cemented an alliance between your father's program, *After Ashley,* and a very important local philanthropist. Do you know the name Aaron Weintraub?

JUSTIN: No.

JULIE: I know the, uh, the Weintraub Center.

DAVID: Weintraub High School, Weintraub Planetarium, The Marissa Weintraub Reilly Theatre, The Sylvia Weintraub Library. The man's a gazillionaire; he's put his name and his kids' names on half the county. This is one of the five richest men in the state.

JUSTIN: OK…

DAVID: Now, we had dinner together one night last week. We have a relationship that allows me to speak frankly with him. I said, "Aaron, your heart's in the right place, but you're embarrassing yourself. You gotta stop putting your name on things. You're making yourself look bad." Now, the man's an ego-maniac but he's not stupid. He knows good sense when he hears it.

JUSTIN: Right.

DAVID: Mr. Weintraub is opening a shelter for battered women and their children. If you've been jogging around the reservoir, you've seen it. It's been under construction all winter. Big salmon-pink building. It's got a great big glass dome...

JULIE: That's a shelter?

ALDEN: It's actually a transitional facility—

JULIE: I thought it was another planetarium.

DAVID: Now you're not using your head. He already built a planetarium.

JULIE: Right. With a big huge glass dome...

DAVID: Justin, this place is gonna be unbelievable. It's unprecedented. It's got a pool. It's got a gym. It has a computer center, a day-care center, a screening room. What am I forgetting?

ALDEN: The dining room...

DAVID: A dining room and a chef. What do you think of that?

JUSTIN: I.... It makes me wish I was a battered woman.

ALDEN: Justin.

DAVID: I understand his meaning. Justin, this place represents a step forward for the state of Florida and the United States and an immeasurable leap for women.

JULIE: Why—because it has a gym?

JUSTIN: No, because it has a screening room.

JULIE: How does any of that stuff help battered women change—

JUSTIN: Julie, use your head. They're gonna buff up, eat a balanced diet, and go beat their husbands back.

ALDEN: Justin, women's shelters have traditionally been... prison like. We have, in a sense, punished women for leaving their abusers. Mr. Weintraub wants to reward a woman for her courage to leave and that's an idea that's long overdue.

JUSTIN: All right, well, good for him. What does this have to do with me?

DAVID: I told him about our show and I told him about your mother. I told him what an incredible woman she was. And we made a deal.

JUSTIN: What kind of deal?

DAVID: Ashley House.

(Pause.)

JUSTIN: What the fuck is Ashley House?

DAVID: It's the Canyon Ranch of women's shelters. It opens one week from tomorrow to national coverage. And it's named after your mother.

JUSTIN: No, it isn't.

DAVID: Yes, it is. Now, Aaron wants his daughter, Alexis, to run it and that's fine. She's full of ideas... about how we can make this house, this... shelter... a tribute to your amazing mother.

JUSTIN: You never met my mother.

DAVID: No, I didn't. But I know her. I know her in you and in your father.

ALDEN: Justin, David and Aaron and Alexis... all of us want you to be a part of this. We want your input and your ideas—

DAVID: Alexis has some ideas I think you're really going to like. She wants to establish a corps of volunteers—female volunteers—called Ashley's Angels. She wants to know your mom's favorite color so the Angels can wear these little wing-shaped things on their collars...

JUSTIN: No—

DAVID: Like the AIDS people had the ribbons, we're gonna have wings. Now, you can take your time and generate some of your own ideas. The only thing I need from you right now is a song. Alexis would like to sing a song, of your choice, at the opening ceremony. She wants to know your mom's favorite song so she can start learning it—

JUSTIN: No. No. I veto. I have veto power and I veto this.

DAVID: Veto what?

JUSTIN: The whole thing. Ashley House. You can't do it.

DAVID: Well, actually we already have. It's done.

JUSTIN: Well, fucking undo it, then.

ALDEN: Justin, this is a tribute with permanence. It's an absolutely tremendous opportunity—

JUSTIN: Yeah—to sell your show.

ALDEN: That is not why we're doing this.

DAVID: Justin, this is a gift to your mother—

JUSTIN: She doesn't want it.

DAVID: Listen, you're a teenager and you're selfish. That's normal. I had a teenager myself—

JUSTIN: Fuck you. You had a teenager you never visited until she was a corpse.

ALDEN: Justin!

JUSTIN: You can't let him do this.

ALDEN: Justin. It's a tribute—

JUSTIN: It's a shelter!

ALDEN: It is a tribute to your mother's memory.

JUSTIN: My mother was killed by a homeless person! Putting her name on a SHELTER is not an appropriate tribute!

ALDEN: We are taking her name and… reclaiming it.

JUSTIN: Does no one here have a problem with the fact that it's A SHELTER!!?

JULIE: I do think there is a way in which it could be construed as bad taste—

DAVID: No one asked you.

JUSTIN: Fuck you! I asked the question and I included her.

DAVID: It's a home for women and children. And your mother loved children.

JUSTIN: My mother hated children! She thought battered women deserved to be hit.

DAVID: *(To ALDEN.)* Is that true?

ALDEN: She never said that.

JUSTIN: Yes, she did!

DAVID: Who did she say it to?

JUSTIN: To me! She said it to me!

DAVID: Alden?

ALDEN: I never heard her say that. Never.

JUSTIN: Yes, you did!

> *(Pause.)*

DAVID: Justin, I'm disappointed. Your father was concerned that you might react badly to this and I told him he was wrong. Now, I need to get back to California. I'll leave you to mull this over and come to the right conclusions. For now I need a song. I need the name of your mother's favorite song so Alexis can start learning it.

JUSTIN: *Hit Me with Your Best Shot* by Pat Benatar.

DAVID: Try again.

JUSTIN: *Hit Me Baby One More Time* by Brittany Spears.

DAVID: One more chance.

JUSTIN: *He Hit Me and It Felt Like a Kiss* by Carole King.

DAVID: Three strikes, you lose. Alden, give me a song.

> *(Pause.)*

ALDEN: I don't know. I mean, we both liked the Beatles, I guess—

JUSTIN: *Maxwell's Silver Hammer.*

DAVID: Alden, you were married to the woman. What was her favorite song?

ALDEN: Well…. Towards the end, she was playing a Joe Jackson record and there was one song—

JUSTIN: *It's Different for Girls.*

ALDEN: That's right!

DAVID: I don't know that song. Is it fitting?

ALDEN: It's very fitting. It's about the... fragility of women and the responsibility men... bear to take care... with them. It's actually a perfect—

DAVID: That sounds fine. I'll tell Alexis. Now, Justin, you're gonna take twenty-four hours and think this all through. You're a smart man. You're going to come to your senses and decide to be a part of this project.

JUSTIN: Not gonna happen.

DAVID: OK. Then at the very least you are going to be respectful. You will attend the ceremony and show your father the respect and support—

JUSTIN: I won't do it.

DAVID: All right, listen to me. You're not fourteen anymore. You've had three years to act out and embarrass yourself and it stops here. You lose someone you love, you get a year to act like a shit head. There's a statute of limitations on grief. You break your leg, you don't get to sit on your ass for the rest of your life. You heal. The world expects it and beyond that it's your goddamn duty. You've reacted long enough; it's time to grow up and act like a man.

JUSTIN: Oh, I intend to.

DAVID: That sounded like a threat. I'm sure you didn't mean it to.

JUSTIN: I don't know, David. I'm an immature teenage shit head. It's hard to say what I might do.

DAVID: I'm gonna give you one last chance now to use your head. I can be your best friend or your worst enemy.

JUSTIN: David, them's fighting words.

DAVID: Son, you've got a BB gun and I've got an A-bomb. Don't go up against me.

JUSTIN: I think that sounded like a threat!

ALDEN: No one is threatening anyone. David, I will speak with Justin. Justin, let's have dinner tonight—

JUSTIN: I have dinner plans.

ALDEN: Well.... What plans?

JUSTIN: Julie and have a lot of work to do.

DAVID: *(To ALDEN.)* I have a plane to catch and I'm not finished with you.

(ALDEN wavers a minute, but follows DAVID to the door.)

ALDEN: I want you to call me on my cell phone after dinner. Will you do that?

JUSTIN: Fine. Go.

(ALDEN and DAVID leave.)

JULIE: Wow.

JUSTIN: We don't have to have dinner. I just needed to stall him.

JULIE: We can have dinner.

JUSTIN: Do you have any thoughts on this?

JULIE: Yeah. It's completely horrible and it should be stopped. *(Pause.)* Also they've got the Joe Jackson song really, really wrong.

JUSTIN: No kidding.

JULIE: It's not about women being fragile; it's about their capacity for... cruelty being equal to men's, if not worse.

JUSTIN: Very good. You're smarter than I thought.

JULIE: For a CFU student.

JUSTIN: I'm sorry I said that. *(Pause.)* I need advice, preferably female, and you're here and you understand Joe Jackson and on a purely gut instinct level, I like you.

JULIE: OK.

JUSTIN: So I'm gonna trust you and if it turns out I'm wrong and you really are just ambulance chasing trash, I will... I will qualify you for Ashley House and I'm not just fucking with you, I'm serious. OK?

JULIE: OK.

JUSTIN: OK. I'm gonna show you something.

(JUSTIN gets up and rifles through some things. He returns with a manila envelope. He takes a cloth-bound book out of the envelope and hands it to JULIE.)

JUSTIN: Read the parts with the sticky notes.

JULIE: *(Paging through; reading)* What is this?

JUSTIN: When I found my mom.... I called the police and when I was waiting for them, I thought.... Before the reality of the situation set in and freaked me out I got really, um, practical. Like literally the first thing I thought was, "My mom's got all this pot in her room and I don't want her to get in trouble." Which is insane, she's dead, but... I found the pot and I took it. A lot later, I smoked it. I found this journal, too, and I took it.

JULIE: I don't think I should read this.

JUSTIN: What's your problem?

JULIE: It's... really personal.

JUSTIN: Skip a couple months.

(JUSTIN flips pages to another marked section. JULIE reads more.)

JULIE: I get the idea.

JUSTIN: What is wrong with you?

JULIE: It's really upsetting, Justin.

JUSTIN: Why? Because she had sex... orgies with strangers?

JULIE: No. I'm not judgmental about stuff like that.

JUSTIN: Is it because they filmed them?

(Pause.)

JULIE: No. None of that stuff is... bad in and of itself. It just doesn't sound like she liked it. I don't know. Doing sexual stuff you don't want to do makes me really upset. It might be a girl thing.

JUSTIN: The re-enactments didn't bother you.

JULIE: Right. You're right. Score one, Justin. You made your point.

JUSTIN: Well. It's my fault she... did it, so... I just wanted to know.

JULIE: How is it your fault?

JUSTIN: I told her to read the *City Paper.* I told her to go to a poetry reading or something and she found this... sex cult... thing.

(Pause.)

JULIE: It's not a terrible thing. It's a sad thing, but... I mean, it's not like this had anything to do with... you know. Did it?

(Pause.)

JUSTIN: She was really unhappy and... bitchy. That's why I told her to go do something, but after she went she got worse. Not to me, but.... You know. To Dad or... whoever happened to be there. She could just cut a person down.

(Pause.)

JULIE: You're not the person who brought him home, you know?

JUSTIN: Yeah, but I also didn't stop it.

JULIE: Neither did she.

(Pause.)

JUSTIN: Before the shelter thing, my dad had a plan to put up a statue in some kiddie park in D.C. It was gonna be Mom feeding the birds which is insane.... She liked birds like she liked kids which is not at all. Anyway, he got the TV show and he blew off the statue, but I had this idea of how to stop it if I had to. *(Pause.)* I was gonna call this guy Roderick and get the videos.

JULIE: Do you know how to contact him?

JUSTIN: His number is in the journal.

JULIE: It might have changed by now.

JUSTIN: As of six months ago, it hadn't.

(Pause.)

JULIE: You would show people those tapes?

(Pause.)

JUSTIN: Yeah, I would. If it would keep her from being… the patron saint of battered women or the earth mother with the birdseed, yeah. I would. I would rather people know her for… herself than for someone else's totally false idea of who she is. Does that make sense?

JULIE: You really think your mom having freaky group sex would bring down Ashley House?

JUSTIN: I think the only way to save her is to trash her. Do you think that's crazy?

JULIE: No. I don't.

(A soft knock on the door. ALDEN enters.)

ALDEN: Am I interrupting…

JULIE: No. Come on in.

ALDEN: I was hoping to have a word with… Justin. I know you two have dinner plans. Do you have time for a coffee or…

JUSTIN: We're really busy.

ALDEN: Quick one?

JULIE: Why don't we take a break and you guys can talk. I was gonna go get some air, so—

JUSTIN: Can you look into the thing we talked about? While you're out?

(JUSTIN hands her the journal which is back in its envelope.)

JUSTIN: The phone number is on the inside back cover.

JULIE: What should I say?

JUSTIN: Just check availability.

(JULIE takes the envelope and leaves.)

JUSTIN: Wallpaper. Shit never ends.

ALDEN: Right. I walked away from here and I couldn't stop thinking… about you. I'm trying to understand your… position here…

JUSTIN: Let's not have the same conversation we've had twenty times since you wrote your book.

ALDEN: No. No, we shouldn't retread old ground…

JUSTIN: Do you have anything new to say on this subject or—

ALDEN: I don't know if it's new, but… I did a lot of thinking and I… *(Pause.)* I think we're wrestling over primacy of experience.

JUSTIN: OK… when you say things like "primacy of experience," I can't talk to you.

ALDEN: Because you don't understand?

JUSTIN: Because when you talk like that you're like… you're fucking twelve orbits away from reality. These discussions accomplish nothing. You just find bigger words to advance the same position—

ALDEN: All right, that's fair. I'll be clearer. Your mother's death meant one thing to you and another thing to me. And you are as entitled to your... experience of this event as I am entitled to mine.

JUSTIN: Incorrect.

ALDEN: Why is that incorrect?

JUSTIN: Your version is not true.

ALDEN: Justin, I have not lied at any point—not in the book, not on the show—

JUSTIN: Where is the scene in the book where she says she doesn't want that guy in our house?!

ALDEN: She never said that.

JUSTIN: Oh, please!

ALDEN: She never—

JUSTIN: I was there!

ALDEN: Justin, if your mother had said no, I would have respected her wishes—

JUSTIN: Editing the truth is just a different way of lying.

ALDEN: Well, there is plenty about your... version of this that I would consider ... less than truthful.

JUSTIN: Really?

ALDEN: Yes.

JUSTIN: For example.

ALDEN: I would prefer... *(Pause.)* Justin, you need to understand that reality is a subjective construct—

JUSTIN: Don't talk like that! Just fucking say what you mean. In what way do I lie about my mother?

(Pause.)

ALDEN: I think you make me the villain in our family. I think that you hold me responsible for your mother's unhappiness...

JUSTIN: My mother's unhappiness is nowhere in your 600-page book and that is the problem. THAT is what I hold you responsible for.

ALDEN: You would like me to tell the world about the various... manifestations of your mother's unhappiness?

JUSTIN: I would rather you tell them that than tell them a load of horse shit about camping in Wyoming.

ALDEN: We camped in Wyoming, Justin.

JUSTIN: Yeah and it was fucking miserable.

ALDEN: That's your experience—

JUSTIN: That's real! She was miserable on that trip and so was I and you were too busy obsessing about dead Indians to fucking notice—

ALDEN: Your mother was unhappy on that trip because she was in drug withdrawal. Would you like that in the book?

JUSTIN: Withdrawal? It was pot, not heroin. Why didn't you just let her—

ALDEN: Take illegal drugs on an airplane? Think about it.

(Pause.)

JUSTIN: They didn't have pot in Wyoming?

ALDEN: That's not the… OK, enough. Impasse reached. We're not going to have a meeting of the minds here so let's just… stop. OK?

JUSTIN: OK.

(ALDEN rises to leave.)

ALDEN: I want to ask you… *(Pause.)* I worked very hard, for many years to get to this place… to have an impact. *(Pause.)* I was in graduate school when your mother became pregnant. I have no regrets. I wouldn't change anything. But the life I had planned for myself was not covering school board meetings. *(Pause.)* We've talked a lot about what this recognition of my work means to you. I'm just asking you to consider what it means to me. You think obsessively about your mother. Can you for one moment think of me?

(Pause.)

JUSTIN: You don't take into consideration what she would want, do you?

(Pause.)

ALDEN: I think I… operate under the assumption that Ashley's feelings died with Ashley.

JUSTIN: Good enough. We're through here.

ALDEN: I just want—

(JULIE enters.)

JULIE: Sorry. Am I back too soon?

JUSTIN: Nope. We're done.

ALDEN: OK. I'll…. Will you call me later this evening?

JUSTIN: Sure.

(ALDEN leaves.)

JULIE: How did it go?

JUSTIN: The peace talks have failed. We're going to war. Did you make any progress?

JULIE: The number is still good. His name is on the machine. Along with some jazz music. I didn't leave a message. *(Pause.)* Are you really gonna call him?

JUSTIN: Give me the number.

(JUSTIN and JULIE in soft freeze— JUSTIN dialing the number, JULIE beside him. We hear Syndrome Z's "Down to Mother" again. [Are we starting to tire of hearing the 911 call? Maybe. It certainly doesn't rally the same emotion it did on page 53.]

Some indication of time [six days] passing... and RODERICK LORD joins them in the apartment. There is a small suitcase at his feet. The three stare at each other for a while.)

RODERICK: Am I not what you expected?

JUSTIN: No. Actually, you're not.

RODERICK: I'm sure you have questions.

JUSTIN: Is Roderick Lord your real name?

RODERICK: I think reality is a subjective—

JUSTIN: —a subjective construct. Fine. It's not your real name.

RODERICK: What did you expect? How did I appear to you in your fantasy?

(Pause.)

JUSTIN: You're younger than I expected.

RODERICK: Interesting.

JUSTIN: What is your…. Can I just get the, uh, Cliffs Notes of who you are?

RODERICK: What kind of information are you craving?

JUSTIN: Nobody here is craving or fantasizing.

RODERICK: No child accepts the parent as sexual animal. Are you jealous? Angry? Are you repelled?

JUSTIN: I am repelled. I will give you that.

RODERICK: Talk about repulsion.

JUSTIN: Talk about who the hell you are.

RODERICK: I can leave any time.

JUSTIN: I can kill you and dump you in the Everglades and my guess is no one would miss you.

RODERICK: And he says he isn't angry.

JULIE: I think it's a matter of just… getting to know each other a little.

RODERICK: What if I'd like to see you make love to him?

JUSTIN: This is pathetic. You're like from a bad Mickey Rourke movie. Does this…. Do people find this exciting?

RODERICK: People find… their own capacity for excitement… with my help.

JUSTIN: Do you have a day job?

(Pause.)

RODERICK: I have an inheritance and a lucrative skill. I'm a fortunate man.

JUSTIN: And the skill is?

RODERICK: I unlock computer code.

JUSTIN: OK! You're a rich computer geek. Thank you. That's all I wanted to know.

RODERICK: My turn. You got one, I get one.

JUSTIN: OK.

RODERICK: What sexual act are you most afraid of?

(JULIE *giggles. She knows his answer.*)

JUSTIN: Do you have any idea how juvenile this is?

RODERICK: Step two. They mock and they giggle because they are afraid.

JUSTIN: Look. You have something we want. We would have preferred a FedEx package, but here you are.

RODERICK: Here I am.

(Pause.)

JULIE: Can you maybe be a little less… cryptic?

RODERICK: Absolutely. *(Long pause.)* I'm getting to know you two in the spaces between your words. Do you want to know what I see?

JUSTIN: No. Can I have the whiskey, please.

(JULIE *passes* JUSTIN *a bottle of whiskey.*)

RODERICK: You're terrified of one another…

JUSTIN: *(Rising.)* I'm not gonna listen to this shit.

JULIE: It's OK…

RODERICK: Right there! He leaps to his feet, ready to race out the door and away from his anger. She leaps to follow him. He fears his capacity for aggression; she is drawn to that aggression from a place so buried, so primal—

JUSTIN: A thousand dollars! A thousand dollars—You give me the tape and get the fuck out of my apartment.

RODERICK: Unfortunately, I have more money than I have use for. The currency I deal in—

JUSTIN: You are pathetic. You're a rich loser who never got laid and you watched some movies and read some porn and you can pass yourself off as the fucking… Marquis de Sade of the suburbs, but it doesn't play here. You're not dealing with bored housewives—

RODERICK: Your mother was bored. I unlocked her…

JUSTIN: You distracted her.

RODERICK: Yes, I did. I take some responsibility for her death. I have accepted my participation in that crime.

JUSTIN: Excuse me—you what?

RODERICK: To unlock her sexuality, I broke down her guards. I took away the resistance that would have alerted her to danger.

JUSTIN: You're a pathetic, impotent computer geek fuck. You would rather take credit for killing my mother than own up to the eunuch loser that you are.

JULIE: Justin!

RODERICK: You share my gift for perception. You're right. Here's my offer. You make love to your girlfriend; I direct. What do you think?

JUSTIN: I met her last week, Mr. Perceptive. She's not my girlfriend.

RODERICK: So much anger. Julie offers you a safe space for your anger. She'd face it with you if you were brave enough to let her.

JUSTIN: Fifteen hundred. Take it or leave it.

(Pause.)

(RODERICK moves towards leaving.)

RODERICK: OK. Give my regards to your father. I'd like to be a part of Ashley House, in some way. Perhaps they'll let me contribute some of your mother's artwork. I have some lovely landscapes in my personal collection.

(Pause.)

JULIE: Wait!

JUSTIN: We don't have to—

RODERICK: She'll do it. Julie wants to do it. Don't you, Julie?

(Pause.)

JULIE: I think it's really important we get the tape.

RODERICK: You were moving so swiftly toward insight. When you begin lying, you shut that door.

(Pause.)

JULIE: I do. I do want to do it.

JUSTIN: Jesus Christ! We're back to this? You think demeaning yourself is… is… poetic?

JULIE: It's only demeaning if I don't want to do it.

JUSTIN: Why would you possibly—

JULIE: It's different! It's… unknown.

RODERICK: Talk about "unknown."

JUSTIN: I still have yet to see the fucking tape!

RODERICK: Julie's spirit for exploration terrifies you. You're afraid we'll awaken a desire you can't satisfy.

JUSTIN: Give me the fucking tape!

(RODERICK takes the tape from his suitcase and hands it to JUSTIN who goes to the television and puts in the tape. JULIE and JUSTIN watch for a few seconds.

They look saddened by it. As they watch the tape, RODERICK *takes a video camera from his bag and begins readying it.)*

RODERICK: Is it all you'd hoped for? Is it scandalous enough to jeopardize Ashley House?

JUSTIN: It'll work.

*(*JUSTIN *turns off the tape, ejects it from the recorder and replaces it in its box.)*

RODERICK: Are you ready to meet your shadows?

JUSTIN: *(Indicating camera.)* Oh, no. Not part of the deal. Put that shit away.

RODERICK: I videotape all of the encounters I facilitate. The tapes remain in my personal collection.

JUSTIN: Amazingly, that doesn't reassure me very much.

RODERICK: The taping is non-negotiable.

JULIE: *(Eager.)* What do you want us to do?

RODERICK: *(Adjusting camera.)* Patience. Patience, child. We begin with a structured interview...

JUSTIN: Interview? This has been done. This has totally been done! There's a movie like this!

RODERICK: I've seen the film and I've taken the next step. Julie, why does Justin excite you sexually?

JUSTIN: We've covered this.

JULIE: We have, actually.

RODERICK: I wasn't here. Summarize.

JULIE: OK.... He accused me of hitting on him in this bar because of his mom, because of her death, and I... eventually owned up to that being part—OK a lot— of the attraction.

RODERICK: You are drawn to his proximity to violence.

JULIE: I don't think that's it.

RODERICK: Does that idea frighten you?

JULIE: A little. Yeah.

RODERICK: Justin, why Julie?

JUSTIN: Because she hit on me really, really hard.

RODERICK: Too easy. Try again.

JUSTIN: Dude, I don't know what your teen years were like before you got into the whole... eunuch voyeur scene, but in my universe when a hot girl plants herself in my lap—

RODERICK: I see. Women rarely notice you. Female attention comes so rarely—

JUSTIN: I didn't say that.

JULIE: You did to me.

JUSTIN: Whatever. I can make something up if you need, like, spicier back story, but the truth is I'm a guy and she hit on me.

JULIE: Then he yelled at me and called me the c-word. He was very threatening.

RODERICK: Excellent. And you responded to that?

JULIE: Yeah, I think I did. That's really crazy, right? That's horrible.

RODERICK: No judgments. Experience the feelings without assigning value to them. Justin, was it exciting for you to engage in sex charged with rage?

JUSTIN: There was no rage. I was very happy and very grateful to be... doing what I was doing.

RODERICK: I don't believe you.

JULIE: I don't either. He made me sleep in a chair afterwards.

RODERICK: No more accusations.

JUSTIN: Yeah. No more accusations.

RODERICK: Justin, are you a coward or an innocent?

JUSTIN: Neither.

RODERICK: Admit your anger.

JUSTIN: No problem. I'm angry.

RODERICK: Admit it to Julie.

JUSTIN: I'm not angry at Julie.

JULIE: You were the other night.

JUSTIN: Not as much as the two of you would like to think. *(Pause.)* Sorry. I know where you're going with this and I'm... not on your trip. *(Pause; to RODERICK.)* That's not my thing. My... dickishness does not extend to... this.

RODERICK: Are you sure?

JUSTIN: I'm... committed.

RODERICK: An important distinction.

JUSTIN: Agreed.

RODERICK: I'm very impressed with both of you.

JUSTIN: That's a judgment!

RODERICK: Correct. I apologize. *(Pause.)* Julie, offer Justin some spirits. Enjoy some with him if you wish.

(Pause.)

JULIE: Do you mean give him a drink?

JUSTIN: Yeah. Give me a drink.

(JULIE and JUSTIN drink whiskey.)

RODERICK: Relax. Imbibe. Begin congress. Begin with each other. Respond to my directions if they inspire you. Press your desire to the fullness—

JUSTIN: I will attempt to take this seriously if you will attempt to not use words like fullness and congress. I think it's in everyone's best interest that I not laugh at you.

RODERICK: Message received. Begin.

(JUSTIN and JULIE begin touching, kissing tentatively. They collapse into making out. RODERICK films them.

In the scene transition, we hear Alexis Weintraub Shelly's rendition of It's Different for Girls. *It's high-pitched and over-wrought. Celine-Dion-inspired.*

It's dedication day at Ashley House. A podium draped with purple ribbons is brought onstage.

DAVID and ALDEN enter and huddle around the podium. DAVID coaches ALDEN on his speech. Minutes 'til showtime.)

ALDEN: … Because coercion and control are antithetical to a loving relationship in all its fullness…

DAVID: Now careful there. Aaron doesn't want a lot of emphasis on the whole abuse thing.

ALDEN: Yes, but it is a battered women's shelter so I thought—

DAVID: He's got all his grandkids coming. No off color talk with the kids there.

ALDEN: I don't have anything off color.

DAVID: The man dropped nine million dollars and he wants a day of positivity. We can give him that. Talk about a new life, talk about a bright future. Keep it future oriented.

ALDEN: I can't… I may have to rethink some of the speech.

DAVID: No, no—you don't rethink, you rewrite. I've got eight generations of Weintraubs to deal with, I can't hold your hand through this.

(DAVID exits. ALDEN, stunned and worried, exits as well.

RODERICK, JULIE, and JUSTIN enter and affix purple ribbons to their clothing. DAVID and ALDEN already wear them.)

RODERICK: Is someone graduating?

JULIE: It does look sort of… convocational. I think it's the purple. Why is everything purple?

JUSTIN: Because my dad told them it was her favorite color.

RODERICK: Your mother favored red, if memory serves.

JUSTIN: AIDS took red, yellow's for missing persons and hostages, breast cancer got pink.... There wasn't a whole lot left.

RODERICK: Purple brings to mind Prince and the Revolution.

JUSTIN: Yeah, my dad must have forgot that.

RODERICK: Look at Julie. Look at her. *(Pause.)* Julie look at Justin. Morning after awkwardness is beneath you. I forbid you to run from one another. Even as your new closeness feels chaffing like a too tight—

JULIE: We went out for coffee while you were sleeping.

JUSTIN: We've been dealing with the closeness since seven-thirty this morning—

JULIE: We're completely fine with it as of like eight-fifteen.

RODERICK: I wish you'd included me in that.

JULIE: You were really helpful. We decided we wanted to tell you that. You should do, like, couples counseling. Seriously. I mean, the language is a little baroque, but your instincts are right on and—

RODERICK: I don't do couples counseling. I'm a guide in erotic exploration.

JULIE: Oh, I know—I'm just saying. If you got a master's in counseling—

(DAVID enters, holding a videotape. He hands the tape to JUSTIN.)

DAVID: OK, everyone. Listen up. Justin, I watched the video. It's terrific. It's a wonderful tribute.

JUSTIN: Yes, it is.

DAVID: Video player is under the podium. The tape is cued to you blowing out the birthday candles. Just push play, give us a few seconds. Half a minute tops. You got it?

JUSTIN: Got it.

DAVID: Alden, get over here.

(While DAVID is distracted, JUSTIN hands the video to JULIE, who pulls the sex video from her shoulder bag. They switch the tapes.)

DAVID: *(Noticing RODERICK.)* Who's he?

JUSTIN: He's my life coach.

DAVID: Well he can't stand up here. He's gonna have to take a seat. Her, too.

RODERICK: Of course.

(RODERICK and JULIE leave the stage, arm-in-arm.)

DAVID: After Alden's opening remarks and the video, I'll introduce Weintraub and Alexis will wheel him on up. He wants top billing here, grand entrance. I'll be back in two minutes; Alden keep cutting that speech.

ALDEN: It's already under five—

DAVID: Get it under three. Weintraub doesn't want his speech upstaged. *60 Minutes* is here. Where the hell is the painting?

ALDEN: *60 Minutes* is here?

JUSTIN: What painting?

DAVID: They're doing a piece on Weintraub. The... the kid painting. Damn it. *(Shouting off.)* I need the painting!

ALDEN: *(Now panic.)* David, I cannot compromise the integrity of my speech. I put my wife's name on this—

DAVID: For free. You got her name up there for free. Now we're gonna show the man the respect he deserves.

(Stagehands (?) enter with the painting and mount it. It is an amateurish work that depicts ASHLEY *playing ring-around-the-rosy with a culturally diverse group of children.)*

JUSTIN: What the hell is that?

DAVID: That is original artwork by Debra Weintraub Pagnozzi and we're very honored to have it. Now keep trimming that speech.

(DAVID exits. ALDEN looks stung.)

ALDEN: He's... under a great deal of stress.

JUSTIN: *(Indicating the painting.)* Did you know about this?

ALDEN: There's... a lot here I was not made privy to. *(Pause.)* It means so much to me that you're supporting this, supporting me.

JUSTIN: I know.

ALDEN: And I've missed you. I've really.... Well, I've missed you. *(Pause.)* Now, how in the devil did you find that tape?

JUSTIN: It was in a box of old... school stuff. I was unpacking and... there it was. Serendipity.

ALDEN: I'll say. Your fifth birthday. How the time does fly.

JUSTIN: I'd like to introduce it if I could.

(ALDEN puts his arm around JUSTIN.)

ALDEN: Terrific! God, that sounds terrific. I mean, I don't seem to be calling the shots here, but.... Let's do this. I'll cut a little more off the speech and leave some of my time for you. I'd like to do that.

JUSTIN: Thanks, Dad.

ALDEN: Oh, it's no problem. I'm just.... *(Pause.)* Sorry. I gotta confess I'm a little... starstruck or something.

JUSTIN: Starstruck?

ALDEN: *60 Minutes.* That's... exciting.

(JUSTIN breaks the embrace. DAVID returns.)

DAVID: What's with that guy you brought? He's down there hitting on the Weintraub girls. I had to move him to the back.

JUSTIN: He's harmless.

DAVID: He's creepy. I don't like him. Are we ready? Let me see what you've got. Give it to me. *(Reading.)* Cut that. That—I told you about that. Cut "murder," cut "violated"—

ALDEN: I cut "rape"! I cut "rape"! Now you cannot—

DAVID: Your wife was lost and taken! Taken and lost! However you want to say it. She was lost and she was taken! Now let's do this. Justin, is the tape in?

JUSTIN: It is.

DAVID: Good. Now, let's go.

(DAVID goes to the podium.)

DAVID: Good morning. I'm David Gavin. I am a producer for the Patterns Network. We have a studio here in Playa Linda where we tape a television program called *After Ashley* which is dedicated to making the America of tomorrow a safer place for women. I lost my daughter, Rachel, in 1992 and I want to tell you that the work we do on *After Ashley* and the work we do here today is not charity. It is intervention and it is salvation and it is made possible by one very extraordinary man. We are here today thanks to the generosity of Aaron Wientraub and the tireless work of his daughter, Alexis Weintraub Shelly. Now I present Alden Hammond, husband of Ashley Hammond and the host of *After Ashley*, to say a few words about the woman whose name graces this center...

ALDEN: How often we wish for the intervention of angels in our troubled world. We yearn for some otherworldly power to assuage our pain. As I spoke with Alexis Weintraub Shelly this morning, I understood that the intervention of angels is more than possible. It is certain. We find them right here among us in everyday clothing, their only wings the purple ribbons on their lapels. I saw my wife for the last time, three years ago and I see her again today in the vitality and passion of these women, her angels: Ashley's Angels. I lost my wife to... trouble... three years ago. It gives me great pleasure to forge an association between the name Ashley Hammond and the... recovery of troubled women. Let me now introduce my son, Justin.

(JUSTIN goes to the podium.)

JUSTIN: I'd like to read an excerpt from a poem. It's called *Diving into the Wreck* and it's by Adrienne Rich.

the thing I came for:
the wreck and not the story of the wreck

the thing itself and not the myth
the drowned face always staring
toward the sun
the evidence of damage
worn by salt and sway into this threadbare beauty

It's important to me that you know my mother. You know her name and you know the way she died. If you read my father's book, you know a little bit more than that, but.... I thought it was important to let my mother speak for herself today. Because she's more than a name or a story or a memory. She's.... She's Ashley Rollins Hammond. *(Pause.)* "The wreck and not the story of the wreck. The thing itself and not the myth." *(Pause.)* So. Without further ado.... Let's dive into the wreck. Lights, please.

(Lights dim. JUSTIN presses "play." We hear the following exchange.

During the video JUSTIN reaches behind the podium and retrieves the scissors to be used in the ribbon cutting. He climbs up to the painting and begins slashing it. DAVID rushes to ALDEN and shakes him to intervene. ALDEN is frozen, unable to stop watching the tape, and does not respond to DAVID. DAVID runs to the VCR. JUSTIN intercepts him and they struggle. DAVID finally succeeds in stopping the tape. ALDEN looks to JUSTIN. He appears stunned and betrayed. JUSTIN meets his stare. It's a painful moment. JUSTIN has no regrets, but takes no pleasure in seeing the damage in his father's face.)

RODERICK: *(V.O.)* Ashley, kneel before Donald. Terrence, join them. From behind. Don't think. Move. Linda, join them. Choice! Make a choice. Ellen, go to the box of adventures. Choose—

ASHLEY: *(V.O.)* This isn't sexy. This is like Twister.

RODERICK: *(V.O.)* We resist what we fear, Ashley.

ASHLEY: *(V.O.)* I can't do this. Get the fuck off me. Stop. This is stupid and gross. Why are we—

RODERICK: *(V.O.)* Ashley—

ASHLEY: *(V.O.)* I have pot! Why can't we just smoke and screw around. Let's have fun! If I wanted sex to be a monotonous chore I'd have stayed home with my husband and just—If I'm gonna be a mindless fuck doll I should get paid—

(After the tape is stopped, there's a moment of awkward silence. It's Different for Girls (Joe Jackson this time) comes on—abruptly—to fill the void.

Through the song, actors clear the stage. JULIE and JUSTIN enter with fold-up beach chairs and coffee cups. They sit by a lake.)

JUSTIN: So. *(Pause.)* Julie Bell.

JULIE: Justin Hammond.

JUSTIN: So. Are you breaking up with me or what?

JULIE: What would you do if you were me?

(Pause.)

JUSTIN: I... I don't know. I'm not you.

JULIE: Do we at least agree that you were a jackass?

JUSTIN: Umm... yeah. If you say so. Sure.

JULIE: Justin, you got grotesquely inebriated and insulted my friends. They made us leave the bar because—

JUSTIN: I remember. I apologize. What do you want me to say?

JULIE: That you'll do better.

(Pause.)

JULIE: That you'll try to do better?

JUSTIN: Look, we barely know each other—

JULIE: I know.

JUSTIN: You helped me get my mom's tapes back and I'm grateful and if you feel like used or something I understand and I'm sorry—

JULIE: I don't feel used. Everything up to and including the dedication, I'm fine with. It's afterwards—

JUSTIN: No more dead mom drama. You lost interest. That's fine.

JULIE: Oh, no. Don't you dare pull that with me—

JUSTIN: You and your fucking friends just come at me with all these expectations of who I am—

JULIE: Yeah, you're absolutely right. We do. We expect you to, like, make small talk without being abrasive and insulting.... *(Pause.)* Look. If you don't want to date me, no hard feelings. But say that. Stop hiding behind what happened to your mom.

(Pause.)

JUSTIN: Fair enough. Anything else?

JULIE: No.

JUSTIN: Do you want money for the coffee?

JULIE: No, I don't want money for the coffee!

JUSTIN: OK.

(Silence.)

JULIE: So, what are you going to do now?

JUSTIN: I don't know. Go home probably. Read. What are you doing?

JULIE: No. I meant generally. Life. Your dad cut you off, right?

JUSTIN: I assume so.

JULIE: Is the show gonna air or—

JUSTIN: It's been delayed. Indefinitely.

JULIE: You got what you wanted.

JUSTIN: Pretty much.

JULIE: But you need a job now, right? If you're cut off.

JUSTIN: Eventually. Yeah. I have some money from my mom's parents but it's supposed to be for college.

JULIE: So maybe do some applications, get something part-time—

JUSTIN: Maybe.

JULIE: No immediate plans?

JUSTIN: No. *(Pause.)* MTV called me.

JULIE: Why?

JUSTIN: To talk. They saw the *60 Minutes* piece, you know. *60 Minutes* filmed the dedication, so—

JULIE: They already aired it?

JUSTIN: No. It's not airing for a couple months, but somebody at MTV saw the tape and... the guy said I'm definitely a person of interest to them. He said I was a... righteous rebel and I wasn't afraid to take it to the wall. He goes, "You're the wrong dude to mess with before breakfast is all I'm saying." The guy does reality programming, so.... I think the idea is to like put me in a house with five other contrasting personalities and have me be the one who kicks the TV in and gets voted out of the house.

JULIE: They already did that show.

JUSTIN: Yes, they did. And the people seem to respond to it.

JULIE: But you said no?

JUSTIN: Of course I said no. I just ruined my father's life because he wanted to be a TV star. It'd be pretty fucked up if I started taking meetings, don't you think?

JULIE: Definitely.

JUSTIN: Anyway, I'm busy. I'm writing a book. It's called *After After Ashley*.

JULIE: Yeah, what happens?

JUSTIN: In my book?

JULIE: In your life. What happens After After Ashley?

JUSTIN: I don't know. I have no fucking idea.

JULIE: Well. Having money for college is a pretty cool thing to have. Being broke and in debt, you know—

JUSTIN: I know. I'm lucky.

JULIE: Just don't piss it away being an angry young drunk man.

JUSTIN: You think that's what I'm gonna do?

JULIE: I think it's a… scenario you should be aware of.

JUSTIN: Right. So, that's it? We're done?

JULIE: Yeah. Class dismissed.

(Silence. He doesn't want to go.)

JUSTIN: I know this is gonna sound like I'm making excuses for myself, but…. I was fourteen when she died. I never did the girl thing.

JULIE: I know.

JUSTIN: And you guys mature faster anyway, so in girl years I was like ten.

JULIE: It's different for girls.

JUSTIN: Right. Right. *(Pause.)* These last three years, she's been like… all the girl I can handle, you know? The way that came out sounds pervy, but—

JULIE: I know. She needed you. And you came through for her.

JUSTIN: Well… I'm just saying that I'm working at about a junior high level as far as dating or whatever, so…. I apologize.

JULIE: I understand. I mean, I'm not asking you to be… all-together or even… half-way together—

JUSTIN: So, what would you need—from me? Aside from like, sobriety and civility.

(Pause.)

JULIE: Just be you. Just be. If you don't know what to say, just be silent.

JUSTIN: People in this country are estranged from silence—

JULIE: Yes, they are. But you're a righteous rebel. You can do better.

(Pause.)

JUSTIN: It's like… in the absence of any coherent idea of who I am, I have assumed all of her worst qualities. The summer she died, all I did was chew her out for everything I do now. I was like… Mom lay off the pot, Mom don't pick fights, if you can't be nice, be quiet. I said everything you're saying to me now.

JULIE: Did she listen?

JUSTIN: Absolutely not.

(Pause.)

JULIE: Well. You being… you know, under the influence and obnoxious is just…. You're either keeping her alive or trying to get yourself killed and either way, it's just…

JUSTIN: It's bad.

JULIE: It isn't you. *(Pause.)* Look, your dad's book is dishonest and all those things you say it is, but the title is…. *(Pause.)* There has to be an after Ashley, you know? You do have to let her die.

(Pause.)

JUSTIN: OK. Now would be one of those times when I choose silence.

JULIE: Great. Silence is great.

(JULIE takes JUSTIN's hand and they zone out, look at the water. ASHLEY enters and stands behind them, watching. She doesn't, by look or gesture, endorse their union. It's more a sense of something unfinished. Not sinister, just… not done. Whether her presence represents a bona fide haunting or a character's preoccupation is up to you.)

END OF PLAY

"Down to Mother" by Syndrome Z

(The tone is intensely sincere as Z reflects on how the memory of his late mother has, time and time again, saved him from making bad choices. Syndrome Z was moved by Justin's 911 call and sampled portions of it into his song.)

Down the barrel of my gun, that man's no mother's son
I got a choice to make. Is this a life I'll take?

It comes down to MOTHER.
(911 sample: "I'm not leaving her! She's my mother")
It comes down to MOTHER.
(911 sample: "I'm not leaving her! Jesus Christ! She's my mother!")

I got no cash to burn, I got nowhere to turn
I turn the gun on me and then her face I see… Mother!

It comes down to MOTHER.
(911 sample: "I'm not leaving her! She's my mother!")
It comes down to MOTHER.
(911 sample: "I'm not leaving her! Jesus Christ! She's my mother!")

Sans-culottes in the Promised Land
by Kirsten Greenidge

BIOGRAPHY

Kirsten Greenidge has enjoyed development experiences at Madison Repertory, Playwrights Horizons, New Dramatists, the Mark Taper Forum, Bay Area Playwright's Festival, Hourglass Theatre, A.S.K. Theater Projects, The O'Neill and the Boston Women on Top Festival. Her work has been read at Playwrights Horizons, New Georges Peformathon 2002, Flirting With the Edge Festival of New Work and the Boston Playwrights Theatre. Recent awards include: The Cherry Lane Theatre Alternative (finalist—2002); The American College Theatre Festival; the University of Iowa (IRAM Award 2000 and Richard Maibaum Award 2001); and the Sundance Theatre Laboratory (Residency at Ucross Ranch, Ucross, Wyoming). Ms. Greenidge earned her M.F.A. from the Playwrights Workshop at the University of Iowa, where she was a Barry Kemp Fellow, and her B.A. from Wesleyan University.

HUMANA FESTIVAL PRODUCTION

Sans-culottes in the Promised Land premiered at the Humana Festival of New American Plays in March 2004. It was directed by Randy White with the following cast:

Carol . . . . Angela Bullock
Greg. . . . . Leon Addison Brown
Lena . . . . April Matthis
Greta . . . . Kibibi Dillon
Carrmel . . . . Sharon Hope
Charlotte . . . . Tamilla Woodard

and the following production staff:
Scenic Designer . . . . Paul Owen
Costume Designer . . . . Junghyun Georgia Lee
Lighting Designer. . . . . Tony Penna
Sound Designer . . . . Vincent Olivieri
Properties Designer . . . . April Hartsook
Stage Manager . . . . Cat Domiano
Dramaturg . . . . Sarah Gubbins
Assistant Dramaturg . . . . Dan LeFranc
Directing Assistant. . . . . Jerry Winters
Casting . . . . Mungioli Theatricals, Inc.

CHARACTERS

LENA, 25

CARRMEL, mid 50s

GRETA, 8

CAROL, early 40s

GREG, early 40s

CHARLOTTE, mid 20s

SETTING

A suburb of Boston, Massachusetts, 1999.

NOTES ON THE TEXT:

Instances where slashes occur (/) indicate where text should overlap.

Instances where pauses occur should not be ignored.

The sounds that occur thoughout the play should not be overlooked. They are an important layer in the piece and should be executed exactly as they appear.

NOTES ON CASTING:

The characterization of Greta is quite intricate and therefore it is highly recommended that Greta be played by an older actor who is able to appropriate the mannerisms of an eight-year-old and grasp the nuances of Greta's character specifically.

NOTES ON TONE, STYLE AND PRESENTATION:

Sans-culottes in the Promised Land is extremely style sensitive. It is *not* meant to be read or performed as a melodrama or family drama. The dialogue should be delivered swiftly and deliberately. Think Pinter. Think Beckett. Do not allow the presentation to delve into the realm of "black-family, kitchen-sink realism" (Not that there's anything wrong with that but...). Let the play be buoyant.

The emotions and issues presented in the text are not to be interpreted as "the tips of ice bergs," they *are* the icebergs: moving quietly but forcefully towards a finite and final destination. The play does not utilize a traditional dramaturgical structure. The characters do not develop in the conventional sense, with one character's story taking precedence over that of other characters'. All the characters and their stories work in concert to propel the play towards its end, which is meant to be inevitable and unavoidable.

Elements in the play, Lena's letters and Charlotte's trees, for example, are absurd. It will frustrate the velocity of the play and cause numerous headaches to the actors and production staff if they are deconstructed before they have the chance to simply exist on their own.

Tamilla Woodard
in *Sans-culottes in the Promised Land*

28th Annual Humana Festival of New American Plays
Actors Theatre of Louisville, 2004
photo by Harlan Taylor

Sans-culottes in the Promised Land

Darkness.
The sound of a dryer buzzer.
Light.
LENA stands in front of a large, oversized washing machine.
She pulls out a piece of discolored clothing, holds it up.

LENA: Oooo. Not again.
   (She pulls out more ripped clothes.)
CARRMEL: *(Offstage.)* Hey.
   (LENA freezes.)
   You.
   (LENA shuts the washer door.)
   Why you leave basement door open? Sign say right here near knob "close
   basement door."
LENA: Next time—
CARRMEL: Next time?: I tell.
   (Door shuts.
   LENA waits to be sure CARRMEL is gone.)
LENA: Next time: I'll *lock* it: 'keep you out of my face. *(LENA opens washer, looks*
   inside, then shuts washer lid.) Stupid machine. Stupid, stupid.
   (The sound of a spray bottle.
   CHARLOTTE sprays the leaves of a plant.
   She steps back, regards the plant, then sprays it again.
   A child's room. Piles of clothes clutter the space. CAROL rifles through a dresser,
   pulls out clothes and tests them against each other to see if they match.)
GRETA: *(Hidden.)* I'm far-away-lost. It's up to you to find me, to discover me.
CAROL: Come *out.*
GRETA: I've got Snow White in here. Want to see her?
CAROL: You know how I feel about that Snow White—
   (GREG enters hurriedly.)
GREG: I can take her but only if we leave now. I have a breakfast meeting.
CAROL: Well, check you out, Mr. Man. Did you hear that Greta? Daddy has a
   breakfast meeting with a new client—
   (She pulls him to her with the loose end of his tie, gives him a kiss.)

GREG: Why is this room such a mess? Don't we pay those nannies to keep it clean?

GRETA: I'm too old for a nanny.

CAROL: *(She straightens his tie.)* What kind of numbers are you—

GREG: The last one kept it clean.

GRETA: But Snow White could watch me. Snow White's perfect to guide me.

GREG: You should have her dressed by now.

GRETA: Or Cinderella? Maybe Cinderella—

CAROL: What does it look like I'm doing?

GRETA: How about Pocahontas? She's not so bad *(Sing-song:)* and she's brow-own.

CAROL: No Cinderella. No Pocahontas. Those movies misrepresent—

GREG: See? See? You're doing it all wrong.

CAROL: Oh?

GREG: You keep talking to her like you're having cocktails and a chat: no wonder she's not dressed. Watch. *(To GRETA.)* Greta? Come Out *Now*. *(To CAROL.)* Get it? No conversation: lots of disciplined love. Right? You know I'm so right. *(To GRETA.)* Now, Greta, sweetheart, this is Daddy speaking and you're to do as you're told.
(Pause.)
Greta?

GRETA: What's wrong with Pocahontas?

CAROL: HA. You know, those nannies don't engage her enough, that's why she reverts to this type of behavior.

GRETA: Since no one will tell me what the problem with Pocahontas is, I'm going back to Snow White in the first place.

CAROL: I'll talk to Lena about this first chance I get.

GREG: Who's Lena?

CAROL: The sitter.

GREG: You got rid of the last one, poof, easy as that?

CAROL: Yes, poof, easy as that.

GRETA: Me and Snow White? We're lost in a wood. We're deep, deep in the forest.

CAROL: Come OUT.

GREG: I liked that last one.

CAROL: Maybe I should make Lena a reading list.

GRETA: Follow Snow White's voice:

GREG: The last one didn't need a list.

GRETA: *(She speaks in an affected "English" accent.)* "Do try ever so hard to find me Father, do try ever so hard to discover me, Mother. Do, please."

CAROL: The last one couldn't follow any of my instructions—

GRETA: "This forest is ever so wretched— "

GREG: When she gets like this, Carol—

GRETA: "—and ever so dreadful."

GREG: When she gets like this, honestly, I can't—

GRETA: "Or perhaps it's a thicket."

GREG: I can't get into this now, I'm *late.*

GRETA: "Oh bother, am I in a thicket, or a forest?"

CAROL: And I'm not?

GRETA: "Perchance it's a *glade.*"

GREG: *(As he exits.)* I *have* a *breakfast* meeting.

CAROL: You can't just walk away from her like that, Greg: you'll damage.
    (She follows GREG.)

GRETA: "Yes, yes, a glade, Father. Mother, do tell Father I'm in a glade and it's his duty to save me, to find me. Mother?"
    (Slight pause.)
    Mom?
    (A dryer buzzer sounds.
    LENA *in the laundry room.*
    The washing machine makes a sickly noise.
    LENA *kicks it.*
    The buzzer sounds again, but does not stop.
    LENA *pushes buttons over and over until the machine stops buzzing.*
    Silence.
    LENA *relaxes a bit.*
    The machine begins to thump, then buzz.
    LENA *hurries away.*
    A dryer buzzer sounds again.
    CHARLOTTE *and* GRETA, *playing mankala.)*

CHARLOTTE: In Africa they didn't use a board.

GRETA: Oh yeah?

CHARLOTTE: They drew the playing area in the dirt.

GRETA: There's a horse the color of dirt at riding. I do more than this class. I do riding. And ballet.

CHARLOTTE: I have diagrams of the playing areas at home in books.

GRETA: That horse isn't my favorite.

CHARLOTTE: I'll bring them in to show you.

GRETA: I feed carrots to my favorite.

CHARLOTTE: I'm trying to teach you things.

GRETA: And apples.

CHARLOTTE: About our heritage, about how strong it is. We have so much to be proud of.

GRETA: Like playing in the dirt?

(*Beat.*)

If you ask me, playing in the dirt's not all so special.

CHARLOTTE: *Mankala* is an ancient game passed down through the *ages*. By *Africans*.

GRETA: My favorite horse is the color of sugar but I don't always get to ride him. Those days I hate riding; I may as well be here. Your turn.

CHARLOTTE: I know what you need. Flashcards. I'll call them Heritage Holders. I'll give them to your parents to do with you at night with your homework.

GRETA: My parents don't do the homework with me, the nannies do.

CHARLOTTE: So I'll give them to one of the nannies. "Heritage Holders." I can't believe I never thought of them before. Our heritage, Greta, is astounding. We come from great traditions, great, great history. Just you wait, these Heritage Holders will show you the real you, the Nubian Princess you, the you that used to walk on wide open planes, dark black skin glistening, glowing, under the steamy su—

GRETA: Are you going to take your turn or not? This game isn't very fun, you know.

(*A cell phone rings.*

CAROL in the kitchen, on the phone, as CARRMEL sweeps around her, getting closer and closer. She hums loudly and without melodic appeal.)

CAROL: He won't *go* any higher.

(*CARRMEL sweeps closer to CAROL. CAROL watches CARRMEL. CARRMEL hums.*)

I'm sorry, what was that?

(*CARRMEL hums.*)

I'm sorry, just a moment.

(*CARRMEL sweeps and hums.*)

Carrmel.

(*CARRMEL stops sweeping and humming. She looks at CAROL.*)

Please.

(*CAROL goes back to her phone call.*)

What were you saying? *(Pause.)* Well that's not my problem.

(CARRMEL sweeps, hums quietly.)

He won't cough up any more so you can take that offer and—

(CARRMEL sweeps closer to CAROL.)

Excuse me. Carr*mel.*

(CARRMEL looks at CAROL. CARRMEL sweeps as she walks away, humming.)

No, no, it's nothing. Just the housekeeper: you know how it is.

(Lets out a skittish laugh.)

Now where were we?

(A car.

GRETA sits in the back seat.)

LENA: How was class?

GRETA: I don't like the clay feeling on my hands. You should drive now.

(Pause.

LENA turns to the steering wheel, prepares to drive. A loud voice is heard in the distance. It is CHARLOTTE.)

CHARLOTTE: *(Offstage.)* Greta? GRETA—

(CHARLOTTE approaches the car, wildly waving a piece of material.

LENA and GRETA stare at her.

CHARLOTTE waves the material.)

GRETA: Drive away, it's only Ms. Grey.

LENA: But she's your teacher.

GRETA: Not a real teacher. This isn't school, it's just a stupid class my mom makes me come to. Drive away or she'll try to talk.

(More wild waving from CHARLOTTE.

LENA pushes the power window button and LENA and CHARLOTTE watch as the window goes all the way down.

Beat.)

CHARLOTTE: She forgot her *ken-tae* cloth.

(CHARLOTTE and LENA look at GRETA who does not move.

CHARLOTTE tries to hand GRETA the material.)

Honey, you forgot your *ken-tae* cloth.

(GRETA does not move.)

LENA: Greta.

(GRETA stares at LENA.)

LENA: *(To CHARLOTTE.)* Sorry. *(To GRETA.)* Greta.

CHARLOTTE: I had them make their own *ken-tae* cloths using dye from vegetables. I didn't read it in a book, I thought it up myself. You're the nanny?

GRETA: I'm hungry.

LENA: Lena.

CHARLOTTE: I'm going to be making some flashcards for Greta. To get her into her heritage. I'm going to call them Heritage Holders. I just came up with it this afternoon during Mankala Monday time. When she does her homework make sure she reviews some of them.

(CHARLOTTE shoves the cloth at LENA. LENA takes the material. Just as she does, CHARLOTTE reaches for her hair.)

It's so *dry*. Like straw, girl. Like any second a cow could walk over and start to chew on your head. But don't you worry I have just the thing.

(A phone rings.

CAROL in the kitchen, on the phone.)

CAROL: …it's nothing, I'm fine. So, yes, go on…well frankly… I don't know why there's a hold up, I've explained McIntyre's position—

(GRETA runs into the kitchen at full speed, backpack strapped on her back. She bombards CAROL with a hug.)

Oh, honey, oh, back so soon? *(Into phone.)* Hold on, it's just Greta…my daughter…that's right, at the Christmas—

(She notices GRETA as she kneels on the floor and opens her backpack. Papers and grade school paraphernalia fly out of the pack.)

Oh, dear, where's Lena?

(GRETA pulls out a purple prize ribbon.)

GRETA: For best posting.

(LENA enters.)

At riding.

CAROL: *(Rushed.)* Fabulous. How absolutely fabulous: a blue ribbon—

GRETA: It's purple.

CAROL: Purple? Oh.

(GRETA holds up the ribbon as LENA bends to pick up the spilled contents of the backpack.)

Not now, sweetie. *(Into the phone.)* Still there?

(GRETA moves closer to CAROL, tries to hug CAROL again.)

Once is good for now, Greta. Mommy's working. *(Into phone.)* Sorry. *(To LENA.)* Why don't you make her a snack? *(Into phone.)* Hello? Yes? Today? No, I can't today I'm taking a personal…a little headache…*(Pause.)* I know that but this is *my* case, I *built* —

(Notices GRETA who hasn't moved. Looks to LENA, then GRETA, then LENA again. Annoyed.)

Snack? Yes?

LENA: I think she wants to share—

CAROL: *Snack.*

> (GRETA *groans. The two exit.*)
>
> Yes, still here.
>
> (*A dryer buzzer.*)
>
> Ooo.
>
> (CAROL *pinches the bridge of her nose.*
>
> CARRMEL *stands in the laundry room. She studies the dials on the machines. The washing machine is making a sickly noise.*
>
> CARRMEL *readjusts the controls and the machine whirs pleasantly.*)

CARRMEL: Wrong, wrong. No, no. Stupid, stupid. This one more than stupid. She think all I know is the cooking and the cleaning. Ha. Every day I knowing more about her. She no good to work with child. Uh-uh. Ha.

> (*The machine "dings" pleasantly.*
>
> GREG *and* LENA *in the hall.*
>
> GREG *walks into* LENA.
>
> *Laundry spills onto the floor.*)

LENA: Sorry.

> (GREG *grins.*)

Um. The clothes are this color... Because I'm using...a special fabric...softener.

> (GREG *grins.*)

Because studies— you know studies? They show that soft fabric is best for little kids, little children. Well. All children. Their skin. All little kids', little children's skin when it gets too close to fabric that's too hard, it can be dangerous: their new skin can get torn. Little children's skin is so new compared to our skin. So this fabric softener—

GREG: You've got a nice neck.

> (CAROL *in her office, standing at her desk, looking over work, fingers on the bridge of her nose.*
>
> *Beat.*
>
> GRETA *in a fit on the floor.*)

GRETA: I'll swallow thorns and be asleep for a hundred *years* if you make me. I can't stand that Ms. Grey. All she does is talk all day about black this and heritage that. She's not even a real teacher. She's probably just some brown person they got off the street. During class, she goes on and on about Africa this, and Africa that: stuff she probably makes up herself. And after class?: she comes up to the car all creepy trying to give me things I don't want, things I forget on purpose. If you make me go today I'll, I'll poison apples and feed them to you when you least *expect* it. I swear I swear I swear I swear I swear. *(She looks up to CAROL.)* Mom?

CAROL: *(Absently.)* Mm?

GRETA: Um. So. Mom.

(CAROL pinches the bridge of her nose, eyes closed.)

Mom?

(CAROL looks at her for the first time.)

So I can skip Heritage class today? So you'll tell Lena to bring me right home after school today? Right? Mom?

CAROL: Go get mummy an aspirin, yes?

(The sound of the spray bottle is heard once, then quickly once again.

CHARLOTTE pulls a leaf off of her plant. She sprays it. She holds it up in two hands, like an offering.

Beat.

She examines it, sprays it again twice, then holds it up again like an offering. She lets her head fall back, eyes closed.)

CHARLOTTE: Yes.

(LENA stands in CAROL's office. CAROL is writing. She looks up at LENA, smiles, then finishes in a flurry. She holds out the list to LENA.

LENA looks at CAROL.

CAROL waves the list.)

CAROL: I hope it's no trouble.

LENA: Oh.

(Takes list.)

No trouble. It's my job, right? But, see, what I was hoping we could talk about is…the washing machine. I…can't seem to—

CAROL: The first item on my list relates to the materials I lent you when you began.

LENA: Yeah. I haven't had a chance to read through that yet—

CAROL: Not even the Coles and Coles?

LENA: But I will, I definitely—

CAROL: That's a shame because the Coles and Coles is the most important. It's dense, I understand, but it's the most thorough aide to child development I know. I only bring it up because we've had some issues with Greta recently. She's been *playing* in the mornings and quite frankly it backs up our entire day. And I developed this headache. I'm dying, I just know it.

Anyway. Coles and Coles. Read it as soon as you can so we can all try to stop this phase. As her primary caregivers it's very important.

LENA: Coles-Coles is the one with the white cover?

CAROL: I don't know. And it isn't Coles-Coles. It's The _Development_ of _Children_ by Coles _and_ Coles.

LENA: Okay. But—

CAROL: Greta's in her middle childhood stage, her sense of self is forming at an accelerated rate. It's very important to keep up. Now, in the Coles and Coles you'll find several charts to help monitor her behavior. What I'd like to do in your free time— when she doesn't need _engagement_— is to watch her, study her. Write anything down that seems noteworthy.

LENA: Um, see, okay, like…like that kind of is what I'd like to talk to you about. But it's about the washing machine—

CAROL: The other item you'll see is toiletries. God bless her but she stinks. Skim down that, how many bars of soap did I say?

LENA: Um…. Six. Bars. Of. Soap, but—

CAROL: Get more, _much_ more. And some powder, some talcum powder. Maybe she's not washing enough. Maybe you can get her to be more thorough.

LENA: I didn't know I was supposed to give her baths.

CAROL: No wonder she stinks.

LENA: But I'm not her mother—

CAROL: I would if I could but I'm very busy, Lena.

LENA: Yes, I know—

CAROL: And the last thing we need at that school is for her to be the black kid who reeks. Right?

(CAROL _laughs lightly._

LENA _echoes uneasily._)

When I was growing up it was private this and private that and there was always one black kid who just reeked. Smelt simply awful. Sour: Sweaty: _God._ She's not going to be the stinky one. So _please_, lots of soap. No one likes a skunk. No one invites a skunk skiing, or sailing, or whatever. Money.

LENA: What?

CAROL: You'll need money.

(Hands LENA _money._)

Don't keep the change.

LENA: I wouldn't.

CAROL: I'm joking. Ha-ha. I feel very friendly with you. It's hard to be friendly with—well, you know. The agency usually sends girls who are simply *tres horible*, ready to disregard me completely and turn this home, my carefully run home, completely upside down. But you're different. I'm so glad we can talk. You're very well-spoken, Lena.

LENA: Um, thanks—

CAROL: I'm telling you some of these girls are really half-monsters. Teeth and claws, I mean it. And dim: you wouldn't *believe*: half illiterate, can hardly put a sentence together.

LENA: I, um, had a teacher who, well, she, you know she spoke really well. I guess I just must have picked it up.

CAROL: See how important middle childhood can be? It's up to us to give Greta the very best. I'm so happy we can agree like this. It means so much to me. Those other girls can't hold a candle to you. I'm glad we can be friends, more than friends, like family, almost.

LENA: That's nice.

CAROL: You know, sometimes I feel like you're my wife.

(A dryer buzzer sounds.)

Oh: God: why's that thing so *loud?* You can hear it through the entire house—

LENA: That's what I want to talk to you about: I can't seem to figure out—

(The doorbell rings.

CAROL pinches the bridge of her nose.)

CAROL: Oo.

(The doorbell rings again.)

Go tell whoever it is that I'm absolutely unavailable. I'm dying, I just know it.

LENA: You want me to answer the—

CAROL: Well it's not going to answer itself.

(GRETA at a large mirror.

She whispers.)

GRETA: Mirror.

(GRETA studies herself. She stands back, makes a circle with her thumb and forefinger and peers through it.

Quiet.

She whispers.)

Mirror.

(GRETA looks at herself with her thumb and finger in the shape of a circle. After a few beats she steps back.)

Thanks. I needed that.

(CHARLOTTE and CARRMEL at the door. CARRMEL gives CHARLOTTE a look, CHARLOTTE returns the look. CARRMEL walks away.)

CHARLOTTE: Nice house.

LENA: Heritage class.

CHARLOTTE: Charlotte. And you're Lena-the-nanny.

(CHARLOTTE extends her hand.)

LENA: Carol's unavailable absolute—

CHARLOTTE: Class just isn't the same without Greta.

LENA: I'll tell Carol you stopped by—

CHARLOTTE: She really shouldn't skip.

(Pushing further into the house.)

She needs to know about her roots. She deserves to be proud. I made these myself.

(Handing Heritage Holders to LENA.)

I call them Heritage Holders. Each kid's going to get their own set because they all have stuff they should be working on. Like this kid I teach on Wednesdays?: Austin Hill? He needs work on realizing how many stringed instruments originally came from parts of Africa. People like to associate Africa with only drums and that's unfair, that's a total misconception. There were stringed instruments all *over* ancient Africa. Not just drums. *What* do you think of *that?*

LENA: These are very colorful. Thank you. See you next week?

CHARLOTTE: *(Pushing herself further into the house.)* And this is for that hair.

(Hands LENA a bottle.)

I made it myself. With plants. I'm very good with plants. Everything I used I grew myself. Go ahead and read the label.

LENA: Wow, thanks.

CHARLOTTE: You can't buy better, not even from those fancy brands. I did research. About ancient African hair care and I came up with this recipe, this fabulous, fabulous recipe. I can grow anything anywhere. Go ahead and read the label.

LENA: *(Looking at label.)* You're very sweet.

CHARLOTTE: This really is a nice house. You must get *paid*, girl, 'cause they got the bling bling goin' *on*, okay?

(CHARLOTTE takes a look around the room.)

LENA: They're nice. Almost as nice as the Carvers. They were two, no, three families ago. But they moved and left me behind. This new family, though, they're alright.

(*CHARLOTTE takes a look around the room again.*)

CHARLOTTE: She *really* shouldn't skip. 'Cause I mean: them being the only people of "col-OR" up in this neighborhood— she *really* needs to know her roots. If I could rope in their parents they'd all be better off. But my adult classes never fill up. They think they can do Kwanzaa once a year, *maybe* even read some book about Juneteenth to stay in touch and it's a shame. Now use this twice a day and your hair will regain its natural strength in no time. Trust me. Read the label.

(*LENA unscrews the bottle and inhales.*)

LENA: Smells good.

CHARLOTTE: You've got to treat yourself like the Nubian Princess you are.

(*LENA giggles.*)

'Cause they won't, let me tell you. I used to do the nanny thing. Couldn't handle it. Could-not-handle-it. Especially with the colored folks, if you know what I mean. They think they're all that just cause they've got some change, right?

LENA: They're not bad.

CHARLOTTE: Make sure she does those flashcards. She needs them.

(*GREG working at a desk. CARRMEL is dusting around him. She watches him. He tries to avoid her. CARRMEL stops dusting and faces him.*)

CARRMEL: No more cleany here, cooky there. I work with the child now.

GREG: Why don't you talk to Carol?

CARRMEL: She hires these fancy girls, stupid girls, and finally my feelings get hurt.

GREG: Talk to Carol—

CARRMEL: I talk to the man. The man decides. When I come work for you it was to soon look after the babies.

GREG: Baby. Now she's eight.

CARRMEL: I come here when de wife big in the belly with the baby. I come here when I think maybe later you going to let me bath the baby, play the baby. But no. Instead you hire all them girls and my feelings, they peel away onto the ground, get smashed up by your expensive-looking shoes. My feelings just peels on the ground. Rubbish: only good for the disposal. (*A sound like a garbage disposal.*) Rrrrrrr.

GREG: Carrmel, we *love* you. Don't be upset, just talk to—

CARRMEL: Rrrrrr. How I be upset? I'm just a peel. Rrrrrrr.

(The sound of the spray bottle is heard once. Then twice.
CHARLOTTE pours a handful of seeds into a glass jar.
The sound of the seeds rushing into the jar.
She holds up the jar in admiration.
The sound of the spray bottle is heard once.
Elsewhere.)

GRETA: *(Whispers.)* Mirror, mirror.

(Listens.)

Lips as red as the rose?

(Looks at herself in the mirror.)

Check.

(Listens.)

Hair as black as ebony?

(Giggles.)

As if you didn't know.

(Giggles.)

Check.

(Listens.)

Skin?…skin as what?

(The dryer buzzer.)

Mirror, mirror?

(CAROL, head between her hands, stands in her office.
CARRMEL enters. She studies CAROL, then leans in and taps the side of CAROL's
head with her finger.)

CARRMEL: Knock-knock. *(CAROL groans.)* I go to Mister and he say I work with child now.

CAROL: Greg gets so mixed up in this house he doesn't know whether to scratch his watch or wind his butt.

CARRMEL: Banana. Orange. Potato. You think I only good to be put in rubbish. Rrrrrr.

CAROL: I beg your pardon.

CARRMEL: Nine years ago you say I work with the childrens.

CAROL: Child.

CARRMEL: You say there are childrens coming and I to work with them.

CAROL: No. We said maybe, after a few years. We said maybe you'd become the nanny after a few years and maybe you will.

CARRMEL: But I sent by God to look after the little ones—

CAROL: Carrmel, if you want a baby so badly go and have one of your own.

CARRMEL: Can't. Dried up. When I was thirteen years old I go to one of those doctors. I couldn't keep my legs together so I end up at one of those doctors. All okay he said. I will forget, I said. I will have other babies and I will forget. A few years later I meet my own Mister, only to find out I got dried up. That doctor was no good: stupid, stupid man. I tell my Mister to leave. I tell him no childrens was a sign for us. From God. For me to take care of the little ones in a nice family like I should have been with in the first place. Or I wouldn't had my legs apart so young—

(Spits.)

CAROL: That was very unpleasant, Carrmel.

CARRMEL: Like a whore. *(Spits twice.)*

CAROL: *Carrmel, **please**.* We like how things are going. Smoothly: with one child.

CARRMEL: But you have more? I will take care of you so, so good when you have more. No need to bring in these fancy girls, loose girls—

CAROL: That was *once.* It was five girls ago and it was only *once.*

CARRMEL: But who tells you about the loose girl? How her fingers go visiting. How your husband plays host.

CAROL: *Played.* Past tense. Past tense. You don't even know how to talk, we don't even know what you're saying. What else are we supposed to let you do if we don't even know if you're speaking English.

(CARRMEL leans in and whispers into CAROL's ear.)

CARRMEL: *I* the best one for the childrens.

(LENA, carrying a laundry basket, bumps into GREG. Papers and laundry go flying.)

LENA: Sorry. Sorry: I'm an idiot, really.

(They both drop to the floor. They pick up articles of clothing and papers. Their heads bump.)

I'm not usually this clumsy.

GREG: I am.

(They work.)

You have a beautiful collarbone. Where your neck meets the rest of you is very—. Since I'm an architect, you know, building buildings—

LENA: I know what an architect is.

GREG: I build buildings all day. I forge reality. From metal. From concrete. I know how things fit together. When I was little I used to take things apart. "I smell an engineer in the family," they used to say. "Well I smell an architect," someone else would answer back. I had many sets of Lincoln logs; I made my own model airplane kits out of balsa wood. Everyone knew I would grow up to insert more metal and concrete and glass into our landscape. Sometimes I like to mix it up a little. Sometimes I get creative: a glass teepee here, a stucco hut there. No matter what I create I always remember those voices calling out my future for me, predicting my path. They trusted me to follow it and I try very hard. Because I never stop thinking about how things fit together. Like right now. How your skin is pulled over your bones so tightly, so smoothly—

(The sound of someone slurping loudly.
It is GRETA, *drinking milk and eating cookies.*
CAROL *is working.*
GRETA *chews loudly.*
Quiet.
GRETA *chews loudly and slurps again, she gets louder.)*

CAROL: *(Annoyed.)* Is your mouth open?

GRETA: *(Mouthful of cookie.)* No.

CAROL: Whatever you're doing with your teeth and tongue, stop. It's disgusting.

(GRETA continues.)

Greta.

(GRETA drinks her milk silently, then eats noisily.)

Eat like a lady, not an animal.

GRETA: We *are* animals.

CAROL: Don't be fresh or I'll give you a time out.

GRETA: My whole life is a time out since none of you will play with me.

CAROL: Where's Lena?

GRETA: What's wrong with you?

CAROL: I am under the weather.

GRETA: How long is under-the-weather going to last?

CAROL: I don't know.

GRETA: Because already it's been a pretty long time. Already it's been two Saturdays in a row I've watched you be sleepy and listened to you make that groaning sound—

CAROL: What are you doing around me? Where's Lena? She's supposed to be *engaging* you and feeding you things besides sugar.

GRETA: She's not here.

CAROL: What? Why?

GRETA: Mom, it's *Saturday.* I *told* you.

CAROL: Oh. Really?

GRETA: I asked for lunch but Dad's in his office and you were asleep here in the kitchen.

CAROL: I was?

GRETA: They're chips-a-hoy-cream in the middle. So it's like an Oreo. And an Oreo is like a sandwich.

CAROL: I'm too dizzy for this.

GRETA: So this is kind of like lunch. A sandwich lunch.

CAROL: Maybe Lena can do overtime next weekend.

(Quiet. GRETA eats.)

Must you continue to chew like that? Each bite is echoing in my head.

GRETA: Is it like a pig?

CAROL: What, no, why, *what?*

GRETA: Would you say my chewing is like a boar's?

CAROL: Just stop or no one will invite you anywhere.

GRETA: Maybe just a little like a boar?

CAROL: Like skiing. Or to a club. A supper club. Don't you want to go to a supper club?

GRETA: Because there's a boar in Snow White—

(CAROL extends her arm and crushes GRETA's cookies.

Pause.

GRETA drinks her milk.

CHARLOTTE pulls leaves off her plant and drops them into a mortar. She sprays them. She grinds them with a pestle.

LENA and GRETA in the laundry room.

LENA folds clothes. GRETA sits on the washer. She lifts her fingers into a circle and begins to peer at LENA through them.)

GRETA: You're very pretty.

LENA: Okay, what do you want?

GRETA: No. I mean it. Really. In fact: I'm going to imagine you.

(She looks through her fingers.)

Very pretty. Only—

LENA: Why aren't you outside?

GRETA: The nanny's supposed to talk with me, that's how it works.

LENA: Don't you have any friends?

GRETA: I invited this girl named Sarah Berkowitz over once. But she was kind of weird. All she wanted to do the whole time was sit under the dining room table and figure out people's half birthdays.

LENA: Call and we'll pick her up.

GRETA: No.

LENA: Come on, girl, you can't stay cooped up in here your whole life.

GRETA: I could. Like Rapunzel. You know Rapunzel?

LENA: You've got to have at least *one* friend from school or riding or that ballet.

GRETA: I'm not like those kids.

LENA: How about Heritage class?

GRETA: Read me a story.

LENA: I'm doing laundry.

(Holds up a piece of laundry.)

You don't want to go to school naked, do you?

GRETA: I bet when you were little you had lots of friends, you're so pretty. Like I bet you lived in a place where you just knocked next door and a friend came out and you didn't have to go to riding and ballet and stinky Heritage class, to try to get people to be with you. Right? Did they live close next door? Or maybe across the street?

LENA: Across the street was an old lady with a smell. But there was a girl next door.

GRETA: Did you play games from a box or in the street?

LENA: I never played in the street.

GRETA: What was she like?

LENA: Mean. Used to take the tails of cats and tie them together with string.

GRETA: Oh.

LENA: But before that, before she started with the cats, I guess we were friends.

GRETA: *Oh.*

LENA: We were only little. Sometimes she'd help me in school. She was friendly at first.

GRETA: What happened to her?

LENA: Well. She was a smart one. Used to get stars on her papers all the time. Used to wave 'em in front of my face, right under my nose, so close I could smell what was under her fingernails until one day? I bit her.

(GRETA giggles. LENA giggles.)

C'mon, let's call that Sarah what's-her-name.

GRETA: Oh no, she can't come back and I told her if she ever told anyone about her coming over here I'd poison her snack milk.

(They look at each other.)

LENA: You did not.

GRETA: She drinks the apple juice at snack now.

LENA: You sound like me.

GRETA: She didn't even tell. Her mom never called here or anything. Besides she deserved it. The half birthday she kept saying over and over was Martin Luther King's. Like she was saying it just for me because…. Like it was special for me because I'm…. Read me a book. I'm bored.

LENA: I'm busy.

(LENA folds. After a beat GRETA lifts her fingers into a circle and begins to peer at LENA again.)

GRETA: You know what I think? I think you're so nice and so pretty, but you'd be just a little prettier with white skin. Like bright white skin? That's what I'm imagining when I look through my fingers like this.

(A dryer buzzer sounds.)

So much prettier. Don't you think?

(LENA takes GRETA's hand gently and smoothes her fingers out of the circle shape.)

I was only pretending.

LENA: Pretend something else.

GRETA: I learned it in a movie. This lady she's a model, right, and she's afraid she's getting ugly, right? And she puts this cream on her face and it burns, right? It's supposed to burn the black right off her. It burns little bits of her self, too. She watches it all happening to her in her mirror. But I don't blame her. I'd like to be pretty too. You can't blame people for wanting things, can you?

LENA: If she burnt her face off she's silly. A burnt face is no good.

GRETA: But what if you really wanted something and to get it you had to burn your face off—

LENA: I *like* my face the way it was *made*: brown. You should like yourself the way you are.

GRETA: You like yourself?

LENA: I'm not ashamed to be brown.

GRETA: But you really like yourself?

LENA: Go-out-side.

GRETA: Read me a story.

LENA: I said I'm busy.

GRETA: You're supposed to do what I want. My mom pays you, you know.

(LENA and CHARLOTTE outside Heritage class.)

CHARLOTTE: Greta'll be right out. How are my Heritage Holders doing?

LENA: She does them every night.

CHARLOTTE: Those parents ever take a peek?

LENA: I don't know. I'm pretty busy with just Greta.

CHARLOTTE: They'll work you, girl. They-will-work each and every bone in your body. Your hair looks fabulous.

LENA: Twice a day.

CHARLOTTE: I'll make something for your split ends next.

(LENA touches her hair.)

LENA: I don't think I have split—

CHARLOTTE: I'm working on a recipe with Slippery Elm. I feel like a cheat, though, because Slippery Elm's not from Africa. It's American. But it works and it's got this amazing history. I…I downloaded it for you so you'll be informed about what's on your head.

(Hands a sheet of paper to LENA.)

LENA: *(Reading.)* Wow. This is…this is great. Slippery Elm, wow.

(CHARLOTTE looks at LENA. She turns the sheet right-side round.)

CHARLOTTE: It was upside down.

(CHARLOTTE and LENA look at each other.

The dryer buzzer.

LENA kneels in front of a laundry basket full of clothes. She pulls out a garment slowly, revealing that it has been discolored in the wash.

LENA pulls out another garment, also ruined.

She pulls out all the laundry, becoming more frenzied as she continues until she finally sits in a pile of discolored clothing.)

LENA: *(This is a chant, a mantra: said quickly and deliberately like hurried "Hail Marys.")* Silly, silly, you're not ugly, you're not ugly at all.

(Pause.)

Silly, silly, you're being silly you're not ugly at all.

(A dryer buzzer.)

Silly.

CARRMEL: What are you stupid?

LENA: Oo, girl you scared me.

CARRMEL: I not the girl, you the girl. Loose girl, stupid girl. All the baby's clothes: *(Spits.)*

LENA: It's this machine. It's because I'm an idiot, really, I can't make out the directions—

CARRMEL: You don't know how to wash clothes.

LENA: It's this machine. Carol explained it to me bu—

CARRMEL: What type of person can't do laundry?

LENA: I can do laundry, okay. I'm not an idiot.

CARRMEL: One minute ago you say you an idiot, now you say you are not an idiot: I know why you can't make up your mind: it's too slow, it's soft and runny like molasses. You soft and runny like molasses, and you should just run home, Molassy girl.

LENA: Exactly what is your problem?

CARRMEL: You leave door open.

LENA: Like *once*.

CARRMEL: You ruin all the baby's clothes.

LENA: I didn't: the machine did. There's no dials, it's all electric, electrical, electricalized. How's somebody supposed to know how to work a machine that's this mechanical, that has no dials like normal?

CARRMEL: Directions don't help?

LENA: It should have dials.

CARRMEL: You must have molassy head to be peeking at those directions all day long and still my baby's clothes get ruined. I see you peeking and peeking: your eyes about to bleed you peek so much.

(LENA picks up laundry basket and tries to leave.)

I watch you.

(LENA is about to leave.) I get rid of you like this *(Spits.)* She get rid of you sooner when I tell her you got to peek cause you too afraid to look those directions straight on. You know how I know?

(LENA does not answer.)

Ask me: How I know?

(Nothing.)

Ask me how I know.

(CARRMEL waits.)

What you peeking at…

(Very slight pause.)

LENA: What about it?

CARRMEL: On that lid? They no directions.

LENA: The directions are always, *always* under the lid.

CARRMEL: They the service dates.

(Lifts the lid.)

December. May. November. June. They when the man come with tools. No directions. All that peeking and you not even getting directions. Ha. You gonna be gone by dinner.

(CARRMEL leans in towards LENA, swabs her ear with her finger. CARRMEL licks her finger.)

Because I gonna tell on you my poor molassy girl.

LENA: I'll do it myself.

(GRETA at her mirror.)

GRETA: *(Whispers.)* Mirror, mirror?

(Listens.)

What?

(Listens. She picks up container of talcum powder.)

What?

(Listens. She squeezes the container, talcum powder puffs up in the air. She watches it fall.)

As long as it helps.

(A dryer buzzer.

GREG and CARRMEL at opposite ends of the hall.

CARRMEL walks at GREG.

GREG walks normally until he sees CARRMEL.

CARRMEL walks at GREG, their eyes meet.

GREG tries to walk around CARRMEL.)

GREG: Excuse me.

(CARRMEL stops moving and GREG tries to edge his way around her.)

Just. Ah. Excuse me. Just. Um. Coming through.

(Once past CARRMEL.)

Good to, uh... .Good to see you, Carrmel.

CARRMEL: The wife sick.

GREG: It's allergies.

CARRMEL: You know what she sick with?

GREG: I've got a conference—

CARRMEL: You know how I know? Poke, poke.

(Holds up a diaphragm.)

GREG: What.... Is thata?... Diaphragm?... You're holding.... I've never even touched that and we've been married twelve years.

CARRMEL: Poke, poke that's all I had to do and now your babies come.

GREG: Give me that.

CARRMEL: The stupid girl can have your old one: the next one? Mine.

GREG: Pardon?

CARRMEL: I come to you and say in a nice way: time for me to work with the children but you too busy. I go to the Missus and say what I need to change and *she* too busy. So I forced to take matter into me own hands.

GREG: We can't have you *deciding* things for us Carrmel.
(*He takes the diaphragm.*)
Now when I tell Carol you've been touching our personal—
CARRMEL: You like new-nanny's skin? You like her bones? If I tell about you to the wife you be out in the street no food, no clothes, so you be careful Mr. Man. It's the wife important. It's her make your money, buy your house, pay for your girls. You gonna like all them skin and bones if you in the street? I no look like peel now, huh?
(*LENA and CHARLOTTE on a park bench.*)
CHARLOTTE: My cousin's all into literacy. Our people need it in the worst way. Education was very important in ancient Africa.
LENA: I'm from St. Louis.
CHARLOTTE: After your education you can get a better job. No more fanny wiping.
LENA: I used to want to be a stewardess. I know I'd look smart in that uniform.
CHARLOTTE: See.
LENA: But there's tests.
CHARLOTTE: But I have this cousin.
LENA: Letters get mixed up before I can make them fit together.
CHARLOTTE: Literacy is our legacy.
LENA: The principal's son was my sweetheart: so I got my diploma: I wasn't one of those drop-outs that smoke behind the Walmart. I found my way. I'm not stupid: I pay attention. I had a teacher who was real into words, real into saying words the right way. I paid close attention to every little thing she said, and it worked: I don't sound like one of those people on the T.V. who can't put a sentence together, can't hardly talk: I'm not stupid. I keep up with everything. Even my bills. Each bill I get I send to my grandmother in Fort Worth. Over the phone she tells me how to make out my checks. The only problem right now is that washing machine. Greta's going to be walking around in rags if I don't tell them about me soon. People usually understand after I explain, after I tell them that letters don't work for me. Letters twist around before my head gets a chance to figure them out. People usually understand, but sometimes, sometimes they don't. That's…that's what happened at my last place. The mother there would write me things. I was really good at figuring them out except this one time, my last time, I wasn't, so good. It was a birthday party. I was supposed to take her two girls to this birthday party. She wrote the directions on this piece of paper. Easy, I thought. I just get the

big one to read it, say my eyes hurt, or I forgot my glasses. I got a whole list of things I can say. And I can drive okay but directions, when they're on paper like that, are no good. So I stay calm. I drive around for a little. I wait. I drive a little more, then I make a joke: I say "Hey, make yourself useful." I give a little laugh, too, to go with the joke. But the big one, the ugly one with the big teeth she says "No." Just "No" flat out like that. She says it's not her job, it's mine. She says it's what her mother pays me good money for. So I ask the little one. I don't get huffy I just ask the little one if she can read. But. She can't. So I drive. Around and around 'til they both fall asleep. Big teeth and her sister. Useless. I drive thinking maybe I'll see a house with balloons. But I don't. Next day the agency calls. They say don't go to work today. They say I get one more chance before they have to let me go. This is my one more chance but that Carrmel's creeping around spying on me and the mother keeps writing me notes. How am I supposed to keep my job if she writes me notes?

(The sound of the spray bottle is heard twice.

GREG *and* CAROL *in the office.)*

GREG: —so the courtyard—I've put in a courtyard—that whole part could be surrounded by murals, like we commission someone to come up with murals, and, see, the image I have in my head is hands, like, all different shaped hands, and those are gonna come out of the walls of the courtyard, right?, so we get the whole idea of community, and nurturing, and history, like hands-of-history, and in between all these hands we'll get someone to sculpt what's gonna look like fabric, like textile fabric, in between these hands. Up top? I'm thinking beams, light beams, which I think they'll go for because it's very inspirational, very reach for the sky/sky's the limit kind of thing.

(He looks at CAROL.)

So? You like it? I love it.

CAROL: That depends. What's the going rate for helping hands and beams of light?

GREG: Just tell me you like it.

CAROL: What I'd *like* is for you to start looking for new clients: the phone bill came in a pink envelope, and I'm not about to give up the help around here—

GREG: Would that be so bad? I mean, Carrmel can be a little rough around the—

(CAROL cuts him off with a look.)

CAROL: I just *said* I'm not about to give up my help.

> *(She works.*
>
> *Pause.)*

GREG: I *am* looking for new clients—

CAROL: Real ones, not rainbow-coalition-helping-hands-up-with-people ones. Oo. My head. From above there's this scraping. From inside there's all this thinking. About being little and hoping: praying. Every little girl grows up hoping, praying, that really, underneath it all, she's Cleopatra. Or Nefertiti. But then life creeps along, sneaks up, and she begins to worry. Maybe she's not Nefertiti at all. Maybe she's one of the peasants who's only heard of Nefertiti. Maybe there's been some cosmic confusion and she's one of the unwashed and nothing like Nefertiti in the least. I am thinking, Greg, that I do not want to be the unwashed. I do not want to be that peasant. I am Nefertiti. And Nefertiti, Greg, would not have her telephone bill delivered in some pink envelope—

> *(LENA enters.)*

LENA: Oh. Sorry.

CAROL: No. Come in.

> *(CAROL watches GREG.)*

LENA: If you're in the middle of something or something—

CAROL: No, Greg was just leaving. He's very busy getting new clients, aren't you, Greg?

> *(He leaves.*
>
> *CAROL groans.)*

LENA: I can really come back.

CAROL: Stay. I have a list. I hope it's not too much trouble.

LENA: No trouble, but, I was hoping I could talk to you about the laundry—

CAROL: Detergent. Yes. You can slip that in right under the salmon.

LENA: She won't eat salmon.

CAROL: It's not for her. Not everything's for her, I live here, too, you know.

LENA: It's just that…I thought my job was—

CAROL: Money. I'm getting riled up and all you asked for is money.

LENA: I didn't. I—

> *(CAROL fishes in her pocket and hands LENA money.*
>
> *LENA stares at it.)*

CAROL: Don't keep the change. Ha-ha, I'm joking. You can get yourself something. Something little.

> *(LENA does not move.)*

Well take it.

LENA: It's just that my job isn't to do any shopping.

CAROL: Sometimes in the middle of the night—

LENA: And what I really want to talk to you about is the washing machine: Carrmel and the washing machine. I'm having trouble—

CAROL: When the sweet smell of my daughter is turning to stench in my nostrils—

LENA: There's no dials.

CAROL: And my husband is building America in his sleep—

LENA: I'm used to dials.

CAROL: I think to myself: where's Lena now? What's she doing now?

LENA: I'm very good with dials because—

CAROL: I think to myself: is her head about to explode? Is she smelling her life rot?

(CAROL lets out an abrupt little laugh that hurts her head. She holds it in place, then leans against the desk.)

You are not smelling your life rot. You're so pure and so fresh. Undeveloped. That's what I like about you: your potential. I want to teach you things. I want you to look up to me. As an example. Of how to succeed. Oooo. My *head*. You should get going.

LENA: I just said shopping isn't part of my job. I want to stick to my job.

CAROL: Can't you see I'm sick?

LENA: I'm not a housekeeper.

CAROL: All I'm asking for is a little favor.

LENA: I'm not anybody's maid, either.

CAROL: I know what you are, I hired you. Why are you being so mean to me? You should be my friend. That's how it works. You girls are supposed to be my friend.

LENA: I'm just the nanny.

CAROL: No. You're my sister. My little pioneer sister. Out on the prairie with nothing around but putrid mountains and futile plains. Vast and empty; dry and thirsty; amber waves waiting; waiting to devour us; amber waves that are eager, *eager* to taste the last drops of moist blood that waits in our cobwebbed marrow. This country is killing me. Work and work but there's no end. I look at you and I see hope. There's so much I can help you with. To succeed. I was just like you girls. But first, you help me: please, Lena: shed your light on me and get me some salmon.

(A dryer buzzer sounds.

GRETA stands in front of her mirror.)

She squeezes the talcum powder, a puff of it shoots into the air. She catches it on her arm and rubs it around on her skin, so that her forearm is now covered with a sheet of powder.

She smiles.)

GRETA: Thanks, Mirror, I certainly did need that.

(The sound of sweeping.

CARRMEL sweeps around CAROL.)

CAROL: Where's Lena?

(LENA at the washer, which churns.

LENA peers at the lid. The sound of an old-fashioned typewriter.)

CARRMEL: I can help you.

LENA: You're not ugly—

CAROL: You're not Lena.

LENA: You're not ugly at all, sill-

(The sound of an old-fashioned typewriter as a large black letter falls from the sky, hits LENA on the head.)

CARRMEL: I'm a peel on the floor.

(LENA smoothes her head where the letter hit.

CARRMEL spits.)

CAROL: Where's Lena?

CARRMEL: She no good—

CAROL: These girls should be grateful to work here. I'm entitled to a little favor here and there. It's a small price to pay for being allowed access into this type of lifestyle. These girls don't know how lucky they are. I used to be just like them. I used to have nothing but I worked. I went to school. I kept my legs shut even though it was the seventies. And nothing went up my nose even though the eighties came after. These girls traipse around here like their presence is some precious gift to us when really it's the other way around.

(A letter falls again.

LENA is still at the washer.)

LENA: Silly.

CARRMEL: I get that salmon. You sick. I get the salmon and cook it for you—

CAROL: No. It's the least she can do. LENA.

(GREG stands in proximity to LENA but not too close to her.)

GREG: Before you we had a girl who had nice wrists. Hills of skin and bone that stuck out of her where normal people keep their arms and hands attached.

CAROL: How is a little salmon too much to ask? Tell me.

(*GRETA enters completely covered in talcum powder.*

CAROL and CARRMEL watch her sit at the kitchen table.)

GRETA: (*In her Snow White voice.*) How do you do, Mother?

CARRMEL: The stupid girl do this: she let my baby walk around like this.

CAROL: Where's Lena? I don't pay her to hide from me in my own house.

GRETA: Mother—

CAROL: I pay her to work.

GREG: I touched them once.

LENA: Silly—

(*The doorbell rings.*)

CAROL: — oo my *head*—

GREG: I managed to brush against them.

CAROL: LENA?

CARRMEL: She too stupid she can't even do what you need.

GRETA: I could fetch a spot of salmon for you, Mother.

GREG: You have a beautiful collarbone—

(*GREG moves towards LENA.*

He walks his index and forefinger towards her in the air.)

CAROL: *LENA.*

CARRMEL: This one a molassy girl.

(*Spits.*

A letter falls on LENA's head.)

LENA: (*In the direction of the letters.*) Would you **leave me alone?**

(*GREG clutches his hand back to himself protectively.*)

GREG: Shhhh: sh.

(*GREG exits.*)

GRETA: Mother?

CAROL: LENA?

(*The doorbell rings.*)

Ooo. My head, my head, my head.

(*She slumps into a chair.*

CARRMEL spits.)

CARRMEL: Stupid, stupid molassy girl.

(*CARRMEL spits twice.*)

LENA: You're not ugly at all, silly—

(*But many, many letters fall on LENA, knocking her to the ground.*)

VOICE: (*From inside the washing machine.*) Silly, silly, silly, silly, silly…

(One last letter falls.
The sound of the washing machine, it begins to sputter and make a sickly noise, as before.
Darkness.
The doorbell rings.
The doorbell rings quickly in succession, three times.
Quiet.
The sound of a spray bottle is heard once.
Lights up on the laundry room.
LENA on the floor covered by letters.
CHARLOTTE sprays the floor with her spray bottle twice.)

CHARLOTTE: *Girrrrl.* This family is *wacked.* I mean they are *gone,* oh my goodness. First I ring the bell for near to an hour before Broomhilda *(Mimics CARRMEL.)* answers the door and I'm like can I *please* talk to Lena, thank you very much. 'Cause I'm gonna hook you up go-*od.* Literacy is legacy and all that so don't you worry but first I have to finish my story, 'cause *then* when I get into the kitchen the mother's like "Lena's *working,* you know"—*you know*—like we're on some English moor, like she's some Parisian aristo-crat or some such nonsense—I minored in French Studies, I know a thing or two about those French rich people. Got their ass *whooped.* She wants to play some role? Okay by me as long as I get a role, too. I'll be a *sans-culotte,* one of those French workers wanted to over-throw every-thang, you know what I'm saying? Natural rights, natural state; none of this abuse of wealth, of privilege, right? *Right?*
(She looks at LENA.)
Why're you on the floor like that?
(LENA brushes the letters off of her and stands.)

LENA: Laundry.

CHARLOTTE: But did you have an accident or something?

LENA: No.

CHARLOTTE: Why're you covered in their dirty clothes?

LENA: I'm not covered in their dirty clothes.

CHARLOTTE: You *are.*
(CAROL and GRETA in the GRETA's bedroom.
GRETA is still covered in powder.)

CAROL: Is it a costume?

GRETA: No.

CAROL: If you like this activity so much I'll sign you up for lessons: Mime lessons.

GRETA: I'm *not* a *mime.*

CAROL: For now go tell Lena to give you a bath.

GRETA: This is me, you don't want to wash *me* away, do you?

CAROL: If it's a costume you can wear it until Lena gives you a bath. But if it's a type of personality you're adopting— Where *is* Lena?
(LENA and CHARLOTTE still in the laundry room. LENA gathers the letters that have accumulated on the floor and throws them in the washer.)

CHARLOTTE: But I'm goin'ta free your mind—

LENA: You and your cousin—

CHARLOTTE: I'm going to take you down to the Y and have one of those counselors—

LENA: I won't do any tests. They make me feel like my blood is on the outside—
(The letters clang in the machine.)

CHARLOTTE: How are you supposed to get work done with a machine that clangs around like that? They probably blame you first chance if something shrinks, if something comes back a little worse for wear when it's not your fault. It's the machine. The system; *their system.* Ah-ha? You know?

LENA: Is this cousin a nice cousin or a mean cousin?
(GRETA and CAROL in GRETA's bedroom, as before.)

GRETA: Now when you don't find me or discover with me it won't matter because I'll blend right into the wood, into the glade.

CAROL: I don't want you blending into any glade.

GRETA: It's impossible to do it with the other me.

CAROL: What are you talking about?

GRETA: The other me that sticks out.

CAROL: You don't stick out.

GRETA: I don't stick in.

CAROL: Greta—
(LENA and CHARLOTTE still in the laundry room.)

LENA: 'Cause I had this mean teacher once, she used to hold pencils under my wrists to make me write better. The school sent me to her because I squeezed through into one of those programs. It was only supposed to be for the smart ones but I squeezed through. I was a cute one. She sharpened the tips real pointy. So as soon as I wrote wrong, soon as my wrist dropped, I would feel those tips scratch and dig their way to my skin. Then it didn't matter how cute I was: I'd made a mistake: stupid, stupid:

silly: silly. Teachers had a way of making you feel like that, if they were mean. So I quit that stupid program. If teachers aren't nice, I quit.

(CHARLOTTE begins to place seeds in the floor.

GRETA and CAROL in GRETA's bedroom, as before.)

CAROL: Greta, honey—

(CAROL gropes for GRETA from her chair.

GRETA does not move.

CAROL strokes the air awkwardly, as if she is stroking GRETA's arm, trying to reach her.)

Honey.

(Gropes for GRETA. Gently.)

Honey.

(CAROL moves a bit closer to GRETA as she continues to grope the air between them.

GRETA inches only a bit closer.

CAROL reaches for her, rises slightly, then stops abruptly, as if she has bumped into something very hard.)

Oooooo.

GRETA: What's wrong with you?

CAROL: We do not subscribe to every black magazine there is to have you blend. Look at our coffee table, have you looked at our coffee table? We don't put those out there for us, we put those out there for you to develop a sense of—. Why haven't you looked at our coffee table?

GRETA: I'm not talking about the coffee table I'm talking about school and riding. And ballet. There's always only me.

(LENA and CHARLOTTE in the laundry room, as before.)

LENA: One doctor said I had a vitamin deficiency. See there was this book I wanted to read when I was in third grade. About this girl named Ramona. Soon as those vitamins kicked in I was going to read that book cover to cover, even use a bookmark. My grandmom was always sending us bookmarks only I never got to use mine. What are you doing?

CHARLOTTE: These are the best seeds I have, these Slippery Elm seeds.

LENA: You're planting them in the house?

(CHARLOTTE reveals the jar full of seeds. She pours a handful into her palm. She holds one up to the light.)

CHARLOTTE: I've been preparing them for a special occasion, coating them with Miracle Grow.

(The sound of the spray bottle is heard twice.)

They should sprout in no time. No time at all.

(She begins to place the seeds into the floor.)

This family's lucky I've *arrived*, honey-child, yes, *yes*. Everythang is going to cha-*ange*, girl, just you wait and see. These seeds I'm planting in their floor, they're going to sprout soon-as-you're-born into a forest: thick and dark. A wilderness so natural, so strong it will take over this entire *house*, girl. It's gonna bust through the walls, through the windows, it's gonna spread down the street, up the block: *Yes.* Turn this whole town, this entire land of McMansions back to its natural state, man, so we can start over up in this here country. This is supposed to be America but eight-year-old-you is stuck lining up books, looking at their pictures instead of being able to read them yourself.

LENA: Yeah.

CHARLOTTE: *(Excited.)* Yeah?

LENA: I'm supposed to learn how to really read, right? No guessing, no making up stories about eye glasses, no driving around in the dark while some snotty-nosed kid makes fun of you, laughs at you while you're just trying to do your job. With your cousin it's going to work this time. I can feel it. I'm going to read everything I get my hands on. Every little thing. But the first thing's going to be that menu at Chili's. The *whole* menu. I'm sick of going to Chili's and ordering the chicken-fried steak. After that cousin, I'll know how to read, really read. Like I should have been taught in the first place, since this is America—

CHARLOTTE: The *Promised* Land: but people like you and me get left out in the cold, get left to ring the bell for an hour while they propagate their precious status quo. Man. These people get to me.

(She squirts her spray bottle into the air. The two watch the spray evaporate.
CAROL and GRETA in GRETA's bedroom, as before.)

CAROL: I want that washed off.

GRETA: Then give me a bath yourself.

CAROL: Not today.

GRETA: I bet you don't even know how. A mommy is supposed to know how.

CAROL: Mommy's tired. Mommy has no energy left.

(She gropes at GRETA, attempts to stand, hits her head, falls on the floor.
GRETA looks down at CAROL's head, pats it.
CARRMEL's non-melodic humming as she enters, sweeping.)

CARRMEL: Mummy sick?

GRETA: I think sleepy.

CARRMEL: You play. I take care of Mummy. When you come, she be as good as new.

GRETA: No. I'm doing it.

CARRMEL: Baby not take care, I take care. When you come back I make you nice dinner. You like my dinner: I cook it just for you.

GRETA: You make everything too spicy.

CARRMEL: This time I make it just for you.

GRETA: You always say that but it never works. I have to take small bites so I don't get sick and throw up all over the table.

CARRMEL: Then I cook the mac and cheese. From the box. And we sit at the table, you tell me all about your day—

GRETA: You'll just start that humming.

(GRETA begins to stomp off.)

CARRMEL: Sh. Sh. You wake the mummy—

CAROL: *(Startled awake.)* Lena? Where's Lena?

CARRMEL: She down there with a pushy girl.

CAROL: I don't pay her to have social hour, do I?

(She scribbles a note on a piece of paper.)

One more chance. I'm too nice to these girls; it's going to kill me, I just know it. *(To GRETA.)* Give this to Lena.

(GRETA exits.)

CARRMEL: A girl like that, she don't listen. Especially when they mix up with the pushy ones: Uh-uh. And no way a stupid girl with a friend who is a pushy girl good enough to take care of that new baby.

CAROL: It's *allergies* and if I wanted to chat about my personal life I'd call you on the phone.

CARRMEL: You can't keep secrets from me.

(Plants have begun to grow out of the floor boards.
The sound of giggling.
GRETA darts in and out of the plants, carrying the note: gleeful. She leaves it on the washer.
The plants grow.
GREG on the phone.)

GREG: ...Greg, that's right...I'm looking at them right now but I don't see.... Well that's not set in—oh: hold? Hold.

(The sound of leaves rustling.
LENA, in the laundry room.
She reads CAROL's note.

The sound of the spray bottle is heard twice.
LENA and CHARLOTTE in the laundry room.
Plants grow through the floorboards.)

CHARLOTTE: Look at that: would you just look at that?

LENA: Are you done? 'Cause if you're done maybe we can give that cousin a call? 'Cause see?

(LENA pulls out CAROL's note. Frantic.)

I'm gonna get fired: I can't get fired: I've never been—

(CHARLOTTE tears the note into pieces, then stuffs the pieces in her mouth.)

CHARLOTTE: You know what *I* want? I want my 1.9% APR. That's what I want. Stupid student loans. Stupid credit card I can't even use anymore. What kind of place is this where I can't get my 1.9% APR because I tried to better myself?

(The dryer buzzer.
Immediately after, a cell phone rings.
CAROL, on the floor in the kitchen, groans.
It rings again.)

CAROL: *(Answering phone.)* Hello?… Of course…. Yes I realize…. First thing tomorrow?…Andrew? … assist *Andrew?* He barely passed the bar…how long have I been with this firm…so assisting some milk-fed bronzed trust fund brat who has failed the bar at *least* four times the last time I checked…. Of course it's temporary, so I don't understand why…I have given…I have given…I have given ten years to this firm. Ten years of being…don't think I don't know how this all works, how you all see me, watch me. All I'm asking for is the common decency, the common courtesy of ooo. Damn ceiling, damn glass ceiling is scraping my, don't think you don't know what I'm talking about, you know exactly what I'm…ooo, ooo…who knew it even existed? Who knew it'd start scraping my…but *this* case I built this—hello?

(She gets frustrated and begins to push buttons on the phone. She pushes many, then flings the phone across the room.
She slumps in her chair.
Silence.
The sound of the spray bottle.
CHARLOTTE enters, spraying the floor, planting seeds.
CAROL looks up.)

CAROL: Just what do you think you're doing? Where's Lena? Tell her I said to tell her she should tell you to go.

CHARLOTTE: I'm gonna free your mind, girl.

CAROL: LENA. Ooo.

CHARLOTTE: It's going to be a whole new world, I'm telling you. Like the pilgrims, right? No, no, no, that's not right, like the Indians *before* the pilgrims, *yes*. Slippery Elm. Healing powers. Under the bark. Natural state. Self-evident truths. I'm endowed by my creator just like you but I get treated like nothing can grow from me. They had it right in France. Liberty. Unity. Distribution was all wacked and they fixed it, man.

(The cell phone rings. CAROL begins to crawl towards it.)

Uh-uh-uh. Don't answer their call. Let them answer your call. The call of the *wild*.

(CAROL kicks at CHARLOTTE with one of her legs from her position on the floor.)

CAROL: *(On phone.)* Yes? Yes, we must have been cut off—

CHARLOTTE: My wilderness is gonna get you, girl—

(CAROL kicks at CHARLOTTE with her heel.)

CAROL: I am not Angela Davis: I-am-*Marie*-Antoin*ette*—

(CHARLOTTE sprays into the floor and air once, each.

CAROL cradles the phone to her ear in a curl on the floor and listens to the phone.)

CHARLOTTE: My wilderness is gonna get you good.

(GREG, sniffs the air.

He examines a draft of his work.

He sniffs the back of his hand, then his elbow.

LENA and CAROL in the kitchen.

CAROL groaning on the floor.)

CAROL: While you and your unfortunate food co-op smelling friend traipse around my house ruining my sealed wood floors, my daughter's running around smothered in powder looking like a cutlet.

LENA: I was in the basement. Trying to work that machine—

CAROL: You're dedicated. I like that. But about that note.

LENA: I have…trouble…with notes.

CAROL: Trouble with notes?

LENA: I've been trying to tell you, see: I can't make out letters very well. I can memorize real good, though. You can test me. Capitols. Dates. I learned all the dates of the Civil War just by watching the History Channel.

CAROL: It's not necessary to test you, Lena, don't be silly.

LENA: I'm not silly.

CAROL: I understand completely. Here you are trying to do your job and I've made it so difficult for you. I apologize. From now on I type.

LENA: Type?

CAROL: My handwriting is *atrocious*. Those notes were probably giving you migraines. I'm not as lucky as Greta. I had twenty-six kids in my class. But Greta gets the very best; which is why she has you.

(The sound of the spray bottle is heard as CHARLOTTE *traverses the house, spraying the floor boards and planting seeds while the leaves rustle and more plants grow to waist height.*

CARRMEL enters.

CARRMEL looks the plants up and down.

Leaves rustle.

CARRMEL examines a plant, starting at the tip and traveling downward to the root.

She pokes the stalk of one plant.

Leaves rustle.

She pokes higher up the stalk, then pulls at the tip, picking a leaf off of the stalk.

Loud rustling.

CARRMEL is startled.

Violent rustling.

CARRMEL hurries away.

The sound of leaves rustling.

LENA and CHARLOTTE.

The plants have grown quite large.)

LENA: —But I've waited long enough.

CHARLOTTE: Natural citizens, that's what we'll all be, it's just going to take time—

LENA: I don't have anymore time—

CHARLOTTE: We shouldn't be reading their notes they should be reading *our*—

LENA: You know what I think? I think there is no cousin.

CHARLOTTE: Of course there's a cousin.

(As LENA *speaks she walks towards* CHARLOTTE, *backing her into the washing machine.*

Its lid is open.)

LENA: Then what's her name? Which side of your family is she on?

CHARLOTTE: She's *on* the side of the revolution—

(LENA presses CHARLOTTE against the washer, and CHARLOTTE is forced to lean more and more towards the open mouth of the machine.)

LENA: You're *fooling* with me.

CHARLOTTE: I'm *uplifting—*

LENA: You don't care if I can read those notes.

CHARLOTTE: I do.

LENA: You tore one up in my face.

CHARLOTTE: I was breaking a chain, destroying a shackle.

LENA: You told me there was a cousin so I'd let you in so you can ruin this family for God knows why—

(CHARLOTTE is leaned over the mouth of the machine.)

VOIE: *(From inside the machine.)* Silly, silly, silly…

(The machine clangs. LENA looks towards the washer, releases CHARLOTTE. Immediately the sound of giggling.

GRETA darts in and out of the plants, playing as CARRMEL enters the kitchen, leaf in hand.

CARRMEL slams leaf on table, near CAROL's head.

CAROL is startled.)

CARRMEL: *(Points to leaf.)* She do this, I know. With that pushy friend. The whole world is a joke to those type of girls.

CAROL: It's a *leaf* Carrmel.

CARRMEL: A leaf yes: but from outside?: no. From those girls. Growing up through the floor: into the house. Not good for you, not good for that baby—

(LENA at the dryer. As CAROL speaks, LENA opens the dryer door, takes out her letters, spreads them on the floor, examines them.

She becomes increasingly frustrated.)

CAROL: You will never touch any babies. I'm dying here on the floor—my head's about to explode into a million pieces—and all you can think of is yourself. The sooner you realize you are just the housekeeper the sooner you'll be useful around here again, so go find something to clean.

(The sound of giggling, then the sound of leaves rustling.

CHARLOTTE, tending to her trees, bumps into GREG.)

CHARLOTTE: Watch it.

GREG: Excuse me.

CHARLOTTE: What, you think you can just run me over? You think I don't even matter so you can walk all over me like I'm dirt? You got another thing coming, Mr. Man, let me tell you.

GREG: *(Extends his hand.)* I'm the father. I'm Greg.

(They shake hands as CHARLOTTE eyes GREG.)

You've got lovely ears. The way they're shaped. Like they're designed in such a way that you're a very good listener, because they hold on to sound so well. I'm an architect. I notice how things are put together. The girl before you had a nice neck.

CHARLOTTE: Girl before me?

(She sprays the spray at him, it coats his skin.)

Oh no, no, *no.*

GREG: There's always girls roaming around the house so I assumed—

CHARLOTTE: What you and your tri-Delta wife don't understand is: I'm on an *errand.* I *am* not and never *will* be one of your *girls.* Couldn't handle it: could-not-handle-it. Besides you're not going to need girls once I'm through, once my errand is complete. This is America, man, and I'm gonna make sure it stays that way.

(GREG looks down at his skin, his arms and legs, where the spray has landed. GREG sniffs his arm.)

GREG: Hm?

(He sniffs his thigh.)

Hmm: I *do* smell an architect.

(He inhales deeply.)

I do, I do.

(Slight pause.)

Carol? I smell an architect.

(He hurries away.

CHARLOTTE darts behind a stalk. Rustling is heard.

A dryer buzzer.

The laundry room.

LENA drops the letters at CHARLOTTE's feet.)

LENA: So. I've decided you're going to teach me.

CHARLOTTE: I'm not trained to help people with— people who have some sort of—

LENA: You teach Greta, you teach all those kids who don't even know how to tie their shoes. I'll be easy.

(She gets on the floor, spreads out her letters.)

So like, I think this is a C, right, I think I remember this is a C.

(Holds out a letter to CHARLOTTE.

Pause.

CHARLOTTE reaches for another letter.)

CHARLOTTE: Um. This…this is a C. You…you have a G.

LENA: Okay, now we're talking. You're gonna teach me. Reading. And writing. I want to learn good writing. I'm missing out on that email people do.

CHARLOTTE: Okay…sure: yes. You're right. This should come first: then: our revolution. So. Where…where should we start? I mean, what do you know?
(LENA shoves the jumble of the letters at CHARLOTTE.

CHARLOTTE picks through the letters. She holds up an A.)
So, um, okay. Um, maybe…we'll just start at the beginning. This is the letter—

LENA: A, it's an A. I already know that.

CHARLOTTE: Okay. So how about we…um…put them together. Right?
(Pulls out paper and a pencil.

Hands pencil to LENA.

LENA looks at these, then back to CHARLOTTE, confused.)

CHARLOTTE: No. No, no, no: *not* right. But: *wait*: I have just the thing you need.
(CHARLOTTE hurries away.

LENA takes the pencil and grips it in her fist. She touches the tip with her finger.)

LENA: Pointy.
(The dryer buzzer.

GRETA darts through the trees, giggling.

GREG in the hallway, hears GRETA's giggle.)

GREG: Greta, have you seen your moth—
(Sees GRETA.)
Look at you.

GRETA: Oh Father, you've found me. I knew you would.

GREG: What's happened to you?

GRETA: It's not a costume.

GREG: But you can't walk around like that. You'll wipe off on the furniture.
(GRETA half giggles.)
You might be mistaken for a cutlet: Carrmel might even cook you. Go find Lena for a—

GRETA: I don't want Lena for a bath. You do it. Or Mommy. No more nannies.

GREG: The nannies aren't so bad. If you put all the best pieces of them together they're like one big mommy, you can have with you all the time.

That's what I think about when I see the nannies. So let's find Lena to clean you up. You don't want to be covered in all this white stuff, do you? Really?

GRETA: I feel much lighter this way. A burden's been lifted, Father, it truly has.

GREG: And stop talking like that, Greta. You should be proud to be you. Just plain, little you. We l...like you. Your mother and I—. I know we don't often say how we…. But things are going to change—

GRETA: Like me. I've changed. See: I've made the powder like my skin, right? So when I run through my glade, little bits of me *fly* away, up, up and away and I get lighter by the moment. It's fantastic, truly. I blend right into the air, into nature.

GREG: But if you blend into the air, into nature, Greta, there'll be no more you. There'll be nothing left.

GRETA: Just a wisp of me.

GREG: Where did you learn this?

GRETA: It will be glorious—

GREG: From school?

GRETA: And if you listen carefully to the wind, Father—

GREG: From us?

GRETA: —you'll be sure to hear just the twinkle of my voice—

GREG: Who taught you this?

GRETA: Now no one will be bothered with the me that sticks out ever again.

GREG: We're not bothered—

GRETA: You want the nannies to give me baths. You have them take me places when instead I would be home—

GREG: But Greta we love you, just plain little you—

(*The leaves rustle.*)

GRETA: Oh, Father, if you'll please excuse me, I must attend to my glade. Nature grew for me right here in my own house, can you believe it? I don't need to worry about sticking out ever again now that I have all these trees, isn't it marvelous?

(*She disappears into the plants, which have grown larger.*)

GREG: Greta? Come back. Please.

(*A giggle.*)

Greta?

(*Leaves rustle.*

The sound of giggling.

The sound of something moving through the leaves.

The sound of the spray bottle, twice.
The plants have grown very tall.
CARRMEL and her broom in front of a tree. She looks at the tree and hits it
with her broom. A great rustling is heard.
CHARLOTTE emerges.)

CHARLOTTE: STOP.

CARRMEL: How you gonta stop me, pushy girl?

(She hits the tree again, angry rustling.)

You can twist the molassy girl this way and that, but not me.

(She goes to hit the tree again, but CHARLOTTE grabs the other end of the
broom. They tug.

CHARLOTTE wins and breaks the broom over her knee.)

CHARLOTTE: Just you wait. You're not going to need this broom when I'm through. There's a place for you in this wilderness. No more scrubbing or sweeping. Once this wilderness is here we'll all start new.

CARRMEL: *(Spits.)* I too old to be starting new.

CHARLOTTE: You need to treat yourself like the Nubian Princess—

CARRMEL: I look like some princess to you? No. I a peel: Rr. New world? Not even good for dis world. HA.

CHARLOTTE: You got to empower yourself, girl—

CARRMEL: I not a girl. I'm a grown woman.

CHARLOTTE: And we could use that maturity in the wilderness—

CARRMEL: You think I wan to be walkin' round in some wilderness? Some dark place where you can't see nothin'? No. I want de light. I want de whole sun on me face. If I could I'd have ten a you girls running 'round after me. No more cooky here, cleany there. I be de fancy one. My whole life I give up pieces of meself, entire slices of meself for dem to eat and what I get? I got-ta keep the little bit I have for meself, no way I going to give any to you if all that's left for me in the end is crawling in de dark like a dog. *(Spits.)*

(CAROL and GREG. CAROL is typing on a manual typewriter.)

GREG: This country's fingers were wrapped around me until now: digging, gouging, spilling my blood so it could feed off me. I couldn't smell. I couldn't even see. But. Something's happened. I *do* smell an architect. No more waiting for someone to tell me *how*, give me permission *to*. Because, for the first time, I've seen Greta: this little thing we created and planned so much for, but who'd rather evaporate like a puddle than live here with us and wait until it's her turn to be devoured. We…we actually had a conversation. She talked, I talked. I enjoyed it. You say we're pioneers but I smell fruited plains that don't grow for *me*, but for wretched people who *ask* instead of demand, *whisper* instead of shout, *crawl* instead of stand. You say we're pioneers but I don't have enough blood to feed this place anymore. Now let's go find Greta—

CAROL: Lena will do it.

CAROL: *(Points to typewriter.)*

LENA—

(Continues typing.)

GREG: No more housekeepers, no more nannies—

CAROL: Don't you dare try to take Lena away from me. I need her under me, or how will I know how far I've come?

(The sound of a giggle.)

GREG: Please, Carol, we've got to find Greta—

CAROL: *I'm* the one who makes the decisions around here. If it were up to you Greta'd be playing in the street, going to public school, and taking lessons from amateurs at the Y—

GREG: You don't understand, she's gone: poof: easy as that and it's up to us to find her—

CAROL: I lost the McIntyre account.

GREG: Please. For Greta.

CAROL: I see you and I hear Greta but I'm a pioneer. We're building America, Greg, not Timbuktu—

GREG: For me.

CAROL: I won't just give up: Nefertiti wouldn't give up.

GREG: Carol.

CAROL: Jackie Kennedy wouldn't give up—

GREG: CAROL.

(They look at one another, then:)

CAROL: I had twenty-six kids in my class. Sour, sweaty: no one likes a skunk. I would have liked a supper club but no one ever invited me, which I don't understand because I'm Nerftiti.

(A faint giggle.

GREG sees the trees.)

GREG: I'm coming Greta.

CAROL: My frontier's turned— there's all this scraping— assist Andrew?— But I'm Marie Antoinette—Damn glass ceiling—who knew it even existed?

(Very slight pause.)

I had twenty-six kids in my class—

(LENA and CHARLOTTE: LENA reads.)

LENA: W…w…hn—

CHARLOTTE: "When."

LENA: I…nnnn.

CHARLOTTE: "In." See? The word is "in."

LENA: How am I supposed to do this with you breathing down my back?

CHARLOTTE: Sorry. So the next word is—

LENA: Tea.

CHARLOTTE: No. That's an h. See: t-h. It's Th-ee. The. Next word:

LENA: Cooo-ur—see.

CHARLOTTE: Course. Maybe we need a break—

LENA: Maybe we need a book instead of some paper from that Internet.

CHARLOTTE: This is *perfect* to start: The Declaration of Independence, man.

LENA: I feel silly.

CHARLOTTE: This time I won't talk. I won't say a word until you ask me.

> *(Pause.*
> *LENA turns to the reading materials again. She holds the pencil in one hand, guiding her work.*
> *CHARLOTTE murmurs over LENA's shoulder.)*

CHARLOTTE: *(Murmuring.)* …"it-becomes-neccesary-for-one-people-to-dissolve-the-political-bands"-hm-*MM*—

LENA: *Stop.*

CHARLOTTE: It's the language I get jazzed about. You'll understand soon—

LENA: I can't concentrate.

CHARLOTTE: Sorry.

> *(LENA works.*
> *CHARLOTTE murmurs to herself, then:)*

LENA: Would you *stop?*

CHARLOTTE: Sorry, sorry.

> *(LENA works.)*
> "…history of unremitting injuries and usurpations…"—
> *(LENA jams the pencil point at CHARLOTTE's neck. CHARLOTTE's hands go to her neck, LENA forcefully keeps the pencil gouged into CHARLOTTE, until CHARLOTTE is still.*
> *Darkness.*
> *The kitchen.*
> *CAROL is on the floor, obscured by many, many tall plants.*

The sound of rustling.

The sound of giggling.)

CAROL: LENA?

(CARRMEL enters, luggage in hand.

To CARRMEL.)

I'm Nefertiti and I need my amber plains. Go find Lena to get me my fruited waves because I'm Cleopatra Roosevelt; I'm Jackie Washington.

(CARRMEL walks past CAROL.

The sound of rustling.

LENA, pencil in hand.

CHARLOTTE's body is in the middle of being sucked into the trees.

LENA watches.

CARRMEL enters, luggage in hand.)

CARRMEL: This family all yours, molassy girl.

LENA: *(Looking at the pencil in her hand.)* Molassy girl—

CARRMEL: They gonta be lost in these trees that gonta grow over the old and bring new days, but dat not for me to see. I give nine years to them. Nine years waiting to get my chance to serve them, to serve God, like I was meant to do. But in de end: noting. So I not going to serve no one but meself from now on. They all yours now, my molassy girl.

LENA: I had a teacher used to hold pencils under my wrists. Teachers have a way of whispering to you: /silly, silly, silly….

VOICE: *(From inside the machine.)* Silly, silly, silly….

LENA: Hear that?

(CARRMEL puts on hat, starts to leave.)

VOICE: *(From inside the machine.)* Silly, silly—

LENA: This is supposed to be a place where eight-year-old me can get taught those letters no problem, right? A place where I get all different chances to choose from, right?

VOICE: *(From inside the machine.)* Silly, silly—

LENA: But I only had one last chance. She was my one last chance but she gave me nonsense to read, nonsense that didn't have anything to do with me, only her, all her, making fun, echoing in my head, I had to make it finally stop.

CARRMEL: We both just peels on de floor in dis world, my molassy girl. And that's no way to live.

(She spits as she leaves.)

LENA: No way to live.

    (CARRMEL leaves.)

VOICE: *(From inside the machine.)* Lena, Lena, Lena…

    (LENA looks at the machine.)

    Lena, Lena, Lena…

    (LENA opens the machine.)

LENA: Yes?

VOICE: *(From inside the machine.)* Yes.

LENA: And the trees will grow?

VOICE: *(From inside the machine.)* Yes.

LENA: And the new world can begin and I'll learn to read?

VOICE: *(From inside the machine.)* Yes.

LENA: *(Takes a deep breath.)* Until then.

    (LENA climbs in the washer.)

VOICE: *(From inside the machine. A hiss.)* Yesss.

    (LENA shuts the lid as the VOICE's hiss ends.

    The sound of the spray bottle.

    Darkness.

    End of play as the new world begins.)

END OF PLAY

The Ruby Sunrise
by Rinne Groff

BIOGRAPHY

Rinne Groff is a playwright and performer. Her plays, including *Jimmy Carter was a Democrat, Orange Lemon Egg Canary* (Humana 2003), *Inky, The Five Hysterical Girls Theorem, House of Wonder, Three Short Plays About Flying* and *The Ruby Sunrise,* have been produced and developed by Trinity Rep, P.S. 122, Target Margin Theater, Clubbed Thumb, HERE, Soho Repertory, and Andy's Summer Playhouse, among others. Ms. Groff is a founding member of Elevator Repair Service Theater Company and has been a part of the writing, staging and performing of their shows since the company's inception in 1991. Ms. Groff is an instructor at New York University Tisch School of the Arts and a member of New Dramatists and the Dramatists Guild. She is a graduate of Yale (1991) and New York University (1999).

HUMANA FESTIVAL PRODUCTION

The Ruby Sunrise premiered at the Humana Festival of New American Plays in March 2004 in co-production with Trinity Repertory Theatre. It was directed by Oskar Eustis with the following cast:

Ruby/Elizabeth Hunter . . . . Julie Jesneck
Henry/ Paul Benjamin . . . . Stephen Thorne
Lois/Ethel Reed. . . . . Anne Scurria
Lulu . . . . Jessica Wortham
Tad Rose . . . . Mauro Hantman
Martin Marcus . . . . Fred Sullivan, Jr.
Suzie Tyrone . . . . Russell Arden Koplin

and the following production staff:

Scenic Designer . . . . Eugene Lee
Costume Designer . . . . Deborah Newhall
Lighting Designer . . . . Deb Sullivan
Sound Designer . . . . Bray Poor
Properties Designer . . . . Doc Manning
Dialect Coach . . . . Thom Jones
Stage Manager . . . . Allison Tkac
Assistant Stage Manager. . . . . Michael Domue
Dramaturg. . . . . Adrien-Alice Hansel
Assistant Dramaturg . . . . Erin Detrick

PART I

CHARACTERS

RUBY, young, maybe 16, maybe 17
HENRY, 21
LOIS, 50s

PLACE

Boarding house in Indiana

TIME

1927

PART II

CHARACTERS

LULU, production girl, 24
TAD ROSE, writer, 28
MARTIN MARCUS, producer, 50s
SUZIE TYRONE, actress, 21
PAUL BENJAMIN, actor who played Henry in Act I
ETHEL REED, actress who played Lois
ELIZABETH HUNTER, actress who played Ruby

PLACE

New York City

TIME

1952

PART III

CHARACTERS, PLACE, TIME

A combination of Parts I and II

Stephen Thorne and Julie Jesneck
in *The Ruby Sunrise*

28th Annual Humana Festival of New American Plays
Actors Theatre of Louisville, 2004
photo by Harlan Taylor

The Ruby Sunrise

PART I
SCENE ONE

A barn in Indiana, early on a January morning in 1927.
RUBY, a young woman, bundled up for warmth, becomes visible in the shadows. She has a rag in her hand. Various parts of a disassembled mechanical generator are strewn before her on the floor. She talks to the audience.

RUBY: It happened just like this. I was on the mower, riding it down the field, each row, all those straight, straight lines. My thoughts, as usual, weren't on farming; I was building something else in my mind. When the reins slipped out of my hands, I didn't even note it, which can be mighty dangerous, specially with a skittish horse like we had. And right then, right as the horse felt its freedom and jerked me forward with its pull...

HENRY: *(From offstage.)* Hey in there!

(RUBY stops still.)

HENRY: Who's messing in there?

(RUBY sits. She begins rubbing kerosene into the generator parts.)

HENRY: You best get out of there. You best move on. I got a gun. You coming out? 'Cause I'm coming in. You coming out? 'Cause I'm coming in.

(HENRY enters with a lantern and a big piece of wood. He sees RUBY.
RUBY continues cleaning the disassembled generator.)

HENRY: What the devil...?

RUBY: Is 'cause of the storm.

HENRY: Huh?

RUBY: Snow storm out there.

HENRY: I know that. Who the heck are you?

RUBY: Miss Haver...

HENRY: You hers?

RUBY: Kind of.

HENRY: What kind?

RUBY: Aunt.

HENRY: You her niece?

RUBY: I been here before, when I was a kid.

HENRY: What are you doing here now?

RUBY: My daddy passed.

HENRY: Miss Haver didn't say about a funeral.

RUBY: Weren't close anymore.

HENRY: Doesn't your mamma need you now?

RUBY: My mamma died before I was rightly born. I'm alone.

HENRY: You got brothers? A sister?

RUBY: Just me now, okay? No one.

HENRY: So you're staying in the house?

RUBY: For a bit.

HENRY: I'm Henry. Henry Hudnut. I board here.

RUBY: Ruby. That your gun?

HENRY: No. Yeah. No.

(HENRY *sets down the piece of wood.*)

HENRY: Sorry about your daddy.

RUBY: Mnnnhmmm.

HENRY: I wouldn't've yelled like that if I'd known. Just it's black dark out
there: our power line is out, on account of the ice.

RUBY: That's what I'm taking care of.

HENRY: What you're taking care of?

RUBY: The Delco.

HENRY: A generator? That right there is a generator? I didn't even know Miss
Haver had one.

RUBY: Mess of grease, isn't working.

HENRY: She'll be peeved you took it to shreds.

RUBY: I'm fixing it.

HENRY: Where'd you learn to do that?

RUBY: My daddy taught me.

HENRY: He's some kind of engineer? Was.

RUBY: Not with a degree kind.

HENRY: You know what you're doing?

RUBY: You partial to degrees?

HENRY: I'm getting one myself. At the School of Agriculture, Purdue. It's a
good time for agro-business. And it's the best school in Indiana. I'll most
like take over my daddy's feed store soon as I'm done—couple months
away is all—not that I need a degree for that, but he wanted me to go
ahead and get it before I go back home for keeps, and I'm learning a lot.
You're making me nervous.

RUBY: Idle hands. Wanna help?

HENRY: Can't say I can. Don't get electricity perfectly.

(RUBY *holds out a pair of wires to* HENRY.)

RUBY: Take these wires here and link 'em up with your tongue.

HENRY: No, sir.

RUBY: Seems like you got it perfect enough.

HENRY: You were kidding with me? About putting it to my tongue?

RUBY: Ummm, yes, I was.

HENRY: That's a good one.

> *(Looking at the equipment.)*

> It sure doesn't look like anything much now, huh?

RUBY: You think?

HENRY: Nothing like something to light up the whole house.

RUBY: That's 'cause of how I took it all apart.

HENRY: But, taken apart, it's not a generator.

RUBY: Is so. Now more than ever, when you can see every inch of how it works.

HENRY: Maybe *you* can see how it works.

RUBY: Maybe I can.

> *(RUBY returns to her work, cleaning the grease of the equipment.)*

HENRY: Be careful with that oil. Farm over in the next county had a fire started that way.

RUBY: What way?

HENRY: *(He doesn't know the details.)* Oil.

RUBY: Uh huh.

HENRY: Just there was a fire.

RUBY: I'll be careful.

> *(She continues with her work.*
> *HENRY picks up a spare rag and, following RUBY's lead, begins to clean the equipment with her.*

HENRY: I'll be careful, too.

SCENE TWO

> *The Kitchen. Later that morning. LOIS, a woman in her early fifties, wearing a housecoat, holds a nearly full coffee pot.*

LOIS: Who the hell made coffee?

> *(HENRY enters.)*

HENRY: Morning, Miss Haver.

LOIS: Don't scream; I got a headache. You make coffee?

HENRY: Must've been Ruby.

LOIS: Ruby?

HENRY: I didn't know you had a generator.

LOIS: What are you talking about?

HENRY: She fixed your generator. Got the lights back on.

(HENRY turns the switch on a light. It works. HENRY and LOIS look at the working light bulb.)

LOIS: I'll be damned.

(RUBY enters. LOIS turns to her.)

LOIS: Ruby Sunrise.

RUBY: Morning.

LOIS: I'm looking at a ghost.

RUBY: Not likely.

LOIS: You got your mamma's hair, her eyes.

RUBY: I got my own eyes.

LOIS: When'd you get here?

HENRY: Imagine me: I found her in the barn.

LOIS: Henry, you're gonna be late for your class.

HENRY: It's not yet seven.

LOIS: You don't wanna be late.

HENRY: Morning, Miss Haver. Morning, Ruby.

RUBY: Morning.

(HENRY leaves.)

LOIS: What'd you do to that boy?

RUBY: Nothing.

LOIS: I don't want you messing with him. He's a good boy.

RUBY: Seems like.

LOIS: Where'd you sleep?

RUBY: You mean last night?

LOIS: It's bitter cold out there.

RUBY: It is.

LOIS: How'd you get here, Ruby?

RUBY: I need a place to stay.

LOIS: Excuse me?

RUBY: I would like to stay with you for a while.

LOIS: For how come?

RUBY: My daddy passed.

LOIS: Son of a bitch passed, huh?

RUBY: Mmmnhmmm.

LOIS: Isn't there folks back in Kokomo who need you?

RUBY: I'm the youngest.

LOIS: 'Course; I knew that. How old are you? You must be... You pregnant?

RUBY: No.

LOIS: You don't look pregnant.

RUBY: I'm not pregnant.

LOIS: You can't stay here.

RUBY: I fixed your Delco.

(LOIS turns the light off.)

LOIS: Don't need a Delco.

RUBY: I could straighten out all your wires. Whole setup is a mess, no wonder it shorts.

LOIS: You some angel sent to look in on my electrical?

RUBY: Didn't say angel.

LOIS: You sure you're not pregnant?

RUBY: I never even kissed somebody.

LOIS: Two weeks. Then you're on your way.

RUBY: Need three months.

LOIS: How come three months?

RUBY: You got a radio here?

LOIS: Who's asking who questions? Two weeks. Is fourteen days, up and over on a Thursday. I can't afford to feed you past then even if I wanted to.

RUBY: I'm gonna make it you got light in every room.

LOIS: I can't pay for that.

RUBY: Who said pay? Electrons running out there all along miles of wire. We'll just borrow them.

LOIS: Take whatever you want and to hell with the consequences. Sounds familiar.

RUBY: I'm not my mamma.

LOIS: Sure got a lot of notions about stealing in common.

RUBY: Electrons ought to be free anyway. Like air, like water. I'll rig it for you.

LOIS: Did I ask you for light?

RUBY: Long as I'm here.

LOIS: Two weeks.

RUBY: Right; long as I'm here right now.

SCENE THREE

Night. The Kitchen.
LOIS sits at a table. She is drinking from an old red glass bottle.
HENRY enters.

HENRY: Hey, Miss Haver, have you seen my radio? It wasn't on my shelf; I thought maybe.... Miss Haver, what are you doing with that bottle?

LOIS: Hello, Henry.

HENRY: That homebrew?

LOIS: I do believe you might say it is.

HENRY: Better put it away. Could get you arrested.

LOIS: Johnny Law understands when a lady needs to pour herself a drink at certain junctures.

HENRY: Junctures?

LOIS: You judging me?

HENRY: No, Miss Haver. I just hate to see you blue.

LOIS: Who says I'm blue?

HENRY: When you're drinking.

LOIS: Maybe I'm celebrating. When's your birthday?

HENRY: Aww, Miss Haver.

LOIS: What, we can't celebrate your birthday?

HENRY: Today's not my birthday.

LOIS: We can celebrate it anyway. Here, have a drink.

HENRY: I couldn't.

LOIS: Easy. You could do it easy. To your twenties.

(LOIS drinks. HENRY doesn't.)

HENRY: How old's Ruby?

LOIS: What?

HENRY: And why do you call her a sunrise?

LOIS: Will you kill that girl for me? Will you set a fire to the barn while she sleeps? If she ever sleeps. Lights on out there all the time.

HENRY: How she got electricity to the barn, I'll never know.

LOIS: Crafty. Like her mamma. And a lot of good it did *her*.

HENRY: I feel sorry for Ruby: she's alone in the world.

LOIS: That's the way they like it. Crafty dreamers. Hungry, so they think the world owes them a meal. They're on a mission.

HENRY: What's Ruby's mission?

LOIS: Who cares; she's leaving in ten days.

HENRY: Mission isn't bad.

LOIS: If you don't care who you hurt to do it, it is. Better not to have hopes.

HENRY: Everybody's got hopes.

LOIS: Not me; no more; no, sir. I'm free. My aspiration crushed a long time ago.

HENRY: Let me take that bottle.

LOIS: I wrapped it up in the prettiest package when I was a girl. Bows and ribbons and fancy paper. And a man took those hopes and sent them away as a wedding gift to someone else.

HENRY: I know, Miss Haver.

LOIS: May you never have to feel what it feels: to want something more than anything in the world, and not only is it ripped from you but then it's exposed as poison, the kind that'll kill you.

HENRY: I know, Miss Haver.

LOIS: What do you know?

HENRY: I know what you told me before.

LOIS: I told you before?

HENRY: Couple times.

LOIS: I must be drunk.

HENRY: Are you going on up to bed now?

LOIS: Do you think I'm terrible?

HENRY: No, Miss Haver.

LOIS: Have you ever called me Lois?

HENRY: No, Miss Haver.

> (LOIS exits. HENRY begins to clean up after her. RUBY enters. She has been loitering just outside the house, waiting for LOIS's departure.
> HENRY has the half-empty liquor bottle in his hand.)

RUBY: You gonna drink that?

HENRY: Ruby.

RUBY: You want it?

HENRY: I was gonna dump it. There are laws. 'Sides, a girl your age.... How old are you?

RUBY: I need that alcohol.

HENRY: Maybe Miss Haver wants it.

RUBY: Be cursing the whole lot in the morning, how much she drank.

HENRY: But she wouldn't want *you* to take it.

RUBY: That's not saying much.

HENRY: What's she got against you?

RUBY: That I look like my mamma.

HENRY: What's she got against your mamma?

RUBY: You bribing me for gossip?

HENRY: Maybe.

RUBY: Aunt Lois used to love my daddy, and then he ran off with her sister. Gonna hand it over now?

HENRY: That was your daddy? Miss Haver talks about that man like the devil himself.

(Catching himself.)

May he rest in peace.

RUBY: Mmmnhmmm.

HENRY: Why'd you come here if that was your daddy?

RUBY: Where'd you want me to go?

HENRY: You got no place to go, huh?

RUBY: Look, I'll return your radio. I was just borrowing it.

HENRY: What?

RUBY: I'll fix the cover back on and everything. You gotta loan me that alcohol to clean out the insides first.

(RUBY holds out various pieces of a disassembled radio.)

HENRY: Is that my Zenith? That's my Zenith! My parents gave me that when I made Dean's List. What'd you do to it?

RUBY: Looked at it.

HENRY: It's in pieces.

RUBY: Looked inside.

HENRY: Boy, I hope you never look inside me.

RUBY: It'll be back brand new soon as I'm done.

HENRY: Done with what?

RUBY: I said I'll return it.

HENRY: No, done with what? What's going on?

RUBY: On where?

HENRY: Out there in that barn.

RUBY: What about it?

HENRY: Here we are, living under the same roof; is it so strange to want to know something?

RUBY: I don't know you neither.

HENRY: Grew up in West Baden. My father runs a Feed and Dried Goods. My mother's a saint. I got six sisters, each of them married already. I could tell you about our swimming hole.

RUBY: Don't.

HENRY: So then you gotta tell me something about who *you* are.

> *(Pause.)*

RUBY: You ever hear people say the word television?

HENRY: What word?

RUBY: Television. It means seeing things that are far away through your radio.

HENRY: What are you talking about?

RUBY: Electromagnetic radiation.

HENRY: What what?

RUBY: Energy in the form of waves. Radio—like how the songs on the radio travel over miles to get to you—is just one example. Light, the kind of light you see, that's another. In radio—okay?—vibrational patterns that are music or speech are converted into a pattern of electromagnetic radiation. It flows from the transmitter at the station to the radio receiver.

HENRY: What do you mean receiver?

RUBY: That's the radio, like your Zenith. The receiver converts the radio waves back into sound by vibrating a membrane, called the speaker. Television aims to work similar, but it's seeking to reproduce visual patterns of dark and light, rather than just sound.

HENRY: Where'd you learn to talk like that?

RUBY: Like what?

HENRY: Membrane.

RUBY: My daddy.

HENRY: But he wasn't an engineer. Miss Haver said you grew up on a farm like me.

RUBY: I said he didn't have a degree. And besides, it was rightly my mamma who gave me lots of technical magazines: *Science and Invention, Popular Mechanics.*

HENRY: I thought you said your mamma died giving birth to you.

RUBY: Not right in birth. Not exactly right then.

HENRY: After.

RUBY: Uh huh, a little after.

HENRY: When you were old enough to read magazines.

> *(Pause.)*

RUBY: Can I take that liquor now like you said was okay?

HENRY: Wait.

RUBY: What?

HENRY: Just explain it all again one more time.

SCENE FOUR

The Barn. Morning.

RUBY has set up an ad-hoc work space. There is a table fitted with several ringstands with clamps. Wires have been diverted from the generator to a wooden framed box.

RUBY and HENRY in the Barn.

HENRY: You ever done this before?

RUBY: Partly.

(RUBY holds up a meshed metal screen with a wire ring around it.)

RUBY: 'Kay, this is the cathode. Here's where the light rays get converted to an electron image. The first step is we gotta get the cathode stuck into one of those glass tube blanks that you borrowed from the University. The heavy wires are the leads.

HENRY: The leads.

RUBY: You gotta seal the leads through the wall of the tube, glass to metal.

HENRY: Uh huh.

(RUBY secures the cathode in a pair of forceps and hands it to HENRY.)

RUBY: Get a firm hold.

(She steadies the tube blank.)

RUBY: Now slip it in.

HENRY: Slip it in?

RUBY: The cathode. I guess about a half-inch from the end.

HENRY: You're asking me?

RUBY: Half an inch.

(HENRY inserts the cathode into the opening in the glass tube.)

RUBY: Good. Don't move.

(RUBY lifts a torch and sets the flame going.)

HENRY: *(Jerking away.)* Hey now.

RUBY: Just do what I tell you.

HENRY: But, careful.

(RUBY applies the flame to the tube.)

RUBY: I gotta get the glass softened before you push the wire right on through.

HENRY: Through what?

RUBY: The glass.

HENRY: Don't get sore.

RUBY: I gotta switch to a hotter flame.

HENRY: Hotter?

(*RUBY takes another torch, gets it going and applies it to the glass.*)

RUBY: The lighter flame is for starting and again at the end in order to prevent strains. Strain causes cracks, and we'll get one of these things blowing up in our face.

HENRY: It will?

RUBY: See that red dot forming?

HENRY: Is that bad?

RUBY: It means we're in business. You ready?

HENRY: If you are.

RUBY: Do it.

(*HENRY slides the wire through the molten spot on the tube.*)

HENRY: (*Excited.*) Oh hell, excuse my language.

RUBY: Straighten it a little? Yeah, flat like that.

(*HENRY does.*)

RUBY: It's in.

HENRY: Like that?

(*RUBY changes back to the cooler flame and bathes the whole tube.*)

RUBY: Now hold still for god's sake while I cool it down.

HENRY: I'm still.

RUBY: You're shaking.

HENRY: I'm still as I get.

(*RUBY turns off the flame. Beat.*)

RUBY: I think it's cooled.

HENRY: Yeah?

RUBY: Yeah.

(*RUBY takes the newly made cathode from HENRY and sets it down.*)

RUBY: That was good.

HENRY: That was great.

RUBY: I get the air pumped out and I'll have my first genuine prototype.

HENRY: Whatta you think of that? I made a photo-cathode tube. Well, we did. But you couldn't've done it alone.

RUBY: Suppose not.

HENRY: Now what?

RUBY: We gotta capture an image—it's gonna take a lot of light, get some more bulbs set up in here—but once we do, we can try sending it over the wires to the receiver.

HENRY: I thought you said the picture would move through the air.

RUBY: It will. But for the testing stage, it doesn't matter how it travels, just that it does, and that it seems like an unbroken image at the other end even though it's not.

HENRY: Why does it seem in a way it's not?

RUBY: 'Cause of your eye.

HENRY: My eye?

RUBY: The human eye retains an image on its retina for about less than a tenth of a second. That's called by Persistence of Vision. See, television doesn't have to show a continuous picture. Instead it replaces each and every line that makes up the image in less than that fraction of time. *(Holding up the cathode.)* That's why we need to coat these cathodes with something that can blink on and turn off. When the electrons light up the phosphorescent dots on the receiving end, your brain can assemble all that into a steady picture 'cause of how the vision persists.

HENRY: *(Looking at the cathode tube.)* What's that?

RUBY: I told you: Persistence of Vision is just...

HENRY: No, that.

RUBY: What's what?

HENRY: That line. That break supposed to be there?

(RUBY looks at the glass tube.)

RUBY: There's a crack.

HENRY: That's what I...

RUBY: I heard you now.

HENRY: Oh, Ruby.

RUBY: It's worthless.

(She throws the tube against the wall. It shatters.)

HENRY: Hey, don't do that. *(RUBY moves away from HENRY to the barn door. HENRY follows her.)* You're sad. Don't be sad. *(Silence. RUBY is looking out at the night.)* I hate to see you sad. *(Silence.)* You'll get it next time. *(Silence.)* Besides, all those wires and stopcocks, no wonder it busted, it looks like something most awful stupid.

RUBY: It is not stupid. You're the one what's stupid.

HENRY: Got you talking.

RUBY: Don't much want to talk about it. Gotta think about it: what went wrong.

(Long silence.)

HENRY: Look: fairies.

RUBY: What?

HENRY: Fairies out there.

> (RUBY *looks out.*)

RUBY: Fireflies.

HENRY: I know. How do they do it?

RUBY: What?

HENRY: Glow like that.

RUBY: Bioluminescence.

HENRY: You got a word for everything.

RUBY: Science has words.

HENRY: It looks nice anyhow. Like fairies making magic.

RUBY: It's a chemical process. Any living thing that glows has a substance inside it whose energy is increased 'cause of a chemical reaction. Then when it's returned to its original level, the substance inside the insect gets rid of the added energy and does it as light, gives off light. It makes the males and females find each other.

> (HENRY *kisses her. He pulls back.*)

HENRY: I'm sorry. I interrupted you.

RUBY: Mnnnhmmm.

HENRY: Can I do it again?

RUBY: I gotta get back to work.

HENRY: Oh, okay. You mean, right now?

RUBY: Yeah. *(Pause.)* You're interested in fireflies.

HENRY: I sure am.

RUBY: Because maybe you could borrow me some potassium hydride from the lab at your school. It releases energy, too.

HENRY: Some what?

RUBY: I'll write it down for you. They're bound to have it in the lab.

HENRY: I don't even take chemistry.

RUBY: Fireflies. It's like fireflies.

> (And they kiss more.)

SCENE FIVE

> The Kitchen. LOIS *sits at the table with a bottle.* HENRY *enters.*

LOIS: You're up late.

HENRY: Could say same to you.

LOIS: How'd that exam fare you?

HENRY: Fine.

LOIS: You're gonna be finished soon, huh? I'll be so proud when you get that degree even though I'll miss you something terrible. Never find another boarder like you.

HENRY: G'night, Miss Haver.

LOIS: *(Seeing his face.)* Oh my lord, you got a shiner coming.

HENRY: Big deal.

LOIS: And been drinking; smell your breath.

HENRY: Smell yours.

LOIS: That's different. You sit down.

HENRY: Don't wanna.

> *(LOIS sits him down.)*

HENRY: Owww.

LOIS: For your own good.

> *(She gets a cold cloth and cleans his eye.)*

LOIS: Now tell me all about it.

HENRY: Nothing to tell.

LOIS: Who socked you?

HENRY: I socked him back.

LOIS: And you're proud of that? It's not like you.

HENRY: A bunch of the kids got together out by Webber's field; I invited Ruby to come along.

LOIS: Ruby.

HENRY: All the fellows were bringing girls. But she's right away brushing me off. What's the point of sitting in a field, she says. Why would I want to do that? I say, what's the point of sitting in a barn? She says, go then, by yourself, go on. I'm so mad. First thing someone says about my mystery girl doesn't exist... next thing I know they're dragging us apart.

LOIS: Ruby is your girl now?

HENRY: I don't know. How can she be my girl when all she wants me to do is stick wires everyplace?

LOIS: You aren't being stupid, are you? Two kids your age...

HENRY: What difference does it make?

LOIS: A big difference if you're being stupid. You'll wind up with a big difference nine months from now.

HENRY: I could have any girl in West Baden. Soon as I finish my degree. But I'm yearning after one who'd rather be messing in a barn on something that won't ever do nothing as far as I can tell than holding my hand in front of my friends. It hurts. Everyone sees it. And all the world knows that I am not worth loving.

LOIS: There, there.

HENRY: I mean what's she doing? What's she doing out there right this minute?

LOIS: Nonsense is what, and don't say I didn't warn you. You know what they used to call her? The Crazy Girl from Kokomo. Oooh, she hated that. The Crazy Crazy Girl.

(She re-applies the cloth to his face.)

HENRY: Stop it.

LOIS: The cool'll take the swelling down.

HENRY: I said get off.

LOIS: Don't be silly.

HENRY: I'm not your boyfriend, Miss Haver. I'm your boarder. I pay you money.

LOIS: I know that.

HENRY: Just because your life was over a long time ago, doesn't mean mine has to be.

(Pause.)

LOIS: I'm sorry, Henry.

HENRY: Oh gosh, I'm a dog. I didn't mean to say mean things, any of that. I'm all mixed up. I better go to bed before I break anything else stupid.

LOIS: Sure, you go on up to bed. Take this. *(Offering the cold cloth.)* If you want.

HENRY: Thank you, Miss Haver. I...

LOIS: Good night, Henry.

SCENE SIX

The Barn. RUBY's television has grown. She is finishing up a demonstration for LOIS.

RUBY: And the rest is a mere matter of dollars, cents, and guts.

(Pause. LOIS walks around the contraption.)

RUBY: Well, aren't you going to say something?

LOIS: Where'd you get all this stuff?

RUBY: Borrowed it.

LOIS: You borrowed a table? Borrowed a... *(Having no words to describe what she sees.)* What is all this stuff?

RUBY: That there's a lens, took it off a bicycle lamp.

LOIS: Borrowed that, too, huh?

RUBY: It's how light from the image gets focused before it's amplified. Amplification's the hardest part. It's why it's been four months 'stead of two.

LOIS: 'Stead of two weeks.

RUBY: Right. But it's gonna be worth it.

LOIS: Worth what?

RUBY: How television's gonna change people. Make a whole different world where people can see the world right in their own homes. Moving pictures in your living room. You'll get to watch a home run while sitting in your favorite chair. See the news as it's happening. Or just listen to somebody talk and be looking at them, too; somebody far far away, maybe with something to teach you. 'Cause if I can broadcast a single point of light from here to there, then anyone can broadcast the bunch of points of light that make up an image, and send it as far as they care to. Soon, we'll get pictures from all over the world, and learn about our comrades in other countries, hell, other planets. If we could see their faces, we'd understand them better, and all our differences could be setled around tables, instead of going to war. Television will be the end of war 'cause who could bear it? Who could bear to see war right in your own living room?

LOIS: What do you know about war?

RUBY: Television'll make for better people.

LOIS: Better people: you sound like a Red.

RUBY: What's so bad about better?

(Beat.)

LOIS: You "borrow" my home brew, too, Miss Sunrise?

RUBY: A little maybe.

LOIS: Care to offer me a glass of my own stock?

(RUBY takes a bottle that's hidden away and offers it to LOIS.)

RUBY: It was almost empty already before.

(LOIS takes a sip).

LOIS: So it's "better" that you got Henry running around like a chicken night and day?

RUBY: Not night and day.

LOIS: That boy cares for you, you know. A whole lot.

RUBY: I do know, and it's slowing me down.

LOIS: Slowing *you* down? He hasn't cracked a book of his own studies in a month.

RUBY: 'Cause this is more interesting, more important than how many oats to feed your cattle to get the fat ratio right.

LOIS: Says you.

RUBY: I wish I didn't need nothing from no one, but now that my daddy's dead and buried, who else am I gonna turn to?

LOIS: Interesting that you mention your daddy.

RUBY: I know there was no love lost between you and him; and same for me.

LOIS: You sure tell Henry nice stories about your daddy: how he taught you things, encouraged you.

RUBY: Sometimes I like to think nice stories, helps me concentrate. And he was my daddy, no matter what.

LOIS: *Is* your daddy.

RUBY: Is, I guess. Always will be, I guess.

LOIS: That's probably why he telephoned.

(*Beat.*)

RUBY: You don't have a telephone.

LOIS: Telephone up at the post office.

RUBY: Must've been a mistake.

LOIS: I don't like liars.

RUBY: Mnnnhmmm.

LOIS: Did he beat you, Ruby?

RUBY: Mnnnhmmm.

LOIS: Son of a bitch. In church when I first saw him, he had a face so sweet, like the sun kept kissing him.

RUBY: Guess the sun went behind a cloud.

LOIS: Your daddy's got rights to claim you. If he wants you home, there's nothing I can do.

RUBY: That's a lie, a bigger lie than I ever told.

LOIS: Ruby, this is just the way things are.

RUBY: But he'll destroy it, Aunt Lois. All over again. I was just getting started in Kokomo. I had my laboratory—and I was doing my chores all the same, I swear I was—but he would get mean drunk, worse than when my mamma was alive, and you know how he used to do her. You saw her face when we came here.

LOIS: You were too young then, to remember that.

RUBY: When she got sick, it stopped for a while. But after she died.... I don't mind the hits; he can smack me all he wants, and scream at me. But my equipment. He smashed everything. My lab in pieces. My notes in the fire. Don't make me go back there.

LOIS: Unmarried girl has got to do what her father says.

RUBY: What's that supposed to mean?

LOIS: You don't want to go back to Kokomo? I bet Henry'll be pleased to hear it.

RUBY: Unmarried girl.

LOIS: I know it's what he wants.

RUBY: But what if I don't want it?

LOIS: I'm offering you something here: the only choice you got, and a good one.

RUBY: Do you believe me, Aunt Lois, believe in all these things I showed you?

LOIS: I don't know the first thing about these wires.

RUBY: Not "know." Believe.

LOIS: Believe in pictures zooming through the sky? Believe in magnets controlling electrons? Seeing other planets? How could I believe in that? Why should I? And I want you to stop stealing my liquor.

RUBY: Yes, ma'am.

LOIS: Now, you think about what I said, Ruby. Lots of girls would be happy for the chance you got.

RUBY: I am thinking, Aunt Lois. All I do is think.

SCENE SEVEN

The Barn.
RUBY is working on her television, connecting the wires in a circuit which links the transmitter, the receiver, and the generator.
HENRY enters. He stands by the barn door for a moment before RUBY sees him.

RUBY: Hey. I thought you were at the library.

HENRY: I was.

RUBY: Don't you have an exam tomorrow?

HENRY: Yeah.

RUBY: Well, Mr. Dean's List, what are you doing back here?

HENRY: Quit.

RUBY: What?

HENRY: Quit messing with the wires for once.

(She looks up from her equipment.)

RUBY: What happened to you?

HENRY: I took a break. When I was studying. I went to the newspapers.

RUBY: Okay.

HENRY: They had the *New York Times.*

RUBY: Okay, the *New York Times.*

HENRY: Ruby, they already did it.

RUBY: Did what?

HENRY: What you're doing. It's done.

RUBY: Nobody's doing what I'm doing.

HENRY: You're wrong.

(He pulls out a piece of paper.)

HENRY: I wrote it down on account of how I knew you wouldn't trust my word. *(Reading.)* Far-off Speakers Seen as Well as Heard in a Test of Television.

RUBY: What are you talking about?

HENRY: *(Still reading.)* Like a Photo Come to Life. Hoover's Face Plainly Imaged as He Speaks in Washington. *(Looking up.)* The American Telegraph and Telephone Company, they did it. The paper explained how and everything. *(Reading.)* Dots of light are put together at a rate of 45,000 a second... *(Looking up.)* And like that. I couldn't get it all down. I'll take you tomorrow. It seems this fellow Dr. Ives...

RUBY: Who?

HENRY: Ives, he's a doctor. *(From the paper.)* And R.C. Mathes...

(RUBY begins to laugh.)

HENRY: Or Maths. Matheez, I guess. Why are you laughing?

RUBY: Henry, it doesn't matter.

HENRY: They did it. They made a television. It's over.

RUBY: Ives and Gray are still working with spinning wooden disks. I read their article eight months ago. It's nothing. Bet the picture was for diddley-squat. What was it: two inches wide?

HENRY: Two by three, it said.

RUBY: Inches. Inches, Henry. Would you go to the the-ater if it was two inches big?

HENRY: By three. And they showed it on a bigger screen, too.

RUBY: It must've looked like hell, all white spots and smudges.

HENRY: It said it was a little unclear.

RUBY: Even they admit that to get a four by four inch picture, they're gonna need a six foot diameter disk. You want a six foot thing spinning in your living room?

HENRY: But they beat you. You can stop now.

RUBY: I'm not making this up. American Telegraph is trying to do it mechanically.

HENRY: The *New York Times* says...

RUBY: The *New York Times*, the *New York Times*, I can say it, too; it don't make it holy. The picture is for squat. I don't need some fancy paper to tell me that. Why don't you have the guts to say that you just don't think I can do it, instead of parading some trash piece of paper like it's the News that's doubting me instead of you.

HENRY: Who the hell gets you those tubes, that wire? For crying out loud, every piece of crap in here came from me whether I bought it or stole it, sorry, "borrowed" it. I did all that.

RUBY: You want it back? You want your share of the investment?

HENRY: Aww, stop it.

RUBY: I buy you out, here and now, you're bought out, I'll pay you back every cent as soon as I file and my patent clears. And when people say my name, you'll be sorry then.

HENRY: Nobody's gonna be saying your name.

RUBY: What do you know? How could I expect you to understand?

HENRY: That phony contraption isn't ever gonna do what you say.

RUBY: And they laughed at Marconi, too.

HENRY: It's too late. Admit it, Ruby. What will it take for you to quit this nonsense?

RUBY: Ignorant cattle farmer.

HENRY: Crazy Girl from Kokomo.

(For a moment RUBY stops her work, stops moving.)

RUBY: Get out.

HENRY: I'm sorry.

RUBY: Get out of my laboratory. I'm working.

(She goes back to adjusting the wires.)

HENRY: Miss Haver let it slip one night. I'm sorry.

RUBY: I don't need any of you.

HENRY: Put down the wires for a minute. I love you. I want to do what's right. Two people who've done what we've done ought to do what's right.

RUBY: Don't come one step closer.

HENRY: What's wrong with that? That's normal. We've known each other.

RUBY: I said, stop.

HENRY: I know the truth about your daddy. I was waiting for you to come clean yourself.

(RUBY begins to prime the generator.)

RUBY: I'm not hearing a thing you're saying.

HENRY: I know he's coming here. Soon.

RUBY: I'm not listening.

HENRY: I'm saying I'll marry you.

(As RUBY gets the generator turning, something shorts. RUBY is thrown across the barn with an electrical shock and slams to the floor. The entire circuit of the TV system sizzles and fumes. The electric lights pop out. RUBY's body is shaking. HENRY rushes to her.)

HENRY: Are you okay? Ruby, honey, are you okay?

RUBY: My baby.

(Realizing what she means.)

HENRY: Oh my god.

PART II
SCENE ONE

New York City, 1952. The office of TV producer MARTIN MARCUS. The writer TAD ROSE sits with MARTIN.

MARTIN: Goddamn it. Whose shitheel idea was it to do the Sea Battle of Bismark? Stupid model ship bobbing up and down like one of my kid's bath toys.

TAD: Naval warfare is popular in the movies, Martin.

MARTIN: This is Television. Tele-Vision. That's ancient Latin for Simple-Story.

TAD: I don't think it's Latin.

MARTIN: Latin, Greek, it's not American. All I know is sponsors are jumping like rats, and the boys upstairs want our slot for a variety show.

TAD: Not another variety show.

MARTIN: Or wrestling. They say the box can't sustain narrative, who needs another narrative in their living room.

TAD: What, the Philco Goodyear Playhouse isn't narrative?

MARTIN: Sure, flaunt the competition in my face; twist the knife a little deeper.

TAD: The problem was the girl can't act.

MARTIN: The problem is never the-girl-can't-act. Who expects Suzie Tyrone to act? She looks good wet.

(LULU enters.)

LULU: Morning, Mr. Marcus, here's your coffee.

MARTIN: Miss Miles. What are you doing bringing the coffee? Where's Mitzie?

LULU: She's here. It's just Allan Wright is visiting Studio Four.

MARTIN: Oh, Allan Wright, heavens forbid I would deprive any girl of a vision of Allan Wright. *(As she sets the coffee down.)* Allan Wright doesn't interest you?

LULU: Between you and me?

MARTIN: And the furniture. And Mr. Rose here.

LULU: Tad Rose?

TAD: How do you do?

LULU: Mr. Rose, I thought "Return to Morgan Hill" was the finest play I've ever seen on television. I'm sorry; I'm gushing.

TAD: No; thank you.

MARTIN: He detests praise.

TAD: Although I think you're alone in your esteemed opinion.

MARTIN: Mr. Rose is going to be writing something for us pronto; isn't that right, Tad?

TAD: Talk to my agent.

LULU: That's wonderful news.

MARTIN: First script I bought off this joker he didn't have an agent. Walked it here himself and put it in Flo's in-box.

LULU: That's the way to do it.

MARTIN: That's how he did it. Flo gives it to me. I have Mitzie call him. "Who's your agent?" "I don't have an agent." "How'd we get your play?" "I brought it up there." "Well, we don't accept unsolicited manuscripts." And she hangs up on him.

TAD: Luckily, the brilliant Martin Marcus...

MARTIN: And that's the real story of how Tad Rose stopped selling appliances for a living.

LULU: You sold appliances?

TAD: Distant, distant past.

MARTIN: Dinosaurs roaming. Cavemen.

TAD: That type of thing.

LULU: If there's anything I can do to assist you, it would be an honor. I do more than fetch coffee.

MARTIN: Mr. Rose doesn't drink coffee since his nervous breakdown.

TAD: I do drink coffee.

LULU: Would you like a cup?

MARTIN: You arrogant son of a bitch, Miss Miles is my new script coordinator, fresh off the boat from Indiana...

TAD: Boat?

LULU: Fresh?

MARTIN: ...my script coordinator, not your secretary.

TAD: I didn't ask for coffee.

LULU: I'd be pleased to.

TAD: *(Rising.)* I'm on my way out.

LULU: Are you sure? It's raining out there.

TAD: Thank you, no.

MARTIN: I want something in my hand the next time I see you.

   (TAD exits.)

LULU: That's a lot of pressure to put on the guy.

MARTIN: Not when I have a slot in two weeks.

LULU: What happened to Joey McCorkle's project?

MARTIN: It was all adultery and alcoholics! Continuity Acceptance will crawl so far up my ass before they approve that shit. I told Joey, patch things up with your wife and give me something when you're sober.

LULU: Did Mr. Rose pitch a play? He can't be working on something new already?

MARTIN: As of fifteen minutes ago he's working on something new: I told him to get right on it.

LULU: Interesting.

MARTIN: What?

LULU: It's an interesting opportunity. For Tad Rose.

MARTIN: You have those reports, Miss Miles?

LULU: I don't.

MARTIN: You don't.

LULU: Mr. Marcus, I didn't even want to waste your time. *Pride and Prejudice* is not a book that makes for a teleplay.

MARTIN: Philco's killing us with the class acts.

LULU: There's more to classy material than rich people in mansions talking in high-class accents. There are stories to tell about the little guy, or girl, and the contributions they make.

MARTIN: No more period pieces?

LULU: *If* they're topical.

MARTIN: Pride and prejudice: sounds topical.

LULU: It's about marriage. Today's audience has more on their mind than who marries who.

(*TAD enters. They turn and look at him.*)

TAD: My umbrella.

MARTIN: You should stay and take notes. Miss Miles is telling us about today's audience.

LULU: I wouldn't presume to tell Mr. Rose what subject matter to address in his writing.

TAD: Please call me Tad.

MARTIN: She calls me Mr. Marcus.

LULU: You're a married man.

MARTIN: How do you know he's not married?

LULU: I don't.

TAD: You can call me Tad.

LULU: (*Handing it to him.*) Your umbrella.

TAD: Thank you.

MARTIN: Two weeks.

(*TAD exits.*)

SCENE TWO

A coffee shop. TAD sits, drinking coffee.
LULU enters and slides into his booth.

LULU: You weren't lying: you do drink coffee.

TAD: Miss Miles.

LULU: Aren't you curious about my first name?

TAD: Lulu. Short for Lois. But no one calls you Lois.

LULU: Quite curious.

TAD: Mitzie loves to gossip.

LULU: And what was the gossip?

TAD: She didn't have much. Evidently, you display a very professional demeanor.

LULU: You dug around?

TAD: I'm a writer.

LULU: That explains it. Did Mitzie tell you she thinks Allan Wright has a funny nose?

TAD: Then why'd she hit Studio Four?

LULU: She didn't. I lied.

TAD: You're a liar?

LULU: When I have a worthy agenda. It runs in the family.

TAD: What's a worthy agenda?

LULU: Something you're trying to accomplish that you believe in desperately. What do you think a worthy agenda is?

TAD: I meant what's *your* worthy agenda?

LULU: Well, for the moment, I wanted the opportunity to meet you; so I engineered it to have Mitzie occupied with a movie star at coffee time.

TAD: Why do I not know how to respond to that revelation?

LULU: I'm sure you can come up with something.

TAD: Allan Wright's given name is Hiram Markowitz.

LULU: No.

TAD: That might account for the funny nose.

LULU: But aren't you Jewish?

TAD: Is that a problem?

LULU: Are you asking me out on a date?

TAD: If I were, would it be a problem?

LULU: I'm a bastard from the Midwest; is that a problem?

TAD: Are you equating Jews and bastards?

LULU: Yes, I'll accept a date with you. Does that answer your Jewish question? Tad.

TAD: My mother named me Tad.

LULU: A likely story.

TAD: How about tomorrow night?

LULU: Don't you have work to do?

TAD: Am I speaking to the attractive young woman who sought me out in my favorite coffee shop, or to Martin Marcus's script girl?

LULU: Same person. How's the soup?

TAD: Watery.

LULU: Fifty-three minutes of material with so few days to write it; I don't know how you do it.

TAD: I imagine each project as an extended sales pitch for the sponsor; that takes the pressure off.

LULU: Baloney. I've seen your work: you've taken on some real topics. I mean aside from the Bismark play.

TAD: Everyone's a critic.

LULU: Even that, with the stuff they can pull off in a studio today, to watch it broadcast live must be tremendous.

TAD: Tremendous isn't the word I would use when your script is cut, mangled, butchered, and lying on the studio floor like a carcass.

LULU: But you've worked with the finest actors.

TAD: Actors as a breed are the least realistic people alive. And somehow they're encouraged to rewrite my dialogue on "instinct."

LULU: Your cynicism is charming, but I know better than to buy it.

TAD: Better based on what?

LULU: *Return to Morgan Hill.*

TAD: Exactly where I learned my lesson. The critics shredded me.

LULU: They missed some of the nuances, but the nuances weren't lost on me. They weren't lost on lots of people.

TAD: "Lots of people" don't write the paychecks.

LULU: But they do. In the long run, they do.

TAD: I'm too out of shape for the long run. Look, I'm sorry to be downbeat— and god forbid the girl doesn't marry the boy at the end, you're forever branded with the adjective "downbeat"—but at 250 a script, Martin doesn't pay me enough to talk about work after seven.

LULU: All right, let's talk about me.

TAD: The Midwest, you said?

LULU: Indianapolis.

TAD: Right, a Hoosier. You miss your family?

LULU: Bastard and orphan. I never met my father and my mother passed.

TAD: I'm sorry.

LULU: About which one?

TAD: That just must be hard.

LULU: Hard, yes.

TAD: But you made it here.

LULU: As fast as I could.

TAD: How does a poor girl from Indiana make her way to the big bad city?

LULU: I bet you eat up every confession you hear and spit it back out as words on the page.

TAD: If it's worthy of the brave new medium of broadcast television.

LULU: Compelling and complex: is that what you're looking for?

TAD: Oh, no, I'm a hack. Martin didn't warn you?

LULU: Warn me? He extols hackdom. I'm working on that. But we were talking about my story not yours.

TAD: Yes, your story.

LULU: You're interested?

TAD: Deeply.

LULU: A man capable of "deeply."

TAD: Do you drink, Miss Miles?

LULU: Only after seven, Mr. Rose.

TAD: I know a place with good soup.

SCENE THREE

> *MARTIN's Office.*
> *TAD enters. MARTIN leaps from behind his desk and kisses him.*

MARTIN: Fantastic. We love it. If the second act is anything like the first, we've got a hit and *Variety* can kiss my pimply ass.

TAD: Settle down, Martin.

MARTIN: I know: you're supposed to be the overly emotional Hebrew.

TAD: Truly. Where's the mythical Southern WASP I was told to expect?

MARTIN: Gone the way of Big Foot, Jew Boy. The script is perfection. Where did you come up with this idea? And the detail is superb.

TAD: That's why you pay me 350 a pop.

MARTIN: Two fifty; nice try. But after this gets on, maybe we can ask for more.

TAD: Maybe.

MARTIN: Wasn't so long ago you were selling door-to-door.

> *(MARTIN picks up the phone.)*

MARTIN: Mitzie, would you get Miss Miles? *(To TAD:)* I want her in on these script change notes.

TAD: Perfection needs alterations?

MARTIN: Do yourself a favor and lose the smart ass. Miss Miles is the best mind I've encountered since I started in this racket. She has a feel for the medium like no one else.

TAD: It's like she was born to do it.

MARTIN: Let's not get philosophical.

TAD: Has Miss Miles read the script?

> *(LULU enters.)*

LULU: She has.

MARTIN: Miss Miles, you remember Mr... oh yes, Tad.

LULU: Mr. Oh-Yes-Tad, surely I do.

MARTIN: Miss Miles had a lot of nice ideas about your script.

TAD: You liked it okay?

LULU: It's a good story.

TAD: I was pretty sure you'd either love it or hate it.

LULU: It had a familiar ring. I won't make a secret of that.

TAD: You don't keep secrets?

LULU: I do when asked. Even implicitly.

TAD: Good to know.

LULU: It's important that this story's being told. We just have to be certain we tell it accurately.

MARTIN: I thought it was fiction.

LULU and TAD: It is.

MARTIN: Jinx. Who owes me a Coca Cola?

LULU: It's fictional, but it speaks to the truth; that's why Tad is so brilliant.

MARTIN: What about me, I hired him?

LULU: You're the most brilliant of all.

MARTIN: Glad we got that straight. Now first off, right off the bat... what do we have, Miss Miles?

LULU: *(Reading from her notes:)* Bastard, page six, twice on page twelve, page twenty, and again on thirty-two.

MARTIN: Right, if you're using it to mean a child born out of wedlock...

LULU: Page nineteen.

MARTIN: But for the rest... you understand. *(Continuing:)* Miss Miles.

LULU: Son of a bitch, page eleven. Comrade, page thirty.

TAD: Comrade?

LULU: Mr. Marcus pointed out that it might lead to unintended interpretations.

MARTIN: It's not a good time for comrade.

TAD: Jesus.

MARTIN: Friend. Why not friend? Who the hell uses the word comrade?

TAD: Are you asking me a loaded question?

MARTIN: Do not even fuck with me for one minute on this communist crap. I had to sign a loyalty oath myself, Miss Miles had to sign one—which reminds me, Miss Miles, they called from upstairs, they didn't get your oath on file.

LULU: Really?

MARTIN: They're sending down another one.

LULU: Okay.

MARTIN: We had to sign oaths, Tad, and we might not have liked it, but there it is. Don't force me into a difficult position.

TAD: Am not now. Have never been.

MARTIN: *(Continuing:)* Miss Miles.

LULU: And too many instances of Jesus, Jesus Christ, God damn, God damn it, and other variations to mention.

TAD: It's a heated story and a feisty character.

LULU: We want to make it beautiful.

MARTIN: We want to make it sale-able.

LULU: And no premarital sex.

TAD: Excuse me?

LULU: In the script.

MARTIN: Oh, yeah, I had an idea on this one, to simplify the change. We don't want to fuck with your words; you're the writer.

TAD: Here it comes.

MARTIN: So how about before the commercial break when the Ruby girl says, "My baby," I thought, why not let that refer to the Tee Vee instead of to her pregnancy?

LULU: That's a great idea.

TAD: What are you talking about?

(MARTIN turns to LULU for help.)

MARTIN: Miss Miles?

LULU: Well, we discussed how driven she is, this character, and how she probably cares more about her new invention than she could ever care about a child.

MARTIN: Yes.

TAD: She cared about her child. How could she not care about her child?

MARTIN: That's gorgeous talk, and we'll use it some time, but this time around, for the sake of Continuity Acceptance, let's smooth out some of the crags and avoid that particular poetry by saying she's not in fact pregnant.

TAD: But the pregnancy's a major part of where the play's headed.

LULU: It doesn't have to be. You get to decide which parts of the story get told.

MARTIN: If we want to see this broadcast to six million homes, we've got to play ball with Continuity Acceptance.

TAD: Continuity Acceptance. It would stick in my craw less if they'd go ahead and call it "The Censorship Office."

MARTIN: *(Dangling a carrot:)* And we'll tell Jerry...

TAD: Jerry Ritt?

MARTIN: Oh, you like Jerry Ritt? Finally, we get a rise out of this guy.

TAD: He would do television?

LULU: If he's directing Elizabeth Hunter as Ruby he would.

TAD: Hot damn.

LULU: She's perfect. I know, she's perfect.

MARTIN: Don't let's get ahead of ourselves. We've got a call in to her agent. But Jerry's in. The first act sold him. Plus he owes me.

TAD: Okay, okay, we soften the pregnancy. Ruby Sunrise goes off at the end of the play to.... I'll think of something.

LULU: I'm sure you will.

MARTIN: And maybe she doesn't have to go off: would it be so terrible if she marries the nice farmer boy? You don't want to be downbeat.

LULU: We want Tad to get his vision across.

TAD: Thank you; I agree with everything Miss Miles says.

LULU: Thank you; you're very wise to say so.

MARTIN: Is the festival of praise over? I talk with Jerry tomorrow. Reading Wednesday.

(The phone rings a quick double ring.)

MARTIN: If we're going with *The Ruby Sunrise*, we've got to move, move. *(Picks up the phone.)* Yeah? *(Listens.)* Christ. Tell him to sit down. I hear you, Mitzie. Give him coffee, black.

(He hangs up.)

MARTIN: Joey McCorkle's in the lobby.

LULU: I'll take it.

MARTIN: Thanks, hon.

(LULU rises and moves to the door.)

TAD: Good-bye, Lulu.

LULU: Good luck, Tad.

(LULU exits. MARTIN looks at TAD, grinning. A beat.)

TAD: What?

MARTIN: Best mind I've encountered: as if I need to be telling you.

TAD: Telling me what?

MARTIN: What else is she "born" to do?

TAD: Who?

MARTIN: Give me a break: I see the score here. Miss Miles is like a daughter to me.

TAD: What are you asking, Martin?

MARTIN: Does she fuck?

TAD: Oh, for Chrissakes.

MARTIN: Come on, does she?

TAD: How would I know? Dad.

(*LULU enters.*)

LULU: I'm sorry to interrupt. What *did* I interrupt?

TAD AND MARTIN: Nothing.

LULU: Who owes me a Coca Cola?

MARTIN: What gives with McCorkle?

LULU: He wants to talk to *you*.

MARTIN: He said that?

LULU: He said he wants to talk to "someone who matters."

MARTIN: Tell him to go home and come back when he's appropriate.

LULU: I did.

TAD: Good for you.

LULU: And he said he wants to talk to someone who matters.

MARTIN: I'll go put him out on his ear. Will you attend to Miss Miles?

LULU: I haven't been damaged.

MARTIN: Be right back.

(*MARTIN exits.*)

LULU: Thus proving the point.

TAD: What point?

LULU: That I am not someone who matters.

TAD: That McCorkle is a drunk is the only thing that's been proved. Thanks for not divulging my, uh, inspiration.

LULU: Mr. Marcus wouldn't care where the story came from, as long as it's good, and Ruby's good.

TAD: Why didn't you ever tell anyone before me?

LULU: Maybe none of them was the right guy. Some secrets, you need to know they'll stay secret.

TAD: But why?

LULU: It's hard enough for a lady to find work in this business without everyone thinking she has an axe to grind.

TAD: Do you have an axe?

LULU: It doesn't need grinding.

TAD: I should have asked before I started typing.

LULU: Guess what, Tad: I had more than a hunch you might take a shine to my mother's story.

TAD: You've got me pegged, huh?

LULU: Not quite pegged; there's a lot I don't know about you.

TAD: So what's next?

LULU: You mean after Ruby's prototype shorted? That's Act Two.

TAD: I mean after I take you out to dinner.

LULU: That is also Act Two.

TAD: I'm looking forward to Act Two.

LULU: Aren't we all?

INTERMISSION

PART II
SCENE FOUR

An office.
TAD and LULU are working on the script.

LULU: What do you mean No?

TAD: Because it can't be a fire.

LULU: Can't? It was.

TAD: A fire destroyed Ruby's lab?

LULU: It happened while she was still in bed, recovering from the electric shock.

TAD: You can't make a fire in a standard issue television studio seven flights above Broadway. The Department of Buildings will close you down. The Fire Department. How about a flood? Throw some water around.

LULU: It doesn't flood outside of Indianapolis in May.

TAD: We call it September.

LULU: By September 1927 Farnsworth had his all-electrical system going in San Francisco.

TAD: That's the Mormon guy?

LULU: Am I talking to the walls here?

TAD: What difference does it make, if the story's "fictional"?

LULU: It needs to operate within the facts that we all know.

TAD: But it's facts that nobody knows. Ask any stranger on the street who invented the television, they couldn't care less.

LULU: If Ruby is going to have her place in history...

TAD: This is a teleplay, not a history lesson.

LULU: But if you ignore actual events on the time line, you undermine her completely, and once again the little guy's story doesn't get a chance. It's the big corporation writing history.

TAD: Martin will laugh me out of the office, I write a fire. Not even Jerry Ritt can make flames fly live.

LULU: If it's a flood, it makes it fate when Ruby's Tee Vee is destroyed. It wasn't her fate. Nothing is fated.

TAD: What was it then: her fault?

LULU: It wasn't her fault.

TAD: Whose fault was it?

LULU: Henry's.

TAD: What's Henry got to do with it?

LULU: How did you think the fire started? Her whole lab, all her equipment burned to the ground.

TAD: A bunch of leads hooked up to an old generator is how. It had already shorted once: we established that before the act break.

LULU: No. Henry.

TAD: You're telling me your father was an arsonist?

LULU: I'm telling you he destroyed the lab.

TAD: Come on; he's our likable college kid.

LULU: It was the only way to insure that Ruby would marry him.

TAD: But she didn't marry him. She took a job in a textile mill.

LULU: He couldn't have known how strong her will would be.

TAD: I don't buy it.

LULU: You weren't doubting my word when Act One showed up on Martin's desk.

TAD: I thought you called him Mr. Marcus.

LULU: If you want to steal someone's story, steal it whole.

TAD: Is that what this is about?

LULU: What?

TAD: Credit.

LULU: Don't be silly. I'm a script girl; I know that.

TAD: You never want more?

LULU: I want someone besides me to know what my mother achieved. A farm girl from the sticks and she figured out this thing which changed our world and which can change our world. When she finally told me her story about a barn and a machine and the girl who built it.... Don't you see how wonderful it will be if other people hear that story, too?

TAD: And you don't care if your name is forgotten?

LULU: I'm not my mother.

TAD: What's that supposed to mean?

LULU: I know when I won't get credit.

TAD: So why do you bother?

LULU: Don't tell me you bother just so you can see your name flicker on a screen for three seconds.

TAD: Five seconds. It's in my contract.

LULU: And creating something good doesn't even cross your mind? Sneaking into people's homes, knocking on the glass screen in their living rooms, really talking to them.

TAD: I think you're wrong.

LULU: About what?

TAD: You are just like your mother.

LULU: I'm not.

TAD: Except she gave up.

LULU: Ruby did not give up. She failed.

TAD: That's better?

LULU: If any of those small-town washouts had recognized her brilliance, she wouldn't have ended her days as an angry drunk.

TAD: You want to stick it to all the people who didn't believe in her? That's called revenge.

LULU: So what?

TAD: So what is you heard Martin: people want a happy ending.

LULU: This is a happy ending.

TAD: A woman dies in obscurity from alcohol poisoning without ever having achieved her goals. Tell me how that's a happy ending.

LULU: It's like that phrase: Persistence of Vision. Sure, it's about the science, it means something technical, but it's also.... There was a girl who ran away from what everyone expected from her, and from her persistence and her vision, she made something fantastic: Television!

TAD: That's ancient Latin, you know.

LULU: Tele is Greek for far and vision is Latin for seeing. Some people say it's wrong to combine two languages in one word like that, but I think it's the perfect name because it's democratic: both languages get a vote.

TAD: Democratic?

LULU: Yes. Tee Vee is democratic: a machine that treats everyone equal, so a girl in Indiana is as important as a fat cat in New Jersey. Tee Vee is free. It moves through the air that we breathe. You don't have to buy a ticket. You don't need a car. We're all together even if we're a thousand miles apart. We all belong. Finally. Don't look at me like I'm crazy.

TAD: That's not how I'm looking at you.

LULU: How then?

TAD: Like you're beautiful.

LULU: Beautiful.

TAD: Martin called you a genius; do you know that? He says you have the best feel for television of anyone he's ever met.

LULU: That doesn't mean he'll promote me. He said that?

TAD: He said more.

LULU: And what do you say?

TAD: I'm here, aren't I? With you, aren't I?

LULU: Yes, you are here with me.

TAD: Yes, I am. Here with you.

(Pause.)

LULU: Do I scare you?

TAD: Yes, but why do you ask?

LULU: Because you still haven't tried to kiss me.

TAD: Do you want me to kiss you?

LULU: Do I have to answer that?

(She waits. He kisses her.)

LULU: Now we've got that out of the way.

TAD: I'm not sure that's out of the way.

LULU: A fire?

TAD: A blazing, booming, hot-as-hell fire.

LULU: Because I'm a genius? And I know how Ruby's story should be told?

TAD: A fire.

(And they kiss again.)

SCENE FIVE

The Rehearsal Hall.
The actor PAUL BENJAMIN (HENRY from Part I) sits in a chair. He eats a sandwich as he reads a script.
MARTIN enters.

PAUL: Morning, Mr. Marcus.

MARTIN: Paul, glad you could join us.

PAUL: Thrilled to. It's just one hell of a script. My agent only gave me Act One.

MARTIN: Yeah. You're the first one here.

PAUL: I'm still doing the voice for the canned beef so I was right around the corner.

MARTIN: That's going well for you.

PAUL: My agent said Elizabeth Hunter's doing the Ruby part. You know in summer stock...

MARTIN: Yeah, uh, Tad Rose, our writer, and the others should be here shortly. You need coffee?

PAUL: I'm good.

MARTIN: Of course, you are, Paul, of course, you are. Give me minute.

PAUL: Sure thing, Mr. Marcus.

(MARTIN exits.
PAUL goes back to his sandwich and script.
ETHEL REED (LOIS) enters. She is smoking.)

ETHEL: Don't get up.

(PAUL sees her and rises.)

PAUL: Hi, I'm Paul Benjamin. I'll be playing Henry.

ETHEL: Is there only one chair?

PAUL: I'm sure they're bringing more.

ETHEL: An optimist.

PAUL: I saw some in the hall. I could...

ETHEL: Would you be a dear?

PAUL: No problem, take a load off. What's your name?

ETHEL: Pardon me?

PAUL: I'm Paul Benjamin.

ETHEL: Yes.

(She looks at him.)

PAUL: I'll go get that chair.

(ETHEL sits and PAUL exits. MARTIN enters.)

MARTIN: Ethel, you look amazing.

ETHEL: Are there no ash trays in this building?

MARTIN: I'll have the girl bring one in.

ETHEL: Don't bother; I'll use my hand.

MARTIN: Don't be surly.

ETHEL: Am I that antique?

MARTIN: As what? As me?

ETHEL: As a young man in the theatrical profession doesn't recognize me.

MARTIN: He'd recognize your voice.

ETHEL: I spoke. Several sentences.

(PAUL returns with a chair.)

MARTIN: Paul, you must know Ethel Reed from the La Tropicale Cigar Smokers Lounge.

ETHEL: Among other credits.

PAUL: What a hoot. My dad loved that show.

ETHEL: When are the others arriving? I hear this Elizabeth Hunter is a modern day marvel, but I was somewhat surprised, Martin, to hear that she'd be working in this production.

PAUL: I did *Seven Messengers* with Liz Hunter in try-outs. I was one of the messengers.

ETHEL: My script ends on page thirty; I assume there's more.

MARTIN: Ethel, you know I adore you.

ETHEL: An ash tray; is *that* too demanding?

MARTIN: I'll be right back.

(MARTIN exits.)

PAUL: I worked with Jerry Ritt's brother once in a radio drama.

(LULU enters with an ash tray which she holds out to ETHEL.)

ETHEL: Ah, you've saved me.

LULU: Miss Reed, it's an honor to meet you.

ETHEL: What a dear. Would you bring me some coffee? Mitzie knows how I like it. Tell her extra sweet.

LULU: Coming right up. *(Shaking PAUL's hand.)* You must be Henry.

PAUL: I am. Paul Benjamin. *(TAD enters.)*

LULU: And may I present Tad Rose?

TAD: *(Shaking hands.)* Pleasure.

(MARTIN enters.)

MARTIN: Miss Miles, we need...

LULU: Six chairs.

TAD: Jerry's not coming?

MARTIN: They held him on the Coast.

(LULU turns to go.)

ETHEL: And my coffee, dear. Extra sweet.

LULU: Yes, Miss Reed.

MARTIN: *(Taking LULU aside.)* There's a flask in my top drawer.

LULU: Excuse me?

MARTIN: "Extra sweet."

LULU: Oh. Right.

(*LULU exits.*)

ETHEL: Well, Mr. Rose, do we have pages?

TAD: Not quite to the end, but almost.

ETHEL: Almost: such an innocuous word.

(*TAD begins distributing scripts. LULU enters with two more chairs.*)

PAUL: I can't wait to see how it all turns out. Do you need help?

LULU: Sit; you're the talent.

(*She exits.*)

TAD: We're only waiting on Miss Hunter?

MARTIN: Can I speak to you for a moment?

(*TAD and MARTIN retreat to a corner.*)

PAUL: Nuts and bolts.

ETHEL: Excuse me?

PAUL: Production talk.

ETHEL: Quite.

(*LULU returns with two more chairs, bringing the total to six.
She is setting them in a circle as an overly sexy young woman whom we
haven't seen before enters. She is SUZIE TYRONE.*)

LULU: Can I help you?

SUZIE: Is this Studio Six? I'm in Studio Six.

LULU: Yes, you are. What are you looking for?

SUZIE: Ummm, hold on... (*Digging into her purse.*) I think my agent said Six.

LULU: This is Studio Six.

SUZIE: (*Still digging.*) For rehearsal. I think it was Six.

LULU: This is Six.

SUZIE: (*Holding up a piece of paper.*) Six!

LULU: We're having a rehearsal in here.

SUZIE: In Six. I'm Ruby.

LULU: Excuse me?

(*MARTIN sees SUZIE.*)

MARTIN: Suzie, is it possible you've grown even more stunning?

SUZIE: Marty.

MARTIN: Ethel Reed, Paul Benjamin; Suzie Tyrone. Lulu Miles, assisting us.
And you've met our writer Tad Rose?

TAD: (*Shaking her hand.*) I never told you you really blew me away in *Bismark.*

ETHEL: That's why you look familiar. Didn't you drown in that one?

MARTIN: Okay, as soon as we get those chairs... great. Today we're going to give Tad a chance to hear what we've got. We'll have a completed script by Thursday.

TAD: Knock wood.

MARTIN: We'll have a completed script by Thursday, when the night crew gets these set pieces in place. Everybody knows Jerry can't be here until day after tomorrow.

LULU: What is going on?

MARTIN: He got held up on the Coast.

LULU: What does she mean she's Ruby?

MARTIN: Yes, we're lucky to have Suzie signed on for the project.

LULU: We agreed on Elizabeth Hunter.

SUZIE: Oh.

MARTIN: Miss Miles, will you take your seat? We can discuss any confusion later.

LULU: Tad.

TAD: What?

LULU: Aren't you going to say something?

TAD: About what?

ETHEL: Liz Hunter's on the list, honey.

LULU: Elizabeth Hunter?

ETHEL: Is blacklist.

MARTIN: Elizabeth Hunter was no longer right for the part.

LULU: There must be a mistake.

ETHEL: She was at that peace conference at the Waldorf three years ago, and that's all it takes.

LULU: When she was a teenager? And it was a peace conference.

PAUL: Elizabeth Hunter's a commie?

LULU: This is ridiculous. *(To MARTIN:)* You've got to do something. No offence to Miss Tyrone here who I'm sure is a terrific performer...

SUZIE: I got very wet on *Bismark* and never complained.

LULU: No one will be getting wet in this story.

SUZIE: My agent said in the flood scene.

LULU: It's a fire.

TAD: We'll see.

LULU: We'll what?

TAD: Budget nixed the fire.

LULU: You promised.

TAD: I didn't promise. We had to make some edits.

LULU: Edits?

MARTIN: The boys upstairs came down hard on the idea that this hick girl had the technology before RCA.

LULU: But she did. I mean, that's the story that we agreed to.

TAD: She had a prototype, right? And she'll still have that. It just won't work as well as she'd have hoped.

LULU: But her prototype would've worked if it hadn't been destroyed.

TAD: Would've, could've, should've.

LULU: No, would've.

TAD: Don't be difficult.

LULU: Oh, I'm sorry, am I inappropriately standing up for what's right?

TAD: Lose the high horse. This is the real world.

LULU: As opposed to the coffee shop; your office; your bedroom.

(ETHEL *begins to cough loudly.*)

MARTIN: Let's suspend budget conversations for now.

LULU: What else has been changed?

TAD: Nothing important.

LULU: Just another "comrade" or two?

PAUL: Comrade?

TAD: You went along with that.

LULU: This is more than a word switch. It's the essence of the story. If you don't let Ruby invent the machine, you're rubbing out her life all over again. And if you allow her to be portrayed by some... someone who might not completely understand Ruby's genius.... *(Stopping herself.)* Liz Hunter can do this part. You don't need to give over to this red-baiting hysteria. I mean, speaking of rubbing out a girl's life. Mr. Marcus, if you don't hire that girl, no one will.

MARTIN: Maybe you haven't heard, Miss Miles, but I have hired a girl.

LULU: Don't let them do this.

MARTIN: Do what?

LULU: Turn you into a coward.

TAD: It's not cowardice.

PAUL: It's patriotism.

LULU: It's not illegal to go to a political conference. It's not illegal to be a communist for crying out loud.

SUZIE: Oh, I think it is.

LULU: This is America.

SUZIE: But not for communists.

PAUL: Don't kid yourself, miss, these people want to infiltrate our way of life.

LULU: Can you even define "infiltrate"?

PAUL: They're trying to infiltrate the Actors Studio.

LULU: Then they really must be a bunch of morons.

TAD: This isn't a joke.

LULU: Isn't it? We're making a piece of art about a visionary betrayed by small minds, and the first thing we do is betray.

PAUL: There is a war going on.

LULU: I know that, but terrorizing some poor actress isn't going to bring those boys home.

MARTIN: We're being asked as Americans to state which side of the fence we're on. If you're not willing to declare your allegiance... then you're bringing this country down.

LULU: Martin, a person is allowed to look at this world and then dream of ways for it to be different. That's Ruby. An uncompromising vision of a changed world. Sabotaged. But it's us sabotaging now. Throwing a blanket over her achievements.

TAD: That's not what we're doing.

LULU: Caving in to self-serving, spineless...

MARTIN: I am doing you a favor here by telling you to sit down and be quiet.

LULU: I should have seen this coming. You just can't let her succeed, can you?

MARTIN: Are you going to force me to throw you out of this studio?

LULU: No one's forcing you to do anything. That's the tragedy here: you're choosing to accept this madness.

TAD: Lulu, please.

LULU: Please what? Please get on board with a bunch of shitheels making a mockery of everything true? No. No, I won't. If it's going to be killed, I'd rather put it out of its misery myself.

MARTIN: What are you talking about?

LULU: Ruby is my story; I want it back.

TAD: Don't do this.

LULU: I won't let you destroy her all over again with condescending endings and some ditzy, soaking dancer.

SUZIE: I'm not a dancer.

(*LULU starts grabbing scripts out of people's hands.*)

TAD: Lu, you're acting crazy.

LULU: They called Marconi crazy, too.

MARTIN: Am I going to have to call Security?

LULU: Sure, call those god damn FBI dropouts who run the upstairs office.

TAD: For god's sake, shut up.

LULU: It's my story. You know that.

TAD: No; *The Ruby Sunrise* is mine.

LULU: But it's not.

TAD: I wrote it; look at the god damn cover page.

> *(Pause.*
>
> *For a moment, it looks as if* LULU *will rip the scripts in half. But she just throws them on the floor; they land in disarray.*
>
> LULU *leaves.* TAD *makes a small move to follow her.)*

MARTIN: Tad, sit down.

> *(*TAD *sits.* MARTIN *pulls the extra chair out of the circle.* PAUL *collects the scripts from the floor.)*

MARTIN: I apologize for the hectic-ness.

PAUL: No problem, Mr. Marcus.

SUZIE: We're all professionals.

MARTIN: Tad?

TAD: We're all professionals.

ETHEL: Where is that coffee?

MARTIN: Coming. Now, are there any logistics I'm forgetting? Paul, I know all this Tee Vee talk is new to you—it's pretty damn new to all of us—but you'll catch on quick.

PAUL: I'm catching on already.

MARTIN: Let's turn to page one.

> *(They all sit. The scripts are redistributed.)*

MARTIN: Go ahead, Suzie.

> *(The read begins.)*

SUZIE: It happened just like this. I was on the mower, riding it down each row, back and forth, all those straight, straight lines. My thoughts, as usual, weren't on farming. I was building something else in my mind.

SCENE SIX

> *A Set in a TV studio: on one side, the Kitchen; on the other, the Barn with all the TV equipment in it.*

SUZIE and PAUL have new script pages in hand. They are rehearsing, not yet in costume. MARTIN and TAD watch.

SUZIE: *(As RUBY:)* What am I doing here?

PAUL: *(As HENRY:)* You had an electrical shock. It threw you halfway across the barn. Don't you remember?

SUZIE: I've been sleeping?

PAUL: A bit.

SUZIE: But what happened?

PAUL: Something must have shorted.

SUZIE: What were we talking about? My father is coming.

PAUL: Don't worry about that now.

SUZIE: My television is waiting.

PAUL: Whoa, lie back, lie back now. You need to rest.

SUZIE: Oh my god. Did the surge... *(Turning out to TAD.)* Surge?

TAD: Yes, surge.

MARTIN: Let's keep going.

SUZIE: Did the surge fry the connections?

PAUL: You know I wouldn't know about that.

SUZIE: I have to get back to work.

PAUL: Rest now. It's not as if that contraption's gonna burst into flames the moment you close your eyes.

SUZIE: Flames. Why do you say flames? Henry, what's become of my television?

PAUL: I'll check on it, okay, I'll check on it.

SUZIE: Unhook the blue leads from the generator. They're tied with blue string; that's how you'll recognize them.

PAUL: What would happen if I connected the yellow leads instead of the blue?

SUZIE: Don't ever do that! If the generator's still running, especially if the more dangerous chemicals were knocked over, the whole thing would blow to Kingdom Come.

TAD: Stop, just stop.

MARTIN: Tad.

SUZIE: What's wrong?

TAD: It's not you; it's me. It's the dialogue.

SUZIE: I think it's great, the dialogue.

(ETHEL enters in LOIS costume.)

ETHEL: Are you on break? Wonderful. I need something addressed: "May you never feel what it feels: to want something more than anything in the world, and not only is it ripped from you, but, also, it's exposed as poison."

TAD: What about it?

ETHEL: Clunk clunk clunk.

MARTIN: We're not quite ready for you, Ethel.

ETHEL: I was told light check at two. And I saw the Technical Supervisor in the hall.

MARTIN: Shit. Who's got blocking notes?

TAD: Audio stuck his head in about ten minutes ago.

MARTIN: I'm talking about the god damn blocking notes.

SUZIE: Marty?

MARTIN: *(Too loud.)* What!

SUZIE: Are you mad at me?

MARTIN: No. No, Suzie. Suzie, go down to Costume. Paul, will you escort Suzie down to Costume?

PAUL: Sure thing, Mr. Marcus.

MARTIN: Tad, get over here.

(SUZIE and PAUL exit.)

TAD: I'm not changing the Lois speech.

MARTIN: Fuck the speech; Ethel can make anything sing. When did we go back to a fire?

TAD: Flood's not working.

MARTIN: Budget's going to lynch me, and that means you.

TAD: It doesn't flood in Indianapolis in May.

MARTIN: It doesn't... what the fuck are you talking about? Are we making a teleplay here or pissing off the Empire State Building? There were no women on the Bismark and that didn't stop us.

TAD: Bad example, Martin.

(ETHEL is seated on set, applying age make-up.)

ETHEL: "All your dreams were built on a basket of lies." Is it me, or is that a mixed metaphor?

TAD: Can someone shut her up?

MARTIN: This is just to test the lights, Ethel.

ETHEL: Never say "just." I have questions; I need them answered.

TAD: Was it Machiavelli who said to get anything done you have to be a son of a bitch?

MARTIN: I don't know; who's Machiavelli?

TAD: What do you think about it really? In your heart?

MARTIN: About what?

TAD: Was Lulu right to make a stand?

MARTIN: Tad, honey, my heart's convulsing too hard with the terror of unemployment to be able to think. I have kids to support; that's what I think in my heart.

TAD: And God forbid you'd have to move from Scarsdale.

MARTIN: Don't knock Scarsdale. Now who's Machiavelli? Should I have a call in to Machiavelli?

TAD: Martin, I'm dreaming about Elizabeth Hunter at night. She's calling me a traitor. She's burning down my office.

MARTIN: You're lucky you have an office. If we can't pull out a winner, believe me you won't; and neither will I.

TAD: And what would make it a winner? It can't only be about the ratings. There's got to be something more than that.

MARTIN: You have a job to do, end of discussion. And so do I: two jobs until Ritt ges his sorry self on an airplane from Los Angeles.

TAD: But what if I can't do the job without Lulu? She knew how to tell this story: the brilliant inventor, going it alone.

MARTIN: I'll get you another script girl. Someone to bounce some ideas around with.

TAD: Yeah, that would be great. If I could just bounce some ideas around, I'm bound to figure it out.

MARTIN: Of course, you will. You got the first act, right?

TAD: I sure did.

MARTIN: Now I miss the girl, too. I know she was the best. But Lulu made her own choice. We can cry over that milk after we broadcast.

TAD: Then we'll cry?

MARTIN: You, me, and a bottle of whiskey.

TAD: That's the answer?

MARTIN: No. The answer is: wipe your ass and get me an ending that works.

(TAD wanders off.

SUZIE enters in costume: a slinky night gown.)

SUZIE: *(To ETHEL:)* Oh, Ethel, you look so old! Do you think this is too see-through? Paul said it was fine.

ETHEL: Dear, this is called rehearsal, and I am preparing.

MARTIN: Why don't you get set, Suzie? You look great.

(SUZIE lies down.)

MARTIN: Who's in the booth? We don't need music. Clear the fucking musicians, and get the contrast man in there.

SUZIE: Good night, Marty.

MARTIN: Good night, dear. *(Calling out:)* We're ready. Let's do it.

*(SUZIE closes her eyes. ETHEL stows her make-up kit away. She positions herself
close to "sleeping" SUZIE.*

The lights close in as if it is late at night.

ETHEL takes a wash cloth and dabs SUZIE's forehead gently.)

ETHEL: *(As LOIS:)* Oh, Ruby. I let you down.

(She strokes SUZIE's hair.)

ETHEL: I wanted for you what I wanted for myself a long time ago. I thought
you could mold your dreams into a more viable form, and that it would
spare you the kind of pain that I felt, that I still feel, every day.

MARTIN: Hold. Hold. "Viable"?

ETHEL: Yes.

MARTIN: What viable?

ETHEL: Viable. It means...

MARTIN: I don't give a damn what it means. Ethel, where are you getting this
dialogue? For scene ten, I have...

ETHEL: I am aware of what is scrawled on the cue cards, Martin, but Instinct. I
have a very strong instinct that issues of viability cut to the heart of this
play.

MARTIN: That's interesting, Ethel, because I, too, have a very strong instinct
right about now.

SUZIE: *(Opening her eyes.)* Me, too. I think Ruby should have really bad teeth.
Like on a farm.

MARTIN: Are the musicians still there? *(Calling out:)* I think it's as good a time
as any to test the score. Music. I said, music!

(And the music comes.)

SCENE SEVEN

*A simply dressed young woman (ELIZABETH HUNTER) stands on the empty
Kitchen/Barn set. She looks around.*

*TAD enters. He seems shocked by the sight of her. He watches her. Finally she
notices him.*

ELIZABETH: I'm sorry; I was only looking around; I'm just leaving.

TAD: No, it's okay.

(TAD stares at her.)

ELIZABETH: Are you Security?

TAD: No.

ELIZABETH: Do I know you?

TAD: No. I don't think so. I mean I recognize you. You're an actress.

ELIZABETH: Guilty as charged. Are you involved in this production?

TAD: No. Are you?

ELIZABETH: No. No.

TAD: What are you doing here then?

ELIZABETH: You're sure you're not Security?

TAD: I hate Security.

ELIZABETH: Do you know Martin Marcus?

TAD: The producer?

ELIZABETH: He tried to get me some extra work on the variety they're shooting upstairs.

TAD: That's great. He did that?

ELIZABETH: It didn't work out so well.

TAD: Why not?

ELIZABETH: The big unanswered question. I'm no longer "right for the part." Any part, it seems. I was literally going to be a pair of legs in a crowd scene. You wouldn't even see my profile. But some agency guy spotted me. "Is that Liz Hunter? Get her out of here." I said, no, I'm nobody, just a brunette trying earn a nickel. "Get her out of here."

TAD: They're maniacs.

ELIZABETH: I think "maniac" is generous.

TAD: Can I have your autograph?

ELIZABETH: My autograph?

TAD: I saw you in *St. Joan* at the Lyceum. You're tremendous.

ELIZABETH: I don't think the autograph will be worth much.

TAD: That can't be true; you're a rising star.

ELIZABETH: I'll let you in on a little secret: my career is officially over. I guess I learned that today.

TAD: You were slated to perform on this set?

ELIZABETH: Slated? I don't know. I read the first act.

TAD: What was it about?

ELIZABETH: Despair. I mean, persistence.

TAD: Huh.

ELIZABETH: "It happened just like this. I was on the mower, riding it down the field, each row, all those straight, straight lines. I didn't even notice that the reins had slipped from my hands until the horse lurched forward. And right then, right as I felt that jerk.... That was my Eureka! You gotta magnetically deflect electrons across the television screen in the same way you plow a field. Back and forth. Line by line. Rows and rows and rows, just like the field. I figured it out. It was mine."

TAD: You must have an amazing memory.

ELIZABETH: It's a curse.

TAD: It seems like you would have nailed the part.

ELIZABETH: The world will never know. You still want that signature?

TAD: *(Searching.)* I don't have any paper.

ELIZABETH: A writer without paper.

TAD: How'd you know I'm a writer?

ELIZABETH: A certain smell: over-worked and under-appreciated. *(Going in her bag.)* I've got a publicity photo in here somewhere; might as well use them up. How would that suit you?

TAD: That would be amazing.

ELIZABETH: Who should I make it out to?

TAD: Mitch.

ELIZABETH: Just Mitch?

TAD: Mitch is good.

(She writes on the picture.)

TAD: I don't believe your career is over. You're too talented; it can't be right.

ELIZABETH: I didn't say it was right; I said it was over.

(She holds the picture out to him. He hesitates.)

ELIZABETH: What's wrong?

TAD: My name is Tad Rose, and I'm sorry.

ELIZABETH: You didn't seem like a Mitch.

TAD: You deserved better. Maybe if I had been more brave...

ELIZABETH: That was pretty brave: confessing. Don't you want to read what I wrote?

TAD: What?

ELIZABETH: My autograph.

(He takes the picture and reads.)

TAD: Dear Mr. Rose, May God Forgive Us All.

ELIZABETH: I had such dreams. New York City. I was going to be the best they'd ever seen.

TAD: You could testify. They'd welcome you back. You were young and made a big mistake. Sign right here.

ELIZABETH: I want a career; I also need to sleep at night.

TAD: I can't get you back on the show. I'm a writer; I'm nothing. You want me to quit, too; quit in protest? It won't make a ripple if I quit. No one will even notice, and it won't change a thing.

ELIZABETH: Who are you trying to convince? I don't want you to quit.

TAD: What do you want me to do?

ELIZABETH: Restore justice and reason to the world, ease my broken heart, and keep up my weekly payments of two bucks fifty to my mother in West Virginia. I don't know, Mr. Rose. I'm not prepared to exhort. I'm not actually St. Joan.

TAD: You would've made a great Ruby.

ELIZABETH: I really liked that play, what I read of it. I found her struggle very moving.

TAD: Yeah, don't you want her to succeed so much? A shame the world's not like that.

ELIZABETH: A crying shame. Ruby believed in people, their capacity for change. Too bad they didn't believe in her.

Is it a true story?

TAD: Does it make a difference?

ELIZABETH: I just wondered how you came up with it.

(Tad looks at her. Silence.)

ELIZABETH: But your name's on it.

TAD: You don't have to worry about me stealing anyone's thunder. I'll mess it up so horribly before I'm done that it will become mine: another failure.

ELIZABETH: Wow. I think you might possibly be in worse shape than me.

TAD: Oh god, I don't deserve your sympathy.

ELIZABETH: I wasn't offering it.

TAD: There were people who tried to fight for you. Not me, I rolled over like a dog.

ELIZABETH: I don't think I can bear any more confessions, Mitch.

TAD: You want me to leave you alone here?

ELIZABETH: No; I'm done.

It's funny. Back home everyone always thought of me as Scaredy Cat Lizzie. Maybe when somebody calls your number, you'll surprise yourself, too.

TAD: You are a hero, Miss Hunter.

ELIZABETH: Yeah, okay, if you say so, Mr. Rose.

(She moves to exit, but stops herself.)

ELIZABETH: Mr. Rose?

TAD: Yeah?

ELIZABETH: Make sure that you say so.

SCENE EIGHT

LULU in a coffee shop, eating soup. ETHEL enters.

ETHEL: How's the soup?

LULU: Watery. *(Looking up.)* Miss Reed. What are you doing in a place like this?

ETHEL: Is that a pick-up line?

LULU: No...

ETHEL: You're throwing a pass at me?

LULU: I'm surprised to see you here. This dump is hardly of your caliber.

(ETHEL sits.)

ETHEL: You think I'm a snob.

LULU: No.

ETHEL: I think you're a snob.

LULU: I'm not a snob.

ETHEL: We are selling a detergent; you are aware of that? That is the purpose of our jobs in this emerging field.

LULU: I don't have a job. I was fired.

ETHEL: You can't be too literal in this business. Fire can mean many things.

LULU: Not to me. I'm finished.

ETHEL: Like your mother.

LULU: Excuse me?

ETHEL: Ruby Sunrise.

LULU: That's the name of a teleplay by Tad Rose; it's got nothing to do with me anymore.

ETHEL: My first husband, some eight hundred years ago, was a writer.

LULU: And?

ETHEL: And he taught me how to "read" a script. Only an unobservant boob could fail to see the familial bond.

LULU: Well, that explains why no one at the studio has figured it out. *(Beat.)* You think I'm like my mother?

ETHEL: Maybe a wee bit.

LULU: I tried to fight it for so long; I wasn't going to make her mistakes. Why'd she have to be so solitary? So bitter?

ETHEL: So self-destructive?

LULU: They destroyed it, not me. I was trying to be rational.

ETHEL: Screaming in a rehearsal hall?

LULU: But I was right!

ETHEL: You called your employer a shitheel.

LULU: I'm unclear about what it is you want, Miss Reed.

ETHEL: I want the rush.

LULU: The rush?

ETHEL: When I'm sitting on set, memorizing the new pages in my hand as the make-up boy sets my curls.

LULU: That's a rush?

ETHEL: When I go out under the lights and I know I have one chance, to get it beautifully and do it effortlessly, live on camera, right now. One shot at nailing it because when this moment passes, it's gone. Everyone from my sister-in-law to the milkman will either get it or not. And praying that the camera focus holds, and no sound bleeds in from the radio Western they're broadcasting down the hall, here it comes: they're shooting. Of course I've got the new script down cold: every line means something. I know precisely what I have to do for all you lovely, sad people at home, and I do, and it goes out on the airwaves, and it's done when Jerry Ritt calls wrap. I want to sell some detergent.

LULU: I wanted that, too. God, the stories I wanted to tell.

ETHEL: Yet off you go throwing tantrums. Not that it wasn't impressive—hell, I've never seen anything like it in my life and I'll remember it until that day I die—but it was foolhardy. You must continue to work; and to work, you must know your place. Even Ethel Reed has to know her place.

LULU: Oh, for heaven's sake: Ethel Reed does exactly what she wants.

ETHEL: No, I do exactly what they want. For me, all this... (Gesturing vaguely to herself.) ...grows a little tiresome.

LULU: You don't look tired.

ETHEL: I'll loan you my make-up.

(Beat.)

LULU: I won't name names.

ETHEL: I don't recall anyone asking you to.

LULU: But isn't that just luck? That I haven't shown up on some radar for crossing some perceived line?

ETHEL: Then it's good luck. Because you can walk back through that door and make things better.

LULU: Better.

ETHEL: Blaming the fire on Henry isn't the answer. It's a yawn.

LULU: But what if it's the truth?

ETHEL: But it's not and you know it.

LULU: What do you know?

ETHEL: I know it's a yawn. It demeans her. Life is more complicated than that. I hardly need to be telling you.

LULU: My mother should have been celebrated. She should have been supported.

ETHEL: So support her. Celebrate.

LULU: Why do you care?

ETHEL: Because the second act is schlock.

LULU: No. Why do you care?

ETHEL: Because I am an old bag who works in the theater; and we can't afford any more losses.

(ETHEL rises.)

ETHEL: Your soup is getting cold.

LULU: It was cold when it arrived.

ETHEL: My advice is: eat it anyway.

SCENE NINE

> *On Set: the Barn and the Kitchen from LOIS's house in Indiana.*
> *TAD sits alone at the kitchen table. There is a red liquor bottle in front of him.*
> *He is looking at LIZ HUNTER's signed photograph and drinking.*
> *LULU enters. He doesn't see her. She hesitates. Finally...*

LULU: Boozing during lunch hour?

(TAD looks up.)

TAD: Lulu.

LULU: You look awful.

TAD: I haven't been sleeping so good.

LULU: I know what that's like.

TAD: I telephoned you. I telephoned twenty times.

LULU: It rang and rang in the hall.

TAD: Why didn't you answer?

(LULU walks over to the Barn area of the set.)

LULU: I didn't know what to say then.

TAD: You know now?

LULU: Yeah, I do.

(LULU hits the prop TV equipment with her fist.)

TAD: Hey.

(She bangs it again.)

TAD: What are you doing?

LULU: *(Banging.)* I'm nothing. Nothing.

TAD: Cut it out.

(LULU pushes the prop over. It falls to the floor.)

LULU: I've failed. I'm nothing.

TAD: Lu.

(She bangs on the equipment. TAD tries to restrain her.)

LULU: It's done for, dead. It's over.

TAD: You want Security to come in here?

LULU: *(Struggling against him.)* You betrayed me. You horrible chicken. You didn't stand up for me.

TAD: I didn't know how. I'm sorry.

LULU: You built something with me. You had a stake in it. Our photo-cathode tube.

TAD: What are you talking about?

(LULU breaks free. She continues banging and overturning props in the Barn set.)

LULU: My career is finished.

TAD: Stop it.

LULU: No one's ever heard of me.

TAD: No.

LULU: I've been erased.

(LULU grabs the liquor bottle which TAD was drinking from and smashes it against the wall. It shatters.)

TAD: What the hell are you doing?

LULU: Working on a scene.

TAD: A scene?

LULU: A scene I never told you about. Where Ruby's boyfriend tried to restrain her, but he couldn't, and she destroyed her own lab.

TAD: Oh my god.

LULU: That's the real story. She smashed the wood, she shattered the glass, she lit a fire, and she ran. And all she had to show for her time in that barn was a little girl who never seemed quite able to please her. What would it have taken to please her?

TAD: Oh, Lulu. If she couldn't see you for what you are, that's the biggest, dumbest loss in her life.

LULU: Yeah, well, just one loss among many.

TAD: No, you don't deserve that. No kid could bear that burden.

LULU: You complained that Henry shouldn't be the bad guy. Now you've got your bad guy. I'm back here to help you finish *The Ruby Sunrise*.

TAD: You're back?

LULU: I talked to Mr. Marcus. I apologized for calling him a shitheel. He said it was his favorite swear word and offered to re-hire me.

TAD: He knows you're a genius. But you're wrong about this.

LULU: About what?

TAD: Ruby didn't have to torch it all.

LULU: What else was she going to do? Marry Henry? Go to work for David Sarnoff over at RCA? Lure investors to the barn to give her seed money?

TAD: I don't know. But I know that her destroying her own creation is not the real story. That's not the fate of Ruby Sunrise.

LULU: But it is. I'm coming down off my high horse to tell you that it is. That's just the way things are.

TAD: We make the way things are. We are making it.

LULU: The fact of the matter is...

TAD: I'm not talking about facts, I'm talking about truth. Self-destruction isn't the essence of Ruby that you've been working towards all this time. That wonderful story you wanted to tell is not about despair.

LULU: No? Look around you. Everywhere we turn, these gaping, horrible holes. Liz Hunter, thrown in the garbage.

TAD: I know. But that's what I'm talking about. That's what she taught me.

LULU: Who?

TAD: Liz Hunter. It's about persistence. She wanted us to make her a hero. She's got to persist.

(*TAD kneels and picks up some of the equipment that she knocked to the floor.*)

LULU: What are you doing?

TAD: There's going to be a rehearsal in here.

LULU: But it's broken; I broke it.

TAD: It's a prop, Lu; it doesn't have to work. *You* have to work.

LULU: I am working. I came back. I know my place.

TAD: You came back, but you're still not daring to tell the story the way you wish it was. That's your place. You can invent.

LULU: I don't even know what I wish the story was. It's impossible to imagine anything hopeful in this mess.

TAD: Because you're lost. You feel lost right now. And it's my fault. I took something from you in front of all those people. But now my number is being called again. I hear it calling. It's my chance.

LULU: To do what?

TAD: What I should have been doing all along: sitting you down in front of a typewriter and bringing you some coffee.

LULU: I should bring you coffee. You're the writer.

TAD: I'm the front. You know that more than I do. You're the writer.

LULU: You're calling me a writer?

TAD: Five seconds in the credits. It's not much, but when we get a better agent...

LULU: You're crazy.

TAD: Don't be cynical. It's losing its charm. This is too important for cynicism. This is television!

LULU: Compromised. It's all so compromised. It's not the dream of what Tee Vee could be.

TAD: Yes, there will be compromises. But I swear we'll sneak some victories in there, too. Knocking on the glass screen.

LULU: Do you think we can actually make something good in all this ridiculousness? Something that matters even one little bit?

TAD: I think we can try.

LULU: Is that enough?

TAD: It's better than the alternative. *(Pause.)* Give me a second chance. Don't throw it all in the fire. Write this story another way.

LULU: A second chance.

TAD: Lu?

LULU: Yeah, Tad?

TAD: Can I ask you something?

LULU: Is it serious?

TAD: Yes.

LULU: Is it personal?

TAD: Very.

LULU: You can ask.

TAD: Why does Lois call her Ruby Sunrise?

LULU: That's what you want to ask me?

TAD: That's where I want to start.

LULU: Are you telling me that my credit is going to be right there next to yours?

TAD: You need credit, and you'll get it. Yes.

LULU: Then we'd better start arguing about what a sunrise means.

PART III

The following scene is played on the Studio Set and simultaneously shown live on a television screen (or screens). All the performances are first-rate.
A countdown to the TV shoot is heard.

COUNTDOWN: Ten seconds!

(and then:) Five, four, three, two…

(A silent beat for "one," and the shoot begins…
The sound of rain falling hard.
ETHEL dressed as LOIS sits at the kitchen table. A red glass bottle of booze before her.
PAUL enters, dressed in costume as HENRY. He is wet.)

PAUL: Where is she?

(ETHEL doesn't respond.)

PAUL: Where the hell is she? My wallet's gone. She might have tried to make it to the train. I had five dollars in there. Where is she, Miss Haver? I think she stole my wallet.

ETHEL: She didn't steal your wallet.

PAUL: Borrowed: did she teach you to say that?

ETHEL: *I* stole your wallet.

PAUL: What?

ETHEL: She had to get out of here before her daddy shows. I sent her to the train and handed over your cash. Don't you think we owe her at least that?

PAUL: You sent her away?

ETHEL: She's gone.

PAUL: I should have believed in her more. For real, believed.

ETHEL: Henry, no way in hell a television was gonna spring forth from that barn. Too much working against it. It just wasn't viable.

PAUL: I wanted to make her my wife.

ETHEL: Well, too bad this ain't a story about who marries who.

PAUL: But I loved Ruby Sunrise.

ETHEL: You know, my sister thought I called her Sunrise because Ruby was always awake so early, never seemed to sleep.

PAUL: That's not why?

ETHEL: She was four years old, scrambling around in my kitchen while her mamma slept off her bruises upstairs. Ruby takes my liquor bottle from the table. She doesn't break it. She holds it up to the window, up to the light and looks on through. "The whole world's made of redness now," she says. "The world's different, Aunt Lois. And everything's a sunrise."

(SUZIE (as RUBY) enters the scene. She is very wet. She carries a suitcase.)

PAUL: Ruby.

SUZIE: I know I'm not supposed to be here still.

PAUL: Miss Haver said you'd already left for the train. I thought...

SUZIE: I had one more thing to do before I say goodbye.

PAUL: So it is goodbye? You're already lost to me.

SUZIE: Please don't think of me as lost.

(SUZIE removes a locket from her pocket and holds it out to PAUL.)

PAUL: What's this?

SUZIE: Open it.

(PAUL does.)

PAUL: It's your picture.

SUZIE: I want you to save it.

PAUL: What for?

SUZIE: To remind you. Even though it hurts. Don't wipe it all away.

PAUL: I don't want a keepsake. I want you.

SUZIE: Just promise me you'll never forget what we did together, everything it meant. You were part of it.

PAUL: I mostly served to mess it up.

SUZIE: That's not how I remember it; it's not how you do either. Promise me.

PAUL: Every time I look at your picture, I'll remember everything you taught me. Bioluminescence. Electromagnetism.

SUZIE: Persistence of Vision.

PAUL: I'm so sorry about what happened to your lab.

SUZIE: Who would've thought it? At this time of year: a flood.

PAUL: Fate, I guess.

SUZIE: Don't say that. You say that, and the game's over; and it's not over because nothing is fated. Not even Tee Vee. Not how it works and, sure as can be, not what it's used for. We can keep making choices about all that stuff.

PAUL: What are your choices?

SUZIE: I took a job at RCA. They saw my patent application. They have the money to make it a reality.

PAUL: But a big corporation like that, they'll own everything you invent.

SUZIE: But *I'll* have invented it. An Indiana farm girl.

ETHEL: She's doing what she has to do.

PAUL: She's destroying the most precious part of herself.

SUZIE: No. This is me trying *not* to destroy. Because if I don't do this, I'll shatter it all in a rage, I swear, every last piece of everything 'til there's nothing left.

PAUL: But what about your dreams?

SUZIE: Those'll have to be my dreams.

PAUL: It's sad, Ruby.

SUZIE: Yeah. But I feel like this is the only way it won't be sad forever. You disappointed in me?

PAUL: Naw. You stay here, you got nothing; I get that. You go out there, maybe you can make a difference, change the way people see things.

SUZIE: I might not get it right off.

PAUL: It'll come. You gotta start where you start. If I had a daughter, I guess I'd tell her to do what you're doing.

SUZIE: You'll have a daughter one day, Henry. She'll be so pretty, and so kind, and your wife will be so lucky.

PAUL: I think you better go now.

SUZIE: Henry.

PAUL: Yeah?

SUZIE: Do I scare you?

PAUL: Yeah, but why do you ask?

SUZIE: Because you still haven't tried to kiss me.

> *(And they kiss.)*

ETHEL: *(Clearing her throat)* A-hem.

> *(The kids stop kissing.* ETHEL *approaches and hands* SUZIE *the bottle of booze.)*

ETHEL: Hide this good. And use it when you're making all your special vacuums.

SUZIE: Thanks for looking out for me.

ETHEL: That was just me looking out for myself.

SUZIE: If you say so. There's gonna be an all-electrical system sending pictures through the air before the year is out. You believe me now?

ETHEL: Not if you miss that train, there's not.

SUZIE: Not gonna. No way I'm gonna miss. Goodbye, Henry.

PAUL: Good luck, Ruby.

(SUZIE exits with her suitcase and the bottle of alcohol.
The rain beats down.)

PAUL: You got a drink, Miss Haver?

ETHEL: No, Henry, I do not. Packed the last away with your girlfriend.

PAUL: You think she's my girlfriend?

ETHEL: As much as she could ever be anybody's.

PAUL: So it's some kind of upbeat ending after all.

ETHEL: Some kind.

PAUL: Hey, someone's coming.

ETHEL: Oh hell.

PAUL: It's her daddy, come to stop her?

ETHEL: Must be.

PAUL: But Ruby's on her way now. She's already on her way.

(ETHEL rises. She crosses to the edge of the set and looks out a window.)

ETHEL: I'll be damned.

PAUL: What?

ETHEL: What a hopeless woman I am.

PAUL: What are you talking about?

ETHEL: That man, he still looks good to me. After all he's done. Hopeless.

PAUL: Maybe he's changed. Maybe you can change him.

ETHEL: Here comes heartache.

PAUL: Make him better.

ETHEL: Here comes pain.

(The camera fades away from ETHEL and HENRY and comes up on SUZIE on a different part of the set. She is walking in place in front of a back-drop of the house which slowly recedes, making it appear on the TV screen(s) that she is walking away from the house. She has a determined step; she is walking towards her dreams.)

SUZIE: *(V.O.)*

Television's gonna change people. I know it can. It'll be a whole different world once people can see the whole world right in their homes.

(LULU approaches a television screen. She watches "RUBY's" departure on the little box.)

SUZIE: *(V.O.)* You'll get to watch the news as it's happening, can you imagine? Get to listen to somebody talk while you're looking at them, too; somebody far far away that you'd never get to meet, and maybe that person has something to teach you. A lecture about science or safety, or just a story.

(TAD, MARTIN, ETHEL, and PAUL gather to watch this final image on the monitor.)

SUZIE: *(V.O.)* Soon, we'll get pictures from all over the world, and learn about our comrades in other countries, hell, other planets.

(The crew watch as well, looking at a different screen.)

SUZIE: *(V.O.)* Everything will be different once we see all those faces. We won't be able to hide anymore. We'll realize how connected we are, how we all want the same things really at the end of the day.

(RUBY enters the space. She crosses to LULU and the TV screen.)

SUZIE: *(V.O.)* Maybe I am crazy, the Crazy Girl from Kokomo, but I just know there'll come a time when all our difference will be settled around tables, instead of going to war. Television's gotta bring the end of war—it stands to reason—'cause who could bear it? Who could bear to see war right in your own living room?

(The music swells over SUZIE's speech.
RUBY and LULU watch together as "The End" flashes on the TV screen. The two women almost touch as the lights begin to fade…
And the credits on the TV screen begin to roll.)

END OF PLAY

KID-SIMPLE,
a radio play in the flesh
by Jordan Harrison

BIOGRAPHY

Jordan Harrison's plays, which include *The Museum Play, Kid-Simple*, and *Finn in the Underworld*, have been produced and developed at Playwrights Horizons, Perishable Theatre, The Empty Space Theatre, Clubbed Thumb, Sledgehammer Theatre and American Theater Company. His ten-minute play *Fit for Feet*, co-winner of the Heideman Award, was produced in the 2003 Humana Festival. A recipient of two Jerome Fellowships from The Playwrights' Center, Mr. Harrison has also received commissions from the Guthrie Theater and Children's Theatre Company, and from the National New Play Network. Mr. Harrison received his M.F.A. in Playwriting from Brown University, where he was a Lucille Lortel Fellow. He is a resident playwright at New Dramatists.

HUMANA FESTIVAL PRODUCTION

Kid-Simple premiered at the Humana Festival of New American Plays in February, 2003. It was directed by Darron L. West with the following cast:

Moll . . . . Maria Dizzia
Oliver . . . . Max Ferguson
The Narrator . . . . Glynis Bell
The Mercenary. . . . . Michael Ray Escamilla
Father, Mr. Wachtel, Voice One . . . . Jason Pugatch
Mother, Miss Kendrick, Voice Two. . . . . Carla Harting
Foley Artist . . . . Clifford Endo Gulibert

and the following production staff:

Scenic Designer . . . . Paul Owen
Costume Designer . . . . Lorraine Venberg
Lighting Designer. . . . . Tony Penna
Sound Designers . . . . Bray Poor, Darron L. West
Properties Designer . . . . Doc Manning
Stage Manager . . . . Paul Mills Holmes
Assistant Stage Manager. . . . . Abigail Wright
Dramaturg. . . . . Tanya Palmer
Assistant Dramaturg . . . . Erin Detrick
Viewpoints Consultant . . . . Will Bond
Directing Assistant. . . . . Emily Wright
Casting . . . . Jerry Ellis Beaver

CHARACTERS

MOLL, a girl who invents things

OLIVER, a virgin

THE NARRATOR, a mellifluous voice (female)

THE MERCENARY, a master of disguises, including:
GARTH
A PAWNSHOP CLERK
A SATYR
A FIG TREE

MR. WACHTEL, a black marketeer
& FATHER
& VOICE ONE
& TRIPLE-A GUIDE

MISS KENDRICK, a music teacher
& MOTHER
& VOICE TWO
& AMWAY SALESLADY

CREEPY PHONE VOICE & CAR SALESMAN VOICE should be played by the actor playing the Mercenary. The COMMERCIAL ANNOUNCER might be played by the Foley Artist or the actor playing Oliver, or else pre-recorded.

NOTES

Microphones. There are at least three free-standing mikes. In the background, a Foley Artist with a baroque assortment of instruments, household objects and noisy junk. As many of the play's sounds as possible should be produced live.

Projections. Sound effects in bold are meant to be seen as well as heard. *Sound of a violent recognition*, for example, indicates that these words are to be projected, so that the audience can see the distance between the intended sound and the actual one. Part of letting them in on the game.

The Narrator. In addition to narrating, she might manipulate the projections, like an ambassador between the machine and the audience.

Onomatopoeia. Late in the play, words become replaced by onomatopoeia, indicated by brackets. For example: "Monday is the first *[clang]* of the week." Produced by the Foley Artist, this is a kind of percussion that seems to come from the actors' mouths.

Michael Ray Escamilla
in *Kid-Simple*

28th Annual Humana Festival of New American Plays
Actors Theatre of Louisville, 2004
photo by Harlan Taylor

Kid-Simple

1.
In Which Books Are Opened and Throats Cleared.

Sound of a great tome opening.

Sound of a throat cleared with majesty.

NARRATOR: Beyond the raging river and the cadaversome chasm, over the mighty mountain, in the finest cul-de-sac of a peaceful town, there lived a clever girl.

MOLL: If a cookie jar contains n gingersnaps, n being more than ten but less than twenty...

NARRATOR: A very clever girl. It seemed the cogs in her brain were never at rest.

MOLL: ...let D^n be a linear differential operator with a continuous right inverse—

NARRATOR: Her parents were very proud.

FATHER: What a clever girl we have, Mother.

MOTHER: Clever but ill-at-ease socially, Father. Why does she have to stay at home with us listening to the "Mystery Radio Nostalgia Hour" instead of necking with boys like I did back when it was way-back-when?

FATHER: In time, Mother. In time.

NARRATOR: Moll is her name.

MOLL: Molly is for simps, so.

NARRATOR: Moll invented things. Instead of softball trophies and hit-parade records, her room was filled with timber and tools...

(Sound of hammering.)

NARRATOR: and Mozart—which they say is good for thinking as well as for making plants grow...

(Sound of the Overture of The Magic Flute.*)*

NARRATOR: and the friction that always exists between fresh contraptions and the world-as-we-knew-it.

(Sound of sandpaper, slowly.)

NARRATOR: But no one really knew what Moll was up to in her head.

(Sound of the Overture in full flight.)

NARRATOR: Sometimes she stayed in her room all day, furiously at work...

(Sound of hammer and nails and Mozart and sandpaper.)

NARRATOR: …but she always emerged in time to sit around the fire with her folks and listen to the "Hilberson's-Brand Hot Dog Mystery Radio Nostalgia Hour."

(Sound of radio static.)

FATHER: There we are.

COMMERCIAL ANNOUNCER: Imagine, for a moment, a hot dog.

If the picture that comes to mind is a wiener in a bun, think again!

There are a zillion ways to prepare this immortal tastebud tempter:

"Take the chill out of winter with a hearty hotdog soup,

Keep your cool in summer with a piquant hotdog salad,

Best of all, satisfy the gourmet inside *you* by whipping up an epicurean hotdog delight"[1] with the help of Hilberson's All-Beef Foot-Long Finest!

And now, sit back and enjoy the fifth nail-biting installment of "*Death and the Music Teacher.*"

(MOTHER and FATHER move into the shadowy space of the radio broadcast, becoming KENDRICK and WACHTEL. We are in a realm where our eyes are less useful now.)

(Sound of empty park swings creaking in the wind. Preferably, a winter wind.)

WACHTEL: How does it feel to be totally in my power?

MISS KENDRICK: It isn't necessary to blindfold me, Mr. Wachtel.

WACHTEL: This is how we do business in this business. The fold comes off once I trust you.

MISS KENDRICK: I came to you to share something extraordinary. Why would I do anything funny?

WACHTEL: Show me something extraordinary then.

(Sound of latches undone, with difficulty.)

MISS KENDRICK: *(Excited.)* Here. The inscription reads Bolokva, and I wondered could it be, really and truly

could it be?—

WACHTEL: Miss Kendrick. What makes you think you say a name like that and Open Sesame? Bolokva is a crucial name, this is true. But it is a city name, not a maker. Say you're here selling me a car. Say you're a salesman saying:

---

[1] Mettja C. Roate, *The New Hotdog Cookbook.*

CAR SALESMAN: *(Slithery and slimy.)* Wachtel buddy, I've got a Detroit here, beautiful '87 Detroit Coupe, runs like molasses in August.

WACHTEL: Sounds dynamite, but how do I know if that coupe's a Ford a Dodge a Pontiac or what? It doesn't make sense in the head, the way you're talking. A woman in your position to a man in mine.

MISS KENDRICK: *(Mustering strength.)* You do relish your little ring of power.

WACHTEL: Miss Kendrick. You play like Casals, you look like Garbo…

CAR SALESMAN: …but that doesn't make you Lee Iacocca in this business.

WACHTEL: *I'm* the smartie in this business. I know a lot. I know about your guy here just by looking. I know from the varnish he's ages old. Late 17th century, could be top of the 18th—any later they don't have this color in the resin. Clearly he's been through a lot. Battle scars here here and here. That stain—blood maybe? Blood of a former owner. Court musician who displeased the queen.

(Sound of a string breaking. *Violent dissonance.)*

WACHTEL: Dainty he ain't, but sometimes deformity yields the most distinctive timbre. But do I know he's what you say he is, sight-unheard? I mean…

CAR SALESMAN: You don't know how a car runs by the paint job.

MISS KENDRICK: Or a book by its cover, I tell my students.

WACHTEL: I've got to protect myself from charlatans, Miss Kendrick. There are three Speechless Cellos in the whole wide world. That we know of. Two are owned by the Chinese government, which has been trying its darndest to get them to mate. It's near unheard-of in captivity. The third one is in the private collection of Baron Von Schygullhösen. And now you come out of the woodwork telling me you just happened upon one quite by accident…

WACHTEL:	CAR SALESMAN:
… well it's just awful fancy to believe	…well it's just awful fancy to believe.

MISS KENDRICK: It would be difficult to believe, if it weren't true.

WACHTEL: Ho—she's feisty, this one…

MISS KENDRICK: I am not.

WACHTEL: …but I can't make exceptions,
even for blue-chip dames like yourself:
If he turns out to be a sham, Miss Kendrick, then my man Big Pete will stuff you in that case there and toss you in the river and you can float back to your kindergartners practicing their "Go Tell Aunt Rhody."

(Sound of sinister music swelling. A minor-key rendition of "Go Tell Aunt Rhody.")

COMMERCIAL ANNOUNCER: Will the sinister Wachtel send sweet Miss Kendrick down the river? Tune in tomorrow, if your spine can take any more tingling, for the next installment of—

(Sound of the radio off with a click.
Mother and Father have returned to their comfy family den.)

MOTHER: That Mister Wachtel gives me the heebie-jeebies.

FATHER: That Miss Kendrick can come serenade me any time.

MOLL: I think you're both loony. Pass me the piquant hot dog salad.

(They laugh wholesomely until everyone feels a bit queasy.)

2.

In Which Moll Discovers Her Own Circuitry.

Sound of hammer and nails and Mozart and sandpaper.

NARRATOR: In preparation for the regional science fair, Moll had taken to staying in her room so long that her hair would become a greasy helmet and the sweat of mental exertion would trickle down her neck and Mother would have to bring her dinner…

MOTHER: Meatloaf and mashers and a heaping pile of succotash.

NARRATOR: …to her room on a tray.

MOTHER: Knock-knock.

(Sound of machinery clattering to the floor.)

MOLL: MOM! I TOLD YOU NEVER INTERRUPT ME WHILE I'M MAKING THINGS.

NARRATOR: Moll's temper was as active as her imagination.

MOLL: NEVER NEVER NEVER, IT'S DANGEROUS.

MOTHER: I don't care if she's some kind of genius, Father. The tone she's been taking—

MOLL: I cannot be distracted—the equilibrium!

FATHER : What the devil is she doing in there?

MOLL: I can't tell anyone til it's finished.

NARRATOR: *(Stage whisper.)* She was making a machine for hearing sounds that can't be heard.

MOLL: It just might be my greatest thing *ever*.

NARRATOR: It should be mentioned that there are two principal schools of inventing. In the Apollonian School, every part has its proper place, every atom is
accounted for. In the Dionysian School, the free-form philosophy...

MOLL: The artistic mess!

NARRATOR: *(Rather impatient.)*...to which Moll chiefly subscribed—the inventor gathers whatever suits her fancy...

(Sound of a creative din.)

NARRATOR: A broken TV antennae.

MOLL: For tuning.

NARRATOR: A woofer (or was it a tweeter?) from her father's old stereo.

MOLL: For amplifying.

NARRATOR: The mouth of an antique Victrola.

MOLL: For listening.

NARRATOR: Nearly a mile of copper plated wire, all told.

MOLL: For wiring.

NARRATOR: And a million more

MOLL: a *zillion*

NARRATOR: more things, all piled high.

MOLL: Glorious! Still...

NARRATOR: Something was missing.

(Sound of an unpromising mechanical whirr.)

MOLL: A human touch
That's all it needs.
A bit of God-designed listening equipment.

NARRATOR: And so Moll contributed a piece of herself, literally...

(Sound of Moll smacking the side of her head.)

MOLL: Come out of there!

NARRATOR: The tiniest bone in her body, deep in the middle ear...

MOLL: The stirrup bone, which is just an eighth of an inch long, and sometimes goes by its Latin name, the *stapes*.
(Sound of more smacking.)

NARRATOR: It took some persuading to dislodge it from her skull. When the
little bone finally emerged...

(Sound of a satisfying "ping.")

NARRATOR: ...she planted it in the mechanical heart of the machine...

MOLL: Now part of me will always be with you.

NARRATOR: And the whole mess seemed to come, improbably, to life.
(Sound of the machine coming to life, creakily.

Lights rise on the Foley table for the first time: It is the Machine.)

NARRATOR: And just like that   MOLL: …Just like that!

Her familiar room quivered and crackled
with previously undiscovered universes:
The aching backs of load-bearing walls,
Dust bunnies stomping like pachyderms
Across the unswept floor.
But nothing was so deafening as the thoughts in her very own head.
(Sound of the cogs turning in her head.)

MOLL: Eureka!

NARRATOR: Finally, the big day of the science fair arrived.

(Moll stands before a chalkboard full of calculations.)

MOLL: It's easy, it's kid-simple.
Tune with the antennae, with the knobs and presto:
You can hear toenails growing on a field mouse.
You can hear if someone's lying by their breath.
You can hear your way through the dark, like bats.
…Um.
(An instant when she seems to lose her way, then:
Sound of cogs in her head.)
ˈIf you listen close, you can even hear an essence inside an accident.

NARRATOR: The panel of judges, glassy-eyed from an afternoon of appraising
potato plants and sea monkeys, snapped suddenly awake.

MOLL: The stethoscope attachment permits high-precision listening:
Objects can tell you what they've overheard.
(Objects are the best eavesdroppers, on account of no one suspects them.)
*(She holds the stethoscope up to the chalkboard. We hear many voices,
swirling and cacophonous, like something from Dante's* Inferno. *Frightening.
Note: A change in font indicates a new voice.)*

CHORUS OF TEACHERS: Missy Sperling, is that gum in your *mouth off one more
time, Mister, and you're headed to detention for the rest of your natural* life is
a great beautiful adventure, except the parts that make you want to end it
all in single file or we won't go out to recess, period, comma, or question
mark? Who can tell me what punctuation belongs *here on the equator, we
find Kenya where it is very hot all the* Time! Pencils down on your desks,
pencils *down the road from the first little pig lived his brother in the house of
sticks who* can tell me if this state of matter is a liquid, a gas, or a *solid citizen wouldn't cut in front of a lady, he would open the door*way to tomorrow

is keyboarding skills—if you don't know your Control from your Caps Lock, how can you expect to plan for the *future of the giant panda is still uncertain, if only man could learn that the world belongs to animals as well as* people may want to have their hair cut nicely before class picture day because a photograph is forever you know *running in the halls, Billy Dumpsch!*

(MOLL removes the stethoscope. Sudden quiet.)

MOLL: Any questions?

NARRATOR: Even without the aid of the machine, one could have heard a pin drop in a haystack.

MOLL: I call it… The Third Ear!

(Sound of applause, overlapping the following lines.)

NARRATOR: Not only did Moll take top honors at the fair…

MOLL: Three years running!

NARRATOR: …the Third Ear landed her on *American Egghead Quarterly's* Junior Overachiever List. She received fourteen fan letters, eight accusations of witchcraft, and one creepy phone call.

CREEPY PHONE VOICE: Ring ring. Ring ring.

MOLL: Moll here.

CREEPY PHONE VOICE: You're the girl with the machine?

MOLL: I have a lot of machines.

CREEPY PHONE VOICE: My clients are prepared to offer a good bit of money for the blueprints.

MOLL: I'm not sure you know what you're dealing with.

CREEPY PHONE VOICE: Kid-simple, you said so yourself.

MOLL: There are still some kinks. It could be very destructive, if—

CREEPY PHONE VOICE: You could be a very rich young lady.

(Pause.)

MOLL: Don't call here again.

(Sound of the receiver put down.)

Creepsters.

NARRATOR: Things went back to normal more or less, until one day she was walking home from Math Club.

(Sound of MOLL's footsteps, then another set of footsteps shadowing her. She stops. Nothing. She starts again and the second steps resume. She stops.)

MOLL: What do you want? *(Silence.)* I can see you behind that telephone pole.

GARTH: I've been following you.

MOLL: Well, cut it out.

GARTH: Are you the girl?

MOLL: I'm *a* girl.

GARTH: The girl with the machine.

MOLL: I have a lot of machines.

GARTH: I'm Garth.

(Sound of hair gel being smoothed back.)

MOLL: I'm Moll. Hi.

GARTH: 'Sup.

NARRATOR: It should be mentioned that these two are at an age of hormonal tumult.

GARTH: Moll.

(Two seconds of silence.)

MOLL: Garth.

NARRATOR: It's possible Moll would have noticed the faintest similarity between Garth's distinctive phonation…

GARTH: 'Sup.

NARRATOR: …and the voice on the phone, earlier that week. But her recent sacrifice in the name of science had left her somewhat deaf in one ear.

MOLL: Pardon?

GARTH : I said maybe I could carry your books?

MOLL: Oh. Here.

(Sound like a great door slamming.)

GARTH: Oof! How many classes are you taking?

MOLL: I like to do a little extra reading.

NARRATOR: Like most people, Moll is susceptible to flattery…

GARTH: I think it's bitchin' the way you use your head and stuff.

NARRATOR: …and things moved quickly for the pair.

GARTH: You're, like, the sun and the moon and the stars and all.

NARRATOR: He touched her on the cheek, lightly.

MOLL: Thank you very much.

NARRATOR: Very quickly indeed. It felt to Moll like the earth was spinning faster than normal.

GARTH: This is my room, so.

(Pause.)

NARRATOR: He touched her on the shoulder, lightly.

(In the following, MOLL's interior thoughts are indicated by italics. Different and reverberant, these should be spoken into a body mike or standing microphone. Still, the overall effect should be a seamless current of speech.)

MOLL: *Back in my room I was safe I was safe and now here I am in his clutches but this is what you wanted didn't you want to know what it feels* like your place a lot, Garth. The Screeching Weasel poster really cozies it up, even if the feng shui could be *better be gentle, he'd better. I'm not one of those smitten by the brute, by the boot, thanks Sylvia Plath, but no* thanks for dinner! I've never had buffalo wings with ranch dressing before, is that a regional delicacy or *what is that rather unpleasant boy-musk is* that cologne you're wearing or what *IS that? probably he slaps a pint of horse piss under his pits every morning before heading out to tear the wings off ladybugs that's what boys do* you think it's hot in here? it seems hot but maybe I just have bad circulation in my extremities it isn't good for the blood to *Stop talking stop talking this instant stop.*

GARTH: Stop talking, babe.

Relax.

Garth's gonna take care of you.

MOLL: *Better take care, you better be delicate. Ms. Hanrahan in Sex Ed said it's like a flower opening inside you but she was probably ordered to say that or else the species would cease to put babies on this* earth feels like it's spinning faster than normal or is it just me*thinks the curious contortions of the human body are not for me, last chance to run to get me to a nunnery go!*

GARTH: I'm gonna go put on some mood tunes. You just lie back and let yourself feel moody-like.

MOLL: *But he's certainly* All right *in the hospitality department maybe you haven't been fair probably he had a maladjusted childhood not everyone has fireside radio family time probably he had a stutter and that's why he doesn't venture words containing more than one syll—*

(Her thoughts are drowned out by the opening guitar lick from the Rolling Stones's "Miss You."

Get-it-on music.

When the music subsides, time has passed.)

GARTH: Oh man, Molls—

Can I call you that now that we're boyfriend and girlfriend?

You, I mean—

I mean, you—

GARTH:	MOLL:
What am I trying to say?	What are you trying to say?

NARRATOR: What did a headstrong inventress see in this ill-groomed monosyllabalizer?,

You might be asking yourselves.

GARTH: What I mean is, you're one-hundred percent sexy.

> (MOLL *doesn't know what to say.*)

MOLL: Thank you very much.

NARRATOR: Perhaps Moll *fancied* being the keener one of the two.

> Or perhaps she just fancied the contrast between the hard metal stud in his brow and his long long eyelashes.

> **(Sound like moving through tall grass.)**

> Perhaps Garth's heart condition made him seem like he needed her protection.

> **(Sound of an irregular heartbeat.)**

> But perhaps most of all, she loved the things Garth was teaching her:

> To hold a cigarette like Jean-Paul Belmondo.

> (Sound of MOLL *coughing.*)

> To walk through the streets of a city like they were nothing but her backyard...

GARTH: Gotcha something.

> (*It is a very cheap ring.*)

MOLL: Um, shiny.

NARRATOR: To put her skepticism away on a high high shelf...

GARTH: I found it on the sidewalk and I thought,

> maybe you can wear it around your neck?

> That way it doesn't mean getting *married*—

MOLL : (*Agreeing very quickly.*) Nooo.

GARTH: But it means I think you're, wow.

> (*Sound of a kiss.*)

NARRATOR: ...To put down her gadgets and pay some attention to her own circuitry. Perhaps.

> (*Another, longer kiss.*)

GARTH: Hey, Moll?

MOLL: Mmm.

GARTH: You mind showing me that Ear doohickey tomorrow?

MOLL: What?

GARTH: I'd be real intrigued to see it.

NARRATOR: At any other time, Garth's mastery of a word like "intrigued" would have raised her suspicions. But Moll was in no state for semantic nit-pickery.

MOLL: Yeah whatever, it's in my locker. Tomorrow. Come here.

> (*The Rolling Stones take over again.*)

3.

In Which Life Imitates Art or Is It The Other Way Around?

NARRATOR: It seemed to Moll's parents that they hardly ever saw her anymore.
   (Very rapidly:)
MOTHER: Peaches.
FATHER: Pumpkin.
MOTHER: Cupcake.
FATHER: Cutiepatootie.
MOTHER AND FATHER: Aren't you going to listen to the "Hilberson's-Brand Hotdog Mystery Radio Nostalgia Hour" with us tonight like always?
MOLL: Garth's gonna call any minute.
MOTHER: *("Yum.")* Garth with the green green eyes.
FATHER: Garth with the *shifty* eyes.
MOLL: I have a problem set due, so. We're going to…study together.
MOTHER: *(Entincingly.)* Invite him over. I made hot dog canapés.
   (Sound of radio static.)
FATHER: It's only just starting.
   (Sound of empty park swings in the wind. *Preferably a winter wind.***)**
MISS KENDRICK: The blindfold, Mr. Wachtel.
WACHTEL: Everything was as you said it would be, Miss Kendrick.
MISS KENDRICK: Why, then, am I still bereft as a bat?
   (Sound of a blindfold removed.)
WACHTEL: Most unusual, a woman who's true to her word.
MISS KENDRICK: Do we have a deal then, Mr. Wachtel?
   Do we have a deal or do you still intend to send me down the river?
WACHTEL: You're a hard-headed woman, Miss Kendrick.
   But my head is even harder.
   I can give you the price we discussed or I can take him from you forceful-like.
MISS KENDRICK: You wouldn't dare.
   Like birdsong, his music depends on his mood.
   He plays Bach when he's blissful
   And Bloch when he's blue.
   But you know as well as I do,
   He won't play if he smells danger.
WACHTEL: He can't smell anything, woman. He's a bloody cello.

MISS KENDRICK: He's a very *special* cello.

He plays notes you can only hear outside your ear.

WACHTEL: What are you riddling for, Kendrick?

You think I don't know what you got here?

MISS KENDRICK: You know years

You know makers

You know *varnish*

But do you know how an instrument can reveal whole worlds of sound?

How it enchants – repels –

Swoops – trembles – triumphs –

Defeats – whispers – thrums!

How it can do such things

That you'd cross the earth to find it?

There are more notes, Mister Wachtel, than you or I are fit to hear.

WACHTEL: You think I can't make him speak, Miss Kendrick,

With my arthritic knuckles and my decidedly unmusical temperament?

Think again, music teacher…

WACHTEL:	CAR SALESMAN:
A Rolls Royce drives just as well for the poor man as it does for the Earl of Ritzyville.	A Rolls Royce drives just as well for the poor man as it does for the Earl of Ritzyville.

MISS KENDRICK: I don't care about your metaphors or your money, Mr. Wachtel.

I just want my cello to have a safe and proper home where all the world can enjoy his music.

(Sound of the phone ringing.)

MISS KENDRICK:	MOLL:
I won't surrender him to a bunch of barbarians, Mr. Wachtel. Yes, thugs and barbarians.	I'll get it! Moll here.
	I told you not to call me again.

WACHTEL: Thin ice, Miss Kendrick. Thin ice.

MISS KENDRICK:	MOLL:
I'd have to be crazy to let you sell him to the highest bidder, piece by piece.	I'd have to be crazy to tell you its secrets; its wires and work-ings.

WACHTEL: On the contrary, Kendrick. You'd be wise to pocket the percentage.

MISS KENDRICK:	MOLL
You can't make me do anything.	What does that mean, "or else"?

WACHTEL: You can be *persuaded*, Miss Kendrick.

MISS KENDRICK:
I know my rights, Mr. Wachtel.

Maybe I should take my business
to the Historical Society.

Goodbye,
Mr. Wachtel.
I won't come calling again.
(Sound of a door slamming.)

MOLL:
It's my machine, mine. It came
from my head fully-formed and it
has enough juice to destroy NOISE
AS WE KNOW IT so you see it's not
going to leave my sight!
GOOD. BYE.

(Sound of the receiver slammed down.)

MOTHER AND FATHER: Who was THAT?

MOLL: Um. Jennie Doherty wanted my Chem notes so I told her she better go
find someone with shakier ethics and copy from them.

FATHER: That's my girl.

(Sound of a dial tone. Quite loud.)

NARRATOR: Moll waited by the phone all that night, but Garth never called.
The next day at school, she opened her locker and found only a note.

(Sound of a locker door opened.)

NARRATOR: A note and a big empty space where her splendid machine,
where...

The Third Ear!
used to be.

MOLL: *(Aghast.)*...the Third Ear

(MOLL begins to read.)

GARTH: Dear Moll:
I'm afraid you've been had.
Our love, I'm afraid, was a hoax.
It was the Ear I wanted all along.
You would have been paid top dollar,
If only you'd cooperated.
I'm not a teen rebel, see.
I'm a secret operative, a master of disguise
With a decade of reconnaissance experience.
You were seduced by my temporary form
As many are.
Sometimes I am a beautiful woman with red hair.
Sometimes I am a salamander.
Other times I am an agitated molecule.

Whatever happens to be useful.

Do not try to find me.

I won't look like me anyway.

Sincerely,

Garth

Or, should I say,

(His voice changing to the MERCENARY's monotone.)

THE MERCENARY.

(Sound of paper torn into very small pieces.)

4.

In Which Things Are Heard Beyond the Reach of Hearing.

NARRATOR: Far from the fine cul-de-sac, past the penumbra of street lamps, a duo with dark intentions was huddling in the darkness. It was so *dark* in fact that no one, including a certain astigmatic Narrator; no one, themselves included, could tell exactly where they were.

> **(Sound of a heartbeat.** *Growing closer, growing louder.*
>
> *Then:*
>
> **Sound of another heartbeat.** *Growing closer and louder.*
>
> *For some moments, they beat a duet.)*

ONE AND TWO: That you?

(Pause.)

ONE AND TWO: Over here.

(Sound of a bump.)

TWO: Ouch! I can't see with all this dark.

ONE: How do you think bats improved? With a lot of darkness. With a lot of patience and a lot of perseverance, that's how.

TWO: It's *eons* to evolve, Number One.

ONE: Soon we'll hear the Grand Design, Number Two. Wait and see.

TWO: But *I* can't see.

(The following very rapidly:)

ONE: Wait.

TWO: What.

ONE: Did you hear?

TWO: No.

ONE: Now.

(*Sound of an irregular heartbeat*. It is GARTH/THE MERCENARY. *For some moments, the hearts beat in a trio*.)

ONE AND TWO: You.

THE MERCENARY: How did you know?

TWO: That beat—

(*Sound of One and Two giggling*.)

ONE: There's no mistaking it.

THE MERCENARY: It's called arrhythmia and it's nothing to laugh about.

ONE: Do you have the device?

THE MERCENARY: I told you I'd get it, didn't I?

TWO: Hand it over!

ONE: Me first!

ONE AND TWO: Me me me me me me me.

THE MERCENARY: We can all listen. It's got an attachment so everyone can listen.

(*Sound of a switch switched*. *Electricity flowing. They listen. What starts as a submerged sound grows slowly audible: Many different voices in a seamless Babble*.)

BABBLE: The House Blend, please, with two percent and no *sugar, you're a real nice girl but I think we should* see low-lying nimbostratus and stratocumulus in the afternoon, giving way this evening to a cold, *clear Filston Ice Draft, the closest thing to drinkin' a glacier this side* of your argument really doesn't hold water, Stanley—if you expect the public to vote *four on the floor, ladies. Always four on the floor and you won't end up changing diapers instead of taking the SATs which are, after all, the key to your* future is shrouded in mystery, the Queen of Pentacles here beside the Hanged Man but—

ONE: So much interference. There must be a way—

TWO: There must be a button?

THE MERCENARY: A tuner, perhaps.

ONE: Don't you know?

TWO: He doesn't know.

THE MERCENARY: Patience. It's simply a matter of fiddling.

ONE: *(Fiddling.)* Fiddling wasn't the plan.

TWO: *(Fiddling.)* I don't remember fiddling.

THE MERCENARY: The girl wouldn't talk.

ONE: What if we

TWO: Try this?

ONE: Ouch!

TWO: Oops.

ONE: How 'bout.

THE MERCENARY: Here.

BABBLE: *(Accelerating.)*—here I see great romance I *see what you're saying, if the GTCWA is to survive, but it just doesn't have the overhead to support what* did you learn in school today *is the first day of the rest of your* life is good *riddance to that dumb mutt I want a cat* scan reveals a growth that must be treated at once with *the crusts cut off please* put down the gun, John, please put it *down the hatch. Delicious.*

ONE AND TWO: That's it, there's the frequency, there—

(The Babble fades to silence—we can hear their heartbeats again. Then:
Sound of a gossamer, almost undetectable, footfall.)

ALL: Did you hear?

THE MERCENARY: Water spider on tippy-toe.

ONE AND TWO: Wow.

(Sound like a great beam of wood straining.)

ALL: Did you hear?

TWO: Roots in the earth.

(Sound like a great beam of wood straining, then a wall of water.)

ALL: Did you hear?

ONE: Shipwreck at sea.

TWO: All ships wreck at sea.

ONE: Some in bays, straits, lagoons. This one far from the reach of hearing—

TWO: Poor souls.

THE MERCENARY: —from *ordinary* hearing, that is.

(Sound like a guillotine chop, then a sickening thud.)

ONE: What—what's that?

THE MERCENARY: That I think it's…

TWO: An execution, maybe?

ONE: A woodchuck chucking wood?

(Again, the sound.)

THE MERCENARY: It's—

ONE: It's—

TWO: It's—

(Light rises on MOLL.)

THE MERCENARY: *(Realizing it's her.)* It's the sound of a broken heart.

5.

In Which Moll Says What She Didn't Get To Say the First Time Around.

(Sound of rage muted by a thick pillow.)

NARRATOR: Back at the cul-de-sac, Moll wished the cogs in her head would stop turning for once.
(Sound of the relentless cogs.)
If only, poor girl, she could murder her memory.
(Sound of a knock.)
MOLL: *(Barely scrutable.)* Goooaway. You're the ENEMY.
GARTH: Moll? 'Sup.
MOLL: Why are you here, you you…FIGMENT.
GARTH: Look who's a mess.
MOLL: Used to be I was your sun and moon and stars. What happened to that?
GARTH: *(Not too sorry.)* Yeah, I'm sorry if that was misleading.
(Pause.)
MOLL: I will get you for this, Garth. The world will have to go without new inventions for some time, because all my ingenuity will be directed toward your undoing. I will GET you for messing with my machine and my sanity.
NARRATOR: Did I mention Moll has a temper?
MOLL: All of CREATION will get you. You will be FOOD. A plane will drop you over the unforgiving Serengeti with a faulty parachute an empty canteen no sunblock, and when one of these circumstances fells you, you will finally do some good on this planet as recycled material. Your meat will invigorate the ecosystem, your eyes will shrivel into tiny raisins, the albino kind no one favors. And you will be alone, totally alone, for so long that proximity to another body is *novel*. And when you think you'll never see a human face again, I'll swoop in, *deus ex machina*, to say simply: 'Sup.
Your stumpy remains are so glad to see me, looking up to me like a God. But instead of kisses or cool clear water I serve you up a subpoena, bringing to the fore your crimes against United States patent law.
MAY ALL THIS COME TO PASS. The loneliness most of all.
GARTH: Kinda sucks you have to curse me with *your* life.
MOLL: What is this back-talk, Garth?
This is my post-facto daydream so…
(Sound of sweaty sweatsocks being removed.)
…you'll say and you'll do what I wish.

(Sound of him pleasuring her toes.)
MOLL: That's better.

Now.

(Sound of a sexhalation from MOLL.)

Would you say I was the sun and the moon and the stars?

GARTH: *(Dreamily.)* You are the sun and the moon and the—

MOLL: Whoa whoa whoa.

This little piggy needs more attention.

This little piggy isn't ready for wee wee wee.

Love my feet, boy-fiend

Love them all night

You greedy man-slut, you!

6.
In Which the Mercenary Learns Fear.

(In the very dark place, just as MOLL says "you," THE MERCENARY cries out.)

NARRATOR: Elsewhere…

ONE: What is it?

THE MERCENARY: There's an awful funny taste in my mouth. Like sweatsocks.
Ack!

TWO: I think I've got gum.

THE MERCENARY: Quick! Ick!

(Sound of a wrapper, then chewing.)

TWO: Better?

THE MERCENARY: Not just the taste. I thought she—I thought I had *her* in
my head.

ONE: Her who?

THE MERCENARY: The girl.

ONE AND TWO: Impossible.

NARRATOR: The two who live in the dark called it impossible,

But the Mercenary was another story.

He had seen Moll at work, you see.   ***(Sound of cogs in her head.)***

He had seen her determine the 139th digit of Pi.

He had seen her petting Schrödinger's cat.   ***(Sound of a content kitty.)***

He had seen her use a particle thrower

To isolate peanut butter from jelly.   ***(Sound of solitary jelly.)***

So you see, he began to believe it *was* possible
For her to enter his skull like a cat burglar
And kick things about as she pleased.
Anyone using the Third Ear might have
heard him quaking in his boots.   *(Sound like an earthquake.)*

7.
In Which Moll Steps Into a Trap.

NARRATOR: Like many compulsive people, Moll was a maker of lists.

MOLL: Objective 1. Locate the Mercenary.

> Objective 2. Destroy him utterly and totally and completely without mercy.

> Objective 3. Locate the Third Ear and rescue it from evil hands before it's too late.

> *(Sound of a pencil scratching.)*

NARRATOR: This she underlined several times.

MOLL: Before. It's. Too. Late.

NARRATOR: But where to begin? Reexamining the Mercenary's note for clues, she found something that had escaped her notice. At the bottom of the page, embossed letters reading:

> *(Sound of a jingly store bell jingling. We see the CLERK. It is the mercenary in DISGUISE.)*

MOLL:
"Friendly Glen's Pawnshop and Nick-Nackery."

CLERK:
Friendly Glen's Pawnshop and Nick-Nackery, How may I help you?

NARRATOR: Behind the counter was exactly the person you'd imagine there. An old widower with smiling cataracts and white hair sprouting everywhere but the top of his head.

CLERK: Miss? Are you looking for anything in particular?

MOLL: I'm looking for a greasy but somehow irresistible boy with a way of looking at you like he's trying to figure out what makes you tick which makes you feel so totally great and GOD HOW I LOATHE HIM.

CLERK: Did you pawn something recently?

MOLL: I said a boy, but he could be a man by now. Or a woman, for all I know. I don't know. Greasy though.

CLERK: A rebel.

MOLL: You remember!

CLERK: Nope. Just I know the type.

MOLL: Maybe you saw the machine, maybe? It has a stethoscope, antennae, headphones big as earmuffs? Disc on top like a satellite dish?

CLERK: Nothing like that. We got a special on musical instruments, though, if music is your thing. We got kazoos up the wazoo. Over here we got pick-wicklers.

(Sound like an ailing oboe.)

We got an old foozharp, belonged to Toskernini himself.

(Sound like a harp played with a tennis racket.)

We got a batwali banjo from the other side of the world.

(Sound of a dull thud.)

All she needs is new strings and…

(His CAR SALESMAN VOICE slipping through.)

she'll be off and running like a Ferrari fresh from a tune-up.

(Sound of a violent recognition.)

CLERK: What's the matter?

You're turning a funny color.

MOLL: You remind me of someone on the radio.

CLERK: People are always telling me I have a face for radio. But I'm very happy here in my shop.

MOLL: You must see a lot of things here.

CLERK: Yup.

(Three seconds of silence.)

MOLL: What have you seen?

is what I mean.

(Sound of a crisp twenty-dollar bill removed from a wallet.)

CLERK: I get your meaning.

MOLL: Do you know where good-looking rebels go when they quit this town?

CLERK: Usually they raft the river, cross the chasm, and mount the mountain.

NARRATOR: *(Trying to be part of the scene.)* It should be noted that in fairy stories, things always come in threes.

MOLL: And after that?

CLERK: They never come back, that's for sure.

MOLL: I had a cousin who rafted crossed and mounted. She was never heard from again.

CLERK: Could be she made it.

MOLL: More likely she was a meal for a mountain goat.

CLERK: I don't want to see a nice girl like you be goat-meal. Here. I have a AAA guide here, it's got all the shortcuts, all the bargains. Give it to you free of charge.

MOLL:

(Examining.)
"Rafting the River,
   Crossing the Chasm,
and Mounting the Mountain."
Ten Bucks a Day."

TRIPLE-A:
Rafting the River,
   Crossing the Chasm,
and Mounting the Mountain!

CLERK: Now don't say Friendly Glen never did anything for you.

MOLL: I can't find my machine.

I can't find my nefarious ex.

You take my money and give me an old travel book.

Friendly Glen, you're a *godsend.*

(Sound of the door jingling, then slamming.
Sound of an old-fashioned rotary phone.)

CLERK: Yeah it's me.

——

She came by.

——

Mousy little thing, yeah. Eyes like hot pokers, like there's something smoking behind there.

——

Just like we said, I pointed her toward certain death. Shouldn't trouble you again.

——

Yeah, but. This thing's starting to get sticky, morally speaking.
(He looks behind him—the coast is clear.)
I think I could use some more…
(Changing back into the MERCENARY.)
incentive.

8.

In Which Moll Consults the Oracle of the Everyday.

NARRATOR: She played tough, but Moll couldn't resist the conquest of a new read.

MOLL: Okay book, time to surrender your secrets to Moll.

(Sound of pages flipping fast.)

NARRATOR: Ever since she had taken that speed-reading course, Moll was accustomed to stripping a book of its meat in minutes, like piranha on an unfortunate heifer.

(Sound of pages flipping faster.
Voice of the Triple-A Guidebook, jolly and well-fed. Midwestern accent, perhaps?)

TRIPLE-A: Just eight miles south of the raging river, a most charming Bed and Breakfast awaits the weary traveler. Owned and operated by the Alteveers, a Dutch couple who cook tremendous, fluffy—

(Pages flipping faster even.)

NARRATOR: At first it seemed a travel guide like any other.

TRIPLE-A: —upstairs, distributed among a dozen nineteenth-century glass cabinets, is a superb selection of soapstones.

(Pages flipping fastest.)

NARRATOR: Until finally something caught her eye.

TRIPLE-A: —Embarking on a journey for business rather than pleasure, it is absolutely essential that one consult the Oracle of the Everyday.

MOLL: Oracle?

TRIPLE-A: The Oracle is not one person or another. The Oracle is whoever. The day before one commences an expedition, one should toss a housecat over one's left shoulder and then—

MOLL: Mom wouldn't like me throwing Muffin around.

NARRATOR: But what other option did she have?

(Sound of an airborne cat, then a gentle landing.)

MOLL: What now?

TRIPLE-A: Following the cat procedure, one should stop up one's ears and wait. The first person who crosses one's path will be the Oracle. When one opens one's ears again, one will be prepared to hear the prophecy.

NARRATOR: It took some time for somebody to come along.

(Sound of MOLL idly whistling.
Sound of muted footsteps—MOLL's ears are covered. Footsteps suddenly louder, to indicate that she has uncovered them.)

AMWAY SALESLADY: Hello, young person. Have you heard the good news about Amway?

MOLL: Was that my path you just crossed?

SALESLADY: Amway products are in over seventy percent of the nation's households. You might have Amway in your home right now and not even know it.

MOLL: I don't think so.

SALESLADY: Sounds like somebody has a case of Strip Mall Sickness. Amway's colorful, easy-to-use catalog should be just the cure you're looking for.

MOLL: Sorry.

SALESLADY: SORRY ISN'T GOOD ENOUGH.

MOLL: I'm going to leave now.

SALESLADY: Wait wait, I promise I'll behave. I just get so EXCITED about these PRODUCTS.

This being the birth month of Virgos, we have a special discount on all virgin items: Virgin of Guadalupe votive candles, extra-virgin olive oil, Madonna's *Like A Virgin* record. Even an acre of virgin forest for sale in the Adirondacks, really lovely property. No one's going anywhere these days without virgin-something, *that's for sure.*

NARRATOR: For an average intellect, this prophesy may have seemed abstruse.

But Moll remembered how in fifteenth-century Romania...

(Sound of cogs in her head.)

NARRATOR:	MOLL:
...boy-virgins were often used as guides when hunting down vampires.	...boy-virgins were often used as guides when hunting down vampires!

NARRATOR: Their purity was thought to attract the undead like bears to honey.

MOLL: Eureka!

NARRATOR: Satisfied, she bought a bottle of the olive oil for her mother and sent the saleslady on her way.

SALESLADY : Thank you, dear — Tell a friend about Amway!

(The cogs in her head again, so loud this time that the NARRATOR has to shout over them:)

NARRATOR: Then she sat down for a GOOD LONG THINK.

MOLL: Do I *know* any boy virgins?

9.

In Which Moll Sets Off Toward Certain Death.

OLIVER: Do I have, like, a sign on my forehead? Is there a big scarlet V up there?

MOLL: Probably it would be a lily-white V. Only the As are scarlet.

OLIVER: Moll.

MOLL: Ollie. We've known each other since Pampers. We talk, right? If something happened, you'd have told me.

OLIVER: Don't be so sure.

MOLL: All right. What's it like then?

OLIVER: What?

MOLL: Fucking.

OLIVER: It's like there's a great beautiful flower opening inside of you.

MOLL: Nobody who had sex would say that.

OLIVER: I'm positive. The flower opens and shoots big blossoms of good feeling all through you.

MOLL: Isn't that what Ms. Hanrahan told us back in Sex Ed?

(A suspicious pause.)

OLIVER: No.

MOLL: That was six years ago!

OLIVER: Stop rubbing it in.

There was Madeline Stokeler, we were close but then—

I'm very picky.

MOLL: Didn't Madeline run off with that kayak instructor?

OLIVER: So why do you need this thing back so bad?

MOLL: This "thing" has power I don't even understand.

In the wrong hands…

(Sound of a portentous musical riff.)

Yeah.

OLIVER: What's in it for me?

MOLL: I'm a very clever girl, Ollie. Maybe you've heard?

I can make a potion so that next time around, Madeline won't be able tell you from Joe Kayak and his rock-hard haunches. Or forget Madeline altogether, and I can invent you an android dominatrix with a hydraulic—

(Sound like a jungle cat.)

OLIVER: Excuse me.

MOLL: That came from you?

OLIVER: That was my libido.

MOLL: *(Amused.)* Oh my god. Gross.

OLIVER: I'll be right back.

(Sound of footsteps, a doorknob, a splash.)

MOLL: What are you doing in there?

OLIVER: A good dunk in cold water, usually that helps me cool down.

MOLL: Then it's all settled. We're questing together.

OLIVER: Wait a minute! I didn't say—

NARRATOR: And so Moll set off on the road, with her guidebook, her virgin and a great sackful of inventor essentials.

(Sound like a door slamming.)

OLIVER: Oof! What do you have in here, bricks?

MOLL: You never know when masonry might come in handy.

NARRATOR: If one were to dig deeper into the sack, one would also find:

MOLL: Double-sided tape,
Five kinds of screwdriver,
Portable fan…

NARRATOR: In case of a desert sojourn.

MOLL: Seam-splitter,
Hot glue gun,
Ceiling wax…

NARRATOR: On the occasion of a drab ceiling.

MOLL: Tupperware,
Twine—

NARRATOR: *Always* twine.

MOLL: Kerosene,
Kindling…

NARRATOR: In the event of a flash Ice Age.

MOLL: My Ls are especially well-stocked:

NARRATOR: Laughing gas,
Lederhosen,
Load-bearing Leechee nuts—

OLIVER: You *alphabetized* it?

MOLL: Yes.

OLIVER: What *are* you, some kind of obsessive?

(Sound of thin ice.)

Some kind of compulsive?
Some kind of obsessive-compulsive—

MOLL: THIS IS MY LIFE, OKAY? THIS IS WHAT I DO.

NARRATOR:

Moll looked at him with her hot poker eyes, *(Sound like a laser pistol.)*
A vein throbbed in her neck,
And Oliver made a mental note to… *(Sound of a pencil scratching.)*

OLIVER AND NARRATOR: … never ever question the girl again.

MOLL: ELSE I MIGHT LOSE MY TEMPER.

10.

In Which We Hear to Fear the Worst.

(Overlapping Moll's last line:)

ONE AND TWO: Owwww!

NARRATOR: Back in their lair, the darkdwellers heard the questers' every step.
Not only that,
They could hear the ghosts of
footfalls felled four hours before;   **(Sound of phantom footfalls.)**
They could hear where the air
Had been wounded stride by stride;   **(Sound like banshee shrieks.)**
They could even hear the slow progress
of yesterday's dinner through mazy intestines.   **(Sound like a hefty earthworm.)**

MOLL: FLEET THOSE FEET, SLOWPOKE!

TWO: Aiyeeeee!

ONE: My ears are ringing!

TWO: She has a *voice* on her, that one.

THE MERCENARY Maybe if we turned down the volume?

TWO: Like she's down deep in the contraption itself.

THE MERCENARY: She's stronger than we expected.

ONE: The virgin will ruin everything.

TWO: Everything will be ruined, yes.

ONE: A proposal, gentlemen.

THE MERCENARY: Clearly it's a matter of seducing the virgin.

TWO: That's what I was going to say.

ONE: But who to do the seducing?

THE MERCENARY: *(Speaking of himself.)* I know just the man for the job.
(Sound of their diabolical laughter.)

NARRATOR: While the Mercenary was happy to do almost anything for mercenary reasons…
(Sound of a cash register's ka-ching.)
…for the opportunity to stretch his dark talent, and for the mean thrill of
messing with innocent heads, he couldn't help wondering why the
machine was so important, so *sacred*, almost, to his employers.

ONE: Not simply sacrosanct

TWO: Nothing simple about it

ONE: No, rather it's

ONE AND TWO: Sacrosanctimonious!

NARRATOR: At this, the Mercenary raised a single eyebrow
   (which is hard to do.)

ONE: You can hear essences inside accidents!

TWO: You can hear ugly things behind everyday talk!

ONE AND TWO: Listen close.

   *(Sound of two sets of footsteps. MOLL's are lighter and quicker, OLIVER already
   lagging.)*

   *(In the following, we hear MOLL's interior thoughts—the truth behind her lie.
   Just as in the interior-monologue scene, she should speak the italized lines into
   a body mike or standing microphone—some kind of reverberant modification
   of her voice.)*

OLIVER: Is it far?

MOLL: Nah. *The farthest.*

OLIVER: Is it steep?

MOLL: Nope. *The steepest.*

OLIVER: Is it dangerous?

MOLL: No sirree. *The dangerousest.*

OLIVER: Is it—

   (MOLL's soothing voice turning into something more dread-inducing.)

MOLL: Listen, *Virgin.*

   You can rest assured that this harmless extended field trip *might quite possibly involve the Raging River*, that it has not a whit to do with the *treach-
   erous maw of the Cadaversome Chasm, and you can bet your life it'll take us*
   safely if circuitously around *the corpifying peaks* of the Mighty Mountain!

OLIVER: *(Nonplussed.)* Um. That's a relief.

MOLL: Would I lie?

ONE AND TWO: Did you hear?

ONE: Fibs are no accident—

TWO: No sir—

ONE AND TWO: They speak the will of the Gods.

ONE: Intention is oracle—

TWO: Decorum is Delphic—

ONE AND TWO: At least to those who have the ears to ear.

TWO: Our ears are not yet capacious enough to hear the Grand Design.

ONE: But if we practice—

TWO: Yes, if—

ONE AND TWO: The God of the Third Ear will make us Perfect,
And we will listen Beyond the Border, Beyond the Order of Things!
NARRATOR: By this point, the Mercenary was sorry he'd asked.

And the Narrator found herself speculating whether the machine's capacity to perceive the imperceptible human interior might very well lead to her very own obsolescence— *(Running out of breath.)* But this grim reverie was mercifully brief, for there was a story that begged telling, and in the dismalest dark, the two listened on…

TWO AND OLIVER: Wait.
ONE AND MOLL: What.
TWO AND OLIVER: Did you hear?
ONE AND TWO: The raging river!

(Five seconds each of:
An educational filmstrip describing a salmon's journey.
Sound of turbines spinning in a hydroelectric plant.
The song "Take Me to the River."
A commercial for an extra-strength feminine hygiene product.
Twain's description of Huck setting out on the river.
An interview with a woman after going over Niagara Falls in a barrel.)

11.
In Which Oliver is Tempted For the First Time, Not the Last.

NARRATOR: The questers cooled their heels in the shallows.
OLIVER: This has to be the place.
MOLL: Lemme find in the book. It says here:
TRIPLE-A: The Raging River carves an S-curve through the picaresque Glendall Forest—
MOLL: Yada yada yada—Ooh, listen to *this!*
TRIPLE-A: The forest, it should be known, is populated with satyrs, who travel in a pack or else not in a pack, but always—
MOLL: Do they travel in "packs," really? There should be a special word.
OLIVER: Whales in a pod. Crows in a murder. Satyrs in a—
TRIPLE-A: —PACK or else not in a pack, but always aroused in beastly lust. Customarily, they will have furred, muscular legs, caprine noses, engorged members, and goatees, twinned at the chin in goatish wisps.[2] Many consider satyrs a danger, but an incident has not occurred since a woman with a

---

[2] Pausanias, *Guide to Greece*

lame leg lagged behind her orienteering group, eleven years past. She was ravished by the satyrs, not only in the usual place but all over her body.[3]

OLIVER: Moll. I don't have a good feeling about this.

MOLL: Eleven *years*, worrywart. Plus, they only go for naiads and draiads and maenads. Only the ads and the nads—*I'm* the one should be worrying.

OLIVER: I guess.

MOLL: I'll go make us a way across. Remember: Don't interrupt me while I'm inventing. It's DANGEROUS.

OLIVER: What's so dangerous about thinking?

MOLL: I can't tell you / it's…

OLIVER: —or you'd have to kill me?

MOLL: …personal. You'll be fine, Ollie. I have every confidence in you. Just holler if there's an emergency. We've got pepper spray in the sack, between paste and pickled plums.

(Sound of her footsteps fading.)

OLIVER: Just me then. Alone in the darkening, spookening forest. Quality time. Me and my solitary brain.

(Sound like a jungle cat.)

OLIVER: Oh, and you too. But not for long…

(Sound of a splash.)

Cold cold COLD raging river!

(Sound of hoofsteps approaching.)

OLIVER: Moll?

(The hoofsteps quite close now. We also hear a jug of liquid, swaying. Slosh slosh slosh. Then stillness. It is the MERCENARY, disguised as a SATYR.)

SATYR: Hullo, pet.

OLIVER: Moll? Emergency!

SATYR: Out of the reach of hearing, pet. We'd ask her along for a toss, but it's just us two for tea.

(Sound of sniffing.)

OLIVER: You smell like a stable.

(Sound of vigorous, animal sniffing.)

SATYR: You smell like clean young man.

(Pause.)

OLIVER: Your breath is like a saloon.

SATYR: Takes an awful lot to get me cock-eyed these days.

OLIVER: Cock—?

---

[3] ibid.

SATYR: Hotsy-totsy, flummoxed, *lubricated.*

OLIVER: You mean drunk?

SATYR: As a skunk.

> Have a sip.

> Makes you see double and feel single, they say.

OLIVER: Ha!

SATYR: Think you're too good for my wine?

OLIVER: I'm questing, so you see it wouldn't *do.*

SATYR: I don't see any quest, I just see a nice young boy-pet in the forest

> With nothing to pass his time and I just thought I'd *share.*

> A cup of the God, a swig of salvation.

OLIVER: I don't think…

SATYR: A drop at least.

> So sweet you'll wish you were all nose.

OLIVER: I guess…

> *(The SATYR tips the flask over OLIVER. Sound of glug glug glug.)*

SATYR: Good stuff, huh?

OLIVER: It's…woodsy.

SATYR: More?

OLIVER: Just another drop—

> *(The SATYR tips the flask again. More glug.)*

OLIVER: —Or two. Ohmigosh. Are those hooves?

> *(OLIVER hiccups.)*

SATYR: All the better for dancing clippety-clop to the panpipes.

> *(Sound of a bar or two on the panpipes.)*

OLIVER: Are those—*(Hiccup.)*—horns?

SATYR: All the better for lancing grapes on the highest vine.

> *(OLIVER hiccups.)*

SATYR: Nasty case of the hickey-ups. Better have more wine to wash 'em down.

> *(OLIVER drinks. Glug.)*

OLIVER: That a tail?

SATYR: All the better for. Hmm.

> **(Sound of his tail wagging in thought.)**

OLIVER: Must be good for—*(Hiccup.)*—something.

SATYR: A tail makes you move different. Like you own the world.

> *(Sound of the SATYR dancing, accompanying himself on his pipe: he plays the guitar lick from the Stones' "Miss You."*
> **Get-it-on music.)**

> Now you.

OLIVER: Like this?

SATYR: Looks like Doris Day doing the cakewalk.

It's all in the pelvis, Elvis. *Move.*

OLIVER: I feel silly.

SATYR: Pretend that it's another time ago

Bacchus has made the river run wine just because he can.

You lap at the grapey goodness and

Soon you're feeling like the fucketeer of the forest

—What else is wine for, right?

Soon your groin is barking for fresh kill:

Cur non tam latera ecfututa[4].

OLIVER: Are you speaking English?

SATYR: *Cur non tam latera ecfututa.*

OLIVER: Ecfuc—? Ecfut toot?

SATYR AND OLIVER: *Ecfututa.*

SATYR: *Good.* Here now.

Just a touch.

(Sound like a society lady luxuriating in a fur coat.)

OLIVER: *(One slushy slurry sentence.)* I knew it I knew what you are Are you one of those YOU'RE NOT HUMAN are you?

SATYR: *Ecfututa.*

OLIVER: But you chase mostly naiads and draiads and maenads Iheardmostly-right?

SATYR: Not many of those about the woods any more.

Nothing but deers and mooses to keep us company.

Anything pink starts to look real nice.

OLIVER: *(Guileless and very drunk.)* I'm pink.

SATYR: I know.

(Sound like a jungle cat.)

OLIVER: Mollllllllllllllllllll!

(Sound like a gust of wind.)

MOLL: I'm here I'm here!

NARRATOR: And just like that...

OLIVER: Um, false alarm?

MOLL: Is that booze on your breath?

(A suspicious pause.)

OLIVER: Maybe.

---

[4] Catullus

MOLL: You just thought, to pass the time?

OLIVER: I had an encounter.

MOLL: *(Quick but grave.)* Was it a salamander, a molecule or a beautiful woman?

OLIVER: No no and no.

MOLL: Then tell me on the way. I made us a raft for crossing.

OLIVER: You "made" a raft.

MOLL: It's no big deal. A couple old rain slickers, some party balloons, fishing line, and a jar of molasses to resin the bottom.

OLIVER: How are we supposed to steer?

MOLL: I carved an oar from one of the saplings down there.

OLIVER: Moll, you *scare* me.

12.
In Which Plots Are Thickened.

NARRATOR: At that same instant, in the very dark place…

TWO: He failed.

ONE: If at first you don't succeed….

TWO: You and your platitudes.

ONE: Patience, Two. Only the faithful will pierce the fold and hear with fiercer ears.

TWO: Wait.

ONE: What.

TWO: Did you hear?

ONE AND TWO: The Chasm.

> *(Five seconds each of:*
> *A news report of a New York City blackout.*
> *A New England matron explaining how to dismember a lobster.*
> *A promo for a television show about Extreeeeme Sports.*
> *A rousing rendition of "There's a Hole in My Bucket, Dear Liza."*
> *Dante describing the lowest circle of Hell.*
> *The echo of the echo of the echo of someone saying "Echo.")*

NARRATOR: Far flung from the chasm and the raging river, in the finest cul-de-sac of the peaceful 'burb, Moll had been missing for one whole day. Apart from notifying the police, calling the PTA phone tree, posting her picture on local telephone poles, and hiring a skywriter to scrawl "Come

Back To Us, Moll" in great puffy clouds from horizon to horizon, her parents didn't know what to do.

FATHER: Into thin air!

MOTHER: That Garth with the shifty eyes is behind this.

FATHER: *(Mocking her earlier assessment.)* Garth with the green green eyes.

(A curdled moment between MOTHER and FATHER.)

NARRATOR: They tried to take comfort in routine.

(Sound of radio static.)

COMMERCIAL ANNOUNCER: ...disappeared last Thursday. She was last seen in the company of a certain Garth,

Last name unknown, 5'8" to 5'10", complexion fair, hair greasy.

This just in: Nine in ten officials agree! Hot dogs are bursting with ultra-healthy supervitamins, which is no surprise, seeing as they contain just about everything.

Starve a cold, maybe, but feed a fever with Hilberson's all-beef foot-long finest!

And now, without further ado, the next give-you-the-creepsing episode of "*Death* and the Music Teacher."

(Sound of a hand slammed on a desk.)

WACHTEL: Cellos don't just up and walk away, Miss Kendrick. Where is your musical chum?

MISS KENDRICK: I helped him escape, Mr. Wachtel. He's free now.

WACHTEL: The Smithsonian offered me seven figures for him, and the Russians even more. You didn't really think you could keep this on the hush?

(Sound of a hush.)

WACHTEL: We have a way of dealing with people who won't give up their deep-and-darks. You ever hear of Cambodian water torture?

MISS KENDRICK: You mean the bit that goes

drip drip drip?

WACHTEL: Someting altogether less simple, Miss Kendrick. First, some not insubstantial body of water is introduced to your petite solar plexus. (I saw a Flemish dignitary swallow thirty-seven liters once, but he was altogether more...voluminous than yourself.) Next, my man Big Pete trusses you with your legs shooting skyward and your head dusting the floor. In this fashion, the full weight of your stomach is permitted to press on the lungs and heart until...kablooie.

MISS KENDRICK: I'm not afraid of a little...trussing.

WACHTEL: Let it begin, Pete.

(Sound of heavy rope.)

WACHTEL: You remember my associate.

MISS KENDRICK: The strong silent type.

(Sound of water flowing.)

WACHTEL: This will hurt, Miss Kendrick. You just give us a scream when you're ready to let the cat out of the bag.

(Sound of spitting.)

MISS KENDRICK: Bullseye.

WACHTEL: *(Wiping his eyes.)* The funnel, Pete. We've got ourselves a spitter.

MISS KENDRICK: Used to be I could hit a tin can at forty yards, back on the farm.

WACHTEL: This is your last chance, Kendrick. Where's our musical friend?

MISS KENDRICK: He's beyond here-or-there. He's past this-or-that.

NARRATOR: At that exact instant…

OLIVER: What's that down in the river?

NARRATOR: Something-or-other was floating in the tall reeds on the riverbank.

MOLL: Like Moses!

OLIVER: Looks like.

MOLL: A body?

OLIVER: A billygoat?

NARRATOR: Upon closer inspection, the something-or-other turned out to be a cello case.

OLIVER: I used to play back in fifth grade but they said
my fingers were too stubby and that was that.

MOLL: There's a note.

(Oliver reads.)

OLIVER: "Whoever you are…"	MISS KENDRICK: Whoever you are, Please make sure he stays in tune. And protect him from the very hot and the very cold. And for heaven's sake treat him well and you will be rewarded with the
"sweetest music you've never heard."	"sweetest music you've never heard."

MOLL: "Never" heard?

OLIVER: Must be a typo.

(Sound of latches undone, with difficulty.)

MOLL: Probably out of tune.

(Oliver plucks a string.
Sound of an A-string.
Although we see this projection, there is no corresponding sound. The FOLEY
ARTIST *and the* NARRATOR *take notice, alarmed.)*

OLIVER: That's strange.

MOLL: What.

OLIVER AND NARRATOR: Not a sound.

(The NARRATOR *covers her own mouth – she hadn't meant to speak.)*

MOLL: Try the other strings.

(He does: One, two, three.
Sound of a D, a G, a C.
Again, the FOLEY ARTIST *doesn't succeed in producing a sound.*
The MERCENARY *listens, at the machine. A three-way split scene, rapidly:)*

THE MERCENARY:

Curious…

| | OLIVER: |
| | What? |

Nothing at all.

| | MOLL: |
| | Wait— |

Something's wrong. Something's there.

You can *feel* it, almost.

Like a thickening of the air.

MISS KENDRICK: I told you, Mr. Wachtel:

He's a very special cello.

NARRATOR: For you see, it seemed the instrument only resonated in the infrasonic realm. The notes, too low to be heard by the ear, could only be felt
on the skin. Instead of high and low, the cello played hot and cold,
smooth and rough. (Infrasonic waves, let it be known, can be quite con-
founding to sonar and other technological listening devices.)

THE MERCENARY: No use fiddling.

WACHTEL: You'll confound me no further, Miss Kendrick.

MOLL: Do you feel?

OLIVER: Like all of a sudden the tropics.

WACHTEL: The funnel, Pete.

MOLL: We're taking it with us.

WACHTEL: Open wide, Miss Kendrick.

MISS KENDRICK: *(Her Oscar-winning moment.)* Tell me, Mr. Wachtel, have you
ever loved something enough to set it—*glurg!*

WACHTEL: There now, nice and snug.

(Sound of water flowing into a funnel.)

NARRATOR: This wasn't the escapist evening Mother and Father had planned.

MOTHER: I'm going to turn it off.

FATHER: No, I want to hear.

(Sound of water crescendos over the following, until the NARRATOR must shout to be heard.)

NARRATOR: Mother looked at her husband and recognized a kind of mad expectation in his eyes. For it seemed to Father that the voices coming from that little box, from that blackest nowhere, were the last whisper-thin thread of the COMFORTABLE LIFE THEY HAD ENJOYED ONLY YESTERDAY.

(The deafening sound subsides. The NARRATOR regains her composure.)

NARRATOR: Back on the wrong side of the river, the questers approached the cadaversome chasm, their backs aching from the extra load…

OLIVER: Why exactly are we bringing the mutant cello?

MOLL: Stop whining.

NARRATOR: …their shoes steaming from traveling on *foot* all day.

(Sound of an automobile.)

They had been traveling on foot all day.

(Sound of an airplane.)

After an entire day on foot…

(Sound of a bicycle horn.)

NARRATOR: At this point, the Narrator wondered what she'd done to deserve this. She wondered why three years at the Royal Speech Academy had so ill-prepared her for the trials of tales that don't behave as they're told.

She wondered on her future career prospects: What was to become of her stint behind the desk at Masterpiece Theater? Her narration of the Great American Novel? On a larger scale, she wondered if a sense of narrative Order would ever return to the universe.

(The NARRATOR is closer to us than she has ever been.)

—Pig-dithers!,

she said to herself, shaking these feckless thoughts from her head.

—There is a deep and secret fountainhead in me: The power of the third person.

Where most could only say something sodden and expected, like "I love you," she could describe the quickening of the pulse, the simmering of the blood above 98.6, the dilating of the pupils, the inevitable goosing of the bumps, and the streak of a vulnerable smile across the face of the smitte-nee.

She was necessary, then. *Eminently* necessary.

Civilized words were more than a match for roguish noises, be they clan-gor or cacophony or something else too terrible to imagine. And this thought made her brave, for the time being.

13.
In Which Oliver Learns a Dark Secret.

NARRATOR: *(Resolutely.)* So the questers continued, one *foot* after another…

MOLL: Let's see some hustle!

NARRATOR: …until they reached a place where
they could quest no further.

OLIVER: I can't see the bottom.

(MOLL *takes* GARTH's *ring from around her neck and drops it.*
They watch it fall and fall and fall and fall.)

MOLL: One Mississippi two Mississippi three Mississippi four Mississippi five Mississippi six

(Sound like a penny off the Empire State Building.)

OLIVER: *(Breathless.)* Holy.

MOLL: *(Breathless.)* Mississippi.

NARRATOR: So it seemed she'd rid herself, unceremoniously, of the last trace of Garth, at the same time deducing…

MOLL: Five-point-five Mississippis at a rate of thirty-two feet-per-second-squared makes

NARRATOR: …the precise depth of the chasm.
They set up camp in the shade of a nearby fig tree.

MOLL: Don't do anything funny, okay? Don't touch anything don't talk to anything don't DO anything.

(*Sound of* OLIVER *plopping down under the* FIG TREE. *It is the* MERCENARY *in disguise.*)

MOLL: Just sit quiet and find us a place to stay tonight in the book.

OLIVER: What if something wants to have sex with me again?

MOLL: That's the *idea.* We want the evil somethings to be attracted to your innocence so that we can capture them and make them hand over the machine, see, but until then you have to resist the bait or you'll lose your special virgin power, see?

OLIVER: *(Skeptical.)* Special virgin power.

MOLL: Just—Be good.

(Sound of MOLL's parting footsteps.)

TRIPLE-A: Wild figs line both sides of the Cadaversome Chasm. While the outside of the ripe fig remains sickly green, the inside flesh is red as strawberries.

OLIVER: Snoozeworthy old book.

TRIPLE-A: The fig's powers to enchant are known as far back as Biblical times…

(We might continue to see TRIPLE-A's mouth moving, silently.)

NARRATOR: Oliver was exhausted from traveling on foot all day…

(Sound of a hovercraft.)

NARRATOR: …and the guidebook was not gripping enough to keep him in the waking world.

(Sound of OLIVER dozing.)

TRIPLE-A: …the tree withered under Christ's righteous gaze, and for evermore, the fig became known as the tree that is not what it seems.

(Sound of ripening figs.

We can detect, faintly, the melody of the Stones' "Miss You.")

FIG TREE: Get a whiff of my big firm figs,

Go daffy, go gaga

For my ready freshfruits.

Furry on the out, flesh on the in

Form a line, come and sniff, be my guinea pig.

OLIVER: *(In his sleep, slowly.)* Don't care for figs. Taste funny.

FIG TREE: Funny perhaps, fragrant for sure.

My fine little wag, you're barely a twig,

In need of feed. Figs

Is food for good fit boys,

Like truffles is for pigs.

You'll go all goosy if you gobble, if if if

If you goible full foosy, giff you fibble gigs if.

OLIVER: *(Enchanted snoring.)* Iffffff—

Guh—

Ifffff—

Guh—

FIG TREE: There's a goody gumdrop.

Just a sniff and you'll go stiff.

Don't be a prig with my fat friendly figs.

OLIVER: Gotta fetch gotta heft gotta lift me a big firm

Thought-fogging tig-snifting gifty-goffing finger-licking fig

Oh friendly fruits—

(Sound of the branch lowering, heavy with figs.)

friendly fruits—

(Branch even lower, fruit even heavier.)

friendly fruits—

(The branch bent almost to his mouth, the figs heavy as bombs. MOLL runs on.)

MOLL We're good to go. I made us a bridge.

Oliver?

(The ripening sound and his breathing.)

What on Earth?

OLIVER: Go all goosy for a folly-gobbing—

(She shakes him.)

MOLL: What's wrong with you? Wake up.

OLIVER: —fifty-giggling, giddy-fisting...

MOLL: *(To the darkness around her.)* I know you're here.

(Shaking him again.)

Oliver!

OLIVER: Giff us a friggin' fig!

MOLL: It's a spell—wake up wake up wake—

OLIVER: Stop the shake,

I'm awake I'm awake!

(Sound like a gust of wind.)

MOLL: Wait a minute. Where'd it go?

OLIVER: I just nodded off for a second.

MOLL: Trees don't just up and disappear. It's not their style.

NARRATOR: Moll lifted a finger in the air, testing the last trace of that suspiciously solitary gust...

MOLL: Didn't they ever warn you about figs in Sunday School? They're never what they seem.

NARRATOR: ...Lifted her nose in the air and detected, she thought, the faintest whiff of styling gel and another, more ineffable presence—a kind of acrid cologne, a kind of

MOLL: *(Under her breath.)* Boy-musk.

OLIVER: What?

MOLL: *(Pointing in direction of the wind.)* Thataway.

OLIVER: Moll. Wait. You're bleeding.

(So she is.)

Your ear.

MOLL: Must be ketchup.

NARRATOR: Reared by trusting parents, Moll had never developed into a deft fibber.

OLIVER: What's going on?

NARRATOR: Maybe it was time he knew.

MOLL: It needed a piece of me.

OLIVER: You are the most baffling person.

MOLL: *(With difficulty.)* I put in everything *and* the kitchen sink and it was shiny and big but still it wouldn't go, so…

(Sound of smacking the side of her head—A remembered sound rather than a live one.)

MOLL All it took was the smallest piece,

But it hurt like…the Devil.

OLIVER: You mean a piece, like, metaphorically?

MOLL: Except sometimes I have trouble hearing on this side, low pitches especially and last week I got a nasty infection and now, with this altitude—would you hand me a Band-Aid?

OLIVER: —

MOLL: Between the backgammon board and the birth control.

(Pause.)

OLIVER: *(Rapidly.)*

This doesn't sound healthy, / no,
if you think I can be some kind of
accessory any longer to this kind of
aggro-pervo Festival of Self-Mutilation.
I mean, it's one thing with you
offering me up as bait to all manner
of man and beast but now —

(Pause.)

MOLL: *(Rapidly.)*

You
think you can tell me about *healthy*,
you neck-deep in your citrus-scented
Mr. Clean Festival of Self-Denial?
I mean, and I don't know how you'd
know what it *is* to be needed the way
the machine NEEDS ME HOW IT
FEEDS on me and I don't want you
to know, I do not want you to, no.

OLIVER: Jesus, Moll.

You're the mad scientist *and* the monster.

You're your own Frankenstein.

(A dark pause.)

MOLL: Excuse me. There's a chasm out there that isn't getting any shallower.

OLIVER: Wait. I didn't mean—

(Sound of her parting footsteps.)

NARRATOR: Meanwhile, in the cozily upholstered but otherwise bereft family den, the radio blathered on.

(Sound like a dam straining against floodwater.)

WACHTEL: Forty liters. I've never seen anyone endure like this.

(MISS KENDRICK speaks with great effort.)

MISS KENDRICK: I'm going to tell you a story I tell my students, Mr. Wachtel. There's no sense in dying quiet.

WACHTEL: There's no sense in dying at all, Miss Kendrick. Talk.

MISS KENDRICK: As long as I have the breath, I'm going to tell you the story of how music was invented.

(Sound like a dam straining.)

It was the god Hermes who first made something mute into something that could sing. The lyre. On the path outside his house one morning, a tortoise was waddling past...

WACHTEL: Is this a children's story?

MISS KENDRICK: Hermes knelt down to the tortoise to say, "Hello there, you shapely creature."[5]

(Sound like a dam.)

"Hel-lo," the tortoise replied, after some time,

for she was slow and steady.

WACHTEL: Is there going to be a hare in this story?

(Silence.)

NARRATOR: But the story never ended, because, quite suddenly…

(Sound like a dam breaking.)

…the sweet schoolteacher expired.

(MISS KENDRICK steps back from her microphone, becoming MOTHER.)

On the other end of the box, Mother and Father didn't know what to make of this. They had listened to the radio every night of their nineteen years of marriage, and they knew how plots were plotted. This was to be

[5] Louis Hyde, *Trickster Makes This World*

the part where the authorities burst into the sinister Wachtel's lair; or else it would be Miss Kendrick's swashbuckling boyfriend who put things right; or, at the very least, sweet Miss Kendrick would go out with a heart-rending speech, but this…

MOTHER: Nothing.

WACHTEL: Miss Kendrick?

(A stage whisper:) It's your line!

NARRATOR: Even Wachtel himself seemed not a little confused by the turn of events.

FATHER: Miss Kendrick?

(Sound of dead air.

In the following scene, a naturalism and a quiet we haven't seen before.)

MOTHER: She's gone.

Our daughter, she's.

Our daughter.

FATHER: What have you done.

MOTHER: What have I?—

FATHER: To encourage this…relationship.

MOTHER: *(A challenge.)* Sixteen years old.

FATHER: You were—living through her or I don't know.

MOTHER: She needed to leave her room and see for herself.

NARRATOR: Mother and Father sat there, in the dead air…

(Sound of dead air.)

MOTHER: Sometimes people need to leave to see.

FATHER: You don't mean…

NARRATOR: …the last remnant of their wholesome aural order…

MOTHER:

These last few days, *your* loss,
your talk the only thing…
of essence.

FATHER:
It doesn't make sense, the
way you're talking…

NARRATOR: …twisted out of shape, as if by a powerful, unseen hand.

FATHER: A woman in your position to a man in mine.

(Pause. She is stung.)

MOTHER: You do relish your little ring of power.

(Sound of dead air.)

NARRATOR: And the foreign words coming out of them felt somehow true, the sharp radio words jumping into their open mouths…

ONE: Soon,

TWO: Any second now,

ONE AND TWO: The God of the Third Ear will Pierce the Fold
And We Will Listen With Fiercer Ears
Beyond the Border, Beyond the Order of Things!

NARRATOR: With time ticking and daylight dwindling, Moll and Oliver set off across the seemingly bottomless chasm…

MOLL: Don't look down.

NARRATOR: …which swirled with the still-echoing voices of the unfortunates it had swallowed over the years.

(Sound of a circus.)

OLIVER: What's that sound?

NARRATOR: *(Impatient.)* The still-echoing voices of the unfortunates it had swallowed.

(Sound of a marching band.)

NARRATOR: *(Even more impatient.)* Horrible mangled voices. Writhing in eternal agony.

(Sound of a sock hop.)

ONE AND TWO: Did you hear?

ONE AND TWO: Yes.

TWO: Sounds starting to mutiny.

(Sound of the sock hop, the marching band, and the circus: a horrible trio.)

OLIVER: What's that awful music?

ONE AND MOLL: It won't be long now.

OLIVER: What do you mean?

MOLL: The oldest rule—*don't monkey with nature*—and I broke it.
It needed a piece of me and I worry.

OLIVER: You worry…

MOLL: That a piece of me will be the only way to stop it.

OLIVER: Stop it *what*.

(MOLL shakes her head.)

MOLL: *(Gravely.)* We may be encountering polyphonic timebleed, we may encounter residual environmental dissonance.

OLIVER: Residjama—?

MOLL: "Side effects." Kinks I could never unkink.

OLIVER: Example.

MOLL: For example:

> The sounds that have already sounded. The last word you said. The first words you ever said. They never went away. They just got smaller and smaller and smaller and smaller and smaller and —

OLIVER: I get it.

MOLL: Do you?

OLIVER: No.

MOLL: It was meant to be used sparingly. The machine—*futzes*, fundamentally, with the boundary between the audible and the inaudible and—once you're playing fast and loose with that boundary.... There's a cost to everything, you see.

OLIVER: You did this?

MOLL: Noise as we know it, the very Order of Things, is at stake.

ONE AND TWO: Did you hear?

MOLL: One day you're listening to toenails on a field mouse, next thing you know the whole world is an ungodly *[clang]*.

> *([ ] indicates a kind of noise pollution, an industrial onomatopoeia that seems to come from the actor's mouth in place of the intended word.)*

OLIVER: Something's the matter *[clash]* your voice.

> *(They look at each other: Uh-oh.)*

NARRATOR: For all of Moll's booksmarts, there was another factor she hadn't factored in.

MOLL: Pre-utterance *[tra-la-la]*-warp—it's incredible!

> *(The NARRATOR is quite close to us again.)*

NARRATOR: With words themselves now sullied, the Narrator suspected that her task could only get thanklesser.

> With the gap between thought and speech ever gaping; with the gulf between sound and action ever gulfing, the Narrator didn't feel so brave as before.

14.

In Which Oliver is Tempted for The Final Time.

ONE AND TWO: Did you hear?

ONE AND TWO: Yes.

ONE: Miss Smartylocks didn't think of *that*.

TWO: Yes but, listen over there.

ONE: Over where?

TWO: Higher there.

ONE: Oh *there.*

ONE AND TWO: The Mountain.

> *(Five seconds each of:*
>
> *The journal of a member of the Donner Party.*
>
> *Sounds of a high-speed ski race, complete with commentators and crowd.*
>
> *An angry Yeti.*
>
> *J.R.R. Tolkien describing Mount Doom.*
>
> *The song "Ain't No Mountain High Enough."*
>
> *A dry lecture explaining how mountains result from shifting tectonic plates.*
>
> *Sound of someone trying to breathe without oxygen.)*

NARRATOR: The mountain soon proved too mountainous for passage.

> *(Sound of OLIVER catching his breath.)*

MOLL: I'll go invent us a way over.

OLIVER: Are you *[gallop]* to *[slash]* yourself up again?

MOLL: Don't *[chatter]* to strangers this time. I'll be back soon.

> *(Sound of fading footsteps.)*

OLIVER: Gonna ace this.

Not gonna *[chatter]*, gonna mind my own business.

[Gallop] to show her she can't be the boss of—

> *(Footsteps approaching, from the other side of the stage. MOLL enters. It is the MERCENARY in disguise.)*

MOLL: Gonna show who, Ollie?

OLIVER: You got back so *[whoosh]!*

MOLL: *[Rumble]* are pretty straightforward.

I converted the raft into a hot-air balloon.

We'll just *[whoosh]* over the mountain, lickety-split.

OLIVER: Great, let's get *[gallop]*.

MOLL: What's the rush?

> *(Sound of an irregular heartbeat.)*

OLIVER: What was that?

MOLL: Nothing. Just a little arrythmia.

NARRATOR: She touched him on the arm, lightly.

> *(Sound of fingernails on a chalkboard.)*

OLIVER: What are *[ping]* doing?

MOLL: Let's listen to our *[growl]*, just this once.

OLIVER: All the *[tick-tock]* we've known each other, you never seemed too interested.

MOLL: Things aren't always *[hiss]* they seem, Ollie.

OLIVER: *[Boink]* been noticing that these last few days.

NARRATOR: She touched him on the cheek, lightly.

(Sound of a slithering tentacle.)

MOLL: Ever since *[boink]* first laid eyes on you...

OLIVER: *[Boink]* dunno. This is weird.

MOLL: Now I know why you're the only *[meeow]* in the eleventh grade.

OLIVER: *[Boink]* been saving myself.

MOLL: *[Hiss]* for?

OLIVER: True *[kazaam]* I guess, if I can find it.

NARRATOR: She touched him on the shoulder, lightly.

(Sound of something pulled up by the roots.)

MOLL: *[Kazaam]* isn't anything special. *[Kazaam]* doesn't make you whole.

[Kazaam] isn't all you need.

NARRATOR: She touched him on the groin, lightly.

(Sound of an ingrown toenail.)

MOLL: But fucking,

[rip] at least is enough to make *[ping]* forget yourself.

(Sound of the irregular heartbeat. They are very close.)

OLIVER: I know you're not her.

MOLL / THE MERCENARY: *(Both voices now.)* Why don't you run away then?

THE MERCENARY: Why don't you scream?

(OLIVER doesn't know.)

Then we proceed.

(The MERCENARY wraps OLIVER up in his shadow.

Sound like a present opened with great haste.)

GARTH	SATYR	FIG TREE	MERCENARY
			This will hurt this will *[slash]* so don't say you didn't ask for *[rip]*.
Just lie back and feel moody-like			

GARTH	SATYR	FIG TREE	MERCENARY
	Just thought I'd *share*		
		Just a sniff and You'll go	
			Easy. Easy. Easy. It's all in the *[gasp].* There. All done. *[Slash]* it, that's all there is to love.

(Sound of footsteps approaching. The real MOLL.)

MOLL: Good to go! *[Boink]* converted the raft into a hot-air balloon. We'll just *[whoosh]* over the mountain, lickety—

THE MERCENARY: You're too *[fizzle]*.

MOLL: *[Hiss]* do you mean?

THE MERCENARY: I taught your *[meeow]* the same lesson *[boink]* taught you.

MOLL: *(To OLIVER.)* You're…
(To the MERCENARY.) You.

THE MERCENARY: Me.

NARRATOR: Moll had anticipated this reunion with her first love, her nemesis. She had run it back and forth through her head many times…

MOLL: You're very *[splish]* at becoming things with two arms and two legs.

THE MERCENARY: I'm *[splish]* at roots and branches too.

MOLL: I *[shuffle]* it's not so easy becoming *[gobble]* abstract.

THE MERCENARY: You wouldn't think, but I can be a trail of *[whistle]*, I can be a gaseous *[psssh]*, I can even be an excited *[buzz]*.

MOLL: I *[shuffle]* there's one thing you can't do.

NARRATOR: …It had looped through her head so many times, it had become like a masterful duet she had written.

MOLL: *[Boink]* bet you couldn't be pure *[tra-la-la]*.

THE MERCENARY: I can be any *[tra-la-la]* I choose. *Pure.*

MOLL: I don't believe *[ping]*.

THE MERCENARY: *[Hiss]* kind of sound do *[ping]* want?

MOLL: How about, *[boink]* don't know, a ripple in a pond?

THE MERCENARY: *(Accepting the challenge.)* A *[ripple]* in a pond.

NARRATOR: The vain Mercenary cracked his knuckles…

(Sound like a man snapped in half, slowly. *)

NARRATOR: …and summoned all his arcane power. He tried to make it look effortless, but Moll, who had once studied the particulars of his face with an *innamorata's* intensity, could see the terrible strain as he fumbled for the frequency.

(Sound like something pulled up by its roots.
Sound of a slithering tentacle.
Sound of ripening.
Sound of panpipes.
Sound of an irregular heartbeat.
Sound of an irregular heartbeat.)

MOLL: *(Very quietly.)* Garth…

MERCENARY AS GARTH: Me babe.

NARRATOR: The very intimacy that brought her to the brink of triumph now caused her to hesitate.

MERCENARY AS GARTH: It was always me.

NARRATOR: And there was an instant…

MOLL: *(Believing a bit.)* **[Boink]** don't *believe* in you…any more.
I don't believe in *[kazaam]*.

NARRATOR: A moment when she felt it would be so easy to surrender to that easy old unction…

MERCENARY AS GARTH: Reform me. Babe.

NARRATOR: …But it was merely an instant.

MOLL: *(Sudden resilience.)* Any *[tick-tock]* now.
I said, pure *[tra-la-la]*.

NARRATOR: And she took a preemptive step back…

THE MERCENARY: Very well.

NARRATOR: Just in time for the Mercenary to rend himself forever from the physical realm…

(Sound of an irregular heartbeat.
Sound of hoofsteps.
Sound of glug glug glug.
Sound of hair gel.
Sound of long long eyelashes.)

---

* "Slowly" might be projected just after the rest of the sentence.

NARRATOR: …catching the perfect sound wave…

(*Sound of a ripple in a pond.*)

…a shapely ripple that diminished with every second…

(*Sound of a ripple,* fainter this time.)

…as ripples do. Softer and softer until he was too faint…

(*Sound of* a ripple, barely there.)

NARRATOR: (*Cont'd.*)

…even for the Third Ear to hear…

(*Sound of nothing there.*)

ONE: Gone!

TWO: Impossible!

NARRATOR: …spread too thin ever to reassemble.

MOLL: (*Exhausted but triumphant.*) Kid-simple.

NARRATOR: The darkdwellers, invisibly shaken, clung to the Third Ear, hoping for some sign of life from their henchman.

ONE: Our *[ripple]* defeated!

TWO: Don't panic, don't *[screech]*. He at least prevailed in the *[rip-slash]*.

NARRATOR: Moll turned to her visibly shaken companion.

MOLL: *[Hiss]* did you think *[ping]* were doing?

OLIVER: Isn't this the part where *[ping]* ask *[plink]* I'm okay?

MOLL: Nobody's *[gallop]* to be okay if the *[beep beep]* isn't stopped.

OLIVER: I didn't *[hiss]* to be part of your *[cuckoo]* mission.

The least *[boink]* could get out of it is some *[kerpow]*.

MOLL: If whoring *[pitter]* to all the flora and fauna *[patter]* as "action."

OLIVER: I'm not like *[ping]*. Most people *[roar]* like you! Most people need *[kazaam]*.

(*This sobers* MOLL.)

MOLL: Are *[ping]* *[gallop]* to be all right?

OLIVER: *[Boink]* think it's gone, my *[meeow]*.

MOLL: Then we're *[fizzle]*. Unless.

OLIVER: *[Hiss]*?

MOLL: *[Boink]* invent one last *[beep beep]*. A Swallower of *[tra-la-la]*.

NARRATOR: Many an intelligent person had set out to create a Sound-Swallowing device. Most likely because intelligent people need quiet for their thinking purposes, so naturally they pursue ways to mute the racket of the urban jungle.

OLIVER: It *[tra-la-la]* ambitious.

NARRATOR: There had been the Realists.

INTELLIGENT PERSON #1: Everything which might make a sharp sound will be covered with a thin layer of rubber.[6]

NARRATOR: There had been the Romantics.

INTELLIGENT PERSON #2: When I was on safari in Africa, all the native tribes wanted to hear about was snow. They were not astonished by its whiteness or its coldness so much as its ability to siphon sound from the air...

NARRATOR: And there had been the Loony Tunes.

INTELLIGENT PERSONS #3 & 4: A giant pair of earmuffs will be sent in to orbit by NASA. These earmuffs would be navigated by remote control or else by—

NARRATOR: Although every previous effort had been for naught, Moll was undaunted.

MOLL: It's simply a matter of collecting the *[tra-la-la]*, analyzing their wavelengths, and *[boomerang]* back exactly *[flip]* waves to meet them, thereby negating that *[tra-la-la]* completely.

OLIVER: Sounds great but *[oof]*—how much *[ugh]* do we have to carry the *[trill]*?

(He gives the cello a slap. Again, no sound.)

MOLL: Ollie, *[ping]* a genius! The *[trill]* is the key!

OLIVER: Thanks, but *[boink]* don't see how it's the *[clink]*.

NARRATOR: Moll, her hand trembling with cogitative adrenaline, pointed to the instrument.

MOLL: *[Trill]* for playing infra-*[tra-la-la]*. Do you feel the *[sizzle]* off it? Those waves are a weapon against *[tinkle]*!

15.
In Which Moll Makes A Sacrifice For the Good of the Planet.

NARRATOR: Moll took a deep breath and drew the bow across the instrument. Instead of music ringing out, they felt a cool stillness like an onsetting snow, then a warm equatorial current, then back again. The air flush with infrasound.

ONE: *[ ]* is that *[ ]*?

TWO: *[ ]* sucking *[ ]* sound!

ONE: Turn *[ ]* *[ ]* volume!

(A collision of voices and sounds, dazzling and almost incomprehensible:)

---

[6] Tristan Tzara, *Approximate Man and Other Writings*

BABBLE: Four score and seven years a*go-go don't leave me hanging*
   there like a yo-yo, wake me uptown on the six train get off
   at the first *stop! in the name of the* Father, the Son, and the
   Holy *Ghost of Christmas Past, Mister* Right is just around
   the corner so never go out without putting on your
   face-*first into the windshield, killing her instantly.*

NARRATOR: Every whatsit and whatnot of the Third Ear was going full throt-
   tle, fighting the silent undertow of the Sound-Swallowing cello, which
   began to rattle and quake from overexertion.

MOLL: *[Trill]* losing. Unless.

NARRATOR: Only two elements are necessary for the production of sound: An
   energy source and a vibrating agent…

MOLL: *[Trill]* needs a *[slash]* of me!

NARRATOR: …but a third element may be desirable:

NARRATOR	MOLL
A resonator,	A resonator!

to refine and project the distinctive
Timbre of the instrument.

OLIVER: No! *[Ping] [screech]* have *[gobble]* to spare!

MOLL: There's a *[ka-ching]* to everything, Ollie.

NARRATOR: *(Pressured.)* There was no time for deliberation, and Moll reached
   down her throat and suppressed her gag reflex and fished for a certain
   aperture in the laryngoid wall.

MOLL: The Ventricle of Morgagni!

NARRATOR: A superfluous organ in humans, very likely a remnant of the air
   sacs from primitive seafaring mammals. A sort of enhancer of noise…

MOLL: Inessential for sound production!

NARRATOR: Moll gave it a hearty tug…

   (From MOLL, a screech that ends abruptly.)

NARRATOR: And twined it to the bow of the cello, and played.

BABBLE: *Two out, bases loaded and he pitches a change*-up, I'm going to
   be a fireman or an astro-*not only is it great tasting, it's*
   full of Vitamin sea, by the sea, by the beautiful
   see the sun rise for the final time to get a new
   watch *where you're going, buddy, you*
   nearly killed me to go but I just
   couldn't abandon *you*
   know what they say:

Good things
come to
be or
not
to
(*A flash, then blackout. Some seconds of silence in the dark.*
Sound of dust settling.)

OLIVER: Moll?
I'm still here.
We're still here!

(*Light slowly returns. The Machine/Foley table is nowhere to be seen. Word projections continue, mute, with no machine to produce the sounds.*)

NARRATOR: Nothing was left of the Third Ear but a crater, thirty feet deep, where the splendid machine had soundlessly exploded, taking two dark-dwellers with it...

ONE AND TWO: (*Heavy echo.*) Beyond the Border, Beyond the Order!—

NARRATOR: ...to their curious notion of the everafter.

OLIVER: Moll? Say something.

(*Moll opens her mouth.*
Sound like a muzzled animal.)

NARRATOR: It seemed she had made a slight miscalculation.

OLIVER: Can't you speak?

(**Sound like a muzzled animal.**)

NARRATOR: The Narrator mopped her brow and looked on helplessly as they veered quite alarmingly—and decisively, this time—from the tale she had so tenaciously told.
Her words were torn from the past tense
and here they land in the present, riven and real.

(*The NARRATOR is close to us for good.*)

NARRATOR The Narrator tore up—the Narrator *tears* up—her elegant old ending into very small pieces. Nothing a Narrator can do now
but listen and wait and watch
and report what she sees.

16.

In Which Sounds Have Their Say.

Moll is paying her last respects to the machine.

OLIVER: This is something you can fix, right?
  (Sound like a muzzled animal.)
  You're not, it's not permanent?
  (Sound of cogs in her head.)
OLIVER: *(Cont'd.)*
  You'll make another something-or-other. You'll make other somethings.
  (Examining MOLL's throat.)
  Not anything quite so *thermonuclear* in proportion, of course,
  But first things first you'll make a prosthetic larynx, clear as a bell, you
  can do that, right?
  (Moll has seen something.
  He sees her seeing something.)
OLIVER: What is it?
NARRATOR: Deep down in the charred rock, beyond the parting smoke, lies
  Moll's stirrup bone, tiny but unmistakable.
OLIVER: What are you doing?
  (MOLL gesticulates.)
NARRATOR: *(Deciphering.)* If she can just reintroduce the bone to her body…
  (Sound like using a razor blade as a Q-tip.)
  Maybe, just maybe, it can tell her what it heard.
  (Sound of a satisfying "ping.")
OLIVER: Can you hear anything?
  (MOLL holds a finger to her lips: "Shhh…")
NARRATOR: She hears a whole world of things.

(Three seconds of quiet. OLIVER and The NARRATOR look on, expectantly.
Lights dim to a spot on MOLL, listening. The following projected, soundlessly:

Sound of a throat cleared.

Sound of cogs in her head.

Sound of radio static.

Sound of a string breaking.

Sound of long eyelashes.

Sound of a heartbeat in the dark.

Sound of an uncertain heart.

Sound of a heart broken.

Sound like a jungle cat.

Sound of footsteps.

Sound of hoofsteps.

Sound of cogs in her head.

Sound like a dam breaking.

Sound of dead air.

Sound of a slithering tentacle.

Sound like a jungle cat

Sound of cogs in her head.

Sound of a ripple in a pond.
Sound of a ripple
Sound of

Sound of the splendid machine exploding.

Sound of dust settling.

Sound of a great tome closing.)

MOLL: *(On microphone.)* Sound of cogs in her head.
Sound of cogs in her head.
Sound of cogs in her head.

(The light fades.)

END OF PLAY

At the Vanishing Point
by Naomi Iizuka

BIOGRAPHY

Naomi Iizuka's other plays include *36 Views*; *Language of Angels*; *Polaroid Stories*; *War of the Worlds* (co-written with Anne Bogart and SITI); *Aloha, Say the Pretty Girls*; *Tattoo Girl* and *Skin*. Her plays have been produced by Actors Theatre of Louisville, Berkeley Rep, the Public, GeVa, Campo Santo, Brooklyn Academy of Music, Dallas Theater Center, Soho Rep, and Tectonic Theater Project; workshopped at the Kennedy Center, the Taper, the McCarter, Hibernatus, Bread Loaf, Sundance, A.S.K. and PlayLabs; and published by Playscripts, Dramatic Publishing and Overlook Press. Iizuka is a member of New Dramatists and the recipient of a Whiting Award, a Stavis Award, a PEN Center/USA West Award for Drama, a Rockefeller MAP grant, an NEA/TCG Artist-in-Residence grant, a McKnight Fellowship, and Princeton's Hodder Fellowship.

HUMANA FESTIVAL PRODUCTION

At the Vanishing Point premiered at the Humana Festival of New American Plays in March 2004. It was directed by Les Waters with the following cast:

The Photographer	Bruce McKenzie
Pete Henzel, Martin Kinflein	Trey Lyford
Ronnie Marston, Ida Miller, Photographer's Wife, Maudie Totten	Claudia Fielding
Nora Holtz, Tessa Rheingold	Suli Holum
Mike Totten, Frank Henzel	Lou Sumrall
School Children, Children's Choir at St. Joe's	A.J. Glaser, Luke Craven Glaser, Madeline Marchal

and the following production staff:

Scenic Designer	Paul Owen
Costume Designer	Connie Furr-Soloman
Lighting Designer	Tony Penna
Sound Designer	John Zalewski
Original Music Composition	Tara Jane O'Neil
Properties Designer	April Hartsook
Stage Manager	Nancy Pittelman
Production Assistant	Brian Duff
Dialect Coach	Rinda Frye
Dramaturg	Tanya Palmer
Assistant Dramaturg	Dan LeFranc
Casting	Orpheus Group Casting
Directing Assistant	Meredith McDonough

CHARACTERS

the PHOTOGRAPHER
PETE HENZEL, a guide at the thomas edison house
    also: MARTIN KINFLEIN, an accountant at oertels brewery
RONNIE MARSTON, a bacon packager at fischers
    also:IDA MILLER, a retired schoolteacher
    MAUDIE TOTTEN, the owner of a bar near the stockyards
    PHOTOGRAPHER's WIFE
NORA HOLTZ, a student at the school for the blind
    also: TESSA RHEINGOLD, a painter at hadley pottery
MIKE TOTTEN, an employee at the impound lot and a painter
    also: FRANK HENZEL, a loin puller at fischers

CHORUS OF CHILDREN (three children):
PHOTOGRAPHER's OLDER SON
    also: MARTIN KINFLEIN's FATHER AS A YOUNG BOY
    the YOUNG FRANK HENZEL
PHOTOGRAPHER's YOUNGER SON
    also: the YOUNG PETE HENZEL
PHOTOGRAPHER's DAUGHTER
    also: the YOUNG NORA HOLTZ
    the YOUNG RONNIE MARSTON

PLACE
Butchertown

TIME
Past and Present

At the Vanishing Point was commissioned by Actors Theatre of Louisville, and developed with support from the NEA/TCG Theatre Residency Program for Playwrights.

Special thanks to: Dan Basila, Holly Becker, Turney Berry, Laura Lee Brown, the Butchertown Neighborhood Association, Emilya Cachapero, Helen Carle, John Catron, Claire Cox, Finn Curtin, Frederic and Julie Davis, Michael Bigelow Dixon, Susannah Engstrom, Caitlin Ferrara, the Filson Club, Mike Flynn, Kendra Foster, Peter and Sarah Fuller, Jen Grigg, Jon Jory, Gene

Hewitt, Fran Kumin, Damon Kustes, Dan LeFranc, the Louisville Public Library, Trey Lyford, Frazier Marsh, Marc Masterson, Guy Mendes, Bruce McKenzie, Elizabeth Nolte, Carrie Nutt, Tara Jane O'Neil, Tom Owen, Tanya Palmer, Alexandra Peterson, Martha and Richard Rivers, Ted and Jackie Rosky, Jim Segrest, Edward P. Seigenfeld, Sharon Sparrow, Sandy Speers, Terry and Mandy Tyler, United Food and Commercial Workers Local 227, the University of Louisville Library, Nancy Vitale, Les Waters, Madeleine Waters, Chloe Webb, Amy Wegener, James Welch, Steve Wilson, all the people at ATL who helped and advised during this residency, and most of all, thank you to the residents of Butchertown past and present for telling me their stories.

Inspired by the photographs of Ralph Eugene Meatyard, 1925–1972.

Bruce McKenzie (foreground), Madeline Marchal, A.J. Glaser and
Luke Glaser (windows/background) in *At the Vanishing Point*

28th Annual Humana Festival of New American Plays
Actors Theatre of Louisville, 2004
photo by Harlan Taylor

At the Vanishing Point

I. self portrait

darkness. the PHOTOGRAPHER *turns on a slide projector. his features are part in light, part in shadow.*

PHOTOGRAPHER: i want to show you something.
   (the PHOTOGRAPHER *clicks the projector forward. a projected image. a pixillated blur of dark and light.)*
PHOTOGRAPHER: now i could ask you what you see, and you might say, well you might say i don't know what i'm looking at, i don't know what that is, what the hell is that. and i could press you on it, and you might think it was some kind of a trick i was playing on you, if you were inclined to think that way, if you were a suspicious sort. but maybe if you kept looking at the thing, after a while, you might begin to see the shape of something, and maybe i tell you it's a person, and so you start looking at the image with that in mind, and you begin to discern the features of some famous figure, some illustrious soul like thomas edison, say. or maybe you see the face of an anonymous stranger, a stockyard worker or a soldier or a young girl in a school play. i think it's about a kind of focus. when you focus on something, what happens is your eye frames it in what is called the fovia which is a section of the retina made up of these cones that are connected to the brain's optical cortex and then your brain takes all your experience and knowledge of the world, and it forms a kind of context by which to process and make sense of that information. so that say you're standing in the middle of a field, and you hold up your hand in front of your eyes
   (the PHOTOGRAPHER *lifts his hand.)*
PHOTOGRAPHER: and everything else, the field and beyond, it becomes a blur, and all you see are the particulars of your own hand, the lines embedded in your palm, the whorls and ridges of your fingertips, and that makes you think of the time you cut yourself with the coping saw or the way the inside of a baseball glove, the way it feels, or the feel of your wife's hair warm from the sun, all of these things, more, and so you understand what it is you're seeing because of all the associations and memories of a whole lifetime, everything that makes you who you are comes together in that instant. but then let's say, let's say you shift your gaze to what lies beyond

your hand, and so the frame, it changes, and what was a blur is now clear and distinct. and what you see is a field, and in the distance,

(a glimpse of a human figure in the darkened place.)

PHOTOGRAPHER: a human figure slowly walking away from you, towards a point far in the distance, a point beyond the horizon line, beyond where you can see, and yet you try. i'm trying to sort this out right now, how the eye selects and organizes the immensity of the world i guess you could say, those parts that stay with you and those that fall away.

(the figure vanishes. the PHOTOGRAPHER clicks forward on the projector. a point of light in a field of darkness. it becomes gradually brighter as he speaks.)

PHOTOGRAPHER: i'm an optician by training, but i'm also, i'm a photographer. i'd say i'm fascinated by light, by the properties of light, by what the eye sees, and also what it misses, and i guess that's how i've gotten to where i am now. there was a young man came into my shop the other day. he was in the army, hundred and first airborne. grew up in louisville he told me. his mom and dad, his wife and kids, they all lived there still. now as it happens, i got family, some of my wife's family, they live in louisville. so we got to talking and we figured out he knew my sister-in-law. she owns a bar just east of downtown, down near where the stockyards are at, and he knew her. anyway this guy, he said he thought he might need glasses. turned out he had a severe astigmatism. how he lived that long seeing so poorly i cannot understand. you'd think someone woulda asked him what he saw when he was trying to read a blackboard or aim a gun. you'd think they would've, but i guess no one did. afterwards he said he never saw so clearly in his life. said he could see the leaves on the trees where before it had just been a wash of green. he could see people's faces really see them. he said it hurt to see everything so sharp and clear. to be that aware was almost too much, it was almost too much to bear. i tell you what, i'm going to pause here for just one second.

(the PHOTOGRAPHER goes to another table upstage on which sits a phonograph circa late 1960s and a cardboard box of lps.)

PHOTOGRAPHER: i have this hi-fi right here and some music. sometimes, sometimes i like to listen to music when i'm looking at my photographs. my wife says the music, it's like the music opens up a valve in your brain so more ideas can flow in, and sensations, too, all different kinds of sensations, and i have to say i'm inclined to agree. i have about a thousand lps i've collected over the years, jazz mostly. duke ellington, louis armstrong, dizzy gillespie, max roach, ornette coleman, you name it. i have it all cross-indexed by title and musician and then by record label, and then i have it cross-referenced so i can see who played on what track, and that's great because that way i can know that fats navarro played on this particular charlie parker song and bud powell was on the piano and i can know that right away. i like knowing that. i like having that information readily accessible. it lets me, it lets me see a bigger picture of how all these different people how they all fit together and intersect in this larger pattern, hold on here. i wanna, i wanna play you something, something you probably never heard before, and may never hear again.

(the PHOTOGRAPHER pulls a record out of the box, slips the record out of its sleeve, and puts it on the turntable with care.)

PHOTOGRAPHER: edgar allen poe's "the raven." as interpreted by buddy morrow and his orchestra with vocal accompaniment by the skip jacks.

(the PHOTOGRAPHER places the needle on the record. the song plays for a bit. he listens.)

PHOTOGRAPHER: isn't that the craziest thing you've ever heard. listen to those harmonies.

(the PHOTOGRAPHER listens for a moment longer. lifts the needle, returns the record to its sleeve, puts it back in the box.)

PHOTOGRAPHER: o man i love that. the craziness. the sheer improbability. i could listen to that all day long. just makes me smile. i stumbled across it in a yard sale. i couldn't believe it. somebody was going to throw it away, consign it to oblivion.

(the PHOTOGRAPHER slips another record out of its sleeve, and puts it on the turntable. he places the needle on the record. the music begins. a piece of jazz plays.)

PHOTOGRAPHER: i guess i like things a little off the beaten path. i like strange names you can pick out of phone books. i keep a list in this little notebook i have:

(the PHOTOGRAPHER retrieves a small notebook from his pocket.)

PHOTOGRAPHER: lummy jean licklighter.

t. bois dangling.

margaret a. ditto ditto.

pharaoh feedback.

connie fongdong.

everette derryberry,

alright that's enough of that. i could go on for hours i tell you. you think i'm kidding you ask my wife, i'm not.

(the PHOTOGRAPHER returns to the slide projector. he switches off the light. he clicks forward the slide projector. a pixillated blur of dark and light takes shape. similar to the first image, but also different.)

PHOTOGRAPHER: this is a self-portrait right here. i took it not too long ago. some fifteen years ago i said i'm going to learn how to take a picture. i'm going to give myself as long as it takes, i'm going to apply myself, and so that's what i did. i use a rolleiflex these days, but my first camera, that was a bolsey 35 mm reflex. i bought it when my oldest son was born.

(a young boy, the PHOTOGRAPHER's OLDER SON, is gradually revealed in the space.)

PHOTOGRAPHER: i wanted to have a memory of him growing up because, well because i loved him very much and i wanted, i wanted to understand what i was seeing when i looked at him. it goes so quickly it seems to me, and there's so much, there's so much to take in.

(a younger boy, the PHOTOGRAPHER's YOUNGER SON, is gradually revealed in the space.)

PHOTOGRAPHER: i have all different kinds i do. i have, well i have a whole series i took of light on water. i have a series i did of twigs that are close-ups of twigs. they don't much look like twigs. get that close to anything, and it doesn't look like what you think it does. my younger son calls them zen twigs and i think that's a pretty good name for them. i have photos of red river gorge i took for a friend, for a book he's writing. mainly, though, i take photos of my wife and kids.

(a young girl, the PHOTOGRAPHER's DAUGHTER, is gradually revealed in the space.)

PHOTOGRAPHER: somebody asked me once why it was i took so many photos of my family, and i guess i'd have to say because they're right there. they're with me every single day of my life, and with my kids, well i'm their father and they kinda have to do what i tell them to — or at least that's the assumption i labor under. i got three of em. two boys and a girl.

(a flurry of movement. like birds shifting in the eaves. the three children vanish.)

PHOTOGRAPHER: i like to take photos of them in old, derelict buildings mostly, where you get nature kinda reclaimin the place, and there's vines and weeds pushin through the windows, and maybe some young, impertinent oak tree shootin up through the floorboards. i like the quality of light in those buildings, and also, of shadow.

(the PHOTOGRAPHER *clicks forward the projector. a square of darkness. a deep enveloping velvet darkness.)*

PHOTOGRAPHER: there was a time, i couldn't take a picture in the sunlight to save my soul. there were all these shadows you had to contend with, and i couldn't figure it out, and i was lost. then after a while, i got a little older, i guess, and well, well it's not that hard to do anything anymore. you make your peace with whatever it is. you find your way.

(the sense of shadows in a ruined, cavernous space. the space grows darker as the PHOTOGRAPHER *speaks. the light on his face grows brighter.)*

PHOTOGRAPHER: i started using masks in my photographs not too long ago, the kind you get at the five and dime. i have this one photo i took of the kids in masks. we were out in a wooded area not too far from where we live, and my younger son had gotten into some poison ivy, and there were tears and fussing, as there often were in those days, and he didn't want to wear his mask, he just wouldn't do it to save his life, and i remember i was pretty mad at the time cause he wasn't doing what i had it in my mind he should be doing, and i had an idea in my head of how this picture was supposed to be, and it wasn't turning out that way at all, and the whole thing was getting on my last nerve, but finally i just took the photo and called it a day. and what struck me, what struck me when i finally got around to developing it — well, it turned out to be a pretty good picture. there's something about seeing a person put on one of those masks, and you can't really see their faces, and there's a kinda mystery and strangeness that comes out of that that i think, well i think is there all the time, it's just the mask, it lets you see it in a way that you couldn't otherwise.

(the jazz begins to fade away. underneath the jazz, the sound of the needle scraping against the void.)

PHOTOGRAPHER: all the everydayness, the realness of it is still there. the poison ivy and the tears and the ice cream afterwards, that's all still there. but it's as if inside of all of that, the masks, they let you see this other thing. for me, i guess, it's about how you see. it's about the act of seeing a thing, and how it connects to other things and is part of a whole. because on some level, how we form connections, how we see a thing and shape it in our minds, it's very personal, i think. it's about who you are and everything that makes you who you are, and how that comes together to form a certain way, a way of looking at the world.

(the PHOTOGRAPHER *clicks the projector forward. a square of light. as he*

speaks, the PHOTOGRAPHER's WIFE *becomes visible. she wears a mask. she wears a dress with sky-blue flowers.)*

PHOTOGRAPHER: this is a photograph of my wife maddie. madelyn. i call her maddie. we've been married twenty-five years. that's a quarter of a century. that's a pretty long time. she's very patient with me and i thank her for that, because sometimes, well sometimes i can be difficult. other people might not know this about me, but maddie does and she's kind enough not to remind me of it too often. we met at her sister's wedding in louisville. my wife has a twin sister lives in louisville. she got married over at st. joes, then they had the party afterwards down by the old water tower. that's where i met maddie. she was dancing with this guy she was going with at the time. i forget his name. he worked at fischers, i remember that. he had scars all along his hands, cuts and burns, the skin all white and smooth, translucent-like. he liked her, too. i could tell. i could tell by his eyes. how he looked at her, shy and hopeful. she was wearing a dress with blue flowers, sky blue, and the way it was cut, you could see her shoulders, the nape of her neck, a wisp of hair, a single strand. and all i wanted, all i wanted was to touch the back of her neck. like this. and i thought, i thought this girl, she's gotta be the most beautiful girl i will ever know in this life or the next, and she doesn't know me yet, but i'm seeing her now across a room of strangers,

(the PHOTOGRAPHER's WIFE *takes her mask off.)*

PHOTOGRAPHER: and i know, i know i'm going to marry her and we're gonna have children together and grow old together, and we're gonna, we're gonna have us a life, a whole entire life together.

(the PHOTOGRAPHER's WIFE *recedes from view.)*

PHOTOGRAPHER: this is a memory. a kind of photograph.

(somewhere in the darkness, a woman begins to sing a cappella a song of eastern mountains. as she sings, the PHOTOGRAPHER *clicks the projector again and again. with each click, we see points of light in a field of darkness in different formations.)*

PHOTOGRAPHER: if i were to give you the facts of my life, i would tell you i was born in normal illinois in the first part of the twentieth century. i would tell you i was an optician and a photographer, and that i've lived in kentucky most all my adult life, and that it is the most beautiful place i know, and i am lucky to call it home. i would tell you i have friends who write poetry and paint, and drink and break bread together, and take long walks in the woods, and raise a little hell because sometimes you need to raise a little hell, you just need to, and that's alright, that's as it should be. i would tell you that i was a husband and a father and that's, that's maybe the most important thing. i would tell you that sometimes, sometimes i think i wasn't as conscious as i should've been. it's something i think about, whether i have taken sufficient care, whether i have done what i should've done. i would tell you that my kids are all grown up now, and that i look at them and i can't even believe it. what a remarkable thing to have your children become people you like and respect, people you would choose as friends. sometimes i wonder what they'll remember, the things they'll take with them. what stays. what falls away.

(the PHOTOGRAPHER *clicks the projector forward one last time. a pixillated blur of light and dark like the first image. the* PHOTOGRAPHER *is part in shadow, part in light. the woman's singing transforms into the song of the river. a wordless song that is the essence of the ohio river on a day in late spring, sunlight on water, the drone of bees, and the sound of unseen birds in the trees, hundreds of birds invisible in the leaves.)*

PHOTOGRAPHER: louisville kentucky. april 1972. down by the point. late afternoon. a field of trees, giant oaks and cottonwood, weeping willow and sycamore. sunlight through the leaves. the sound of birds high above, hundreds of starlings invisible, unseen. the sound of the creek flowing into the river, the sound of water rushing, sunlight shimmering on the water. the scent of livestock and dead leaves and earth, the scent of earth. in the distance, i see my wife. she's standing on the edge of the woods, and beyond the trees, sky as far as the eye can see. i go to her, across a field of tall grass, the sssssh of the grass, and the wind, the sound of the wind like voices from across the river, and when i get to her at last, i lean in close, i lean in close and whisper in her ear. this is what i say.

(the PHOTOGRAPHER *recedes from view. the song of the river ends.)*

II. snapshots from a family album

projection: pete henzel, edison house. PETE HENZEL *enters the space. he's carrying a small gym bag. he begins disassembling the projection screen and putting away the slide projector.*

PETE HENZEL: so what it is alright, what happened was, i was walking out on the point, and i saw this thing that i can't explain in a logical way, and it's been on my mind, and the more i think about it, the more i'm convinced, the more i know, i just know, i just know in the way you know when you really know a thing — well, ok, let me backtrack here for a second because i think in order for you to process what it is i have to say to you, it's important to say up front that i'm a very sensitive individual. i have been all my life. i've always been predisposed in some way or maybe more aware, i'm more aware of certain vibrations, i guess you would say, vibrational movements in the atmosphere. i'm talking about a kind of energy, a kind of manifestation of displaced energy and the harnessing of a kind of flow or wave of charged particles of human consciousness — are you following me here? cause you're lookin at me like you're not following me. let me put it another way: you know how like some folks, how they have perfect pitch? i had an uncle like that used to sing in the choir over at st. joes when he was a little boy, he could pick out a d sharp or a g flat or middle c, just hear it in his head and he'd come back and go:

(PETE HENZEL *vocalizes a note.*)

PETE HENZEL: or

(PETE HENZEL *vocalizes another note.*)

PETE HENZEL: or

(PETE HENZEL *vocalizes another note.*)

PETE HENZEL: and it never failed, he always got the note, he always got it, he got it perfect. my uncle he used to work over at the old hellmuellers bakery. it's closed down now, but it used to be, you could smell the bread a block away, and everybody, well that's where everybody went for their loaves and dinner rolls and such, and during hard times, you could get a whole basket of day-old rolls for free, they'd just give em away. my uncle hewdie used to make kuchen — you know what kuchen is? it's like a, like a sweet roll with the cinnamon and the brown sugar and it's kinda buttery, and it just like melts in your mouth, o man it's so good. hewdie'd always bring us a sack of kuchen when he came over. he was alright hewdie was. he never married. they say he was engaged to some blind girl, went to the school for the blind over on frankfort. he had an older brother carl went there and i guess that's how they met up. carl lost his sight, y'know, in a fire when he was a little kid. he was a grown man already when i knew him. real natty dresser. tuned pianos all around town. i think he made out pretty good with that. uncle carl used to give me silver dollars and i remember his eyeballs'd kinda roll around some when he was looking at you — well i mean he wasn't looking at you cause he was blind, but you know what i'm getting at. he's dead now, carl is, he died.

he's dead. my uncle hewdie, he's dead too. they're all dead, every single one of em, dead dead dead. i don't know about the girl. she's probably dead, too. that's what happens. alright i need, i need to backtrack, i need to situate myself. let me, let me explain. see what it is, i'm a volunteer, y'see, at the thomas edison house over on washington street which is where thomas edison where he lived when he lived in louisville, which he did, he lived right here in butchertown in 1866, lots of people don't know that but it's a fact. he was working for western union as a telegraph operator at the time, and then he got fired under murky and unjust circumstances which i know what that is, i think many of us know what that is when an employer does not, does not fully appreciate who it is we are and what it is we have to offer, and lacks any kind of imagination or vision and is just a narrow-minded kinda person who can't stand to be challenged in any way and is just waiting for us to make a mistake, just one tiny slip, because they're unable, y'see, to go beyond their own tiny little view of the world and they wouldn't know a good idea if it came up and punched em in the face. i know i certainly know what that is, to be in that situation. but of course edison went on to become one of the most famous americans there ever was, and he went on to invent, o many many things, the phonograph and the light bulb, the moving picture camera, and he made a fortune and was beloved by millions, and who remembers that little shit who fired him, i'll tell you who, nobody that's who. thomas edison is my personal hero.

(PETE HENZEL retrieves objects from a gym bag, one by one as he speaks.)

PETE HENZEL: this is his shoe. this is thomas edison's shoe. this is his fork. he used this fork to eat, i don't know what, pie. this is his comb. he used this comb. i know i'm not supposed to have these things like this, but that's alright. it's not like i'm gonna abscond with them or nothing like that. i just — i guess — well i guess i just wanted — well there's something about a thing you can touch and you know this other person, this person who lived once, this person you maybe look up to or admire, they touched this same thing, and it's like they left some part of themselves, some kinda residue, and now they're dead and in the ground, but the thing's still here, it's still here. what i'm getting at, what i'm trying to get at it, y'see, at the end of his life, thomas edison, he was in the process of inventing a machine, a machine in which the dead would be able to talk to the living. he called it a thanaphone and he believed that when he was finished, we would be able to hear the dead talking to us, kinda like voices through a telephone.

(the lights begin to flicker. the thrumming of an electrical current can be heard. PETE HENZEL begins to recede from view.)

PETE HENZEL: and the phone would ring, and you'd hear it like this faint *ring, ring,* and you'd pick it up and on the other end would be this person you knew from a long time ago, someone who was already old when you were just a little kid, somebody who had to be dead, no way they could still be living cause if you did the math, if you worked it out in your head, they'd be way too old to be alive, but there they were, talking to you like it was no big thing, like it was the most natural thing in the world. cause the dead, y'see, they're like an electrical current or a sound wave, and all you gotta do all you gotta be able to do is plug in, and that's what i think happened, i plugged in, i was plugged in, and that's what i was thinking when i saw this thing, that i had somehow plugged in and i didn't even know, i didn't even realize.

(the sound of the electrical current grows louder. voices, static, the sound of ancient radio transmissions. a phone starts ringing. PETE HENZEL exits. the sounds cut out. RONNIE MARSTON enters. she wears a windbreaker, jeans, work boots. she has a six pack of a beer in a plastic bag. she lights up a smoke.)

RONNIE MARSTON: i got a cousin pete. i nearly ran him over the other day in my truck.

(projection: ronnie marston, story avenue.)

RONNIE MARSTON: i was on story avenue up where the road curves round real sharp, down by the greenway, where the pumping station's at, and you know how the cars, how they're always taking that turn a little too fast and some of em, they go skidding and they crash straight into that house that's right there with the brick that's all messed up from the cars that keep crashing into it, but that's all beside the point cause i wasn't speeding. i never speed. i'm a good driver, i never had a ticket in my life not a one, except for some dumb-ass parking tickets i never shoulda gotten in the first place, and then they had the nerve to tow my truck and that made me so mad, but i didn't have nothing to do with that little a-hole falling down, i did not push him, i did not lay a hand on him, but that's a whole other story i don't want to get into on account of a pending legal action. anway this incident i'm talking about right now, this was all my cousin pete, it was all his fault. pete's got about ten lugnuts loose in his head, no common sense none at all. my sisters, they're all like, o poor pete. poor poor pete. and i'm like, to hell with pete. pete pisses me off. cause it ain't like he's slow. he ain't slow. he's just a screw-up is all. always gettin himself into some kind of trouble cause he doesn't use his head, he doesn't think. pete volunteers now full time at the edison house over on washington. he's some kinda tour guide or something like that. he has this thing, see, he knows everything there is to know about thomas edison. you just ask him whatever you want to know, and he'll tell you. pete used to work at fischers, but then he got let go on account of some situation i don't know the full details of. i work at fischers, too. a lot of my family do — well two of my sisters and my brother-in-law, and his dad, and my dad, and my dad's brother, pete's dad, and pete's brother frank — anyway there i was, driving down story rounding that curve, and suddenly pete's right in front of me, he's just there all of a sudden running into the middle of the road, and thank god i got fast reflexes or i woulda run him over, so i slam on my breaks hard and i'm outta the truck in a flash, and i grab him and i'm up in his face shaking him and i'm like, what the hell is wrong with you i coulda run you over i coulda killed you just now. but pete he ain't even listening to me. he's babbling about seeing something down by the point, down by where beargrass creek lets out into the river, and did i know that the dead live on as particles of free-floating energy in the atmosphere like an electrical current or a sound wave and that's what ghosts are and do i wanna see what he's talking about, come see, ronnie, come and see. and i'm just looking at him, and i'm thinking, this person, i'm related to this person. i'm related to him by blood and that just, that disturbs me. and i look at pete and he's still talking and finally i'm just like: pete. you know what, pete. i really don't need this right now. i just got off work and it was one of those days. the feed tube broke, then the chlorine pump gave out, then the ammo line went tits up for three hours, and then if that weren't bad enough, the goddamn power goes out, some kinda short, who the hell knows. it's out all along mellwood and frankfort, all the way over to crescent hill. fifty-nine condemned hogs. we dumped near five thousand pounds of meat, and now my carpal tunnel is acting up and i don't even want to talk about the smell, you don't even want to know about the smell. so right now, pete, it's really not a good time for you to share with me your thoughts about the afterlife.

(pause. RONNIE MARSTON drinks her beer. she drinks.)
RONNIE MARSTON: you know sometimes, sometimes i speak out of turn. i get

impatient and angry. not just with pete. with my kids, with the guys at work, with just about everybody. and i ain't sayin that to make excuses. that's who i am, take it or leave it. cause i hear em talk, yknow, all these years. i ain't deaf. god took him so young and it's sad, it's a sad thing. and i just wanna say to them, i don't need your pity. i don't need no one's pity. i raise my kids, i go to work, i do just fine, thank you very much. everything, everything's just fine. and now i see, i see pete he's starting to say something and that's the last thing i need. so i just tell him: pete. don't you say another word. why don't you just get in the truck. just get in the truck and i'll take you home.

(a BOY gradually appears in the darkened space. he wears a windbreaker, corduroy pants, sneakers. he is the young PETE HENZEL.)

RONNIE MARSTON: and so that's what i do. and as we're driving down the interstate, i look over at him, and i'm thinking to myself i don't understand a damn thing about anything. here's this man, this grown man, and i've known him all his life, since he was a baby, and i can hardly understand the inside of his head, and how can that be? how can that be? and i think what a beautiful little boy he was.

(a german lieder begins. it plays on the phonograph. it sounds faint and crackling, faraway.)

RONNIE MARSTON: so sweet and smart. big brown eyes and a smile that'd light up a room. he had such a light in him, he was so full of light. and i think where did that boy get to? where did he go?

(the BOY vanishes. RONNIE MARSTON exits as NORA HOLTZ enters. the german lieder continues.)

NORA HOLTZ: my name is nora holtz. i'm fifteen years old. i was born in louisville, kentucky january 15th, 1921.

(projection: nora holtz, school for the blind.)

NORA HOLTZ: i had scarlet fever when i was a baby and that's how i lost my sight. i have no memory of what it was to see, and so i never think what if, what could've been. i don't think like that. i go to the school for the blind on frankfort. at school, we study music and grammar and composition. we study history. every year in springtime we do a play. we do it outdoors. we have a stage and we have costumes and everybody, everybody comes to see it. this year we're doing *the tempest* by mister william shakespeare. i'm playing miranda. hewdie says i'll be a beautiful miranda. hewdie's my friend carl's brother. i think hewdie, i think he's sweet on me. but like i told him, i have things to do and so he better be alright with that cause that's how it's gotta be. i'm learning shorthand, and i already type seventy-two words a minute and that's pretty good. my teacher miss miller says i can learn a skill and work downtown at an insurance office or a bank or maybe even the brown hotel, no reason why not.

(a male tenor rises above the rest.)

NORA HOLTZ: you hear that? that's my father, georg holtz. he came from germany to america in 1882. travelled inland to pittsburgh to where the allegheny and the ohio meet, then he sailed down the ohio all the way to louisville. he had the most beautiful voice you'll ever hear. you'd never think a butcher'd have such a beautiful voice. cut up hogs all day long, and still he sang like an angel. he was in the orpheus society. do you know orpheus, do you know the story of orpheus? on his wedding day, his bride, she got bit by a snake and died, and orpheus, he was so full of grief, he followed her down to the underworld, and he sang to the spirits of the dead, and his songs were so beautiful even the queen of the dead, her heart softened, and she said to him, you can have your wife back. go back to the world of the living, and your wife, she'll be right behind you, but if you turn, if you turn to look at her before you reach the sunlight, she'll vanish forever. and of course, orpheus, he does the one thing he's not supposed to do, and in that moment he lays eyes on her, he sees and he knows, all of a sudden he knows he's made a terrible mistake. and there's no going back, there's no undoing what he's done.

(the german lieder ends. the sound at the end of a record, needle scraping against the void.)

NORA HOLTZ: and he replays that moment in his mind, the moment right before she goes. and in his mind it's like an old photograph of a girl he used to know.

(a GIRL appears. she wears a white dress with beads sewn in that sparkle in the light.)

NORA HOLTZ: and she's standing on the lawn in front of the school and she's wearing a white dress with tiny beads stitched in all along the hem and the sleeves. they shimmer in the light. sun against her face. the smell of honeysuckle and clover. and she can hear the birds in the trees. and she can hear their tiny hearts racing. she can feel the rough edges of their wings against her skin. what if you could read the future? what if you could go back? what if you could change one thing? how do you go on knowing you can't? how do you bear it? he thinks these things. he thinks: i am looking into the eyes of a ghost.

(NORA HOLTZ recedes from view. the GIRL runs towards the audience. she runs a great distance very fast. she is a blur of light and flesh in a field of darkness. and then she's gone. a thousand birds explode into the sky. the sound their wings make. the sound of the wings dies down. a bird song. light on MIKE TOTTEN. he's eating a sandwich. next to him is a shopping bag.)

MIKE TOTTEN: i saw this thing down by the point this morning. all these birds, small like starlings, only that's not what they were. and the sound they made, it sounded kinda like voices, like human voices whispering. i never saw birds like that around here before. they flew up and out of the trees and filled the sky. hundreds of birds, thousands even. and i had this sense, i had this feeling — well i can't, i can't put it into words exactly, but it was strange. the whole thing, it was just, it was kinda strange.

(projection: mike totten, the greenway.)

MIKE TOTTEN: i work at the impound lot over by the greenway. you get all kinds of birds down there. swallow-tailed kites and red-tailed hawks, i see hawks all the time. i just sit and sketch birds all day long and nobody tells me what to do, which i appreciate. and then, you know, every so often someone comes along for their car, and i take their check and give em their keys and that's about it. it's a pretty good job as jobs go. only thing is sometimes, y'know, you get these people, and they got all this anger, they're all pent up and pissed off at the world and they'll just take it out on you and that just, well that just kinda sucks. there was this one woman, and she comes in raising hell about her truck and how she ain't gonna pay any dumbass parking tickets and i better give her her keys or she's gonna hurt me, and i tell her to calm down, and she says something i ain't gonna repeat here in mixed company, and then she starts pushing and shoving on me, and she's strong, too, and before i know it, i'm on the pavement staring up at the sky. i hit my head, i got a concussion. i also bruised my ulna. that's this bone right here. hurts like hell. now i'm suing her ass, you bet i am. it's my legal right as an american and i'm gonna exercise it. i'm gonna have my day in court, cause that kinda shit, that's just uncalled for.

(MIKE TOTTEN retrieves a stuffed bird from the shopping bag.)

MIKE TOTTEN: this is a hooded merganser. i shot it, i stuffed it, and then i painted it. my friend tessa thinks that's fucked up. she can keep her opinions to herself as far as i'm concerned. that's how i gotta do it, see, otherwise i can't get up close, i can't see what i need to see to get everything, to get it all just right. to make it look alive, i gotta shoot it and stuff it. that's the paradoxical nature of the whole endeavor, see. i was inspired in my technique by john james audubon. audubon lived right here in louisville, i don't know if you knew that. he painted birds up and down beargrass creek and the river and down by the point. his painting of the carolina parakeet, he did that here, and his painting of the kingfisher, and the whipporwhill, and the oriole, he did them all right here, right here in louisville. tessa don't give a damn. i mean i tell her all this stuff cause i think it's pretty cool and it's our history, it's like our fuckin forefathers, it's like our fuckin history, but she's just like whatever. personally, i think that way of thinking, that's just ignorant. she don't care. tessa's a painter, too. we're friends. no romance, it ain't nothing like that. i mean we make out sometimes yknow, but it's just, well it's no big thing. tessa works over at hadley pottery painting little piglets and chickens and shit on all the pitchers and the soup tureens. tessa keeps trying to paint her own original designs, like a kinda abstract expressionist effect is what she's going after. but see now every time she tries to do her own thing, tessa's mom and all the other hadley ladies, they about have a fit. they just shut her down. fear of the new, yknow what i'm saying. fear of change. that's all it is. sometimes people, they can be so close minded. it's like their brain's wearing a girdle and it's like cutting off all the circulation. her mom got her that job at hadley pottery, and it pays pretty good but it's, well it's a job, you know what i'm saying? sometimes tessa and me, we smoke out, up on the hill by the impound lot and we laugh at all the crap we gotta deal with. my older sister mary catherine and her husband kevin, they're just over the river in indiana. they got some land up in the knobs and they grow this weed, and it's like the most intense shit you will ever partake of. this stuff, this stuff will impair you, it'll humble your ass. i smoke out and i think sometimes i'm seeing god or something. well not god cause i don't know about god, but like, like the tendrils of the universe, like the arteries and synapses and ganglia. i fuckin love that word. ganglia.

(the sound of a violin. as MIKE speaks, the violin melody begins to break down and distort.)

MIKE TOTTEN: you want an experience, i tell you what, you go up on that hill by the impound lot at sunset. you roll some of kevin's weed and you smoke out, and you look at all those cars down below, hundreds of fords and chevys and oldsmobiles in every color you can imagine, new cars and old dented up cars, every make and model and they're all there, they're all down there arrayed before you, and the sun's low in the sky, and the light's shimmering off the metal and the glass, and the cars, they're all kinda all melding together, reflecting the sky, the beautiful enormity of the sky, all fuschia and tangerine and deep deep purple, just seeping into the horizon line, and it's about the most amazing thing, it's about the most amazing thing you'll ever see, it's like the whole universe is there, it's right there in front of you, reflecting back at you, and it's everything, it's the cars and it's the sky and the trees and the creek and the river and tessa's freckles and the little scar she has above her eye, every single eyelash, and her lips, the feel of her lips, and the feel of the grass and the earth and the sound of the pump station and the river and the scent of mud and leaves and birds all those crazyass birds, so many i can't even count them all —

(the violin grows louder. if chaos were a song. light streams in through cracks in the walls. MIKE TOTTEN disappears through a wall. music ends. a mirror is revealed in the darkness where once there had been just a solid wall. light on MARTIN KINFLEIN.)

MARTIN KINFLEIN: my dad tells this story of how he bought this mirror from the devil.
(projection: martin kinflein, oertels brewing company.)
MARTIN KINFLEIN: the devil, as it turned out, was a gypsy woman travelling through town. i said, dad, how did you know she was the devil. and he said: son, some things you just know. see now what you gotta understand is that my dad's mom, she was church of christ, and some of her people were holy rollers, handled serpents, spoke in tongues, the whole nine yards, and some of that fire and brimstone, i guess some of it musta stuck. anyway the devil tells my dad, you can pay some now, pay the rest later. i'll be back through the following spring. my dad says, fine. so a year passes. and then another and another one after that, and before you know it, ten years have gone by, and it gets so that my dad, he forgets about the whole thing. then one day, there's a knock on the door, and it's the devil, and she says to him: mister, i'm here to collect. and my dad says: ok, now, see, this

is the thing, times have gotten hard since last we spoke, i've been laid off from my job at oertels. i make beer see, that's what i do, that's all i know how to do is make beer, that's what my father and his father and his father did, and now all of a sudden drinking beer's against the law, and i gotta say i don't know what kinda country goes and makes drinking beer against the law, i think that's maybe the stupidest thing i've ever heard in my life, so now we're supposed to be making pop, 'cept see i don't make pop, i make beer, that's what i do, that's all i know how to do and i'm too old to change. that's what i told the foreman, and the foreman told me: henry. henry. you don't like it, there's the door right there. and so i walked right out that door, and i haven't been back since. to hell with them is what i say, cause i got my pride, 'cept pride don't come cheap, and now i'm down to my last nickel, and that's how it stands with me that's how it is, and so basically, basically what i'm tryin to say to you is i don't have your money. and the devil says: mister, that's a problem. how about i give back the mirror, says my dad. and the devil says, i don't want the mirror. i want my money. and my dad, he's startin to get a little nervous. he's thinkin, i'm gonna have to give up my firstborn child or my eternal soul or somethin i know it's gonna hurt to give up, and i don't want to do it, i'm afraid, he said. i'm afraid. they worked it out in the end. turns out the devil, she had a little boy. and when she learned my dad played the fiddle, they struck a deal. teach my boy to play, she said, and we'll call it even. by the end of the week, he had that little gypsy boy playing "turkey in the straw." by the end of the year, he was playing mozart. i work at the brewery where my dad used to work. i'm no master brewer like he was. i'm nothing like him really. i'm just an accountant. i do the books. i can't play the fiddle or nothing like that, not like my dad. my dad, he was something else. he lived to be a hundred and four. died on derby day 1949. said he was feeling a little tired, lay down for a nap and never woke up. just like that. peaceful. my dad was from a different time, a whole different place in time. when he came up, it was people riding around in horse and buggy. that's how old he was. he could remember the civil war. he could remember the boys coming back home with wooden legs and empty sleeves, half their faces blown away. sometimes he would talk about the riots in the summer of 1855. this was all over louisville, west side, east side. they called it bloody monday when the mobs came hunting for germans and irish and set the town on fire. that was when that irish fella quinn died. my dad was just a little boy.

(a young BOY *becomes visible in the darkness. he wears clothes from the last century. he is* MARTIN KINFLEIN'S FATHER *as a boy.)*

MARTIN KINFLEIN: he hid in an ice cellar by the river, near where the heigold house is now far as i can figure. he hid behind a giant block of ice and he was so cold, even though it was summer. he stayed down there for a day and a night and into the next day, and then he went home. i don't know if that ice cellar, if it's even there anymore.

(the sound of a violin playing mozart.)

MARTIN KINFLEIN: i went once to look for it. i walked all through thruston park, down by the point, but i couldn't find it.

(the young GIRL *in the white dress appears as a reflection in the mirror. she gradually comes into view as* MARTIN KINFLEIN *speaks.)*

MARTIN KINFLEIN: i did see something that struck me as being, well, kinda strange. there were all these children. i didn't think much of it at the time, but then later i thought how odd it was to see all those children there like that in the middle of a school day. they musta been on a field trip or something. but there was something about the whole thing, well it was just, it was off. they were running through the trees. i could hear them laughing and shouting. they were running so fast, it was hard to see them. all i could see were glimpses of them through the leaves. then all of a sudden one of them, this little girl, she just stopped and she stared at me from across the field, she stared at me for the longest time as if she knew who i was, as if she knew me, and then she turned and ran away.

(flash from a camera. MARTIN KINFLEIN *turns and walks away. as he walks away, his image frays and dissolves. he vanishes from view. the* BOY *in clothes from the last century runs into the shadows. the* GIRL *in the white dress follows him. the sound of distant thunder. the* BOY *and the* GIRL *run through the shadows. in the space, we hear the sound of children whispering facts one after the next. a susurration of historical facts underneath everything: "linden hill was built in 1815. bourbon stockyards were established in 1834. the kentucky distillery company burned to the ground august 14, 1840. the school for the blind was established in 1842. woodland gardens were opened in 1848. the german american civic school opened in 1854. the heigold house was built by christian heigold in 1865. c.f. vissman packing company was established in 1876. the home of the innocents was built in 1880. st. josephs church went up in 1883. oertels brewing company was incorporated in 1906. fischer packing was founded in 1909. the great flood occured in january 1937. the interstate was built in 1965. mary alice hadley founded hadley pottery in 1939. it*

still exists today." as the facts are read, the BOY in clothes from the last century emerges from the darkness. the GIRL in the white dress follows him. they play orpheus and eurydice. the BOY walks ahead of the GIRL.)

A BOY: there used to be a man named william wells. he ran a ferry cross the river. he lived in linden hill right in the heart of butchertown. they say he married an indian maiden. sweet breeze was her name. and that she died of typhoid fever before the year was out. they say her soul left her body, and turned into a bird, and flew away.
(the sound of thunder grows closer.)

A GIRL: we used to go down when we were kids and swim in the river. the water was so cold, even in the summertime. and deep, deeper than you ever thought. the mud would give beneath your feet and you'd suddenly, you'd drop off and you'd fall and you'd fall and you'd fall and you'd fall until all you saw was green black water.
(the BOY turns around and looks at the GIRL. lightning. thunder. the GIRL vanishes. the BOY vanishes. rain. rain. rain. the walls buckle and crack. a terrible creaking sound. wood cracking. the walls explode. water comes rushing in. the song of the flood. a final thunderclap. the rain, the thunder, everything cuts out. silence. light on IDA MILLER sitting in a chair.)

IDA MILLER: in '37 we'd be underwater where we're sitting now. that's a fact.
(projection: ida miller, wesley community house.)

IDA MILLER: 52 feet and 6 inches, that's how high the river rose. it rained for forty days straight. we lived down four blocks on washington, 1500 block near where the interstate, near where it cuts through. the water was up to our backyard. my sisters and i we had a marker set out, a little stick where you could see how far the water rose. and it just rose and rose and rose. we got around by rowboat. we rowed down main street, can you believe it. we'd wave at the guardsman on the pontoon bridge. we saw all kinds of things floating by. we saw a cow on top of a roof. we saw whole houses floating downstream. we even saw a couple of nuns paddling by in a canoe. my sister hazel gotta hold of a barrel of pickles, it was just floating by, and we pried it open and we ate those pickles, we ate so many pickles, we just stuffed ourselves with pickles. i got so sick on pickles and i never ate a pickle again. that's a true story. i'm a teacher. i have been all my life. i never married. never had children of my own. me and my sisters none of us did. we were what they used to call maiden ladies. hazel worked at the seelbach, dorothy worked at kauffman strauss, and me, i taught down at the school for the blind.

(the german lieder begins.)

IDA MILLER: there was this one girl i think about sometimes. her name was nora holtz.

(the young GIRL in the white dress playing the young NORA HOLTZ comes into view.)

IDA MILLER: i see her like i see you. she's standing on the front lawn waiting for me. it's like a photograph in my mind. it's late spring and i can the smell the honeysuckle and the clover, and the sun, the sun is so bright, it's so bright. this was june 1936. she's miranda in *the tempest* and her costume, i sewed it myself. a white dress with tiny beads stitched in that shimmered in the light. i can see her clear as i'm seeing you. just the way she was. come the flood that winter, in the panic of the first night, nora crept down into the old root cellar at her uncle's place down on quincy. she stopped her ears against the thunder and curled up on the hard earth, and fell asleep to the sound of the rain above her. no one knew to look for her, no one knew till after. but by then, it was too late. by then she was already gone.

(the german lieder gets caught in a groove. the same phrase repeats in a loop and begins to break down and disintegrate. IDA MILLER slowly exits. the young GIRL playing NORA HOLTZ spins. She spins faster and faster. the skirt of her dress is a blur. her face is a blur. TESSA RHEINGOLD enters the space as the GIRL vanishes. she's in the middle of packing cardboard boxes.)

TESSA RHEINGOLD: ok here's the deal, ladies: this is my art we're talking about. this is my artistic vision. and this is the fuckin future. you're looking at the future, right here, that's me, and if you don't like it, well that's too damn bad. cause time's on my side. so you better get with the program or you gonna be fuckin obsolete. like, like fuckin eight track tapes. hell yeah. fuck yeah.

(projection: tessa rheingold, hadley pottery.)

TESSA RHEINGOLD: that's exactly what i said to them just like that. you shoulda seen their faces. my mom's been working at hadley pottery practically all her life, and she was looking at me right then like i was like devil's spawn or something, like my head was about to spin round and green gunk was gonna come shooting outta my mouth. they fired me right on the spot. whatever. me and that job, it just wasn't meant to be. but you know what gets me, the thing that burns my ass — if she was alive, mrs. hadley, she would've totally backed me up. mary alice was hip, y'know what i'm sayin. she was cool. i seen those pictures of her with the weird little hats and the little mona lisa smile. i know she had a wild side. you can tell just lookin at her. and she woulda dug my shit. i know she woulda, too. alright, look, i know, i know i give my mom, i give her way too much grief, i know that. but see now i justify it in my mind, cause my mom was a hellraiser when she was comin up, way worse than i ever was, staying out late and drinkin and smokin and carryin on. her dad, my grandpa kinflein, she drove that poor man crazy. he was like an accountant. he worked at oertels his whole life. he passed away last year. he was walking out by thruston park down by the point, and he had a heart attack and he died. he just died there on the spot. these little kids found him. my mom was pretty torn up about it. i guess i was, too. he was sweet y'know, and kinda crazy. he was a real pack rat. he had all this stuff crammed into his house. he had this big old mirror in a gilt frame. i don't know where he got that thing. i wonder.

(TESSA RHEINGOLD begins to recede from view.)

TESSA RHEINGOLD: he'd tell stories about his dad or the way things were back in the day, just little things. i don't remember all that much. i wish i remembered more. i wish i'd paid more attention. sometimes when i'm down at the point, i picture him walking along the railroad tracks.

(the thrumming of an electrical current begins.)

TESSA RHEINGOLD: it's like i can almost see him. he's walking away real slow and steady towards the horizon line. and i'm standing there watching him, and i can't move. and i know if i call out, he won't hear me, so i just stand there, watching. i watch him as he walks away, till he's just a tiny speck, so small i can hardly see. i watch till my eyes ache. i watch till there's nothing left but sky.

(the sound of the electrical current grows and cuts out. TESSA RHEINGOLD vanishes. light on FRANK HENZEL.)

FRANK HENZEL: the power went out today. some kinda short. nobody knows for sure.

(projection: frank henzel, fischer meatpacking plant.)

FRANK HENZEL: it was out all along mellwood and up frankfort, all the way over to crescent hill. they shut down the cut floor. we had to dump near five thousand pounds of meat. it was bad, stank to high heaven. afterwards i kinda, well i kinda had it. i went for a walk down by the greenway, and ended up down at the point. i saw a guy down there taking pictures. i watched him a while. finally he looked over at me and he said: c'mere. i want to show you something. and so i went and looked into the camera, and i saw this thing. the bark of a tree but close, so close that you could see all the patterns the wood made, layer upon layer, swirled and jagged. it looked like something i can't put into words, and it was, it was beautiful. later the guy, he asked if he could take my picture and i said alright. and so he did and we got to talking. he wanted to know what i did for a livin, and i told him: mister, i kill hogs is what i do. i kill em and i cut em up. and he asked, what's that like. and i ended up telling him about this old guy i used to know, worked at the same plant i work at. we called him old man holtz. old man holtz, he knew the score. my first day i go in, i see him sittin there and i say, i'm lookin for a job. and he says to me, i never hire someone lookin for a job, I hire someone lookin for *work*. he wasn't kiddin either. kill floor, cut floor. i don't care what the hell you're doin on the line, you're gonna work. old man holtz knew. he'd been there forever and a day. he sang. i remember that. he had a beautiful voice. i heard him sing karaoke one night. you'd never guess he'd have a voice like that. cut up hogs all day long, and sang like an angel. i started on the kill floor. worked my way up from scalder to splitter to loin puller. i even worked in the order room boxing up the quick-cut hams. i did just about everything. it's a system, yknow, it's a whole system. you know what a dark cut is? it's when the animal gets scared and the adrenaline gets released into its system, and it stains the meat, and you can taste it. you can taste the fear in the meat. old man holtz, he always said, talk to em soft, soft and sweet. don't be yellin and cursin. talk to em soft and gentle, as you would a child. i used to pull loins. i used to use what they call a draw knife. now i work splitting and i use a chainsaw, and it's different, well it's a different kind of thing. these days you take what you can get. i'm lucky i got a job. at least that's what they tell me. sometimes you think about things, you can't help but think about things. work here long enough, and you're gonna get messed up, ain't no way around it. i saw a man once, his hand slipped, he was working the band saw, took two fingers clean off, knuckle on down. tore the skin all along his hand. you could see underneath, you could see the muscle and bone. just takes one slip, one slip is all. you can tell a man, i think, by the scars on his hands. by the cuts and burns, and how they turn, how they turn all white and smooth, translucent-like. like you can see, like you can see straight through.

(the BOY playing the young PETE HENZEL gradually emerges from view. he wears a windbreaker, corduroys, and sneakers. he wears a mask.)

FRANK HENZEL: see, i wonder how you tell a stranger about yourself, who you are and what you know of the world. everything you've seen and all the people you've known. i wonder what you tell em, so that they can understand. i was driving down story avenue the other day and i thought of this thing i hadn't thought about in years. when we were kids, my brother pete and me, we used to go to this halloween party.

(an older BOY playing the young FRANK HENZEL emerges into view. he wears a mask. he wears the same clothes as the PHOTOGRAPHER's OLDER SON.)

FRANK HENZEL: mrs. hadley, she used to have this halloween party for all the kids in the neighborhood all along story. powder donuts and apple cider, and all the children wore costumes, and mrs. hadley she gave a prize to the best one. and one year, i remember, me and my brother pete we went, and i didn't even have a costume, and pete, all's he had was this plastic mask the color of skin, and it was a shitty costume cause you could tell, you could tell it was him. and he'd been cryin, cause somebody was makin fun of him. kids were always makin fun of him cause he was kinda strange. he's still kinda strange. i mean he's pete, and he's my brother and i love him, but yeah he's fucked up. something's broken and it ain't getting fixed, and that's just, well that's just the way it goes. so there he was, standin there with tears and snot runnin down his face, and our cousin ronnie, she came over.

(a GIRL appears. she wears the same clothes as the PHOTOGRAPHER's DAUGHTER. she wears a mask.)

FRANK HENZEL: and ronnie, she always looked out for us, me and pete both, and she cracked some joke about some smart-ass kid we all hated, and before we knew it, we were all crackin up, we were laughin so hard, and somebody, i forget who, they took a picture. pete. and ronnie. and me. just like that. and if you look real close, you can see right there at the edge of the picture, you can see ronnie's husband jimmy. they weren't married yet. i mean they were just kids, we were all just kids. later, they'd get married and have kids of their own and jimmy, he'd enlist. one hundred and first airborne division stationed out of fort campbell. shot and killed in an ambush outside a place called hung nhon, 400 miles north of saigon, somewhere on the other side of the world. this was april 1972.

(a woman sings a cappella. a song of eastern mountains, a song of loved ones gone away.)

FRANK HENZEL: i remember right before he shipped out, jimmy got glasses. he was already a grown man and he never even knew he needed them. all those years and nobody knew. i remember he said, he put em on, and he was amazed. how everything, how it was all so clear.

(the BOY playing the young PETE HENZEL takes off his mask.)

FRANK HENZEL: he said it hurt, it hurt to see everything so sharp and clear. to be that aware, it was almost too much, it was almost too much to bear.

(FRANK HENZEL vanishes. the CHILDREN remain. the PHOTOGRAPHER appears. he approaches the CHILDREN across a field of darkness. as he approaches the children, the song fades away. the PHOTOGRAPHER stares into the light. the light gets brighter and brighter.)

PHOTOGRAPHER: what do you see, i asked him. and he said, i see my wife. i see my children, i see the faces of my children. i see my mom and dad. i see the place where i grew up. i see the trees and the river and how the light, the way the light, how it sparkles on the water. and it's so beautiful, it's so beautiful, you never realize, you never even realize till it's gone —

(the young PETE HENZEL sings a cappella the hymn "o god our help in ages past." the PHOTOGRAPHER recedes from view. the young PETE HENZEL finishes singing. the CHILDREN turn into birds and fly away. a blur of skin and color scattering in all directions. silence and stillness. in the stillness, you can hear the sound of louisville, kentucky at nightfall. cars passing on the street outside. and beyond the cars, the stirring of leaves. the sound of breathing. if breathing were a song. a cavernous space, a wrecked and ancient space. the sound of a light switch being turned on. a simple prop that indicates a bar. think a neon michelob sign. think a coors sign with a holographic waterfall. the sound of footsteps. MAUDIE TOTTEN enters the space. she has a bottle of bourbon and a shot glass. a painting of a hooded merganser hangs in the void.)

MAUDIE TOTTEN: my stepson mike painted this. it's a kinda bird. i forget what it's called.

(projection: maudie totten, johnson's bait and beer.)

MAUDIE TOTTEN: i tell him, mike, you paint it and i'll hang it on my wall, and maybe one of these days, some patron'll come in for a nice cold beer and look up and see your painting and say: i like that. i would like to purchase that. that has not as of yet happened, but that don't mean a thing. i think he's pretty good. my husband, mike's dad, he says don't encourage him.

he says mike and mary catherine, that's mike's older sister, he says they're a never-ending source of irritation and dismay. my husband is entitled to his opinions, but this is my place and i'm gonna do what i'm gonna do, and if i wanna hang mike's paintings on every square inch of my damn wall, then that's what i'm gonna do. my name is maudie. maudie totten. i've lived here my whole life. i own this place. i own it free and clear. it used to be called the last chance and the drovers comin through, they'd stop for a pint. totten is my married name. i've had five of em. i was an epperson, i was a kirchner, i was a krebs, i was a miller. my current husband, mike's dad, he worked over at fischers. his name's roy totten. they called him hubcap, don't ask me why. started on the kill floor, worked his way up. that's how it used to go over there. you started at the bottom, worked your way up. when we got married, roy was working the cut floor, pulling loins. that's a bracket one job. good money. hard work. you gotta be quick and strong. the speed of the rail is 300 hog an hour. you got twenty-five men workin the rail, that's five hogs per minute, twelve second per hog. and you gotta do it right the first time out, cause i'll tell you what, you don't get a second chance. roy had a friend named frank henzel. he worked the kill floor splitting hogs. they used chainsaws, and they didn't have the automatic brakes back then, and the saw, it got away from him, and it's on a pulley right, on a chain, and it flew up and coasted see, turned all around, turned back on him, and tore him up, it tore him to pieces. only family he had when i knew him was his brother pete. pete's a little touched i guess you would say. used to work at the plant, but then he got fired. he let out all the hogs. he just opened up the gate in the holding pen and shooed them out, and out they went, trotting down the road, and then running, hogs everywhere, in the streets blocking traffic, chasing people down the sidewalk, everybody shoutin and runnin. it was a mess. after that, pete he got fired, o you bet he did. the plant's closed down now. it's different now, it's all, well it's just different. a whole new world. nothing stays the same, and maybe that's not a bad thing. it just is. i'm still here. me and my sister both. i have a twin sister. her name is maddie. everybody used to get a kick outta that when we were comin up. maddie and maudie. maudie and maddie. o how we hated that. now we don't mind hardly so much, but then, then it was like nails on a chalkboard. maddie lives in lexington. she moved there with her husband gene. i liked gene. i met him at my wedding, my first of many. it was a church wedding. i got married over at st. joes. i had a nice white dress. and we had the kids choir, yknow, and they sang. and then we had the reception out by the old water tower. gene was from normal, illinois and i thought that was very odd. he used to take photographs, and he liked jazz, ornette coleman and dizzy gillespie, and i didn't know much about jazz, but i learned. gene was a good teacher. he'd blast that jazz on his old phonograph and then he's show you his pictures. he'd want to know what you saw. and i'll tell you what, they were like no pictures i'd ever seen. gene, he had all these photos of twigs. i swear to god, i've never seen so many damn twigs in my life. but the thing — this was the thing — gene could make you see a twig like you had never seen a twig before. like it was some kinda alien life form, like it was the most amazing thing in the world. gene went through his days seeing the world like that. all the little league games and the kids' birthday parties, all the camping trips down in red river gorge. that was a time. that was a good time.

(darkness gradually falls. the circumference of light which MAUDIE TOTTEN *occupies gets smaller and smaller.* MAUDIE TOTTEN *is alone in a vast darkness.)*

MAUDIE TOTTEN: the last year of his life, he took pictures of all of us. he was making a family album, he said. not like a regular family album. different. i remember he took a picture of himself and maddie. this was right before he died. we knew he was leaving us, we knew that, and it was hard, it was so hard. they'd come to visit one last time, and we'd gone out to the point. we'd brought all of our kids, and it was such a beautiful day, so clear and bright, and the kids were laughing and horsing around, and the sky was so blue, and the smell of grass and earth and new leaves. and underneath it all, you could hear the river. but the thing i remember most, what i remember was looking across a field, and seeing my sister and gene, these two people who loved each other and who had built a life together, a whole entire life, and he's leaning towards her, and he's saying something i can't hear, and as i watch them, i think of all the things that pass between them, all the things i have no words for, all the things alive in that precise point in time, the tiniest things.

*(*MAUDIE TOTTEN *turns and goes. she turns out the last light remaining. darkness.)*

END OF PLAY

Song List

"The Raven" by Edgar Allen Poe, instrumentals by Buddy Morrow and his
  orchestra with vocals by the Skip Jacks
"When Angels Speak of Love" by Sun Ra
"River Song" by Tara Jane O'Neil
"If Chaos Were A Song" by Tara Jane O'Neil
"Flood Song" by Tara Jane O'Neil
"Your Long Journey" folk song by anonymous, sung by Tara Jane O'Neil
"O God Our Help in Ages Past"
"Stardust" sung by Louis Armstrong
"An Die Entfernte" by Shubert
The Adagio from "Violin Concerto #3 in G" by Mozart

Tallgrass Gothic
by Melanie Marnich

An adaptation of The Changeling
by Thomas Middleton and William Rowley

BIOGRAPHY

Melanie Marnich is the author of *Blur, Quake, Beautiful Again* and *The Sparrow Project. Quake* premiered at the 2001 Humana Festival and has since received over a dozen productions here and in Europe. *Blur* was included in the Public Theater's New Work Now! Festival, the U.S. West Festival of New Plays and premiered at Manhattan Theatre Club in 2001. Her work has also been seen at the Guthrie Theater, Dallas Theater Center, London's Royal Court Theatre, Mixed Blood Theatre, HERE, Hypothetical Theatre, Salvage Vanguard Theater, Quantum Theatre, Undermain Theatre, Hyde Park Theatre and American Theatre Company. Her awards include two Jerome Fellowships and two McKnight Advancement Grants from The Playwrights' Center, two Samuel Goldwyn Awards, the Selma Melvoin Award and the Francesca Primus Prize.

HUMANA FESTIVAL PRODUCTION

Tallgrass Gothic premiered at the Humana Festival of New American Plays in March, 2004. It was directed by Marc Masterson with the following cast:

Laura . . . . Lia Aprile
Tin . . . . Michael A. Newcomer
Daniel . . . . Asa Somers
Mary . . . . Tonya Cornelisse
Scotto . . . . David Wagner
Filene . . . . Jesse Lenat

and the following production staff:

Scenic Designer . . . . Paul Owen
Costume Designer . . . . Lorraine Venberg
Lighting Designer . . . . Deb Sullivan
Sound Designer . . . . Vincent Olivieri
Properties Designer . . . . Mark Walston
Stage Manager . . . . Debra A. Freeman
Assistant Stage Manager . . . . Brady Ellen Poole
Dialect Coach . . . . Rinda Frye
Fight Director . . . . Drew Fracher
Dramaturg . . . . Mead Hunter
Assistant Dramaturg . . . . Erin Detrick
Viewpoints Consultant . . . . Will Bond
Casting . . . . Orpheus Group Casting
Directing Assistant . . . . Keith McCormick

CHARACTERS

LAURA

TIN

DANIEL

MARY

SCOTTO

FILENE

Everyone is in their mid-twenties.

PLACE

Laura and Tin's porch and bed.

An old church.

A corner of a dilapidated barn.

Junked back seat of a car.

All of it in an open tallgrass field.

* (All of it may be minimally suggested and not literal.)

This is the Americana of the Great Plains, fields of wheat and tallgrass, crumbling barns and stone walls, peeling white paint around old windows. There are places of brilliant sunlight, rolling clouds, and dusty shadows. Rural, stark, beautiful and violent.

TIME

The present.

Perhaps everybody has a Garden of Eden, I don't know; but they have scarcely seen their garden before they see the flaming sword.

James Baldwin
Giovanni's Room

Tallgrass Gothic was
Written with the support of The Playwrights' Center's Jerome and McKnight fellowship programs, Minneapolis, MN.
First developed at The Playwrights' Center's PlayLabs, August 1999.
Workshopped at Portland Center Stage's Just Add Water/West Festival, July 2003.

Asa Somers and Lia Aprile
in *Tallgrass Gothic*

28th Annual Humana Festival of New American Plays
Actors Theatre of Louisville, 2004
photo by Harlan Taylor

Tallgrass Gothic

1.

Pre-dawn in the field.
LAURA stands alone, in silhouette, watching the dawn-gold clouds pass over-head.
She wants to move as fast as they do.
She tries to touch them.

LAURA: *(Singing.)* Oh my darlin'
Oh my darlin'
Oh my darlin' Clementine
You are lost and gone forever
Oh so sorry Clementine
(She turns around, looking for someone.
What she's looking for isn't there.
DANIEL enters. She turns to face him.)
I was—
DANIEL: Stop.
(She does.)
Turn around.
LAURA: I—
DANIEL: I said turn.
(She does.)
Stop.
(She stops with her back to him.)
LAURA: But—
DANIEL: This isn't you. This isn't me.
We're not here.
This isn't dirt and dust and grass.
This isn't now.
It's then.
When the clock stopped.
When I saw you for the first time
and think There she is.
LAURA: God.
DANIEL: There she is.
Everything.

You hit me like a train.

I'm wrecked by you and you have no idea.

No more seasons.

Just before you and now.

I can't hear you breathing.

LAURA: Because I'm not.

DANIEL: No one can see us.

We're not here.

You don't have to do a thing.

LAURA: What if I want to?

DANIEL: No.

LAURA: What if—

DANIEL: Lift your arms.

(She raises her arms straight over her head.

No one moves, then—)

LAURA: Can I smile?

DANIEL: Oh, you better.

(She giggles as he slides his hands under her dress.

He lays on top of her.

They each love the feel, the length, and the press of the other's body.

She rolls them over so she's on top.)

LAURA: I like the view from up here.

(He kisses her throat.)

(Laughing.) No biting!

DANIEL: Love bite.

(He rolls her over so he's on top again. He keeps kissing her.

She wiggles out from under him and sits up. He sits behind her, wraps his arms around her, and kisses the hair away from her neck.)

LAURA: It's so hot out.

(He tries to lift up her dress. She pulls it down.)

DANIEL: You'd be cooler.

LAURA: No…hotter.

DANIEL: You're getting shy.

LAURA: It's hard to be naked under a clear sky. Sometimes I feel better under a few clouds.

DANIEL: I'll blow them in.

(He blows gently on her neck.)

A wind from the East…

(He blows on the opposite side of her neck.)
From the West…
(He blows on the back of her neck.)
From the North…
(He blows on the front of her neck.)
From the South. There. Better?

LAURA: Lots. Thanks.

(He runs his hands over her breasts.)
I feel greedy when I'm with you. More.
(He touches her more.)
That's better.

DANIEL: You're getting spoiled.

LAURA: That bother you?

DANIEL: Not even a little.

LAURA: Me either.
What? What are you looking at?

DANIEL: A tornado went through the last place I lived. An act of God. It was the most beautiful thing I'd ever seen. Just like you. I love you like that. I saw you like that when I first laid eyes on you. You cut a path. You could throw the roof off a house. A wall in your way is just…gone.

LAURA: Then why am I so scared?

DANIEL: There's a place I know with just one house. One white house and a river. We can go there.

LAURA: How far?

DANIEL: Far if we drive slow. Closer if we go fast.

LAURA: Is it nice there?

DANIEL: Beautiful.

LAURA: Will we be happy?

DANIEL: Yes.
(He kisses her.)

LAURA: Will we be safe?

DANIEL: Yes.
(He kisses her.)

LAURA: Together?

DANIEL: Yes.
(He kisses her.)

LAURA: Always?
(He kisses her.)
Promise?

DANIEL: Come on, Laura. Come out and play.
> (*He moves to kiss her.*
> *She pulls back.*
> *Waits.*
> *She makes her decision.*
> *Yes.*
> *Then kisses him.*
> *Darkness.*)

2.

> *Lights up.*
> *A few mornings later.*
> *MARY sits on the porch waiting for LAURA, who's inside.*

MARY: Laura? You in there? (*No answer.*)
> Rise and shine. Bring me a light, will ya?
> (*LAURA finally comes out and hands MARY a lighter. MARY lights up, inhales, gets a good look at LAURA.*)
> Wow.

LAURA: What.

MARY: No offense, but you look really…not good.

LAURA: I couldn't sleep. I haven't slept for weeks.

MARY: Huh.

LAURA: "Huh" what?

MARY: I have a theory.

LAURA: Your theories always suck.

MARY: Because they're always right. Want to hear it?

LAURA: No.
> (*Silence for a second.*)

MARY: Want to hear my suggestion?

LAURA: Does it have anything to do with your theory?

MARY: No.

LAURA: Alright.

MARY: I think you need to just, you know, drink more.

LAURA: Great advice.

MARY: Ever hear me complaining?

LAURA: No. You're a drunk.

MARY: See. Even, like, one beer. Just bring it to bed with you and it's sweet dreams.

LAURA: *(Laughing.)* You drink in bed, too?

MARY: You know that.

LAURA: Alone?

MARY: Takes the edge off.

LAURA: Off of what?

MARY: Of drinking in bed alone.

(LAURA *fishes around in one of* MARY's *pockets, pulls out a pack of cigarettes and takes one out.*

MARY *lights it for her.*)

What's wrong.

LAURA: Nothing. I just—My head hurts.

MARY: Come here.

(MARY *rubs* LAURA's *neck and shoulders.*)

Feel good?

LAURA: Mmm.

MARY: You grind your teeth.

LAURA: What?

MARY: Since we were little. I've heard you. Sometimes, when you fall asleep. Maybe that's why you get so many headaches.

LAURA: Maybe.

MARY: All that tension. Your neck.... All the way up here, down here.... You're tight.

LAURA: If I could sleep for a long time, no dreams...

MARY: You'd be fine. You *are* fine.

LAURA: Pull my hair like you do.

(MARY *gently pulls* LAURA's *hair out to the sides like wings and lets it fan and tumble.*)

A little harder...

MARY: Doesn't hurt?

LAURA: Takes my mind off my headache.

MARY: I don't want to ever *be* married. I just want to have *been* married. Like it all happened in my sleep, by accident, so I'd never have to deal with the whole mess.

LAURA: I think that's what it's like in California.

MARY: But here we marry for life. Amen.

LAURA: And afterlife. Amen.

MARY: That means in heaven we're still stuck doing the dishes. Amen.

LAURA: No. That's hell. Amen.

(LAURA opens a bottle of aspirin, swallows a few with some coffee.)

I was watching this show last night. It said if you stand too close to an explosion, it'll suck you right in.

MARY: He scares you that much?

(LAURA nods.)

But he's your husband.

LAURA: I know.

MARY: Here. Lean back.

My dad just bought another horse. Mom asked him why and he said because she's beautiful. And she is. Beautiful when she runs, when she eats. The kind of beautiful only animals can be.

Why can't it be just us, Laura? We'd be happy then.

3.

The Church.
A few days later.
Enter SCOTTO, FILENE, DANIEL and MARY. TIN enters with LAURA.
The men clip on ties.
The women put clips in their hair.
All kneel.

ALL TOGETHER: …And it shall come to pass that from one new Sabbath to another shall all flesh come to worship before me, saith the Lord. / Our Father, who art in heaven, hallowed be Thy name Thy Kingdom come Thy will be done on earth as it is in heaven give us this day our daily bread and forgive us our debts as we forgive our debtors and lead us not into temptation but deliver us from evil, for thine is the Kingdom and the Power and the Glory, forever and ever. Amen.

(TIN begins at /. The others keep praying until they are indicated to speak. They may overlap a bit, one after the other.)

TIN: Can't keep my eyes open.

SCOTTO: My back. My fuckin' back.

LAURA: Don't touch me don't touch me here don't—

FILENE: *(Feeling his pulse at his wrist.)* …fourteen, fifteen, sixteen, seventeen…

MARY: …then I could swing from my hair.

SCOTTO: …maybe a ghost maybe a tree in the dark.

ALL: Amen.

LAURA: *(Toward DANIEL.)* Look at me.

MARY: *(At LAURA and DANIEL.)* Look at that.

TIN: *(Toward LAURA.)* Look at me.

ALL: Amen.

LAURA: *(Toward DANIEL.)* You're beautiful.

DANIEL: *(Looking at LAURA.)* You're beautiful.

TIN: *(Toward LAURA.)* You're mine.

ALL: Amen.

FILENE: …twenty-seven, twenty-eight, twenty-nine, thirty, thirty-one, thirty-two…

LAURA: *(Looking at DANIEL.)* Look at me.

ALL: Amen.

(All rise. LAURA and TIN leave as a couple. She and DANIEL get one last look at each other.)

4.

Night. That same day.
TIN and LAURA on their bed, kissing.
He's much more excited than she is. She's going through the motions.
She rolls her eyes.

TIN: What? Come here. Come here. Close your eyes. Your eyes closed?

LAURA: *(Eyes open.)* Yeah.

TIN: *(Eyes closed.)* Oh yeah…. What are you thinking about?
(No answer.)
(More insistent.) Out loud.

LAURA: I don't want to.

TIN: *(Breathlessly going at it.)* I'm thinking of you. You in white. In lace. In skin. In your smell. Tight. Oh God. I can't fucking take this. Take off your panties.

LAURA: No.

TIN: Laura—

LAURA: Stop it.

TIN: Come on.

LAURA: Not now!

*(He tries to pull down her panties. She struggles to keep them on. It becomes a fight, a near rape. She wins. Besides, he's not **that** bad of a guy.)*

He pulls back.)

TIN: 'the fuck's your problem? You're mean, you know that? You might be the meanest person in this entire state.

LAURA: Asshole.

TIN: Bitch.

LAURA: Cave man.

TIN: I'll do it with someone else.

LAURA: Go ahead.

TIN: Don't think I won't.

LAURA: No one'll do it with you.

TIN: Mary will. You know it. Women always do it with their best friend's husband.

(This stops her.)

(Laughing.) Mean girl's got a weak spot.

LAURA: No I don't.

TIN: You're jealous.

LAURA: Not of her.

TIN: Please please please please please blow me.

LAURA: No.

TIN: Yes.

(He untucks his T-shirt.)

LAURA: *No.*

(He unzips.
She gets on her knees.)

5.

That night.
DANIEL, SCOTTO, FILENE and MARY in a corner of the barn.
They drink beer, smoke.

FILENE: I don't believe in that shit. Metaphysical's just another word for bullshit.

SCOTTO: *(To FILENE.)* I believe.

MARY: Me too.

FILENE: It's all bullshit.

DANIEL: She'd been dead twenty years. When they dug her up and opened the lid there was glass over the body. She was under glass so no air could get in. They said she looked exactly like she did when they buried her. Then they raised the glass and it all went flat, to nothing. They saw her leave her grave.

SCOTTO: There was one time. I thought it was a ghost but it was a white dog in the dark.

DANIEL: That happened to me once with a cat.

SCOTTO: But sometimes it's real.

FILENE: You're just hoping for a phenomenon, aren't you?

MARY: One time I felt something at my heels. Tiny feet. I was too scared to turn around and look. But it stayed on my heels up the side of the hill and down the other side to the river. I saw the bridge and ran. When I got to the other side I turned around and looked. A tiny girl. She just spread out her arms, fell down, gone.

(Silence.)

SCOTTO: I believe.

FILENE: You would.

DANIEL: I know a guy who drank Holy Water.

FILENE: What'd he do? Piss out the Apostles?

DANIEL: You are such an asshole.

(MARY pops open a can of beer.)

MARY: Anyone got a Valium?

(No offers.)

Vicodin?

(No offers.)

Percocet?

(FILENE hands her a couple pills.
She downs them with beer.)

DANIEL: Did she spread her arms like this?

MARY: Who?

DANIEL: The little girl.

MARY: Like this.

DANIEL: *(Shuddering.)* Shit.

(SCOTTO stands to leave.)

MARY: Scared?

SCOTTO: Got stuff to do.

DANIEL: Right.

SCOTTO: Some people actually work you know.

FILENE: I work.

MARY: Jackin' off doesn't count.

SCOTTO: Promised Gary I'd help him with his truck.

MARY: Now?

FILENE: Hasn't run for two years. What's a few more minutes.

MARY: Blow him off.

DANIEL: Come on.

FILENE: Blow him off.

SCOTTO: You think?

MARY: Yeah.

DANIEL: Blow him off.

> *(SCOTTO thinks, then sits back down.*
>
> *MARY's drugs start working.)*

MARY: Man, I feel soooo much better. I was sooooo tense. Like, in my neck. I gotta go home.

DANIEL AND SCOTTO: *(Ad lib.)* No. Stay. Come on. Few more minutes.

MARY: Gotta go.

FILENE: *(To MARY.)* Walk you home.

MARY: No thanks.

FILENE: Come on.

MARY: *(Moving away from him.)* Go play in the road.

DANIEL AND SCOTTO: *(Ad lib.)* God, Filene. Leave her alone. You dog. Back off.

> *(Etc...)*

MARY: Yeah.

> *(SCOTTO puts chewing tobacco in his mouth.)*

DANIEL: That stuff'll give you jaw cancer. Have to get your jaw whacked off.

FILENE: Whole lower half of your face.

MARY: Lips, too.

FILENE: Like Chuck's grandpa, Top-Jaw Johnson.

MARY: Top-Jaw Johnson.

FILENE: All started with a pinch between the cheek and gum.

MARY: Now he doesn't have either one.

FILENE: Smoke. It's better for you.

> *(SCOTTO spits out the wad.*
>
> *FILENE hands him a cigarette.*
>
> *SCOTTO lights up.)*

SCOTTO: Pussies.

DANIEL: *(Emptying his beer.)* Beer run?

FILENE: No one sells on Sunday.

DANIEL: Shit.

SCOTTO: Got a case in my trunk.

DANIEL: Case?

SCOTTO: Well. A six-pack.

(*MARY has climbed onto a bench. She spreads her arms like the ghost from her story.*)

MARY: Hey. Hey. Watch me.

SCOTTO: Mary.

FILENE: Stop it.

MARY: Watch.

DANIEL: Knock it off.

(*She persists more beautifully, fiercely.*)

MARY: Watch me!

FILENE: Knock it off!

SCOTTO: You're freakin' me out.

(*With her arms wide, she leans forward*
Falling.
Falls.
She lies still for a moment.
The guys stare down at her. Then…)

SCOTTO: Mary?

(*He pokes at her with his toes.*)

Mary?

(*She stirs. Finally sits up.*)

MARY: I gotta go meet Laura.

(*As she crawls away…*)

…And then she was gone.

(*They stare after her in silence, then recover.*)

SCOTTO: Why are farm girls so much crazier than farm guys?

FILENE: She's not crazy.

DANIEL: What is she, then?

FILENE: Not crazy.

DANIEL: Look at you.

SCOTTO: Fucked-up girl walking home alone…. You can barely keep your tongue in your mouth.

FILENE: Shut up.

DANIEL: True. Look at him.

SCOTTO: Yeah.

FILENE: Faggots.

> *(DANIEL and SCOTTO laugh this off.)*

SCOTTO: Dog.

> *(FILENE waits as long as he can stand it.)*

FILENE: Jesus Christ…

> *(He goes after MARY.*
>
> *SCOTTO and DANIEL bark and howl after him.)*

DANIEL: She gonna be okay?

SCOTTO: She can take care of herself.

> *(SCOTTO inhales deeply.)*
>
> Smell that?

DANIEL: No.

SCOTTO: Rain.

DANIEL: Yeah. Somewhere. Come on. Let's go. I'm hungry.

> *(DANIEL starts to walk away.)*

SCOTTO: Wait.

DANIEL: I'm starving.

> *(SCOTTO catches up to DANIEL.*
>
> *They stop.)*

SCOTTO: I—

> *(They face each other. DANIEL waits for SCOTTO to speak.)*
>
> I saw you in church today. I watched you watch her.

DANIEL: Who?

SCOTTO: Don't bullshit me.

DANIEL: Who?

SCOTTO: Laura. That's who.

DANIEL: No harm in looking.

SCOTTO: Aw, man. Don't be so—

DANIEL: *(Feigning ignorance.)* What?

SCOTTO: I'm not fuckin' around.

DANIEL: Me neither. Lighten up. Come on.

SCOTTO: You're an asshole if you do this.

> *(They both kick at stuff on the ground for a moment.)*

DANIEL: You ever watch her in church?

SCOTTO: Absolutely not. No. I don't know. Yeah.

DANIEL: The sun, the light, the holy, the mighty….

> She looks…biblical.

SCOTTO: *(Sarcastically.)* What? Like Eve?

DANIEL: Like all of fucking Eden.

> *(And they walk away.)*

6.

> *Later that night.* LAURA *and* MARY *walk through the field.*
> MARY *is really tipsy.*
> FILENE *catches up.*

FILENE: *(To LAURA.)* I can walk her home.

LAURA: She can barely stand.

MARY: He can walk me home.

LAURA: No he can't.

FILENE: It's on my way.

MARY: It's on his way.

LAURA: Come on, Mary.

FILENE: *(To MARY.)* She doesn't want me to walk you home.

MARY: Laura!

LAURA: *(To FILENE.)* Go away.

FILENE: *(To MARY.)* See.

> *(MARY weaves toward FILENE.)*

MARY: I see three of him and they're pretty cute.

LAURA: He's disgusting.

FILENE: Mary?

LAURA: Mary.

MARY: You two fighting over me? Whose sweet dream is *this?*
I think it's...yours.

> *(She points to LAURA then walks off in the direction they were originally headed then stops, waiting for LAURA.*
> LAURA *and* FILENE *face each other. He grabs a handful of dead grass and hands it to her, like a bouquet, bows and exits.*
> LAURA *drops the grass.)*

He gave you flowers.

LAURA: Promise you won't touch him.

MARY: Swear. Not with a gun to my head.

> *(MARY walks off. LAURA runs after her.)*

7.

> *Late. That same night.*
> *TIN asleep in bed. LAURA enters. She watches him sleeping.*

LAURA: *(Quietly.)* I can't do this.
> *(She slips out of her dress and lays down on top of the covers, her back to TIN.*
> *Then, sleepily—)*

TIN: Laura?
> *(No answer.)*
> Laura?

LAURA: Right here.

TIN: Where you been?

LAURA: With Mary.

TIN: I heard something—

LAURA: Go back to sleep.

TIN: Come here.

LAURA: No. I—

TIN: Sleep.

LAURA: I'm gonna get a beer.

TIN: Then bring me one.

LAURA: I was gonna drink it on the porch.

TIN: I'm too far out of your way?

LAURA: No.
> *(She stands up. He stands up. She starts to leave the room, he blocks her way.*
> *He walks forward, forcing her to walk backward toward the bed. At the bed,*
> *he turns her around and bends her over it. He watches her from behind for*
> *what feels like a long time.*
> *He then turns and as he walks out of the room…)*

TIN: I'll get the beer.
> *(She slowly straightens up.)*

8.

> *Morning.*
> *LAURA and DANIEL approach each other from opposite sides of the field.*
> *They stop.*

LAURA: Do you know what your body, there, does to mine, here?
> *(He shakes his head "no," smiling.)*

From fifteen paces?

(He shakes his head.

They take a few steps closer to each other.)

Ten?

(He shakes his head. They step closer.)

Five?

(Closer.)

Two?

(Closer.)

One?

(Closer. Touching.)

You don't know?

(He shakes his head "no.")

I melt. From the ground up. In waves. If the ocean could feel, it would feel like that. If it was lucky. Before you came here, did you ever see the ocean?

(He shakes his head "no.")

The mountains?

(He shakes his head "no.")

We'll go.

(He moves to kiss her.)

Daniel?

(He stops.)

Say "yes."

DANIEL: Yes.

(He kisses her.)

LAURA: When I was a little girl, I always dreamed of someone like you. Someone new, always wearing new clothes and clean shoes. Your skin was smooth and smelled like something nice I didn't know. Soft eyes, soft hands, nothing broken. And you came and fell in love with me. You told me I made you feel like the luckiest man in the world. You would do anything for me.

Daniel.

Miracles happen out here. I've seen it rain grass and shadows.

My mom used to say there's nothing here between us and heaven. The angels twist our arms. Prayers go straight up. Judgment comes straight down. Loving you breaks everything I know.

(A noise in the near distance.

DANIEL jumps. For the first time, he's scared.)
What?

DANIEL: Somebody's there.

LAURA: Nobody.

DANIEL: Wait.

LAURA: Daniel—

DANIEL: Wait.

LAURA: You're scared.

DANIEL: I thought I heard someone.

LAURA: You are.

DANIEL: No.

LAURA: You can't be. Don't you dare. Not now. Look at me.

(He won't.)
Look at me.
(He finally does.)
God, you really are.

DANIEL: Aren't you?

LAURA: That won't stop me.

DANIEL: You can't tell a breeze from a body out here. What if somebody sees? Think about it. This isn't a good place to be a homewrecker. Do you think he knows?

LAURA: No.

DANIEL: Are you sure?

LAURA: No.

(He touches her.)

DANIEL: Should we stop?

(She shakes her head "yes."
He stops.
Then she shakes her head "no" and he continues.)

9.

Later that morning.
MARY is twirling a baton at the junked car seat. Waiting.
LAURA enters.

MARY: You're late.

LAURA: I know.

MARY: Look at you…

LAURA: Oh yeah?

MARY: Yeah.

LAURA: He kissed me here. He kissed me here. He kissed here. Here. Here.

MARY: Mmm…

LAURA: And under here…

MARY: What are you gonna do?

LAURA: I don't know.

MARY: What do you *think* you're gonna do?

LAURA: I don't *know.*

MARY: I've never cheated on someone before.

LAURA: You've never had anyone to cheat *with.*

MARY: How does it feel?

LAURA: Like there's been a big storm. Everything's down: the trees, the power, the phones. So everything has to be said face-to-face in the dark. It's the scariest thing in the world.

> *(LAURA sits. MARY stands and starts twirling a baton.)*

MARY: Do you love him?

LAURA: Yes.

MARY: Do you trust him?

LAURA: What's that supposed to mean?

MARY: It's pretty clear.

LAURA: I wouldn't love him if I couldn't trust him.

MARY: Think Tin knows anything?

LAURA: No. I don't know.

MARY: I think this affair's good for you. Never seen you so pretty, so sexy. Getting away with it does you wonders.

> *(Silence as the air between them becomes tense. MARY twirls the baton then uses it like a scepter.)*

I hereby dub you Queen of the Fling and Princess of Pulling the Fast One.

LAURA: Fuck you.

MARY: Don't you feel even a little bad?

LAURA: Shut up.

MARY: Not even a little?

LAURA: No.

MARY: People like you make the locusts come.

LAURA: Don't say that.

MARY: You make the black flies and the blue flies cover the walls.

LAURA: Stop.

MARY: You bring the fire down.

LAURA: You're crazy.

MARY: That's not news.

LAURA: People do what I'm doing all the time.

MARY: Not around here.

LAURA: Maybe that's the problem with this place.

MARY: For every step taketh the liar, taketh the lie till their steps become one. So saith the Lord in Heaven.

LAURA: So saith you.

MARY: A little g-u-i-l-t nippin' at your heels?

(She pokes LAURA in the side. LAURA is ticklish and giggles.)

Huh? Huh? Huh?

(A poke for each "huh" continues. Not very nice, really.)

LAURA: *(Giggling.)* Stop it.

MARY: Huh huh huh huh huh?

LAURA: *(Over above.)* Stop it. Stop it!

(LAURA shoves MARY away hard. Harder than she means to.
MARY puts more space between them.
LAURA rolls her eyes.)

Mary… I'm sorry. Come here.

(MARY sort of pouts.)

Please?

MARY: You're already gone, aren't you?

LAURA: Closer.

(They hold each other.)

Feel this.

(She presses MARY's hand to her heart.)

Feel it beating?

(MARY nods.)

And now when I think of Daniel?

MARY: It stopped.

(MARY keeps her hand over LAURA's heart, waits for it to start beating again.
It does.)

LAURA: You can stop your heart whenever you want to. Doesn't even hurt.

MARY: Sounds like death.

LAURA: Feels like sleep.

I think about his hands, legs, back. How good it feels with him.

MARY: Yeah. Lucky bitch.

10.

A few nights later.
SCOTTO and TIN on the porch.

TIN: You prick.

SCOTTO: I apologize.

TIN: You fuckin' prick.

SCOTTO: I'm wrong—

TIN: You are so wrong.

SCOTTO: And outta line—

TIN: Completely outta fuckin' line.

SCOTTO: I'm sorry, man.

TIN: I mean, how dare you.

SCOTTO: I just—I'm your friend and…

TIN: She loves me.

SCOTTO: I know. She loves you.

TIN: She loves me like crazy.

SCOTTO: She just seems a little—

TIN: What?

SCOTTO: A little…

TIN: What?!

SCOTTO: Nothing.

TIN: You don't talk shit about a guy's wife. You don't even *think* shit. Because you don't *know* shit. And that's the truth. You don't know shit about women. You don't know *anything* about Laura.

SCOTTO: You're right. I'm wrong. Sorry, man. Sorry.
(Silence.)
She's pretty intense, huh.

TIN: God, you don't know…. Sometimes—I shouldn't tell you this—sometimes when we're messing around, she gets this look. Her eyes. They go dark and explode. Then I explode. I wish I could take a picture of her right then, with those eyes. It's like fear. It's like fuck me. Aw God, I'm getting hard.
(SCOTTO shifts away from TIN and his hard-on.)

11.

A few days later.
LAURA and DANIEL kneeling in the field, kissing.
He stops.

LAURA: What?

DANIEL: What?

LAURA: I asked you first.

DANIEL: Nothing.

LAURA: There's something.

DANIEL: You can read my mind?

LAURA: No. Your eyes. You didn't close them.
(She kisses him.)
What?
(She tries to kiss him again.)
Come on.

DANIEL: Laura…

LAURA: It won't hurt, I promise.

DANIEL: Stop.

LAURA: Come here.

DANIEL: Stop it.
(He steps back.)

LAURA: What's wrong?

DANIEL: It's just— It's stupid…

LAURA: I did something.

DANIEL: No.

LAURA: What?

DANIEL: Do you—Do you ever think that you go from him to me. From me to him?

LAURA: I can't.

DANIEL: That he touches you, then I touch you. He kisses you, I kiss you.

LAURA: You're jealous?

DANIEL: No.

LAURA: You are.

DANIEL: That's not it.

LAURA: It's kind of cute.

DANIEL: I am not *jealous.*

LAURA: Wow. This is really really—

DANIEL: *(Harshly.)* How long since you fucked him?

LAURA: What?

DANIEL: How long?

LAURA: I don't know, I—

DANIEL: Two weeks?

LAURA: No. I—

DANIEL: One week?

LAURA: I don't want to think about him when I'm—

DANIEL: Couple days?

LAURA: Maybe, I don't know…

DANIEL: Hours?

LAURA: Fine. Every night. He makes me. Every fucking night. There. You happy?

DANIEL: No.

LAURA: Daniel—

DANIEL: I don't like sharing.

LAURA: I don't like being shared.

DANIEL: Your hands go from him to me. When I'm in you, I'm an echo of him.

LAURA: When you're in me, I forget him.

DANIEL: One body. With so many hands on it.

LAURA: I try not to let him. You know that.

DANIEL: No. I don't.

I love your heat and your smells. But I'm sick of scraping them up from the dirt when we're done. I want to be clean. What if I said "now." What if I wanted us to leave now?

(Silence.

Then he scoops up some dirt
and puts it in her lap, like he's handing
her a gift.

He walks away.

She stands, brushes herself off and starts to walk off.

FILENE appears.)

LAURA: Oh God.

FILENE: Hey.

LAURA: What are you doing here?

FILENE: Stalking you. What are you doing here?

LAURA: Walking home.

FILENE: Mind if I stalk you the rest of the way?

LAURA: Yes.

FILENE: Come on. Do me the honor. I'm on good behavior. Swear.

LAURA: Go steal some gas. Chickens. Whatever it is you do.

FILENE: You're really funny.

LAURA: *(Flatly.)* Thanks.

FILENE: How's Tin?

LAURA: Fine.

FILENE: Glad to hear it. He's a good guy.

LAURA: You wouldn't know good if it hit you in the face.

FILENE: You're crackin' me up.

(She starts to walk away.)

Wait. I want to walk you home. Honest.

LAURA: Wanna carry my books, too.

FILENE: I mean it.

LAURA: You're pathetic.

FILENE: Thanks. I do my best.

LAURA: I'm serious.

FILENE: So am I.

(Silence.)

You think you're better than me, don't you? That's okay. So do I.

(She takes a stick and lifts his shirt up his belly. It's horribly scarred from burns.)

LAURA: Someone didn't like you very much.

(He doesn't respond—but doesn't flinch or hide, either.)

Does it hurt?

FILENE: *(Without self-pity.)* Some of the nerves are still burning. Some still smell smoke. The rest are dead.

LAURA: How far up does it go?

(She starts to peer up his shirt. He lets her.)

How far down?

(No answer.)

Can I?

(She starts to pull at his belt buckle. He lets her.)

You'd really let me?

(No answer.

She stops.

He takes the stick from her and uses it to lift her dress a few inches.

She doesn't stop him.

He goes a few inches higher.)

She doesn't stop him.
Higher.
Higher.
Higher.)
Your hair is dirty. Your shirt's rotting. I should feel sorry for you but I don't. You're not a body with a scar. You're a scar with a body.
(She starts to leave.)
FILENE: Just remember, I don't care how many hands've been on you. What I wouldn't give to touch your foot.
(She runs away.
FILENE is happy.)

12.

That night. The bedroom.
TIN is asleep.
LAURA enters and tries not to wake him as she gets ready for bed.
His eyes open. He watches her.

LAURA: I'm sorry.
TIN: For what?
(This seems much more loaded to her than it really is.)
For what?
(As she crawls under the sheets…)
LAURA: For waking you.
TIN: Mm.
LAURA: Go back to sleep.
TIN: You think the pillows smell more like you or me?
LAURA: I— I don't know.
TIN: Like you, I think. They smell sweet.
(And he falls back to sleep.
She lays next to him, wide awake.
She smells her pillow and starts to cry.)
LAURA: I'm not afraid.
I'm not cold.
I am loved.
I'm not sick.
I'm not lost.
I am loved.
I'm a storm.

13.

A few days later.
LAURA and MARY in LAURA's bedroom.
They sit facing each other, legs extended, painting each other's toenails.

LAURA: If this place went down in flames, what would be left?

MARY: Bones if we stayed. Nothing if we didn't. You know, in some places, ashes on your forehead mean you're a saint.

LAURA: Or an arsonist.

MARY: Pessimist.

LAURA: Question.

MARY: Hm.

LAURA: Would you sleep with Tin?

MARY: That a trick question?

LAURA: He thinks you would.

MARY: He probably thinks everybody would.

LAURA: Well? Would you?

MARY: *(Rolling her eyes.)* God.

LAURA: That's a no?

MARY: Big no.

(LAURA pretends to smudge dirt on MARY's forehead, sainting her.)

LAURA: I sainted you.

(MARY rubs her forehead.)

It's a compliment.

MARY: Not to me.

(LAURA blows on MARY's polished toenails.)

LAURA: I like this color.

MARY: It's not too…slutty?

LAURA: Not on you.

MARY: Mm.

LAURA: What about Filene? Heard he's up to something.

MARY: Always is.

LAURA: Wonder who he'd love.

MARY: Who cares.

LAURA: Think about it.

MARY: Do I have to?

LAURA: Yeah.

MARY: She'd look like us on the outside, but be something else on the inside. Maybe her bones would be animal, or her blood would be thick. Something. She'd have to be from another place, because we don't make them like that around here.

(*MARY blows on LAURA's wet toenails.*)

LAURA: Am I a good liar?

MARY: You're a great liar.

LAURA: Really?

MARY: I'm lying. You're awful.

LAURA: I'm serious.

MARY: Me too. You suck as a liar.

LAURA: How'd you know? I never lied to you.

MARY: Have too.

LAURA: Name once.

MARY: Every time you say "Sorry I'm late."

LAURA: 'Cause I'm late all the time.

MARY: But you're never sorry.

LAURA: Your toes are fucked up.

MARY: Are not.

LAURA: Compared to mine. Look.

(*They closely compare toes.*)

See. Yours look like skinny people with big heads.

MARY: But yours are all the same length. That's just *wrong*.

(*She blows on LAURA's toes.*)

I don't know how you've walked on these things all these years.

(*She plays with LAURA's toes.*)

This little piggy went to market. This little piggy stayed home.

(*As she tweaks LAURA's toe—*)

This little piggy ate roast beef. This little piggy had none.

(*TIN enters.*)

TIN: The hell's this?

MARY: Speaking of piggies…

(*TIN kisses LAURA on the top of her head.*)

TIN: (*To MARY.*) Two options. One: I can pretend you're not here. Or two: I don't have to pretend.

(*The women roll their eyes.*)

MARY: (*To LAURA.*) Call you later.

LAURA: Yeah.

MARY: And this little piggy went wee wee wee all the way home.

(And she exits.

LAURA stands up. TIN grabs her hand or the hem of her dress.)

TIN: Sit.

LAURA: I just thought—

TIN: Sit for a minute.

LAURA: Thought I'd start dinner.

TIN: I'm not hungry. You?

LAURA: Guess not.

TIN: I like that smell.

LAURA: What?

TIN: Nail polish. It's so…girly.

LAURA: Mary says I have ugly feet.

TIN: She's a liar. What do you two talk about.

LAURA: Stuff.

TIN: Like…?

LAURA: Like what do you think? That we exchange recipes and sewing patterns? We talk about things.

TIN: You ever talk about me?

LAURA: Tomorrow we'll talk about what an ass you just were just now.

TIN: She's always here. This is my house. I wanna know what you talk about in my house.

(She ignores him and fans at the wet nail polish on her toes.

TIN slaps the side of her head roughly. She ignores it. She's used to it.

He does it again.)

LAURA: Knock it off.

TIN: Then answer me.

LAURA: I don't know what we talk about. Shit shit and more shit. Useless, boring, stupid, day-to-day shit. Believe it or not, it doesn't include you.

TIN: Good. She gives me the creeps. Always has. I don't like her in here.

LAURA: Yes, sir.

(She stands.)

I'm hungry.

TIN: You just said you weren't.

LAURA: Well I am now.

(She starts to exit.)

TIN: Wait. Come here.

LAURA: What?

TIN: Come here.

(He pulls her down to his eye-level.)

Look at me.

(She can't meet his eyes.)

Look. At. Me.

(He looks closely into her eyes and runs the tip of a finger along the inner edge of her eyelid. He shows her what's on his fingertip.)

There. An eyelash. It could've hurt.

(She stands up and moves slowly away.)

14.

Later. Dusk.
The car seat in the field.
DANIEL sits waiting for LAURA.
A noise.
He turns.
MARY approaches.

MARY: She's gonna be late.

DANIEL: Fuck.

MARY: I'm just the messenger.

DANIEL: She tell you to tell me?

MARY: No. It's just my good deed for the day. You're hogging the seat.

(He makes room for her.
She sits next to him.)

I make you nervous.

DANIEL: I guess. A little.

MARY: Why? Because I know?

DANIEL: Because you want to know more.

MARY: She's late 'cause hubby's home. He's "high-maintenance." She might be really late. She might not come at all.

DANIEL: That's okay.

MARY: You're patient.

DANIEL: You're a pest.

MARY: I know, I know. I have to get a hobby.

DANIEL: She's your best friend, isn't she?

MARY: Since forever.

DANIEL: You're lucky.

MARY: I think maybe you're luckier.

DANIEL: Yeah.

MARY: When she talks to you, does she touch you right here a lot?

(She touches his arm.)

DANIEL: Sometimes.

MARY: Me, too. What about here?

(She touches his shoulder.)

DANIEL: Sometimes.

MARY: Where does she touch you the most?

DANIEL: I'm done playing.

MARY: I want to know where her fingers go.

DANIEL: Get the fuck—

(He roughly shoves her hand away.)

MARY: You're the luckiest of all. You know that?

15.

A few nights later.
SCOTTO and TIN in the barn.

SCOTTO: ...and if the woman you're sleeping with is thinking of another guy while you're sleeping with her, it's like she's really sleeping with him. Literally. Or maybe it's like *you're* sleeping with him.

TIN: You are such a fuck.

SCOTTO: I am not, man.

TIN: Are fucking too.

SCOTTO: Fine.

TIN: You got a one-track mind these days, Scotto. You know that?

SCOTTO: I just think—

TIN: What?!

(Tense silence while SCOTTO tries to bite his tongue.)

SCOTTO: I just mean, how could you *really* know.

TIN: I *know!* I *know!* I'm there! With her! And it's just the two of us in that bed.

(Silence. Then...)

Something you wanna tell me then spit it out.

(SCOTTO decides not to interfere with TIN's cluelessness/denial.)

You don't understand women and you sure don't understand her.

SCOTTO: You're right.

TIN: You okay?

SCOTTO: Yeah. Fine.

(TIN *hands* SCOTTO *a beer.*)

TIN: You're my best friend.

SCOTTO: Yeah.

TIN: So don't say any more.

16.

Later that night.
In the field.
MARY *and* SCOTTO *cross paths.*

MARY: Hey.

SCOTTO: Hey.

MARY: What're you doing?

SCOTTO: Walking home.

MARY: Me too.

SCOTTO: Doing anything later?

MARY: No.

SCOTTO: I'm bored.

MARY: Me too.

SCOTTO: Maybe I could, you know, go home with you. We could fool around or something…

MARY: Nah. I'll take a smoke if you have one, though.

(*He hands her a cigarette and lights it for her. He smokes one too.*)
So where you been?

SCOTTO: With Tin. You?

MARY: With Laura.

SCOTTO: Oh.

MARY: Yeah.

(*They linger, like they're dying to spill the beans.*)
Had bugs all over the screen door last night. Dozens of them.

SCOTTO: Means it's gonna be a bad winter.

MARY: Yeah.

SCOTTO: Guaranteed.

MARY: Long way off, though.

SCOTTO: Yeah.

MARY: Yeah.

SCOTTO: Yeah. So…

MARY: So it's none of our business, okay?

  (*Silence.*)

  Okay?

SCOTTO: You're right.

MARY: So. You can come over. Just to kill some time. That's all.

SCOTTO: Thanks. That'd be nice.

17.

  LAURA and DANIEL at the car seat watching clouds take on shapes.

LAURA: There. A tree.

DANIEL: A horse.

LAURA: A house.

DANIEL: A river.

LAURA: Our house on the river. And those clouds, those shapes moving into each other. Us. Finally there.

  (*Silence.*)

  Your turn.

  (*Silence.*)

  Hello?

DANIEL: I'm here.

LAURA: You're quiet.

DANIEL: I know.

LAURA: When you're quiet, I'm alone. What?

DANIEL: I'm…bored.

LAURA: That's mean.

DANIEL: It's honest.

LAURA: You like it out here.

DANIEL: It's getting old.

LAURA: Fine. Let's do something else.

DANIEL: Like what?

LAURA: We could…

DANIEL: Go for a walk?

LAURA: No. But we could—

DANIEL: (*Increasingly sarcastic.*) Go for a drive?

LAURA: No.

DANIEL: A swim? A movie?

LAURA: We can't. You know that.

DANIEL: No. *You* can't. I can. Other people can. Scotto can. Mary can.

> *(This hurts.)*

LAURA: How do you know? You ask her?

> *(He rolls his eyes.)*

Did you? What'd she say? Sure she said yes. I mean, if it's a matter of convenience—

DANIEL: You know what I mean.

LAURA: —of availability—

DANIEL: Laura—

LAURA: —then she's the girl for you. It sure wouldn't be me.

> *(This thought stops her in her tracks.)*

Tell me what you want.

DANIEL: I don't know.

LAURA: Anything. What is it.

DANIEL: I feel like a coward.

LAURA: Don't.

DANIEL: Like a cheat.

LAURA: Why should you if I don't?

DANIEL: I know you don't. That bothers me, too.

LAURA: What can I do? Not be with you? Go back to him? We'll leave. Tomorrow. The next day. In a month. Whenever we can. Soon.

> *(He stands to leave.)*

DANIEL: I said I'd help Scotto with something.

LAURA: Stay.

DANIEL: I promised him.

LAURA: Meet me later?

DANIEL: I don't know when we'll be done.

> *(He turns to go.)*

LAURA: Daniel?

> *(He stops.)*

The things I'd do to be with you.

DANIEL: I just want to spend the night with you.

> *(He exits, leaving her alone.*
> *She starts to exit in opposite direction.*
> FILENE *enters.)*

FILENE: You can tell me.

    Ask me anything.

    I'm always up.

    (He starts to walk away.)

LAURA: Wait.

    (He stops.

    She tries, but says nothing.

    He leaves.)

    Help me?

18.

A few days later.

MARY stands in the field.

She tilts her head way back, pulls a sword from behind her back and begins to swallow it. It's difficult, but she does it and finishes with a flourish and a cough.

LAURA who'd been invisible in the grass, sits up.

LAURA: Oh my God.

MARY: Told you I could do it.

LAURA: God.

MARY: I had to practice for a few hours, though.

LAURA: But you didn't *really* swallow it.

MARY: What did I do then?

LAURA: You shoved it in and pulled it out.

MARY: So?

LAURA: If you swallowed it, it'd be gone.

MARY: If I swallowed it, I'd be dead.

LAURA: I guess.

MARY: It's a *trick.*

LAURA: *(Grabbing sword.)* It's got bite marks all over it.

MARY: It's my brother's. He brought it home with him when he quit the car-
nival. Having a side-show for a brother has its advantages.

    (LAURA flicks at the edge of the blade.)

LAURA: Ow. Thought you said it was fake.

MARY: I said it was a trick.

LAURA: Same thing.

MARY: Obviously not.

(MARY grabs the sword and twirls it around expertly.)

LAURA: You been hearing anything?

MARY: About what?

LAURA: You know.

MARY: No.

LAURA: "No" you don't know? Or "no" you haven't heard anything?

MARY: *(Tossing the sword like a baton into the air.)* Haven't heard a thing. Not a fucking thing, princess.

LAURA: You'd tell me though if you did.

MARY: Yes.

LAURA: Promise.

MARY: *(Losing patience.)* Yes!

LAURA: Swear you—

MARY: Shut up!

LAURA: Sorry.

MARY: God! I am so tired of talking about it. Maybe no one gives a shit about what you do! Maybe you're just one more stupid chick, obsessed with her—her *obsession.*

LAURA: I'm in love with him!

MARY: *(Sarcastically.)* That's a good one.

LAURA: He loves me!

MARY: You think so? You don't think you're just a little piece of married ass—

LAURA: Fuck you.

MARY: —piece of ass. Pretty ass, maybe. But just ass. A-S-S.

(LAURA lunges at MARY and gets in a few good blows before MARY strikes back with the sword.
The blade catches LAURA in the arm—she bleeds.
They're both shocked.)

This is a trick. This is only a trick. Should this be something serious you should proceed to the nearest place of safety and tune your radio to something that will tell you what to do. Repeat: This is only a trick.

LAURA: Mary—

MARY: Call Tin. Call Daniel. Get them both here and have them fight it out. That's what you want. That'll get you off. Two guys beating the shit out of each other over you. Then all you'd have to do is lay back and enjoy. Some prize you are.

(MARY swings at some grass with the sword. Calming down.)

Fuck you. Fuck me. So there.

LAURA: The sky is falling, the sky is falling. Who said that?

MARY: I can't remember.

LAURA: I've really started something, haven't I?

MARY: *(Handing LAURA a tissue.)* Put this on your cut.

LAURA: Mary? Will you do me a favor?

MARY: Suppose I have to, now that I almost cut your arm off with my not-so-fake trick sword.

LAURA: Don't talk to Daniel.

MARY: Why not?

LAURA: Don't talk to him, don't look at him, stay away from him. I just— I don't want you anywhere near him.

MARY: You think I'd?—

LAURA: Just promise.

MARY: That me and him—?

LAURA: I don't know.

MARY: You're an idiot, you know that?

(MARY checks LAURA's cut. It's fine.)

MARY: Chicken Little.

LAURA: Hm?

MARY: The sky is falling, the sky is falling…

LAURA: Thanks.

MARY: Could he have remembered that?

19.

Church.

All file in, sit, and cross themselves.

They are reverent, nervous, very different from the earlier church scene.

Silence.

Breath.

They hold their eyes straight ahead, not because they should, but because they don't dare look at one another. No one wants to meet someone else's gaze.

A sense of collective guilt, collective inside knowledge is possessed by everyone—except by TIN.

SCOTTO's eyes shift a bit.

MARY's gaze wanders.

FILENE watches it all.

LAURA tries to look at DANIEL, but he won't look back.

LAURA can't stand it. She blatently stares at DANIEL. He adamantly doesn't return the look. This hurts her so much. It's a change in him, in what she thought was her control of him.

LAURA: *(To DANIEL.)* I don't even have a shadow without you.
    (She turns her eyes to the front.)
ALL: Amen.

20.

LAURA in bed. TIN enters carrying a few beers.
She watches him.
He watches her.
He stomps dirt off of his boots then peels his dirty shirt off and tosses it on the bed.
She gives him a look.

TIN: Sorry.
    (He takes the dirty shirt off the bed and tosses it on the floor.)
    How was your day?
LAURA: Fine.
TIN: You look so…clean.
    (Silence as he looks down at the palms of his hands, picks and scratches at them.)
    "And how was your day?"
    Horseshit.
    "Really honey? And why was that?"
    Because I was thirsty all day and hungry all day and all I could think of was this, walking in here, and it seemed like a hundred years away…
    (He pops open a beer and drinks hard.)
    Work in grain all day, come home at night and drink it. I'm gonna turn into some kind of grain…thing.
    (This makes him laugh. She doesn't join in.)
    Have you ever worked so hard, your bones try to mutiny?
LAURA: No.
TIN: Cut up my hands today. Look.
    (He shows her—she winces.)
LAURA: Wear the gloves they gave you.
TIN: Thanks for the sympathy.

LAURA: What d'you want me to say, if you won't bother—

TIN: When they're shredded like this, when I touch you, I feel you on my inside. Then when I heal it's like you stay inside me. Man and wife, over and over again. I can be so romantic sometimes.

(He finishes that beer and starts another.)

This is the part where you run into my arms. This is the part where you bury your face in my neck. This is the part where you say I love you. It's that part. Can you say it?

(He leans over her. She gets off the bed.)

LAURA: Go get cleaned up.

TIN: Say it.

(She tries to walk away. He pulls her back roughly.)

LAURA: That hurt.

TIN: Say I love you.

(Again she tries to leave. He pulls her back hard. She falls.)

I love you.

(She tries to crawl away. He drags her back.)

I love you.

(She tries to kick him and crawl away. He grabs her and pulls her back.)

I love you!

LAURA: Get off—!

(Same thing. Only by now they're both crying.)

TIN: I love you!

(They're both on the floor. She's getting bloody.)

LAURA: Stop it!

TIN: I love you!

(She stops crying, but he continues. He seems small, pathetic, vulnerable.)

LAURA: Oh God.

TIN: I'm sorry.

LAURA: *(Noticing the blood on her.)* What did you do?

TIN: I didn't mean it.

LAURA: Oh…God…

TIN: I didn't.

LAURA: I'm bleeding.

TIN: Can you say it? Please?

LAURA: I'm bleeding.

(She starts to clean herself.)

TIN: It's not you. It's my hands.

21.

The next day. The car seat.
LAURA and FILENE.
She tries to act in control. Doesn't fool him.

FILENE: It's all hypothetical, of course.

LAURA: Why do you always have to use big words.

FILENE: You know what they say. Big words, big...

LAURA: So... you'll do it? Right?

FILENE: Yeah.

LAURA: Jesus. God. Then, you'll do it. God. I can't believe this.

    (She starts to get sick. She covers her mouth and calms down. Barely.)

    Why are you smiling?

FILENE: If I said, you'd slap my face.

LAURA: Fuck you.

FILENE: You are not from this dip-shit, church-picnic pie-eating, cow-fart of a
town, are you? You are a sharp, shining thing from somewhere else. Your
feet are always clean. I just think about thinking about you and I get off.
We'd be a force of nature. Better. We'd be unnatural. I'm not afraid of anything, except you. You are the biggest bitch I know and you blow me away.

LAURA: Can we get away with it?

FILENE: That's just a state of mind.

    (He turns to leave. She takes a few steps after him, like a lost dog.)

    I like you but not at my back. Go home. Go on. What are you thinking?
What's your favorite flower? What's your favorite color? What time do
you have to be home, little girl?

LAURA: You know what Tin does to me.

FILENE: I have an idea of what he doesn't do.

LAURA: I fell in love.

FILENE: Shit happens.

LAURA: I love him.

FILENE: But I'm gonna be your hero. Your super hero. Off I go to save the day.

    Stop me.... Stop me...

    (She doesn't.

    He leaves with a smile.)

22.

Later that day.
LAURA and DANIEL in the field.

LAURA: Would you love me if I was blind?

DANIEL: Yes.

LAURA: Would you love me if I was deaf?

DANIEL: Yes.

LAURA: If I was dumb?

DANIEL: Yes.

LAURA: If I was different?

DANIEL: You mean if you changed?

LAURA: If I was different.

DANIEL: You're the same.

LAURA: Do you think there's such a thing as a person who's unlovable?

DANIEL: No. Maybe.

LAURA: Would you love me if I was innocent?

DANIEL: You are.

LAURA: Would you love me if I was guilty?

DANIEL: Sometimes I feel sorry for him.

LAURA: Don't you dare. Not now.

DANIEL: How'd you feel if—

LAURA: I wouldn't. I'd only feel if it were you.

DANIEL: Guess that's a compliment.

LAURA: Come here—

DANIEL: Stop—

LAURA: Don't you want me to?

DANIEL: You don't always *have* to—

LAURA: I *want* to.

(*He tries to put some distance, some air between them.*)
What? What's the matter?

DANIEL: Nothing.

LAURA: Did I do something? If I did—

DANIEL: No. Nothing.

LAURA: —tell me.

DANIEL: I just don't feel like it. That's all.

LAURA: I did something.

DANIEL: No.

LAURA: You sure?

DANIEL: Yes.

LAURA: Because a   about is that place. The house. The river. And us. Washing. Eating. Sleeping. Breathing there. You said it was close if we went fast. Do you think about it?

DANIEL: It was my idea in the first place.

LAURA: Don't sound like that.

DANIEL: Like what?

LAURA: Different.

DANIEL: I'm the same.

(He kisses her.)

I'm just—

LAURA: What?

DANIEL: Would you love me if I was…tired?

LAURA: Yes.

DANIEL: Would you love me if I was hungry?

LAURA: Yes.

DANIEL: Would you love me if I had to go?

LAURA: Stay.

DANIEL: I can't.

LAURA: Then you have to come back. Meet me later. You have to.

DANIEL: When?

LAURA: Tonight. Late. And wait for me.

(He turns to go.)

You said once—

(He stops. Turns.)

This isn't here. This isn't now. That you love me like a storm.

(He leaves.)

23.

The barn. TIN *and* FILENE. *They sit quietly, in dimming sunlight.*
They really don't have anything to say to each other.
One whistles softly. The other chews on grass. Sigh. Sigh.
Finally…

TIN: *When* was everyone gonna meet here?

FILENE: Around now, I thought.

TIN: Guess they're late, huh?

FILENE: Guess so.

TIN: Anyway, thanks for calling me at the l‌‌‌‌‌‌‌‌‌‌e ever invites me anyway, so, you know, thanks man.

(They clink beer cans in a toast and wait.

Blackout.)

24.

A little while later. Dusk.

The car seat.

LAURA waits.

FILENE approaches.

He presents a box to her.

FILENE: For you.

(She sets it down without opening it.)

Not even curious?

(She shakes her head "no.")

Come on. Open it.

LAURA: No.

FILENE: I'll open it for you.

(She picks it up, hesitates.)

Go on. It won't bite.

(She finally opens it and immediately drops it, horrified, sickened.)

LAURA: Oh God! Oh God!

FILENE: Surprise.

LAURA: You're sick! This is sick!

FILENE: What did you think was in there?

LAURA: Not this! Never, never…You're an animal!

FILENE: I only did what you asked me to do.

LAURA: I didn't ask for this.

FILENE: I wanted to bring back his wedding ring. For proof, you know.

LAURA: I didn't want this!

FILENE: But it wouldn't come off so I had to take his finger.

LAURA: You didn't *have* to!

FILENE: So you could see what we did.

LAURA: *You* did this!

FILENE: We. Now look at it.

LAURA: Get away—

FILENE: Look!

LAURA: I swear to fucking God I'll call the police!

FILENE: On who? Yourself?

LAURA: But I didn't—It wasn't me—

> (She starts to cry.)

> You made everything worse than I ever dreamed.

FILENE: No. I just made it happen.

> I wish you could see yourself right now.

> Panic becomes you.

> (He holds out an arm to her.)

> Come here.

LAURA: I don't need your shoulder.

FILENE: Or I can come there.

LAURA: Get away.

FILENE: We can go somewhere else.

LAURA: I'll give you money. Tomorrow.

FILENE: I didn't do this for money any more than you did it for love.

> (He touches her hair.

> She slaps his hand away.

> He tries again. She lets him.)

> Are you scared?

> (She lets him keep touching her.

> His hand slips under her skirt.)

LAURA: I did it for Daniel.

FILENE: Whatever you say.

> (He kisses her then stops and waits for her response.)

LAURA: Harder.

> (They kiss harder.

> Darkness.

> Lights up on MARY on porch. Waiting.

> She lights a cigarette and smokes.

> She gets up and goes inside to the bedroom.

> She looks around.

> She stands at the side of the bed. LAURA's side.

> She pulls back the covers, inhales from her cigarette, then leans down and exhales the smoke into the sheets.

> She leaves.

> Later.

Lights up on them at the car seat.
LAURA and FILENE as they get dressed.)

LAURA: Your skin has no smell. Not even sweat. The only smell here is me, isn't it?

(He's not looking at her. She grabs his face and turns it toward her.)

This is our secret, right?

FILENE: Sure.

LAURA: Promise.

FILENE: Nothing to brag about.

LAURA: You keep turning away.

FILENE: Do I?

LAURA: Look at me.

(He does.)

Say something then.

FILENE: A little pillow talk? Okay. Once there was a boy who always wanted a diamond. He wanted and wanted and wanted until finally he got one. Then he looked at it and saw it was glass. He was mad but at least it was pretty glass. Then he looked closer, and saw the glass was only sand. But at least it was pretty sand. Then he looked again and saw the sand was just dirt. The end.

LAURA: Feel better?

FILENE: A little. I gotta go.

(He leaves her alone.)

25.

Later. The bedroom.
LAURA lifts a suitcase onto the bed and starts packing.
MARY approaches from behind—LAURA doesn't hear her.

MARY: Well.

LAURA: *(Jumping.)* God.

MARY: Look at you.

LAURA: What are you doing here?

MARY: I'm always here.

LAURA: You should've called.

MARY: I never call.

(MARY looks around.)

Man, the sex smells so strong around here you can practically walk on it. He just makes you all sexy sexy sexy, doesn't he.

LAURA: Move.

(MARY *keeps getting in the way as* LAURA *tries to walk past her.*)

MARY: Sexy sexy sexy—

LAURA: *Move!*

MARY: You're not really doing this.

LAURA: What's it look like.

MARY: Can't you be like a normal adulteress and just live in shame down the street?

LAURA: No.

MARY: Stay with me.

LAURA: No.

MARY: Come on.

LAURA: No.

MARY: Where are you going? I won't tell. Promise.

LAURA: There's a place he knows about.

MARY: Where?

(*No answer.*)

When'll you get there?

LAURA: A little while.

MARY: Show me your map.

(MARY *grabs* LAURA's *suitcase.* LAURA *grabs it back.*)

I get it. Romeo doesn't need one.

LAURA: Get drunk somewhere else.

(LAURA *tries to step around* MARY. MARY *blocks her.*)

MARY: So tell me. How much money do you have? How much do you need? How much food? How much fuel? How many miles do you have to go? East or west? What happens when you get there?

LAURA: I— I'll call you.

MARY: You'll *call* me?

LAURA: When I get there.

MARY: Oh. This is good. "I'll call you." Isn't that some kiss-off line you give to someone as you crawl out of the back seat? Answer me? Or are you in too big of a hurry?

LAURA: Yeah, I am.

MARY: How long you think he'll wait? An hour? Ten minutes? Till midnight? Till morning?

(LAURA *gets past* MARY.)

Wait! Come here. If you're leaving, if this is it…

MARY: *(Cont'd.)* There's something I've always wanted to tell you.

Closer. Closer. Listen.

(MARY takes LAURA's face and gently, sensuously kisses her ear, like a lover would.)

Did you hear that?

LAURA: No.

MARY: You would've. You could've. Before. I don't know who you are anymore.

LAURA: Get out.

MARY: I'm gonna climb a tree and watch the two of you run.

Then I'll tell everything to anyone who'll listen.

(MARY turns to leave then stops.)

You think he loves you. He barely likes you.

(MARY runs off.

LAURA is panicking. She starts to cry then stops herself.

FILENE enters.)

FILENE: Honey, I'm home.

LAURA: Get away from me.

FILENE: Miss me?

LAURA: Bastard.

(He kicks at the suitcase.)

FILENE: You travel light.

I suppose you'll be warm enough. I suppose you can, you know, live on love. Isn't that what they say?

(Silence.)

Isn't it?

LAURA: Yeah.

FILENE: You'll be fine. You'll land on your feet. But Mary.... Poor Mary.

LAURA: How much did you hear?

FILENE: A little. Enough.

LAURA: But what she said—

FILENE: You broke her heart.

LAURA: Is she right? About Daniel?

FILENE: I wouldn't know.

(She picks up her suitcase.)

LAURA: Don't follow me. Don't look for me. Don't try to find me.

FILENE: Wasn't planning on it.

(Silence.)

LAURA: She said she'll tell.

FILENE: Then she probably will.

LAURA: But she's my friend.

FILENE: No such things as friends where you are now. You're off the map.

(The only option dawns on her.)

LAURA: Stop her.

(She exits.)

26.

LAURA enters the barn.
She's looking for DANIEL.
He's not coming.

LAURA: Daniel? Daniel?

(A noise.
TIN appears.)

TIN: Laura.

(She sees him and screams.)

Laura.

LAURA: Oh God!

TIN: Look at me.

(She won't. She can't.)

LAURA: God!

TIN: Look.

LAURA: Get away from me!

TIN: Look at me!

LAURA: You're dead you're dead go away.

TIN: Look at me! Please.

(She does.)

I loved you. I loved you and look what you did to me. You stupid, stupid... Laura.

LAURA: No. No.

TIN: Do you feel this?

(He hits himself.)

This?

(He hits himself harder.)

You feel anything when I died?

Now I know you didn't love me. Now I can see everything. I'm there. Above you. In the corner of the ceiling, outside the window...

LAURA: Get away—

TIN: Not a pretty picture, watching you. But I can't close my eyes. Why him?

LAURA: I can't—

TIN: Why?

LAURA: You're not alive. You're not.

TIN: Where I am, I can watch it all. I can see it coming. "Tornado...." "A wall in your way...." "Don't want him inside me...."

(She's backed into the corner.)

LAURA: You can't hurt me you're a ghost. You can't hurt me.

(He moves toward her.)

Get away from me!

(He stops.)

TIN: I think I'm in hell. Want to know how I can tell? I'm so tired. So tired and there are millions and millions of pillows everywhere. But they all smell like you. Laura. I can't find any place to sleep.

(He's gone.

Terrified, she starts to pray.)

LAURA: Oh Thou from whom can come the dream, and the courage to make the dream come true, hear my prayer. The prayer that we may hear even at this hour, thy knock upon the door of our hearts. That we may hear— and open—open unto Thee O Jesus Christ Our Lord. Amen. Amen. Amen. Amen.

(She runs into the field.

She finds MARY there, silhouetted against the sunset sky.)

Mary?

(The ghost of MARY turns to face LAURA, revealing her bloody "trick sword" thrust down her throat. Blood runs from her mouth.

LAURA screams.

MARY slowly twists the sword out of her throat.

LAURA is sick, terrified.)

MARY: Laura.

LAURA: Oh God.

MARY: Look.

LAURA: God. Mary.

MARY: I never made it to the tree.

LAURA: It can't be you. This isn't you.

MARY: You stopped me.

LAURA: No! He—

MARY: You did this.

LAURA: I didn't mean—

MARY: All of this.

LAURA: I didn't!

MARY: All for a boy.

LAURA: Get away—

MARY: How could you?

LAURA: Don't—

MARY: I loved you more than anyone.

LAURA: Oh Mary—

MARY: I loved you most.

LAURA: Don't touch me!

MARY: Touch me—and I'll leave you alone. Touch me and I'll stop aching. Please touch me. Touch me.

(*LAURA tries to but can't.*

MARY curses her.)

Your breath will kill the crops. Turn the water black. You've burned down your own house. The one you did this for isn't worth it. He's sound asleep. You're not going anywhere.

(*She drops the sword at LAURA's feet and leaves.*

LAURA is all alone.)

LAURA: This isn't me.

This isn't here.

This isn't now.

I am not lost.

I am a storm.

(*Faster and faster, a desperate prayer, through the night all the way to the morning.*)

This isn't me.

This isn't here.

I am a storm.

I am not lost.

This isn't now.

This isn't here.

This isn't me.

I am not lost.

I am a storm.

This isn't now.

This isn't here.

This isn't me.

LAURA: *(Cont'd.)* I am not lost.

This isn't now.

This isn't now.

I am not here.

I am not here.

I am not here.

This isn't me…

(The night ends and the day breaks at the horizon.

FILENE appears with the sun.)

LAURA: God.

FILENE: What's all this?

LAURA: I thought you were him.

FILENE: Sorry.

LAURA: What time is it.

FILENE: My watch stopped.

(Silence.)

LAURA: Did you know I'd still be here?

FILENE: I'm just on my way home.

LAURA: I—I saw them.

FILENE: Who?

LAURA: The ghosts. Did you?

FILENE: No such thing as ghosts.

LAURA: Why did you do this to me?

FILENE: To you? For you.

LAURA: You're the only one left who could make me cry. Will you leave me?

FILENE: We're not even together.

(Silence.)

LAURA: There's this place I heard about. Just one house and a river.

(The silence of revelation.)

But I don't know where it is.

(Breath.)

Filene?

FILENE: What.

LAURA: Are you looking at me?

FILENE: Yes.

(The silence of recognition.)

LAURA: Don't.

END OF PLAY

Foul Territory
by Craig Wright

BIOGRAPHY

Craig Wright's plays include *The Pavilion* (City Theatre, Actors Theatre of Louisville, the Glove Theatres); *Main Street* (Great American History Theatre); *Orange Flower Water* (Contemporary American Theater Festival, the Jungle, Steppenwolf); *Recent Tragic Events* (Woolly Mammoth, Playwrights Horizons); and *Melissa Arctic* (Folger Theatre). He has received commissions from Contemporary American Theater Festival, Woolly Mammoth and Actors Theatre. His plays are published by Dramatists Play Service, Playscripts Inc., Dramatic Publishing, and Smith and Kraus. He has received several awards for his writing, including fellowships from the McKnight Foundation and the National Endowment for the Arts. He holds an M.Div. degree from United Theological Seminary and lives in Los Angeles with his wife, Lorraine LeBlanc, and their son, Louis.

HUMANA FESTIVAL PRODUCTION

Foul Territory was produced at the Humana Festival of New American Plays in April 2004. It was directed by Sturgis Warner with the following cast:

Ruth. . . . . Russell Arden Koplin
Owen . . . . Jesse Lenat

and the following production staff:

Scenic Designer . . . . Paul Owen
Costume Designer. . . . . Andrea Scott
Lighting Designer . . . . Paul Werner
Sound Designer . . . . Benjamin Marcum
Properties Designer . . . . Doc Manning
Stage Manager . . . . Debra A. Freeman
Assistant Stage Managers . . . . Michael Domue
                                                                    Brady Ellen Poole
Ball Handler . . . . Sturgis Warner
Dramaturg . . . . Steve Moulds
Assistant Dramaturg . . . . Erin Detrick

PLAYWRIGHT'S NOTE

The playwright wishes to thank director Sturgis Warner for all the hard work and imagination he brought to the process of giving this little play a life. It truly would not have happened without him.

CHARACTERS
RUTH, 30s-40s
OWEN, 30s-40s

SETTING
A row of far-left-field seats at Yankee Stadium.

NOTES
Words and phrases contained within [brackets] may be changed to suit a production's discretion.

For the Humana Festival production a third character, the Ball Handler, was added to provide all baseball-related effects. The Ball Handler stood off to the side, dressed in white, barefoot, with a waist-high, white bucket roped around his neck. In each hand he held a thick wooden dowel. The crack-of-the-bat sounds were made by emphatically hitting the dowels together. The Ball Handler would also make the player announcements by speaking into the bucket, creating a loudspeaker effect. He held a foam baseball in one hand along the dowel. Other foam baseballs were kept in the bucket.

For each of the three foul balls that wind up hitting Owen, the Ball Handler, after striking the dowels together, would immediately switch them to one hand and raise the foam baseball high in the other. He would then carry the ball in slow motion toward Owen and Ruth as their dialogue continued. On cue, a foot or two away, the Ball Handler would fling the ball sharply off of Owen's head, then turn and make his way back to the side. He would reach into the bucket for the next ball and resume his position, a dowel once again in each hand. On the third foul, the Ball Handler would guide the ball seemingly into Owen's outstretched hands before slamming it into his face at the last possible moment.

Stylistically, the Ball Handler was played in a somewhat Kabuki manner—formal, deadly serious, exacting in focus and intent.

Foul Territory was commissioned by Mile Square Theatre of Hoboken, New Jersey, for *7th Inning Stretch: 7 10-minute plays about baseball*, where it received its first performance on August 23, 2003.

Sturgis Werner, Jesse Lenat and Russell Arden Koplin
in *Foul Territory*

28th Annual Humana Festival of New American Plays
Actors Theatre of Louisville, 2004
photo by Harlan Taylor

Foul Territory

The scene is a row of far-left-field seats at [Yankee Stadium]. OWEN (30s-40s) is seated next to RUTH (30s-40s). Throughout the scene we can hear a baseball game in progress; the distant drone of the announcer giving the play-by-play; the general crowd roar; and the periodic crack of the bat hitting the ball. OWEN and RUTH are both eating popcorn or peanuts.

We hear the crack of the bat hitting the ball. Ruth jumps out of her seat.

RUTH: Yeah, [Bernie]! Way to go! Way to bloop that ball in there!!!
(She settles back into her seat.)
I think they're gonna do it this year, Owen. I can feel it. They're going all the way. Three months from now, mark my words, it's the World Series, and we'll be sitting here winnin' it…
(She eats a mouthful of popcorn, then finishes her thought with her mouth full.)
ANNOUNCER: NOW BATTING… NUMBER [TWO]… [DEREK JETER].
RUTH: Woo-hoo, [Derek]! …Mark my words.
(Another big mouthful—and she turns to OWEN—)
Don'tcha think?
(—to catch him eyeing her with pity.)
What? What are you looking at? What?
OWEN: *(After a beat, pityingly.)* You're so brave.
RUTH: Gimme a break.
OWEN: No, I mean it, Ruth, you are—
RUTH: Because I think the [Yankees] have a chance? It doesn't take a genius—
OWEN: No, to be out here like this, like you are.
RUTH: At the game?
OWEN: At the game, at the whole thing!
(We hear the crack of the bat hitting the ball.)
To be getting back on your feet the way you're getting—after what Tom did to you—you're so sweet and brave—
(He eats a single piece of popcorn, gazing at her. She tracks the approaching ball with her eyes.)
—so sweet and brave.
RUTH: Stop it.

OWEN: No, I mean it, you're, like, straight outta Laura Ingalls Wilder, I'm so proud of you, to bounce back like this. After Monty left me—

(A ball sails in and cracks OWEN loudly on the head—)

OW!

RUTH: Oh God! Oh God, Owen, are you alright? Oh God!

OWEN: *(Holding his head.)* I'm fine, I'm fine—

RUTH: Didn't you see that coming?

OWEN: Yeah, I, I kinda did…

RUTH: It was coming right at you—

OWEN: I know—

RUTH: Oh my God… do you need anything? Ice, or—

OWEN: No—

RUTH: Should we take you to First Aid or something?

OWEN: No, I'm fine! I'm good. Really. Just watch your game, honey. Enjoy yourself. It's your night. It's your night.

RUTH: You're sure?

OWEN: Yes—

RUTH: Because we can go, really—

OWEN: *(Still rocking, in terrible pain.)* No, I'm shakin' it off. I'm a trooper. I'm fine.

RUTH: *(Double-checking.)* You're absolutely sure?

OWEN: Yes.

RUTH: *(Doubtfully.)* Ok. Ok. You're sure you're alright?

OWEN: Yep. Par for the course. I'm fine.

RUTH: Ok. Ok.

(She settles back into watching the game. A moment passes. Something catches her eye.)

Did you see that?

OWEN: No, what?

RUTH: He balked. *(To the field.)* Stay on the rubber! *(After a long beat.)* Look, he did it again—

(She stands and screams at the field.)

Stay on the rubber! This isn't Cuba, pal! *(To OWEN.)* Do you see what I'm talkin' about?

OWEN: *(Still rubbing his head.)* No, I—I missed it—

RUTH: He balks, like, every third pitch, this guy, and no one calls it! No one ever calls it! *(Amazed.)* Jesus.

(She sits back down, eats some popcorn.)

What's the point of having a rule if no one's gonna call it?

OWEN: Have you heard from him? At all?

RUTH: I don't want to talk about it—

OWEN: Wouldja take him back?

RUTH: No!

(We hear the crack of the bat hitting the ball.)

You don't get it, Owen, Tom Scintilla leaving me is the *best thing* that ever could have happened—to me or the kids—

OWEN: But you miss him—

RUTH: I don't—

OWEN: Oh, come on, you miss him and you want him back, just admit it. When Monty left me—

(The ball sails in and hits him hard in the face.)

OW!!

RUTH: (*Angry and concerned.*) Owen, move!!

(Blood sprays from his nose. He clutches it in agony.)

OWEN: When?

RUTH: *When you see the ball coming!* God! Are you alright? You're bleeding!

OWEN: I am?

RUTH: Is anything broken?

OWEN: No, it just… it just kinda… *hurts…*

(She pulls a napkin from her popcorn container and anxiously dabs his nose, trying to soak up some of the blood.)

Ow, ow, ow…

RUTH: (*After a beat, with one eye on the game.*) So you saw that coming?

OWEN: Of course!

RUTH: So why didn't you *move?*

OWEN: What would be the point?

RUTH: What the hell does that mean? Jesus—

(She suddenly stands up and screams at the field.)

Would someone please nail this guy's feet to the motherfuckin' rubber or make the call?? Jesus Christ!

(RUTH sits back down, annoyed with the game.)

I mean, this guy's not gonna cost us the game, but *shit!*

(A moment passes as she eats some popcorn and looks at OWEN.)

So what do you mean, "What would be the point?"

OWEN: It doesn't matter—

RUTH: Sure it does—

OWEN: No, you're enjoying the game—

RUTH: No, tell me! I've been going to baseball games for thirty-five years, Owen, I never caught a foul ball once and I just saw you get hit twice in one game!

OWEN: That's life—

RUTH: No, it's not life, it's fuckin' weird! *(Then, responding approvingly to the field.)* Ball four! There! Thank you! Thank you! *(To OWEN.)* Do you realize, now, with [Bernie] and [Derek] on base, if [A-Rod] hits a home run, it's over, right?

OWEN: Yeah—

RUTH: This is a good game— All right! They're changing pitchers! Boo! Boo! Take a hike, you bum!

OWEN: When I got hit in the face with a baseball the *first* time—

RUTH: *(Caught off guard.)* How many times have you been hit?

OWEN: I don't know, a lot.

RUTH: You never told me this—

OWEN: It never came up—we never went to a game—

RUTH: I guess you're right—

OWEN: —the first time I was eleven years old, trying to catch a pop fly in the street—

RUTH: You played baseball?

OWEN: I know, it's unlikely—

RUTH: It's mega-unlikely—

OWEN: Well, I did, and this kid hit a pop fly and I must have misjudged or something, the important part is BANG, I got hit right between the eyes.

RUTH: Ouch.

OWEN: Yeah. There was blood everywhere, my eyes were swollen shut—

RUTH: God—

OWEN: Yeah, and I got totally spooked.

(He blows his nose and the napkin fills with blood.)

RUTH: Are you sure you're alright?

OWEN: Yeah, I just feel a little… a little faint, anyway, a couple days later, I was at a baseball game for my school—not even playing, I was just doing stats, because my vision was still a little screwed up, and Jonny Blank hit a high foul and I freaked out. Everyone else was just sitting there, and I'm screaming, running around like a bee is chasing me and I'm ALREADY crying and I finally find the spot where I'm safe and I crouch down and cover my ears, but then I hear somebody catch it, so I look up and BANG, it hits me in the face!

RUTH: Oh my God!

OWEN: I know!

RUTH: What are the chances?

OWEN: Very high, obviously—

RUTH: *(Affirmatively.)* I guess—

OWEN: Anyway, I spent the next week in the hospital.

RUTH: The hospital?

OWEN: Kind of a... mental hospital—

RUTH: Oh—

OWEN: —and when I got out, my father, my beloved father whom I must have generated in my previous life in some evil DUNGEON, fabricated him from trash like some Golem, you know, to torture me later in case I forgot what was true about GOD, my beloved father decided to take me to a baseball game. He told me I had to get back on the horse. I cried the whole way in the car, "Don't take me. Turn around. I want to go home." He didn't care. We got to the game and lo and behold—

RUTH: You got hit—

OWEN: No. Nothing happened. *(After a beat.)* For eight innings.

RUTH: Oh no—

OWEN: And then [Lou Piniella] hit a high foul into the stands, and my father said, "Just sit still," and I did—for two seconds—and then I RAN up the stairs into an empty row that looked safe and BANG, it caught me right in the ear!

RUTH: No!

OWEN: Yes! I still can't hear anything in this ear! I point this ear at something, I hear the ocean. MAYBE.

RUTH: That's amazing.

ANNOUNCER: NOW BATTING... NUMBER [THIRTEEN]...

RUTH: Yeah!

ANNOUNCER: [ALEX RODRIGUEZ].

RUTH: Yeah, [A-Rod]! Yeah!

OWEN: We can't run, Ruth, that's my point. Whether it's baseballs or heartbreak, whether it's your Tom or my Monty, there's no escaping it. Life is going to destroy us. It's going to. Letting it happen is the only freedom we have.

RUTH: But Owen, that's absurd—

OWEN: It's the truth!

RUTH: But Owen, I'm happier now than I've been in ten years! The house is clean, all of Tom's stupid model train stuff is outta there; the kids are doing better in school; Carla Kendall is setting me up next week with a really nice guy—

OWEN: *(Doubtful.)* Oh, right—

RUTH: He sounds really sweet, he's a personal trainer—

OWEN: Sure he is—

RUTH: I think things are really looking up!

OWEN: And I think you're kidding yourself! I think you're seriously kidding yourself.

(We hear a loud crack of the bat hitting the ball.)

(Fatalistically.) See, here it comes again—

(RUTH stands up.)

RUTH: Catch it!

OWEN: No, there's no point!

RUTH: Owen, stand up, put out your hands and catch it!

(She pulls him up.)

OWEN: But if I reach here, the ball goes there, Ruth, wherever I reach is where it won't be!

RUTH: That can't be true!

OWEN: *(Indicating his bloody nose.)* Look at me, Ruth, if anything's true, it's true, I know my own life—

RUTH: Put out your hands!

(She puts out his hands.)

Now keep your eyes open, keep your eye on the ball, and catch it!

OWEN: Ok, I'll try!

RUTH: Here it comes… here it comes… here it comes…

(Their eyes track the incoming ball. OWEN's ready to catch it. Boom, it hits OWEN in the face with a loud smack. He falls over, clutching his face in quiet agony. RUTH doesn't react in horror this time. She just looks down at him. After a long beat.) But see, aren't you glad you made the *effort*?

OWEN: *(From down on the ground, curled up in pain, after a beat.)* Yeah, I'm glad.

RUTH: You'll get the next one. Just tell yourself, "I'll get the next one."

OWEN: "I'll get the next one."

RUTH: You can't lose hope, Owen. That's what I tell the kids. We can't lose hope. It's all we've got.

(She sits down, eats some popcorn, watches the field with interest.)

I really think we have a shot this year. I think we're really gonna go all the way.

(Loud crack of the bat hitting the ball.)

END OF PLAY

Fast and Loose
an ethical collaboration by
José Cruz González, Kirsten Greenidge, Julie Marie Myatt and John Walch

Fast and Loose
an ethical collaboration

If you found out a terrible secret that might hurt the ones you love, would you expose it? Would you choose what served the greatest good for the most people, even if it violated the rights of an individual? Is it ever okay to apply your own ethical standards to another culture, group or home? And in the end, why should any of us care one bit about what might benefit other people?

These are the questions at the center of *Fast and Loose*, a provocative experiment in dramatic form that was performed by Actors Theatre's Apprentice Company at the 2004 Humana Festival. Actors Theatre asked four playwrights—José Cruz González, Julie Marie Myatt, John Walch and Kirsten Greenidge (also author of this year's *Sans-culottes in the Promised Land*)—to combine their efforts and tackle several classic ethical dilemmas.

Starting with four questions that examine the depths and limits of personal responsibility in a morally complex world, these authors crafted four storylines—one for each dilemma—that interweave throughout the performance. Each playwright started one of the storylines and relied on their fellow writers to continue the narrative in their own way, from their unique perspectives. By the end, all four of them had put their individual stamps on each of these quandaries, both illuminating issues and uncovering new ambiguities.

With situations as thorny as a family coping with an ugly truth from their past, or as intricate as the politics surrounding a labor union in a small town, *Fast and Loose* gets at what makes ethics such suitable theatrical fodder. These fundamental questions of human conduct, right and wrong, are the very stuff of drama—choices and their outcomes, the effects of our actions (intended and otherwise), and the place each individual holds in the world at large. These playwrights may not have the answers to these intriguing problems, but the worlds they've created promise to be equally fascinating.

—*Steve Moulds*

BIOGRAPHIES

José Cruz González's plays include *September Shoes, Always Running, Two Donuts, Salt & Pepper, The Highest Heaven, La Posada, Harvest Moon, Calabasas Street* and *Odysseus Cruz.* Mr. González has written for PAZ, produced by Discovery Kids for The Learning Channel. In 2004, *Lily Plants a Garden* premiered at the Mark Taper Forum's P.L.A.Y. program. Mr. González was a recipient of a 1997 NEA/TCG Theatre Residency for Playwrights. In 1985, Mr. González was an NEA Director Fellow. He is a graduate of the University of California, Irvine. He teaches theatre at California State University at Los Angeles and is a member of The Dramatists Guild of America, Inc., ASSITEJ/USA, and an Associate Artist with Cornerstone Theater Company.

Kirsten Greenidge has enjoyed development experiences at Madison Repertory, Playwrights Horizons, New Dramatists, the Taper, Bay Area Playwright's Festival, Hourglass Theatre, A.S.K. Theater Projects, The O'Neill and the Boston Women On Top Festival. Her work has been read at Playwrights Horizons, New Georges Performathon 2002, Flirting With the Edge Festival of New Work and the Boston Playwrights Theatre. Recent awards include: The Cherry Lane Theatre Alternative (finalist—2002); The American College Theatre Festival; the University of Iowa (IRAM Award 2000 and Richard Maibaum Award 2001); and the Sundance Theatre Laboratory (Residency at Ucross Ranch, Ucross, Wyoming). Ms. Greenidge earned her M.F.A. from the Playwrights Workshop at the University of Iowa, where she was a Barry Kemp Fellow, and her B.A. from Wesleyan University.

Julie Marie Myatt has had plays produced in New York, Los Angeles, Minneapolis, and at Actors Theatre of Louisville. Her play *The Sex Habits of American Women* premiered at San Francisco's Magic Theatre. Published plays include *Lift and Bang* in *30 Ten-Minute Plays for 2 Actors* from Actors Theatre; *What He Sent* in *The Best American Short Plays, 2000-2001*; and *Cowbird* in the new anthology *Breaking Ground.* She received a 1992-93 Walt Disney Studios Screenwriting Fellowship, a 1999-2000 Jerome Fellowship at the Playwrights' Center and a 2001-2002 McKnight Advancement Grant. She participates in the Guthrie New Play Project funded by the Bush Foundation. Her other plays include *August is a thin girl, The Pink Factor, Alice in the Badlands* and *49 Days to the Sun.*

John Walch's plays include *The Dinosaur Within, Circumference of a Squirrel, Jesting with Edged Tools, Craving Gravy, The Elements of Style* (an adaptation) and numerous one-acts and shorts. His plays have been produced by the Mark Taper Forum, Zachary Scott Theatre, and Off-Broadway at Urban Stages, and have been developed by the Public Theater, A.S.K. Theater Projects and others. Awards include the Kennedy Center Fund for New American Plays, the Osborn Award from the American Theatre Critics Association, and the Charlotte Woolard Award recognizing a promising new voice. Mr. Walch recently relocated to New York from Austin, Texas, where he was artistic director of Austin Script Works and taught playwriting at the University of Texas, Austin. Commissions include Actors Theatre of Louisville, Manhattan Theatre Club and the Playwrights' Center of Minneapolis.

HUMANA FESTIVAL PRODUCTION

Fast and Loose was commissioned by Actors Theatre of Louisville and premiered at the Humana Festival of New American Plays in March 2004. It was directed by Wendy McClellan with the following cast:

Wake God's Man
Sarah	Natalie Arnold
Brian	Max Ferguson
Ricardo	Clifford Endo Gulibert
Man	Tom Kelley
Annie	Sarah Ann Kinsey
Beth	Laura Riley

Union
Simon	Ryan Barret
Camille	Kibibi Dillon
Les	Jesse Hooker
Margaret	Emily Ruddock
Harry	Adam Suritz
Jane	Mary Tuomanen

In This House

Kathy . . . . Lisa Benner
Lynne / Claire . . . . Jody Christopherson
Kayla . . . . Wendy Gaunt
Robert / Cook . . . . Matthew Goldsborough
Bill . . . . David Wagner

The Mating Habits of the Sage Grouse

Adrian . . . . Sasha Andreev
Charley . . . . Gabel Eiben
Haley . . . . Marianna Frendo
Doug . . . . Patrick Hogan
Danielle . . . . Pirronne Yousefzadeh

and the following production staff:

Scenic Designer . . . . Brenda Ellis
Costume Designer . . . . John P. White
Lighting Designer . . . . Paul Werner
Sound Designer . . . . Benjamin Marcum
Properties Designer . . . . Mark Walston
Stage Manager . . . . Abigail Wright
Fight Director . . . . Drew Fracher
Ethics Consultant . . . . David Osipovich
Dramaturg . . . . Steve Moulds
Directing Assistant . . . . Gil Reyes

The Questions

Fast and Loose is comprised of four storylines, each of which explores a different ethical question. Each playwright contributed one piece to each storyline. Although the storylines were written separately, in performance the storylines interweave. (Note: Although the complete text of *Fast and Loose* contains four interweaving storylines, each storyline may be performed individually.) Story by story, these are the ethical questions that *Fast and Loose* explores.

Wake God's Man

The Question: If you discover an awful secret, should you tell?

The Characters:

> BETH, eldest sister of Annie and Sarah. Nervous type. Ready to confront her past.
>
> ANNIE, middle sister. A young mother. Constantly dealing with migraines.
>
> SARAH, youngest sister. Works for the local parish.
>
> MAN, a lost soul. Pecan aficionado.
>
> RICARDO, Annie's husband. Unemployed, has time on his hands and things on his mind.
>
> BRIAN, Sarah's ex-fiancé. Back home for the first time in years.

Setting: An empty room in a church, a food bank, Annie and Ricardo's home, and the church's sanctuary.

Union

The Question: Should we base our ethical decisions on principles, or solely on the consequences of the decisions?

The Characters:

> JANE, early twenties.
>
> LES, early twenties, engaged to marry Jane.
>
> CAMILLE, early twenties.
>
> SIMON, late teens to early twenties.
>
> HARRY, early twenties, factory owner's son.
>
> MARGARET, early twenties, Simon's older sister.

Setting: A small factory town in the mountains of North Carolina.

In This House

The Question: Are there intrinsically right and wrong acts, or is it all just social convention?

The Characters:

    LYNNE, late twenties/early thirties; also plays CLAIRE.

    KATHY, her friend, late twenties/early thirties.

    BILL, Kathy's husband, late twenties/early thirties.

    KAYLA, early twenties.

    ROBERT, also plays COOK.

Setting: Present; Kathy and Bill's kitchen, outdoors, and a restaurant, respectively.

The Mating Habits of the Sage Grouse

The Question: Is altruism possible, or is all selfless action just disguised self-interest?

The Characters:

    ADRIAN, male, 23.

    DOUG, male, 26.

    CHARLEY, male, 24.

    HALEY, female, 22.

    DANIELLE, female, 23.

Setting A lek, of sorts.

David Wagner and Lisa Benner
in *Fast and Loose*

28th Annual Humana Festival of New American Plays
Actors Theatre of Louisville, 2004
photo by Harlan Taylor

Wake God's Man
Scene Zero
By José Cruz González

The shape of a human body is suspended horizontally above the stage. The body is wrapped in shards of white cloth like a mummy. Green weeds grow out of it. Onstage is a small, delicate table with a vase filled with Easter lilies. BETH and ANNIE stand onstage. They are sisters. BETH is older. They are dressed in black.

BETH: *(To ANNIE.)* She's late.

ANNIE: Don't start.

BETH: She's never on time. It's embarrassing. I'm always the first to arrive. Call her.

ANNIE: Don't start, Beth. Sarah will be here.

BETH: Why must you always protect her?

ANNIE: Look, don't even go there.

Union
Scene Zero
By Julie Marie Myatt

Outside the doors of a small t-shirt and underwear factory in a small town in the North Carolina mountains. The factory sign reads "CAROLINA COTTON CO.", and in smaller print below that reads "We know what fits Below the Bible Belt!"

LES and JANE pace excitedly in front of Camille as she tries to read The Union Steward's Complete Guide *by David Prosten, while Simon sits with face in hands. They've just (successfully) organized a walkout of the factory, but many of the older workers, including their family members, did not walk out.*

Every once in a while, you'll see JANE or LES wave, or yell out a "Hey Will," "Hey Sarah!" etc., to fellow workers across the stage. The sound of the small crowd runs through the scene.

JANE: I feel like Norma Rae—
LES: I'm Warren Beatty in *Reds*—
JANE: I could be the next Erin Brockovich.
LES: No.
JANE: What?
LES: Your tits are too small.
JANE: Fuck you.

In This House
Scene Zero
By Kirsten Greenidge

KATHY and BILL's kitchen.

KATHY: Isn't she adorable?

LYNNE: So tiny.

BILL: Not for long. She eats a *ton*.
(Imitates a baby drinking voraciously.)

KATHY: Stop that.

LYNNE: "Claire." I think I had an aunt named Claire. After the county. In Ireland.

KATHY: "Claire Anna Thomas." Doesn't it sound like she could be a senator?

BILL: *I* wanted to name her Lola—

KATHY: Sounds like a stripper.

BILL: So Claire it is.

The Mating Habits of the Sage Grouse
Scene Zero
By John Walch

Light rises on ADRIAN on a bar stool, looking through a book, nursing a beer.

ADRIAN: There's two types of leks. That's Lek. L-E-K.

The first is the basic monetary unit of Albania. One lek = 100 quintars, so I guess a lek is like a penny, or maybe a dollar. I don't really know, it doesn't really matter. I'm getting confused. This isn't about Albanian currency, I'm stalling. Scratch all that. This is never going to work. I'm such an idiot for letting them talk me into this.

(Light rises on DANIELLE.)

DANIELLE: …I'm such an idiot for letting her talk me into this…

Union
Scene One
By Julie Marie Myatt

LES picks JANE up.

LES: I love you for your brains.

CAMILLE: Too bad she can't say the same.

JANE: Love is blind.

CAMILLE: Cupid must be Helen Keller.

(*LES kisses JANE and lets her go. LES looks out across the stage. He raises his fist.*)

LES: Look at this! Power to the people! UNITE!

(*LES shakes SIMON's shoulders. Raises SIMON's hand in the air.*)

Simon! Simon says, "Power to the people!"

SIMON: Ouch.

LES: We did it, man.

SIMON: Uh-huh.

JANE: C'mon Simon. Aren't you proud of yourself?

SIMON: It took me years to get that job. My sister—Margaret finally talks them into giving it to me, and not one month later, you two "revolutionaries" decide the place has got to get a union to protect everybody, and tell me to start walking.

LES: You took a stand, Simon. That took courage.

SIMON: You pushed me out the door.

LES: Even sheep need a little prodding.

SIMON: I'm hungry. And it's cold out here.

LES: Where're your balls, man?

(*SIMON just looks at him.*)

SIMON: Inside my Carolina Cotton briefs. Where they're paid to be.

(*CAMILLE laughs.*)

JANE: That's where they want them.

LES: They got them wedged right up your ass, tight and squeezed. Believing all their bullshit: "Economy is tough, folks. We can't afford health benefits."

JANE: "Health benefits are a thing of the past. We're just keeping up with the times."

LES: "Maybe you should consider taking better care of yourselves, folks. Then you wouldn't worry so much. Try a low-fat diet."

JANE: "You're just lucky you have a job here."

SIMON: I *am* lucky I have a job. *Had* a job.

LES: They're not going to fire us. They can't. We're just showing them we're serious about what we deserve.

SIMON: What do you care? You never go to the doctor.

LES: I'm getting married, man. We want to have kids.

JANE: It's very expensive.

SIMON: So don't have them. Get a dog—

JANE: We want kids! No one here is going to be able to afford health insurance on their own. *No one.* We've got to get a union in here to protect ourselves. UNITE will help us do that. I've been working here since I was sixteen and I've seen how people begin to believe they can't do anything else but pump pedals and sew seams, and walk fabric for miles a day.

SIMON: All those people still working?

JANE: Scared to death.

SIMON: My sister's in there.

JANE: Margaret's got three kids at home.

LES: Who need health insurance.

SIMON: Still.

LES: Still what?

SIMON: You didn't have to push me.

(*CAMILLE closes her book.*)

CAMILLE: This is going to be tedious, I can tell. At least with a proper picket sign you've got an activity, carrying it back and forth, leaning it on your shoulder. Shouting and so on. With a walkout, hell, what've you got?

(*JANE grabs the book.*)

JANE: Solidarity.

SIMON: Is there gonna be food?

LES: Not ten minutes out here, and you two shitheads are already complaining.

CAMILLE: I just think this whole thing should have been better organized. Where's the coffee? The support system? Where are those UNITE reps Jane was supposed to call?

JANE: I called them.

CAMILLE: So?

JANE: They, they were—they are very busy. They said they couldn't make it up here until June. I—we couldn't wait that long.

CAMILLE: You said they'd be waiting.

JANE: But *I* couldn't wait.

CAMILLE: Then you should have planned *some kind* of more meaningful social activity than just walking out and standing around outside the factory. It makes us look like idiots.

LES: If you're so smart, why didn't you plan it?

CAMILLE: This is Jane's baby—

LES: No it's not—

JANE: This *is* meaningful. You said so yourself—you need those health benefits to keep your mother alive... but—besides, yeah, I don't see you contributing anything—

CAMILLE: You're the one with all the big ideas! You're the one who passed out "secret" flyers in the break room, you're the one who whispered, and made Les whisper all around the plant, "walk out," "if you think you deserve to keep your health benefits, walk out with us," "at three o'clock tomorrow, we're going to walk out of here and UNITE representatives will be waiting to help you"—

JANE: No one pushed you out the door—

CAMILLE: But, whoops, nope, sorry. They're not here. Sorry. Too busy.

JANE: I can handle it—

LES: Hey, I did all the legwork. Most of these people are out here because of me—

CAMILLE: Look around, Jane! Don't you think pretty soon folks are gonna start to wonder? Start looking over here, thinking, "Where's all the help she promised? All those experts that 'really know the law, workers' rights'?" Start looking at their watches. Wondering what's next. Pretty soon, every one of them is going to start thinking, "Man, I was pretty stupid to believe that Jane. She was just full of shit and promises like the rest of 'em."

LES: Shut up, Camille.

JANE: I've got it under control.

CAMILLE: This isn't a movie.

JANE: I know.

CAMILLE: You made promises. To your friends.

JANE: And I'm going to keep them.

CAMILLE: You have anything *real* planned for these people? Water? Dinner?

LES: We never promised dinner.

SIMON: No dinner?

CAMILLE: And what about tomorrow? What then? And the day after that?

JANE: I said, I've got it under control, Camille—

LES: *I* have it under control.

(JANE steps up to meet the crowd. LES steps up beside her.
JANE subtly pushes LES behind her—)

JANE: I've got it, honey.

LES: That's OK, baby, I'll take it from here—

(And what starts calmly, the two of them politely trying to keep the other from stepping forward—)

JANE: Les—

(Soon becomes a pushing match—)

LES: Jane!

(Neither can make it far enough to address the crowd.)

The Mating Habits of the Sage Grouse
Scene One
By John Walch

ADRIAN on the bar stool.

ADRIAN: Do over.

The second type of lek, or the type I'm thinking about anyway, is a small patch of ground that's used for communal display in the breeding season by the males of certain birds and mammals. In other words, it's a strutting ground, a place to hook up. A place, like, say, oh I don't know, Jinx's Bar. *(Lights broaden to reveal Jinx's Bar. Nothing much, perhaps a splash of neon from a beer sign, a bar stool and table.)* You know Jinx's… or you know the type anyway. A classic lek: cheap beer, a dart board without any darts, pool cues without any tips, low lights and high stools—a place where the romantically jinxed come to get lucky. For some time now, Jinx's has been our little lek. By *our,* I mean: me, Charley, and Doug.
(Lights rise on CHARLEY and DOUG sipping beers at the table and talking conspiratorially.)

DOUG: I'm telling you, Charley, she's perfect for him.

CHARLEY: I don't know, Doug, maybe this wasn't such a good idea. We can't force him on someone.

DOUG: We won't need to force jack once he sees her—Haley…
(On a separate part of the stage, lights rise on HALEY, a cell phone glued to her ear.)

HALEY: We're going out tonight…

DOUG: …Nurse Haley.
(On "Nurse," HALEY reveals a stethoscope around her neck; she takes it off as she talks into the phone.)

CHARLEY: How'd you meet a nurse named Haley?

DOUG: Installed her cable modem, and check it out, after I finished—I browsed her browser. You know just "checking to make sure all the protocols are correct" and, well let's just say Haley's protocol is to hook up; her favorites file reads like a wine list for online dating services. I got a feeling Nurse Haley is ready and willing to heal what ails our man, Adrian.

HALEY: *(Into phone.)* I'll bring you some pseudoephedrine from the hospital…

CHARLEY: I don't know if a setup's such a good idea, Doug.

HALEY: *(Into phone.)* ...I don't know, some dive called Jinx's.

DOUG: Come on, man, we're doing this for him.

HALEY: *(Into phone.)* Do it for me. Come on, Danielle.

CHARLEY: I just thought we were going to try and meet someone here, let it happen naturally.

DOUG: Naturally? We're talking about Adrian. I went preemptive.

CHARLEY: So you invited a total stranger? What if they don't click?

DOUG: Plan B. I told her to bring a friend.

HALEY: *(Into phone.)* Thanks, Danielle. So pick me up after yoga, around nine. *(. . .)* Oh, you don't mind driving do you?

CHARLEY: Oh Doug, you didn't—

DOUG: I did. I did, 'cause I love that guy and I want him to be happy, to find someone. So I went out and found him someone. My present to him— Haley.

HALEY: *(Into phone.)* See you tonight. *(. . .)* Yeah, I'll bring the Sudafed. *(HALEY hangs up. Her light fades.)*

DOUG: So, what'd you get him for his birthday?

CHARLEY: That coffee-table book he wanted: *Birds of the Great Plains*—

ADRIAN: All sorts of animals have these leks: antelopes, bats, the red deer, but the one I'm thinking about right now is the sage grouse. Sometimes called the sage hen, cock-of-the-plains, old tom, and/or turkey buzzard, what distinguishes the male sage grouse is its courtship behavior, particularly its peculiar form of altruism.

DOUG: Adrian, you going to join us over here or what?

ADRIAN: In a minute.

DOUG: What are you doing?

ADRIAN: I don't know. Reading. Thinking.

DOUG: Thinking about birds?

(Pause. ADRIAN sips his beer.)

Adrian, you thinking about birds again?

(Pause. ADRIAN sips his beer.)

You know if you spent half the time you spent thinking about *bagging a bird* as you did thinking about birds, you'd be laid by now.

CHARLEY: Lay off the kid, Doug, he'll come around when he's ready.

DOUG: He's ready, he's more than ready. He's twenty-three for Christ's sake and never been laid. It's sick.

CHARLEY: He's a late bloomer, has been since we were kids. Hell, he didn't really start shaving till last year.

DOUG: Listen to you turning into his mother: "A late bloomer." Well, he's bloomed. And he knows it. And he knows tonight's the night. It's his twenty-third birthday and tonight he's getting laid. No more stalling, isn't that right Adrian? Adrian? … He hears me.

ADRIAN: This is so embarrassing. Doug can be… well… Doug. But ever since we were kids—scouts—he's been like a big brother to me. And it doesn't all come from some weird macho bullshit—well it does come from some of that—but it has more to do with the sage grouse. That's my thinking anyway. This warped form of altruism we have developed over the years which leads me to ask: Can we ever act on another's behalf or is there always some animal instinct that tells us we'll get something in return? Is our instinct for self-promotion stronger than our will to help others? Case in point: the sage grouse. See, male sage grouses get together on these leks and female grouses then come to the leks to find a mate.

(As ADRIAN says this we see HALEY join CHARLEY and DOUG at the table. They greet each other.)

Seems pretty ordinary. A bunch of guys hanging out meet a bunch of girls, they engage first in some awkward conversation—

HALEY: This beer is really good, what flavor is it?

DOUG: It's Budweiser flavor.

HALEY:

Oh, well it tastes good. Really yellow.

ADRIAN:

—then some witty banter—

HALEY:

I just can't believe I've never been to this bar.
I thought I'd been to all the bars down here,
and I mean—bar none.

ADRIAN:

—then a spark—

CHARLEY:

So Doug says you're a nurse?

HALEY:

In training.

ADRIAN:

—and people start to pair off—

CHARLEY:

Yeah? I'm in training too, training to be a—

DOUG:

—Charley, why don't you tell Haley about what *Adrian's* training for?

CHARLEY:

Right, Adrian.

(. . .)

Adrian's training to be an ornithologist. You know, birds.

ADRIAN:

—BUT—

ADRIAN:

—that's not how it works for the sage grouse.

ADRIAN: *(Shows picture from book.)* See, of the group of sage grouses hanging out, there's only one grouse in the center of the lek that scores. The males on the fringes attract females in their own subtle way, but ultimately deliver the female to the central grouse. And that's been the system since as far back as I can remember. Center guys like Doug or Charley score, while wing-men like me assist. Altruism in its purest form! But here's the twist—

DOUG: Slide over Charley, make some room for our man Adrian.

(DOUG and CHARLEY slide over leaving the center seat open.)

ADRIAN: Each season, the wing-man moves closer and closer to the center until finally he's dead center and in a position to receive that which he gave. Is this altruism or just some seriously self-denying apprenticeship? Did he know he was assisting with the hope he would be assisted later?

DOUG: Adrian, come over here, we got someone who wants to meet you.

HALEY: Hello, Adrian.

CHARLEY: Come on Adrian, it's cool. Relax, man, I'll get you another beer.

(CHARLEY goes to get a beer.)

ADRIAN: And what of the female grouses? What do they think of this? Do any of them realize this is even happening?

(Light rises on DANIELLE, wearing a thick overcoat. She blows her nose loudly, pockets her car keys, and pops a pseudoephedrine. HALEY waves to her across the bar.)

DANIELLE: Jesus Christ…

DOUG: *(To HALEY.)* That your friend?

HALEY: Danielle! Danielle! Over here.

ADRIAN: And what if the now-central grouse doesn't want to be in the center? What if he's not ready, what if he was happy on the fringe, whatifhe'sembarrassedtohavediscoveredthathe'spartofthiswhole—warped—system? WHAT IF HE WANTS OUT?! I'm such an idiot for letting them talk me into this!

DANIELLE: ... I'm such an idiot for letting her talk me into this.

DOUG: Adrian, come on, man! A bird in hand is worth two in the books!

ADRIAN: *(A quick mantra.)* I am not a sage grouse... I am not a sage grouse... I am not a sage grouse!

DOUG: That's it. I'm not kidding, man, no more stalling. Ditch the book, get over there and meet Haley.

(DOUG takes ADRIAN's book from him; ADRIAN takes a step towards the door. CHARLEY is right behind him, stops him. Hands him a fresh beer and leads him to the table.)

CHARLEY: Don't worry, man, I got your back. And she's cool, you'll like her.

(They arrive at the table.)

DOUG: Haley this is Adrian; Adrian this is Haley.

HALEY: Hi Adrian.

(ADRIAN opens his mouth. Lights shift.)

Wake God's Man
Scene One
By José Cruz González

BETH and ANNIE still wait.

BETH: This isn't easy for me, you know?

ANNIE: You think I want to be here? My kid's sick. Ricardo's out of a job and I've got a migraine coming on. Oh, wait. It's arrived! Thanks!
(Beat.)

BETH: You really should see a doctor about that.

ANNIE: I'll call one when I get health insurance.

BETH: If it's about money—

ANNIE: Please. I can take care of myself. You needn't concern yourself.
(Beat. BETH opens a small bottle of prescription pills. She hands one to ANNIE.)

BETH: Here. It'll help your migraine.

ANNIE: What is it?

BETH: Just shut up and take it. *(ANNIE swallows the pill.)* Oh, my god, you swallowed it without water?

ANNIE: I don't have time to fuss. I have a two-month-old baby.
(Beat.)

BETH: We're not going to let Sarah do this. We've got to end it today. Annie?

ANNIE: You were his favorite. I was so jealous because he'd take you out for pecan pie and ice cream.

BETH: I didn't have a choice. Mom made me go with him.

ANNIE: After you left home she always kept a quart in the refrigerator just for him. We could never touch it.

BETH: I hope he rots in Hell.
(SARAH, the youngest sister, rushes in. She is also dressed in black.)

SARAH: I'm sorry! So sorry! Totally sorry!

BETH: You always do this to us.

SARAH: It's my fault. I'm to blame.

BETH: It doesn't mean anything when you keep doing it over and over.

SARAH: I said I was sorry!

BETH: *(Fed up.)* Oh, please!

SARAH: I'm glad you're both here. I've written something for us to read together.

ANNIE: You've got to be kidding?

SARAH: They'll be others speaking about him at the memorial.

BETH: Let me see that.

SARAH: Our family's got to be included.

BETH: I'm not reading this!

(BETH *tears the paper into shreds.*)

SARAH: What's wrong with you? That man was a saint!

BETH: *(Exploding.)* He was a vampire! I tried protecting you two but I couldn't! I was twelve watching over an eight- and six-year-old! I told Mom and she punished me. Said I was making up lies. When I was old enough I left.

SARAH: What are you talking about?

BETH: You know those ice cream trips he'd always take me on? He was groping me in his car. I couldn't move. I just sat there while he did it. "We'll keep this our little secret. We're good at keeping secrets. Would you like for me to take you out again?"

SARAH: Stop it! Enough!

ANNIE: He'd put us to bed, read us a book and help us with our prayers. Mom was in the kitchen making him coffee to go along with his pecan pie. He'd rub our backs and then—

SARAH: That never happened!

ANNIE: Yes, it did! When you were asleep he'd whisper into my ear, "Annie, be open to my touch and experience God's love." I did what he asked. I was afraid to tell Mom!

SARAH: He never did that to us!

BETH: Sarah, if it happened to Annie and I, it happened to you too.

SARAH: No, he never touched me! He was a good man! He was a priest!

BETH: He was a monster!

ANNIE: I know he's not the devil but he did evil.

SARAH: No, I'm not listening to you! I'll do this without you! I'll go up there alone!

ANNIE: No, Sarah, don't.

BETH: You'll be lying to yourself and us.

SARAH: No, no, no! He was a dear sweet man! He'd read books to me, we'd sing songs together and he'd share his silly Irish jokes!

ANNIE: I'm still haunted by him.

BETH: I won't hide from it or feel dirty or ashamed anymore!

SARAH: We grew up in this community. I work for the parish. Don't you dare ruin this for me! Don't you dare!

(SARAH drops the paper and runs out.)

BETH: Sarah!

ANNIE: I can't handle this!

BETH: Annie, I'm sorry I couldn't stop him. I'm so sorry—

ANNIE: I've got to go! I can't stay!

BETH: Please wait!

ANNIE: No, I've got my own family now!

(ANNIE exits. Lights fade on BETH.)

In This House
Scene One
By Kirsten Greenidge

KATHY and BILL's kitchen.

LYNNE: She's beautiful. Really.
(BILL kisses KATHY's forehead and gives her a squeeze.)
KATHY: She's perfect.
LYNNE: You both—
KAYLA: *(Elsewhere on stage, speaks into a phone:)* —sound so nice. Not that I didn't think you wouldn't be: they told me you were, are, but, when I saw your pictures, in the book? with the big house and the trees? ... that's how I grew up so that's why I just had to choose you: in your pictures you both—
LYNNE: —look so *happy. Claire* Anna *Thomas.* That's an awfully big name for such a little girl.
BILL: She'll grow into it. Check out those shoulders. She could be a line-backer—
KATHY: She's *healthy.*
KAYLA: —real healthy. When I first got those tests, all those tests done they said so. Oh, and a girl. Ten fingers; ten toes; little girl, just like they say when you have it and keep it: I wish I could, but I *(Exhales.)* can't, so—
LYNNE: So you said the Claire's for Bill's mother.
(The sound of wood about to break.)
BILL: I think I hear her.
KATHY: He's worse than I am.
LYNNE: And the middle's for—?
KAYLA: —and that's what I want to talk to you about, since you two look so— hello?—Can you—
(BILL sighs heavily.)
KATHY: *(To BILL.)* Don't start: We're having a nice time.
(BILL looks at KATHY. LYNNE looks at BILL.)
BILL: Didn't you hear her? I think I—
KAYLA: —hear me? Good, because what I want to know is if, like after we meet, because we're all supposed to meet? In like a neutral place? Which I can totally pay my share— Barbecue? I guess that's okay, but what I want to ask, in case I agree it's okay for you to have her, and even though she

wouldn't be mine anymore, that well, see: she can have any first name and like *duh*, of course your last name, but, see, it's important... see all the girls, all the women in my family have this certain middle name, 'cause way back, we were, like, Native American, you know Indians, so *(Exhales deeply.)* I was hoping *(Inhales deeply.)* that whoever gets her would let me give her just this one thing, this one name, which would be Anna—

LYNNE: I didn't know Anna was Indian.

KAYLA: Anna-Achak-Nuttah-Numees-Nadie-Alsoonse-Hurit-Hausis.

LYNNE: I knew Anna wasn't *Indian.*

KATHY: I definitely hear her, Bill. Go check.

(KATHY watches BILL as he leaves.)

KAYLA: Beautiful spirit-my-heart's-sister-wise-independent-beautiful as an old woman. Cool, right?

KATHY: It'd be one thing if we'd been like everyone else and gotten one of those Chinese babies. But that list was way too long. We couldn't wait that long. I don't want to be one of those old mothers, and there's no way I'm going to let every doctor from here to Maine look at my who-ha.

LYNNE: So it's Anna for short?

(The sound of wood about to break.)

KATHY: It's Anna just Anna.

(They look at each other.)

LYNNE: Is that legal?

KATHY: It's not *illegal.*

LYNNE: But it's not moral. You promised—

KATHY: This is not writing the Dean and demanding veal-free Sunday dinners and goddamn hummus burgers—

LYNNE: That was ten years ago, and it wasn't real life—

KATHY: Exactly: she's fitting into *our* family, not hanging onto some old pretend one. Bill feels badly—

LYNNE: Because you *promised*—

KATHY: It's nobody's business what we do with our own child in our own house.

LYNNE: You sound like one of those Montana people, with the guns and the creepy kids who are homespun.

KATHY: Home-*schooled.*

LYNNE: Like you have the right to do whatever you want because you're "building a family."

KATHY: The Sopranos do it and everybody *loves* them. The Sopranos do it and they get Emmys. Whose side are you on exactly?

LYNNE: I get creeped out by the "this is my house, this is my way" thing. The, "I'm gonna buy a huge SUV so I can get my kids to basket weaving in a rain storm or whatever so they'll grow up well-rounded and get into the Ivy League so who cares if my car's so big I could kill you if I ran into you or I spew so much crap out of my exhaust that the ozone'll be gone in fifty years because I've got family values."

KATHY: We don't drive an SUV.

LYNNE: *(As she speaks a tiny pink clapboard house floats deliberately from above, like a spider.)* It's like, my dad, you know how I get along with my dad right? Yeah, right, well: he had this thing about manners, because if you had bad manners people would think you came from a crappy family and then the *rest* of your family couldn't show their faces in town ever again and everyone's ruined. So one day we had company, relatives I think, and I said damn. My bad manners bounced out by accident. So my dad marches me into the kitchen and takes out the pepper, not the black kind but the red kind from the cupboard, and he puts it on my tongue. To teach me to pay attention to what's in my mouth. So I'm standing there, pepper sliding down my tongue, tears streaming down my cheeks and you know what? Not one person said a single word. It was like, "Oh, this is Tony's house, this is Tony's way. We're military; it's tradition." When, it's like, um, no, it's wrong to abuse your kid. So I just... I get creeped out by that "family values"/"my house" thing.

KATHY: Well maybe you should move to Canada where everyone keeps their door unlocked like in the Michael Moore movie about the guns.

LYNNE: Maybe.

KAYLA: Really, really? That's so... oh, thank you... you're so nice.

KATHY: *She's ours:* It's not wrong. She can't grow up with a sign around her that says she belongs in some box marked "other"? No: she's mine now.

KAYLA: I was so worried but, you guys are so... so um, so yeah: Barbecue.

(The sound of wood about to break.

The tiny pink clapboard house falls from above and breaks into splinters on the ground.)

Wake God's Man
Scene Two
By John Walch

An intense light begins to shine from the mummified form hanging over the stage. The light is white hot. Something begins spilling from the mummified form—pecans. The pecans hit the stage deck and scatter. The spilling pecans stop as quickly as they started; the body remains full. A MAN wearing a hat enters carrying a bucket. He steps on one of the pecans. CRACK. He picks up the pecan and eats the nut inside. He gathers all the pecans that have spilled on stage in his hat. He moves just off, sits on the bucket, pulls out a nutcracker, and begins shelling pecans.

MAN: One thing nobody ever tells you about pecans is that they're a powerful aphrodisiac, lot like oysters. Stronger than oysters—more zinc, I think. See it's a chemical thing, scientific fact, nothing to do with ethics or God. Nobody ever tells you that though, 'cause who would want to blame what they done wrong on a pecan?
(The MAN cracks another pecan. He shells pecans throughout the following scene.)

ANNIE and SARAH in flight. The scene exists in two separate halves.

Two spaces: ANNIE and RICARDO's home, delineated by the small table, which now has a family picture on it and a receiver for a baby monitor, and the Food Bank in the church, delineated by a small stepladder. SARAH sits on the bottom step of the ladder in the Food Bank. RICARDO is home when ANNIE enters.

SARAH: *Ladies and gentlemen, friends and family, I'm honored to have a chance to say a few words on behalf of the most generous soul—*
(CRACK from a pecan.)
No. No.
RICARDO: That was quick.
ANNIE: Short service.
RICARDO: World record—forty minutes door to door. I guess when you bury a priest there's not a whole lot of explaining to do.
ANNIE: I've got a terrible headache.

(CRACK. ANNIE exits. BRIAN enters the Food Bank, unseen.)

SARAH: *Me and my family are grateful— My sisters and I—* Remember. Remember. Please God, help me remember.

BRIAN: *(Touching SARAH on the shoulder.)* Remember what, Sarah?

(SARAH jumps at the touch.)

Sorry, I didn't mean to scare you—

SARAH: Scare— Brian. No. It's just been— I can't believe you're here, I didn't know— Your mom didn't tell me you were coming.

BRIAN: She didn't know. I didn't know myself till yesterday, got lucky with a last-minute fare.

SARAH: He'd be glad you're here. It's . . . good to see you again.

BRIAN: You too. I've been looking all over for you. The place is filling up fast, hard to get a seat if we don't hurry.

SARAH: You go ahead, I'm not quite ready.

BRIAN: That's right, I almost forgot: the girl who's late to everything, even her own wedding. But I guess, technically, there's a difference between being late and not showing.

SARAH: Brian—

BRIAN: Sorry, just awkward. It's been— Guess I'll see you in there. *(. . .)* Sarah? Sarah, hey? You okay?

SARAH: Yeah, I just need some time to sort things out. Stay with me…

(CRACK. ANNIE reenters with water and aspirin.)

RICARDO: Was it a nice funeral?

ANNIE: Nice?

RICARDO: I meant: well-attended.

ANNIE: Where's Monica?

RICARDO: Napping.

ANNIE: She go down okay?

RICARDO: Still a little fussy, but better. Listen.

(Hands ANNIE baby monitor. ANNIE listens. CRACK.)

BRIAN: Figured I'd find you in here. Even when we were kids, you'd sneak in the Food Bank to hide.

ANNIE: I like to hear her breathe.

SARAH: I like being surrounded by all the cans and bags and jars. So much generosity.

BRIAN: My mom tells me you've done a great job since taking it over. Expanded it beyond our parish.

SARAH: It was his idea, to expand the Food Bank. He was good, wasn't he? I mean of course I know he was, but I— I can't seem to remember…

BRIAN: Remember what? Everything he did for your family after your dad died?

SARAH: No, no… my speech, talk, remarks. You know: what I'm going to say. I wrote it out last night, printed it on linen paper, but I lost it. And now, I can't remember what I was going to say. Sure, I remember a couple of the words—

(CRACK.)

—but now they're all jumbled in my head, and I can't seem to remember how I ever put them together. Nothing makes sense anymore.

BRIAN: Sarah, you don't need a speech. Just speak from your heart, you'll do great.

SARAH: Is that what you're doing?

BRIAN: Oh no, no, no. I have prepared remarks—minus the linen paper.
(He shows a cocktail napkin from the plane. They smile.)

SARAH: Let me see.
(SARAH playfully snatches for it. BRIAN climbs a few rungs of the ladder, holding the napkin above her. SARAH climbs up after him. This is playful, pushing them higher and higher on the ladder and closer and closer together.)

BRIAN: I'm afraid you'll have to wait like all the other poor souls.

SARAH: *(A childhood game.)* Pretty please with, um, cinnamon and strawberries on top?

BRIAN: Nope said the Pope when he was served a cantaloupe.

SARAH: With caramel and apples on top?

BRIAN: Nope said the Pope when he was served a roasted goat.

SARAH: With pralines and, and, and pecans—
(CRACK. They have reached the top of the ladder and can go no higher. They are sort of holding on to each other there.)

ANNIE: She sounds better. Clearer.

RICARDO: How about you?

ANNIE: Fine. Just this headache.
(The phone rings. Neither moves.)

BRIAN: Uh… Sarah. We should get down… before one or both of us gets hurt.
(SARAH and BRIAN climb down the ladder. The phone rings again.)

ANNIE: Could you get that, please?

RICARDO: It's for you. Beth. She's called twice in the last ten minutes, hysterical, demanding you come back, she says she's not going to the service alone.

ANNIE: Get it before it wakes the baby.

RICARDO: And tell her what?

ANNIE: I don't care, just don't make me talk to her.

RICARDO: What's going on, Annie? Why'd you leave before the service even started?

ANNIE: JUST GET IT!

(*RICARDO exits. ANNIE looks at the picture of her family, listens to the baby monitor again. CRACK.*)

SARAH: Did… ummm… Judy come?

BRIAN: Trudy. Nope, just me.

SARAH: Your mom told me she's pregnant again.

BRIAN: Yeah, look at me. A wife, two kids, three-bedroom house. A happy family.

SARAH: Just what you always wanted—a family.

BRIAN: Lucky me.

SARAH: Brian—

BRIAN: I'm sorry, Sarah, but I see you and I can't help but wonder how different it could have been.

SARAH: You would have resented me your whole life, it would have been a disaster.

BRIAN: But why?

SARAH: You know why. I told you a million times why. You wanted children, I didn't.

BRIAN: Yes, a million times, but never once did you tell me *why* you didn't want children. You're great with kids, everybody knows that, it doesn't make sense!

SARAH: I DON'T KNOW… okay?

BRIAN: How can't you know?… I'm sorry. I just wanted to… see him, pay my last respects. He meant a lot to me too. I mean after you left me he was the only one there for me, and we did a lot of soul searching. I was so bitter—

SARAH: *Was?*

BRIAN: You don't even know. But *he* did, and he helped me not so much understand, but accept that for whatever reason what you did was all somehow part of God's plan. Helped me open my heart again, so I could experience God's love. Not long after that I met Trudy, and she wanted kids and well, here I am. Happy, all thanks to him. We should go.

(*CRACK. RICARDO returns.*)

ANNIE: What did she say?

SARAH: What did you say?

RICARDO: She wants you to come back.

BRIAN: We should get back…

RICARDO: She says you are all going to have to face it at some point, might as well be today.

BRIAN: Sarah, you coming?

RICARDO: —Then she just kept telling me to tell you that she was sorry. Sorry she didn't protect you and that you had to forgive her. Forgive her for what? Face what?

ANNIE: It doesn't matter. What matters is now. Especially now. We have a family together, and I'm not ruining it over something that doesn't matter.

(The phone rings again. Neither moves for it.)

SARAH: You said he helped you? …

BRIAN: Yeah, helped me accept, not understand.

RICARDO: You know I could just answer and find out what this is all about.

ANNIE: You don't want to know.

RICARDO: Yes I do—tell me.

ANNIE: I can't.

RICARDO: Why?

ANNIE: Because if I do, you'll never love me the same.

(The phone rings again. Neither moves. CRACK.)

SARAH: No, no. After that. Something about love?

BRIAN: God's love. He helped me open my heart so I could experience God's love.

SARAH: … Experience God's love.

(CRACK. The phone rings; a baby cries in the monitor.)

Oh my God, I remember.

BRIAN: Remember what?

SARAH: Everything.

ANNIE: Great. Now, we've woken the baby.

(The MAN has finished cracking all the pecans. Shift to:)

Union
Scene Two
By José Cruz González

Two weeks later at the factory gates. Late night. A small fire glows in an old barrel. LES *and* JANE *try to keep warm.* LES *holds a two-by-four.*

LES: Who's there!

HARRY: It's me, Harry. You going to beat me with that?

JANE: Les, put it down.

(*HARRY enters. He is the factory owner's son.*)

LES: Where's your old man? I thought he was coming.

HARRY: I had to rush him to the hospital tonight. He couldn't take it anymore. His blood pressure went off the chart. He was babbling like a baby. "How can they do this to me? After everything I've done for them." The doctor says he'll have to stay in the hospital. Who knows for how long. They got more tests to run.

LES: Harry, everybody's got a sad, heartbreak story.

JANE: Lester!

LES: What?

JANE: I'm real sorry about your dad, Harry.

HARRY: Thank you, Jane.

LES: Why'd you call us here tonight?

HARRY: My old man sent me down here to fix things.

LES: Well?

HARRY: I want your keys to the factory.

LES: You called us here for that? Let's get out of here.

HARRY: Now, wait just a minute. There's something else. I heard you two got engaged.

LES: So what about it?

HARRY: I want to wish you congratulations and give you this.

(*HARRY holds out an envelope.*)

LES: What is it?

HARRY: It's a check for five thousand dollars.

JANE: Harry, we can't take that.

HARRY: Of course you can. It's a weddin' present, Jane. After all, that's what the walkout is all about, health insurance, right? Look, business is business and family is family. My granddad and dad have always taken care of their people in good times and bad. It's my family's tradition. Here. Take it.

LES: What's the catch?

HARRY: There's no catch. This is going to help you start that family you want.

(Beat.)

LES: All right, suit yourself.

JANE: Lester, what are you doin'?

LES: You know we can use it.

JANE: We're not taking it.

LES: Jane, you can have the wedding you want and all the things we planned.

JANE: I don't care! Give it back!

LES: There's nothing wrong with taking it. It's his family—

HARRY: Tradition.

LES: Besides they can afford it. It's nothing to them.

JANE: How's this going to look to everybody if we take it? I won't do it! I won't be bought off!

LES: Hey, nobody is buying me off! It's free and clear. He said it. Besides after we get our union he's still going to have to deal with me!

JANE: Give it here!

LES: No! Are you crazy?

JANE: I can't believe you're doing this, Lester!

LES: Hey, I'm taking care of business!

JANE: Are you?

(JANE exits.)

LES: Jane! Jane!

(Lights fade.)

In This House
Scene Two
By Julie Marie Myatt

ROBERT, construction worker, enters in a hard hat, carrying a thermos, and wearing a tool belt, heavy with tools. He looks at the small house, looks up to the sky, and sighs.

To add emphasis or atmosphere to his argument, ROBERT mimics a woman's voice whenever quoting a woman. And mimics his own voice when quoting a man or himself.

ROBERT: A woman has got choices.... But. *(He shrugs... pours himself a cup of coffee. Takes out his smallest hammer, nails, and glue, bends down, and begins to put the house back together.)* I'm not telling that story. I'm telling the other one. I'm telling the one that everyone loves to shake their head, *(He shakes his head, back and forth, disappointed.)* "tsk, tsk, tsk," and some bitter know-it-all bitch pipes in with, "typical," and another sorry-ass woman, adds, "uh-huh," and the heads keep shaking back and forth, and suddenly my name becomes synonymous with a string of obscenities... like all the unsung heroes of the broken fairytale. We're the "assholes," the "fuckheads," and "who does that son-of-a-bitch think he is?" who don't stick around for the happily ever after. We're the frogs who don't turn into princes. We're the smart guys who pass those inbreds kissing Sleeping Beauty, and yell, "Hell Mac, if the girl's tired, let her sleep!", and when we ride past those "valiant" cats climbing up those long, blond, ponytails, we can state, for a fact, "Rapunzel's a slut!" *(He can't help but smile at himself... and shrugs.)* We don't wear tights, break spells, or save the day.... We look at our finger, and speak the truth, "I don't see a wedding ring, do you?", and look at her, "If you would have taken that pill, you wouldn't be crying now, would you?" and slide on out the door, "Sorry, Baby. I don't want it."... *(He concentrates on the house for a moment.)* But. I don't hit women, or whistle at tight shorts, even when I'm enjoying the view, or get drunk and embarrass myself in public. I don't watch sports and hoot and holler. I don't even stay up all that late. I make an honest living. I pay my rent, I have a savings account, I buy my mother Mother's Day cards, and remember her birthday. I pet a dog when I meet him, and smile at strangers, and cry at sad movies. I eat right. I shave regularly. I open doors for old people. I like to cook for a woman, and make her feel good, and I like to wake up in the morning beside her. I like to talk sweet to her. And mean it. I like calling her up from work, just because I'm thinking about her. I like to tell her I love her. And mean it. But that doesn't mean I want a kid. It doesn't mean I'd make a good father. Sure I feel bad. Sure I feel guilty. But I can live with that. It's not that hard.... The way I look at it, it's better to make just one grown person cry, even a person I love... and get her and her friends and relatives all heated up and full of hate and vengeance, heads shaking back and forth like angry trees, *(He shakes his head back and forth.)* "that god-damn motherfucker Robert, got our precious Kayla pregnant, and then the cocksucker just up and waves good-bye"... "What's she gonna do with a baby all by herself"... "I'd like to get my hands on that Robert, I'd show him what's what"... "I never did like him"... "uh-huh"... than it is a little kid. Better to hurt the woman once, than punish the kid for a lifetime. Better to never know your father, never lay eyes on him, and imagine the best—believe he could be a decent guy, could love animals and cooking spaghetti—than know from one-on-one, personal experience that he's an asshole. I'm not going to make a kid grow up with someone who doesn't want to be her father. I've seen what that can do. I'm saving that kid a bundle in therapy. Believe me. I'm sure you're assuming I had a shitty father, "Yep, that'll do it." But I didn't. My father was a good man. Loyal. He ran an honest household. He played ball with us, built tree houses, all that kind of thing. He was a do-the-right-thing kind of dad. He did all the right things, and I still didn't want to stick around and raise that baby. Kids just aren't in the plan for my life. A man has to recognize that in himself, and respect it, or really fuck up a whole lot of people. And I'm sure you're thinking that I should have thought of that before... "You should have thought of that before you fucked her, ass-hole"... "uh-huh"... but don't tell me you've never laid down with someone in such a hurry to get her clothes off that you weren't terribly interested in doing what's right, saving the day, or planning for the future... you're both just trying to get arms out of sleeves, hooks unhooked, and the zipper down fast enough to get that warm skin next to yours. *(He shrugs. The house is finished—crooked, not perfect, but together. He finishes off his coffee... puts the cup back on the thermos.)* I've got choices too.

(BILL enters and tries to pick up the fragile house, as if he's just picked out the perfect dollhouse to bring home to his daughter.)

Union
Scene Three
By John Walch

Apply Pressure.

The sound of an industrial loom. Lights rise on MARGARET *carrying a heavy bolt of stark-white fabric across the stage. She wears a pair of coveralls. She struggles under the weight of the fabric until she reaches her station and can set it down. Relief, then an ache—somewhere in her shoulder. She shrugs off the ache, then begins measuring yards of fabric by the arm length. Yard after yard. After each arm, she makes a quick slit in the fabric with a pair of scissors. She does this with the efficiency and speed of someone who has performed the same task day in and day out for the last eleven years. But she's tired, more so than usual, and as she makes a slit, she slips and nicks her finger. She drops the scissors, looks at the wound, tries to keep the blood away from the fabric, sucks on the wound, but it continues to bleed. As this has been going on,* HARRY, *the owner's son, has appeared behind her. He comes up and offers her a handkerchief, cut of the exact same cloth as the bolt of fabric.*

HARRY: Apply pressure. "To slow the flow of blood, apply direct pressure to the wound." … That's what the first-aid kit in the break room says anyway.

MARGARET: *(Not taking the handkerchief.)* Thanks, Harry, but I got three kids at home, I think I know how to take care of a scratch.

HARRY: Go on, Margaret, no use letting your pride stand in the way, just take it.

MARGARET: If I were worried about my pride, you think I'd be working for you today?

HARRY: Margaret, you're bleeding. Besides, we got a whole bolt here.

(MARGARET takes handkerchief.)

Good, now wrap it around there—good and tight.

MARGARET: I seriously doubt this is what the folks outside the gate had in mind. When they said HMO, they didn't mean Harry's Health Maintenance Organization. What're you doing down here, Harry?

HARRY: I'm just trying to take care of my own.

MARGARET: I hear that. … This walkout must be squeezing you pretty tight, last time I saw you on the floor was that summer before you went off to college and your daddy made you rip seams and, as I recall, you weren't too good at it then.

HARRY: No, but he always said: "You can't expect to run the store, if you never stood behind the register."

MARGARET: He's a good man, Harry. Strong. I'm sure he'll recover and quick.

HARRY: Oh, yeah. A good man. And you're right; he will *recover*. I just hope you and the kids don't mind moving to Mexico after he does.

MARGARET: Your daddy'd slap you into next week hearing you talk about moving his mill to Mexico.

HARRY: *¿Entonces, por qué está en Mexico ahora mismo?*

MARGARET: Just 'cause I'm punching your clock, don't mean I have to play your games—

HARRY: Sorry, I just thought you might like a Spanish lesson. We'll be looking to take a skeleton crew down with us to help train. And your loyalty to the mill has not gone unrecognized, couple that with some familiarity with Spanish and you'd really have an edge.

MARGARET: Screw you, Harry, your daddy's not moving this plant to Mexico.

HARRY: *¿Entonces, por qué está—*

MARGARET: Translate, Harry.

HARRY: *Entonces* means: Then. *Por qué* … try it with me: *por qué.*

MARGARET: Poor-kay.

HARRY: *POR-QUÉ…*

MARGARET: I am poor, okay? And now I'm pissed, so just tell me what you're talking about.

HARRY: *Por qué* means: why; *por qué está en Mexico ahora mismo* — why is he in Mexico right now?

MARGARET: Your daddy's in Mexico?

HARRY: Scouting out a site, meeting with some people. *¿Comprendes?*

MARGARET: You're running around telling everybody he's in the hospital, had a heart attack, when the truth is—

HARRY: I'm trying to buy some time.

MARGARET: What are you doing down here, Harry, what do you want?

HARRY: To keep jobs in this town.

MARGARET: That's the first sensible thing you said; what's the catch?

HARRY: No catch, really, just facts and stats. The clean-lean truth, something practical-minded folks like you and me can understand. Stats, like how over the last two years more than 125 textile mills have closed in North Carolina, knocking over twenty thousand folks like yourself out of a job.

Facts like how cheap Asian imports are flooding the market making it impossible for our products to compete—

MARGARET: But ours say: Made in the U.S.A.

HARRY: People could give a god damn where something is made, or who made it, as long as it's cheap. We've been able to stay in the game so far 'cause we've kept our overhead low, but this union'll kill us, Margaret.

MARGARET: So what do you want?

HARRY: To keep jobs right here. Read this, it'll explain everything.

(HARRY hands her a flyer; MARGARET reads.)

MARGARET: Harry, you can't— This legal?

HARRY: To the letter. North Carolina is a right-to-work state.

MARGARET: Translate.

HARRY: No worker, new or current, can be forced to join a union, even if it's a union shop.

MARGARET: You know this union is long overdue. First salary freezes and now no more benefits—

HARRY: You think those folks in Mexico are asking for *benefits?* And don't you think we want to keep giving you benefits? Hell yes, but we also want to keep jobs in this town and we can't do both.

MARGARET: So no union?

HARRY: Did I say that? No, I never said that. Last thing I want is anybody in this town thinking that management stands against the union. Hell, I met with Jane and Les last night and told them to go ahead—

MARGARET: So we can have a union, but if we join your daddy'll move to Mexico.

HARRY: I am simply informing you of the reality of our situation and of your legal rights—reminding you that you have a right to work in the good state of North Carolina no matter what Les, Jane or anyone says.

(HARRY produces a stack of fliers.)

MARGARET: You want me pass these out?

HARRY: You know I can't. Be stoned to death before I gave out a dozen. But if it comes from someone who's... closer to the people, someone like you or Simon maybe, then folks might take this thing seriously.

MARGARET: Simon's gone, Harry, I haven't seen him in two days.

HARRY: All the more reason you should pass these out. This thing is ripping this community apart by the seams.

MARGARET: You can't ask me to hand out these fliers. I'm already breaking ranks. I do this, no one'll ever talk to me again, much less my kids.

(Beat.)

HARRY: How's that finger?

MARGARET: *(Unwraps fabric.)* Stopped.

HARRY: See there, just a little pressure, Margaret.

(HARRY looks at the handkerchief; it is stained with blood.)

And all it cost us was this much fabric, and when you look at it against the whole bolt, I'd say that was damn well worth it.

MARGARET: Harry, I—

HARRY: Don't tell me you can or you can't. I don't want to know what you do on your own time. I just want to know that you and everybody else has got the facts they need.

(HARRY rolls fliers and places them in MARGARET's hand, making a fist.)

You do whatever you think is right. *Buénos noches.*

(HARRY exits. MARGARET freezes, a deer in the headlights, with the fliers clenched in her fist.)

The Mating Habits of the Sage Grouse
Scene Two
By Kirsten Greenidge

On a yoga mat. A box of tissues is on the floor next to the yoga mat. MANY *crumpled tissues litter the floor. As* DANIELLE *speaks, she completes simple yoga/Pilates moves.*

DANIELLE: *(Blows her nose loudly.)* So I told her no. Flat out. *(Blows, throws tissue into her "pile" around the mat.)* But *(Blows.)* does she listen? I've got my class, I tell her. And I can't get rid of this cold. That pseudo-feta-whatever isn't going to be enough: I need something to knock me out, like have me speaking in tongues drooling on the floor as long as I can breathe out of my nose again out. So I can't sit at the bar drinking piss-warm beer while you go chat up some yahoo who routinely mistakes breasts for welcome mats. But she doesn't listen. Tonight we're going out, she *announces* to me, like it was never up to me in the first place to say yes *or* no. See, this is what we do. To *not* continue to do it would mean I've violated some sort of sacred oath. *(Blows.)* Haley eats, drinks, dreams about hooking some guy, any guy, so it's "we're going out" like every other night. It's "oh, he's cute, go talk to his friend for me." Because if there's one thing I've learned it's this: in this moveable feast for the yahoos, I am not the entrée. I am the garnish. My function is to attract the eye to the main course, which, in this case, is Haley. *(Blows hard.)* But I think of it this way: *(Blows.)* while the main course sits there on the plate *(Blows.)* getting cold and slick from congealing grease, it's the garnish that gets preserved, all sexy and inviting, all "look at me, I'm not like the parsley they decorate with at Denny's." I'm not talking about parsley at all. I'm talking about, like, rosemary, or sage. Arranged in some sort of pattern around the edge of the plate, you know? I like to think of myself like that. The essence of me wafting up so that I'm still doing my "job," still getting Haley closer to her dream yahoo, but, I'm not on the side—in fact, I'm enjoyable—so some lousy stinking "I still live with my parents so we can't go to my place" so *I* end up with seat belt marks on my *ass* that stay for like a week afterwards which is how long I waited for you to pick up the goddamn phone and freaking *dial* realizes I'm more than just a short cut. *(Blows.)* That's not entirely generous of me. But since girl scouts, second grade, we've been friends so if it makes her happy to rub into all these guys while I drink warm beer until my insides *plead* for one sip of something that isn't domestic, then, as her friend, I guess I should shut up and do that. But there's this little voice inside that says "yeah, sure, do it, but what do you get in return?" Not very altruistic. But then, who doesn't have that tugging, pulling, little bit inside them? Nobody's my guess.

Wake God's Man
Scene Three
By Kirsten Greenidge

Above the stage the body seems to inhale, then exhale. Hat in hand, the MAN *climbs the Food Bank ladder, up to where the body is suspended. He uses a knife to cut a hole in the face of the body (the body's eyes or mouth is a suggestion). He carefully sifts pecan shells into the body from his hat.*

MAN: Nobody wants to blame it on a pecan. *(Sifts/pours.)* But. You could. *(Sifts/pours.)* "Not me. Whatever happened it wasn't me, don't blame me. It was something I ate, something I thought when I ate, something I thought before I ate: a mistake. Not the real me." We do it all the time. Instead of accept. Instead of listening and accepting, we explain and explain. Or try to explain and explain. That's got nothing to do with God, either. *(Sifts/pours.)*
(The body expands. The sound of something about to burst/stretched to its limit. It grows louder. Bright light fills the stage.
We hear the telephone again. Then the baby's wails again.
ANNIE *and* RICARDO's *home. From the baby monitor we hear* ANNIE's *footsteps, then her making soft sounds as she soothes the baby.* RICARDO *watches the monitor.*
The phone rings.
RICARDO *goes to the monitor, turns it up.* ANNIE's *soothing gets louder, the baby calms.*
The phone rings.
RICARDO *stares at the monitor.*
A pecan shell falls to the ground.
RICARDO *turns off the monitor, carefully.*
In mid-ring, RICARDO *picks up the phone.)*
RICARDO: Oh, Beth, sorry—. Yeah, she's here but I'm a little confused—. No, wait, don't go—
(A pecan shell drops from above.)
No, please, Beth, because I've been wondering… about the memorial, yeah, but also about before—
(A pecan shell drops from above.)
Well, like the christening. The wedding was easy. No family. We're not practicing, so no priest. But the christening: for some reason Annie want-

ed Monica blessed. Even though around here Sunday is the day we mow the lawn, you know? We light candles when a fuse blows. But Annie was sure. The only problem was who. A perfect stranger from some no-name parish? Or him: the saint who loved your mother's pecan pies almost more than God Himself. The saint your mom couldn't stop gushing about. See, early on I noticed how Annie would get when your mother would do that. Every muscle under her skin would start to pulse. But with the christening, I think Annie wanted to see a new start to everything, so when your mother insisted on him, after Annie tensed up like she does, somehow she calmed down and said yes. Even though the very fabric of her changes when he's around, when your mother mentions his name. And maybe it's just this day and age— when you're taught to think the very worst about a person—

(The body creaks, begins to tremble, and continues throughout:)

—your blood asks the deepest part of you when you see someone's entire being turn cold, even if just for a split moment and somewhere there's a part of you that knows the answer…. Beth? Still—? Good, because, see, Annie marches home from the church today, and every muscle under her skin is pulsing like they're about to spill onto the floor, and I ask her how the service was, make her lie to me about how the service was— I try to make her tell me even though I already know and I'm wondering, Beth, what's wrong with me that I would agree to that christening, that I would try to make her flat-out tell me—

(A torrent of pecan shells falls from the body. The gauze and weeds float from above. The floor is littered with shells, white gauze, dead weeds, and dirt.)

—when maybe… I should tell her myself. That's what I'm wondering, Beth. Why would I do that?

(The stage grows white and hot.)

In This House
Scene Three
By José Cruz González

BILL's Dream. Stars fill the stage. The sound of a Native American drum beating and the chanting of old men. BILL *enters in his pajamas carrying a house on his back. He is bent over. The house is heavy. He crosses the stage slowly. He stops occasionally to wipe his brow. An eagle's cry pierces the night.* BILL *stops to look up. A large eagle feather falls from the sky landing on the stage.* EAGLE WOMAN *appears. It is* KAYLA *dressed in a long Native-American-type coat with American product icons (GE, Apple, Chevron, etc.) painted over it. She wears long white hair.* BILL *hides behind the house.* EAGLE WOMAN *lifts her arm up, holding a very expensive cooking pot in her hand and a whisk in the other.*

EAGLE WOMAN: Anna!

BILL: Oh, shit!

(BILL *immediately opens the house and removes a small baby doll.* EAGLE WOMAN *yelps a warrior's cry, circling around him beating the whisk into the cooking pot.* BILL *clutches the doll and starts to crawl away.* EAGLE WOMAN *chases after him, grabbing him by the hair. She pulls out a large kitchen knife, holding it to his throat.*)

EAGLE WOMAN: Your family speaks with a snake's tongue!

BILL: No!

EAGLE WOMAN: Yes!

BILL: Well, maybe so, just that one time but we're good, honest people! Honest!

EAGLE WOMAN: Hah!

BILL: You're not going to kill me are you?

EAGLE WOMAN: You have betrayed the ancestors by taking away the child's given name. Our ancestors' tears rain on a land of sorrow. Their cries are carried to the Four Directions. The Sun God is angry with you. And for that a sacrifice must be made.

BILL: But it was Kathy's idea!

EAGLE WOMAN: Do you not live under the same roof?

BILL: Yes, but things are complicated.

EAGLE WOMAN: Are you not the master?

BILL: Yes, sometimes.

EAGLE WOMAN: Your path is crooked like a stream littered with lies.

BILL: What do you want of me?

EAGLE WOMAN: A curse will be put upon your lodge unless the child gets back her full name.

BILL: But how? I don't even remember all of it. And there's Kathy—

EAGLE WOMAN: Your lodge will unravel if you do not!

BILL: Unravel?

EAGLE WOMAN: You must become a warrior.

BILL: Yes, I will.

EAGLE WOMAN: Succeed or I will haunt you and pick at your heart and eyes with my expensive Chicago Cutlery!

BILL: What?

EAGLE WOMAN: Agreed?

BILL: I'll do as you say.

(*EAGLE WOMAN takes the doll from* BILL. *She places the doll inside the pot and stirs it. She smells it and then holds it up to the sky.*)

EAGLE WOMAN: Anna-Achak-Nuttah-Numees-Nadie-Alsoonse-Hurit-Hausis! (*The crack of thunder and lightning.*) Now say it!

BILL: Claire Anna-Achak-Nuttah-Numees-Nadie-Alsoonse-Hurit-Hausis Thomas! Okay? Is that okay?

(*A cooking timer goes off.* EAGLE WOMAN *pulls it out of her coat pocket to check it.*)

EAGLE WOMAN: Well done!

(*Drumming and chanting are heard.* EAGLE WOMAN *hands back the doll to* BILL.)

Go now and remember Pajama Warrior what I have said or else!

(*The house bursts into flames. An eagle's piercing cry is heard once again. She looks up to the sky. Blackout.*)

The Mating Habits of the Sage Grouse
Scene Three
By Julie Marie Myatt

CHARLEY and HALEY make out in a dark corner. They speak in-between kisses.

CHARLEY: He's a great guy.

HALEY: Seems like it. I'm sure he's wonderful—

CHARLEY: One of my best friends.

HALEY: Friends are important.

CHARLEY: He loves birds.

HALEY: I love birds.

CHARLEY: Wow.

HALEY: I know.

CHARLEY: God, you're beautiful.

HALEY: You think so?

CHARLEY: You two would—really will make a perfect couple.

HALEY: Thank you.

CHARLEY: I hear you're a nurse?

HALEY: Yes.

CHARLEY: Important work.

HALEY: Very.

CHARLEY: Saving people's lives.

HALEY: Someone's gotta do it.

CHARLEY: It's a good thing it's you.

HALEY: Thank you.

CHARLEY: It must be satisfying.

HALEY: What?

CHARLEY: Helping people.

HALEY: Incredibly.

CHARLEY: You must sleep well at night.

HALEY: When I sleep.

   (They both giggle.)

CHARLEY: I see.

HALEY: I heard someone call you "the priest."

CHARLEY: Minister. In training.

HALEY: God.

CHARLEY: Yes.

(They giggle some more.)

HALEY: Can you *save* me?

CHARLEY: From?

(She looks at him, pulls him closer. He kisses her neck.)

HALEY: Andy seems like a great guy—

CHARLEY: *ADRIAN.* He's the best. Really.

HALEY: He's very attractive. I'll probably fall head over heels for him.

CHARLEY: You will.

HALEY: God.

(He stops.)

CHARLEY: Yes?

HALEY: Think they're wondering where we—

CHARLEY: Smokers have to smoke.

(They resume their roaming hands and lips.)

HALEY: Should I feel guilty?

CHARLEY: Hmm?

HALEY: Do you feel guilty?

CHARLEY: About smoking?

HALEY: No—

CHARLEY: Oh. This? Yes. Of course.

(They stop kissing.)

HALEY: Good. I mean, I think one of us should, and I guess guilt kinda goes with your job, doesn't it?

(CHARLEY lights a cigarette. Offering one to HALEY.)

CHARLEY: Yes. I suppose. Indirectly.

HALEY: You deal with that. A lot. In your profession.

CHARLEY: To an extent. Often. Yes.

HALEY: I deal with bodies. Blood. Flesh. Monitors. Medicine. Science. Facts. It's very different.

(HALEY lights a cigarette.)

CHARLEY: Sometimes. Yes. Circumstantially.

HALEY: I know that certain things just can't be helped. Physically. Or, if they are to be helped, you have to take certain actions. Quickly. Physically. If you want to save lives.

CHARLEY: Definitely. And. Prayer is helpful.

HALEY: Doesn't hurt.

CHARLEY: Why not put the old hands together, just in case.

HALEY: Couldn't hurt.

CHARLEY: People do it all the time. Pray. All over the world. Someone could be praying for us, right now, and we don't even know it.

HALEY: Who?

CHARLEY: People you'll never meet—

HALEY: Wild—

CHARLEY: Yes. And people you know. Are just getting to know. Right now—

HALEY: Yes. Great. Thank you. So. If you look at this brand-new relationship as a *life,* a life that is very important—

CHARLEY: A baby—

HALEY: Yes. Babies are fragile as hell—

CHARLEY: A relationship is a fragile new life… it has a spirit—

HALEY: Yes, and fragile as it is, the new life has to be nurtured, saved from harm, daily… but, to save it, naturally, from my point of view, you need more than prayers. You gotta take some *physical* action.

CHARLEY: Naturally. From your point of view.

HALEY: For example, if this new partner, in this new relationship—

CHARLEY: You and Adrian really are going to make a great couple—

HALEY: Thank you—

CHARLEY: He'll make you very happy—

HALEY: Of course. But. If this new partner, Alex?

CHARLEY: *ADRIAN*—

HALEY: With the dark hair and dark eyes—very nice—but if he—new partner—in this new relationship, fragile as it is, if he isn't interested in having sex as often as I might like to, have sex—

(CHARLEY drops his cigarette.)

CHARLEY: Uh-huh.

(HALEY crushes it out for him. CHARLEY moves closer to her. CHARLEY begins to kiss her again.)

HALEY: I'm sure he's wonderful in many ways, on the inside too, of course, and I'm sure once I've really gotten to know him, I'm not going to want to lose him—

CHARLEY: He's super. Definitely a keeper—

HALEY: Your best friend—

CHARLEY: We go way back—

HALEY: But, if I've really got to have sex, much more often than he might be interested in having it, (some shy guys are like that)

CHARLEY: (Rare, but, possible—)

HALEY: And of course, I would want to save this new relationship, his sanity, and mine—I wouldn't want to be a bother in bed—

CHARLEY: Bad for both—

HALEY: Yes. Hard on your souls, so to speak—in your language—

(Their hands are all over each other.)

CHARLEY: Your soul is very important, very important—

HALEY: Yet. I've got to get it, sex, *somewhere.*

CHARLEY: But not just *anywhere.*

HALEY: No, no. Heavens no.

CHARLEY: One wants to be particular.

HALEY: Very. One wants to know you have someone to call. In these *physical* matters. For help. To help save, to help nurture this fragile new life, this—

CHARLEY: Budding relationship.

HALEY: Yes. Why not a minister?

CHARLEY: You really only want to do what's best.

HALEY: For Allen—

CHARLEY: Adrian— The new relationship is a very important life. The entire future of every society depends on the *new* relationship to be successful. How else would it thrive?

HALEY: Yes! You don't want it to die. You can't let it—

CHARLEY: No. You must—you want to help it any way you can.

HALEY: People need help.

CHARLEY: You have to save it.

HALEY: We're really just doing what's best for—

CHARLEY: Adrian.

HALEY: Yes! For Adrian.

CHARLEY: Yes—

HALEY: For his sanity. For the future—

CHARLEY: I'm here for you—

HALEY: Our future—

CHARLEY: Amen.

The Mating Habits of the Sage Grouse
Scene Four
By José Cruz González

Later in the evening. Loud music. The bar is packed with people. DOUG and DANIELLE are at a table.

DOUG: I think Adrian likes Haley a lot. I see it in his eyes.

DANIELLE: She's not going home with him tonight.

DOUG: What?

DANIELLE: She likes Charley.

DOUG: No way?

DANIELLE: I saw in the way she looked at him.

DOUG: No way! Really?

DANIELLE: Yeah.

DOUG: But it's Adrian's night.

DANIELLE: Sorry.

DOUG: Why isn't she attracted to him?

DANIELLE: What?

DOUG: What did he do wrong?

DANIELLE: Nothing. He's cute.

DOUG: Yeah, but…

DANIELLE: He's sending mixed signals.

DOUG: I knew it! He's gay!

DANIELLE: No. Maybe he's not ready to date yet.

DOUG: Are you interested?

DANIELLE: Sorry. He's not my type.

DOUG: Adrian is a great guy, a real thinker, deep too.

DANIELLE: You care a lot for your friend. That's sweet.

DOUG: Maybe you're right. Maybe he's not ready.

(*DANIELLE drinks her wine. Music soars and then fades.*)

DANIELLE: Doug, you like to dance?

DOUG: Me?

DANIELLE: Yeah?

DOUG: I don't really know how.

DANIELLE: I like dancing.

DOUG: Yeah?

DANIELLE: Yeah. Maybe I could show you.

(ADRIAN enters with a couple more beers. He looks upset.)

DOUG: My man is back! It took you long enough!

DANIELLE: It's busy tonight.

DOUG: What?

DANIELLE: Busy tonight!

DOUG: Busy!

ADRIAN: Whatever.

DOUG: Hey, where's Haley and Charley?

ADRIAN: They're making out!

DOUG AND DANIELLE: What?

ADRIAN: Yeah. I saw them.

DOUG: No way!

ADRIAN: Can you believe that?

DANIELLE: Maybe I better leave.

DOUG: I'm going to kick Charley's ass!

ADRIAN: Let it go. It's just my luck. It's okay!

DOUG: No, it's not okay! Haley and you are supposed to hook up. Charley and
    I set this up. Where is that son-of-a-bitch?

ADRIAN: It's no big deal.

DOUG: Hey, I'm doing this for you!

ADRIAN: I don't need your help!

DOUG: Dude, you need all the help you can get! I mean what's up with you?
    Don't you like girls?

ADRIAN: Fuck you!

DOUG: No, fuck you! All you do is talk shit about birds! What's that all about?

DANIELLE: Hey, hey, hey!

ADRIAN: Go to hell!

(ADRIAN swings at DOUG and misses. DOUG decks ADRIAN.)

DANIELLE: Oh, my god!

DOUG: Oh, shit! I'm sorry Adrian!

ADRIAN: Leave me alone!

DOUG: I didn't mean it! It's Charley I'm pissed at.

ADRIAN: Back off!

DOUG: Come on, man, talk to me.

ADRIAN: I'm all right!

DOUG: Hey, I'm really sorry.

ADRIAN: It's okay. You didn't hit me that hard. I swung at you first.

DOUG: This is supposed to be your night.

ADRIAN: I'm cool. Really.

DOUG: Are we still buds?

ADRIAN: Yeah.

DOUG: Let me buy a beer. What do you say?

ADRIAN: Sure.

DOUG: Danielle, I'm sorry. That wasn't me. It's Charley's fault. Will you please stay?

DANIELLE: I don't know.

DOUG: Please? Tell her Adrian we talk shit all the time.

ADRIAN: Yeah, we talk shit.

DANIELLE: Are you all right?

ADRIAN: I'm fine, Danielle.

DANIELLE: Yeah?

ADRIAN: Yeah.

DANIELLE: Okay, I'll stay.

DOUG: Great, two beers and another glass of wine, Danielle?

DANIELLE: Sure.

(Dance music is heard.)

DOUG: Hey, Adrian why don't you go dance with Danielle?

ADRIAN: What?

DOUG: Yeah, she loves to dance.

ADRIAN: No, really?

DANIELLE: Yeah, but I thought we were—

DOUG: It's Adrian's night.

ADRIAN: If Danielle doesn't want to—

DANIELLE: No, no, I do.

ADRIAN: Okay.

DOUG: Yeah, I'll get us some drinks. You dance.

DANIELLE: Okay…

DOUG: Okay!

(ADRIAN and DANIELLE get up to dance as DOUG looks on. End.)

Union
Scene Four
By Kirsten Greenidge

A bus station bench. SIMON *sits, duffel bag at his feet.* SIMON *writes.*

SIMON: "Dear Maggie…" no. "Dear Margaret…" no. "Dearest…" ah, who the heck writes "Dearest"? Shoot.

(CAMILLE stands behind JANE. JANE types at an old computer with two fingers. CAMILLE reads over JANE's shoulder.)

JANE: Wait'll everyone reads this. They'll love it; *I* love it; who couldn't love it?

CAMILLE: You need two s's there.

JANE: I didn't ask for help.

CAMILLE: You want it to sound right or not?

(JANE and CAMILLE look at each other.
MARGARET, envelope in hand. Turns it over, then opens it carefully and reads.)

SIMON: "Hey Maggie." *(Considers this. Likes it.)* "It's me, Simon. Never written a letter before. Except that time the Sunday school teacher made us write to Baby Jesus. At least I think you'll get this."

JANE: Well how's it supposed to sound, if you're so smart?

CAMILLE: Move over.

JANE: *(As she moves over:)* Don't erase any— *(With flourish,* CAMILLE *presses delete.)* Camille—

CAMILLE: Fresh start. *(JANE watches as CAMILLE types.)* If we want people to vote for this thing, we gotta give them something real to believe in. Your movie's over, my friend.

JANE: *(Reads as CAMILLE types.)* Oh. *(Reads. Nodding:)* Oh. *(Reads.)* How'd you get good at this?

CAMILLE: I'm a genius.

(CAMILLE laughs. JANE laughs. CAMILLE types.)

JANE: Heard from Les?

CAMILLE: You?

JANE: My movie's over. You said it yourself.

CAMILLE: Two weeks ago he was Warren Beatty.

JANE: I don't make a good Norma Rae. I can't even write a manifesto, never mind get a whole town to believe it.

CAMILLE: We should have waited—

SIMON: "—I was never so good at waiting, Maggie, you know that. On the team, in high school, when Les used to run the field, flying past everyone like he was on fire, I used to get clobbered, just pummeled. Wind knocked out of me; the taste of blood on my tongue; and I'd wait there, in the grass, in the mud, to see if someone'd come see about me, help me up. I'd wait only a little bit, because in the pit of my stomach I would always worry no one would, that everyone'd leave me for hours, not even miss me, carry on with the game 'cause when it came right down to it, I didn't matter. And I'm no genius but the way I figure there's no reason to wait to find out no one cares about you, that no one's gonna come down that field and hold out their hand to help you up, make sure your wind comes back, make sure you swallow the blood so your tongue can taste like normal again. These last two weeks I been thinking: some things never/change—"

JANE: Change can't wait, Camille. The more I thought about it, the more Les and I talked about it—we used to have these great talks. Late at night—

CAMILLE: Spare me the details.

JANE: It wasn't like that. It was… it was like the chance, for the first time in our lives, to be a part of something bigger than ourselves, than this stupid little factory/.

SIMON: "…/factory ain't got enough for me right now. The way I see things, that factory's watching me lie on the ground, in the mud, stomach empty and rumbling. While Harry and the old man cut corners and stay made in the shade, we're all waiting it out in the heat. Well I'm not so stupid I'm gonna sit around and fry, so I'm gonna try my hand out West. Farms. Or. Other people's farms. Way I figure, you got enough mouths to worry about. Don't need one more. This way I don't have to cross lines, don't have to get Jane and Les all upset, but I don't have to become some other mouth to feed, neither. 'Cause the thing is, I won't go hungry for some fancy noble cause—"

JANE: Because I'm tired of giving myself up to it. I've done that enough already. Since I was sixteen. My first day of work?: my momma had this half-frown on her face the minute I got home. I spent the whole day walking fabric up and down the floor. Left foot bloody from three blisters. Shirt collar soaked with sweat. My momma just pulled out the washtub she keeps under the footstool, in the kitchen, that half-frown frozen on her face, Epsom salts in her fist. Her eyes were talking to me: This is the way of the world. Like a brick it hit me. Pow. Right square in my middle. It was like, this is why that teacher in the ninth grade, 'member her?

CAMILLE: Miss Olson.

JANE: Yeah, her. I thought: this is why she brought in all those community college pamphlets. 'Member how she did that?

CAMILLE: She didn't last but six months.

JANE: Never listened to her anyway. Maybe should've. But my whole family works at this mill. Until we started those meetings I didn't think I had a choice. Brick nearly crumbled to pieces when we started those meetings.

SIMON: "People got to eat, I used to say at those meetings. What about them? We walk out, we start something too big to cook all the way through and then what we got? No food but plenty of mouths. No work but too many hands."

JANE: For the first time in my entire life I feel bigger than one of those needles in those machines. I thought Les understood that. I thought we were the same.

SIMON: "I'll send word when I settle—"

JANE: But his spine's as slithery as Harry's.

SIMON: "—you take care of those kids of yours and send word when everything's over, when I can come back."

(MARGARET folds the letter, places it back in the envelope, takes out the fliers, looks at them.)

CAMILLE: And done.

(Pushes a button on the computer. It prints.

CAMILLE hands it to JANE.

JANE reads.)

JANE: *How'd* you get good at this?

CAMILLE: Well let's hurry and make copies. We've got a union to vote in.

(JANE and CAMILLE leave, manifesto in hand, bump into MARGARET, whose fliers spill everywhere.)

MARGARET: Sorry—

CAMILLE: *(Reading a flier:)* What is this?

MARGARET: Harry. He said if I—. The whole factory—. Mexico—: I just want my brother to come home.

(JANE holds up the manifesto, Norma-Rae-style, to the audience.)

JANE: But our movie's not over.

(Lights out.

End.)

Wake God's Man

Scene Four
By Julie Marie Myatt

The body bag is empty, and the body is gone from above the stage. The MAN enters with a broom and sweeps the pecan shells across the stage.

MAN: There's always a trace of something left behind from the appetites of man. Always a crack or a shell or a wrapper or a sock or a feather or a trail of blood. A laugh. A scream. A voice…. Unheard. Somewhere. Left behind. Somewhere in the wake. Of the action…. *(Continues to sweep.)* …what a mess, these nuts—so much trouble just to get that little bit of pleasure—I call them *pecans,* while some call them *peecans*—I guess I can't help myself. I must have a few guilty pleasures. You think you can give them all up, and you do, you do, give them up, but the appetite— the appetite has a mind of its own, and I'm not sure I was expecting that—I was a young man when I was called, Idealist, what did I know?— and I'm not sure God understands how powerful that appetite is, that to give it up is—is not always possible.

(BETH enters. Kicks a pecan shell towards him.)

BETH: You missed one.

MAN: Thank you.

BETH: Who you talking to?

MAN: No one.

BETH: God abandon you?

MAN: Perhaps.

BETH: Good.

(He continues to sweep.)

MAN: You always did have a sharp tongue…. Of course, I always liked your family. Good sense of humor. I enjoyed your company.

BETH: I am aware of that tragedy. Your hatred would have been more welcome. Sir.

MAN: Well, your hatred is not welcome here, at the moment, if that's what you've come for. I'm tired. Confused. And dead.

BETH: No kidding.

(She looks him over.)

So this is what you looked like as a young man?

MAN: This is the way I remember. Myself.

BETH: Dig the hair. Very stylish.

MAN: I thought so.

BETH: Hell. At least you had hair then. I still want to vomit every time I think of the top of your bald head. The way the sweat would bead up on that oily skin. Bastard—

MAN: Move along. I don't like that kind of talk. I've got work to do.

BETH: Oh?

MAN: There's mess everywhere.

BETH: God making you earn your keep now? Or is that the devil's work? Or. Could be Limbo. I've heard that's a pretty irritating place to be.

(He looks at her.)

MAN: Depends on the company.... You know, I worked hard every day of my life—

BETH: At hiding things—

MAN: Serving people—

BETH: Silencing—

MAN: Bringing God into open hearts—

BETH: Putting fear into sacred places—

MAN: Providing refuge—

BETH: Stealing childhoods.

MAN: And this is the thanks I get.

BETH: You want wings?

MAN: Do you want revenge?

BETH: I want my childhood back.

MAN: Who doesn't?

(BETH hadn't considered that.

Silence. MAN keeps sweeping.)

We all suffer something. I had my faults, but what I gave to so many cannot be compared to what I might have—what you think I've taken from you.... I was the eyes and ears and conscience of this town, without judgment—

BETH: How could you judge, when your sins were worse, were greater, so much more serious than any you might have heard?

MAN: I was a good man.

BETH: No. You were not.

MAN: I was a good man with, with, appetites that I tried to control, I tried very hard, but even I could not control some things—I gave up everything for this church. For this occupation. I gave up everything that I watched my congregation enjoy.

BETH: You picked the job. No one put a gun to your head and made you be a priest—

MAN: He made me. He picked me. I was Called. Do you know how much pressure, how much sacrifice, how much responsibility that is?

BETH: That sacrifice, that responsibility was just too much? Keeping your hands off young girls was just too much to ask, too much pressure?—

MAN: I once tried to kill myself. Does that make you feel better?

BETH: No.

MAN: But I was afraid of what would happen. After.

BETH: Fire and brimstone?

MAN: Worse. This. Cold reunion. The infinity of disgust.

(He looks directly at her.)

I am, I was a good man. So very many prayers brushed across my lips in one lifetime—kisses to the heavens—but, those, those... I don't know what to call them—did not, could not, come close enough for discussion. It was lonely. To tell Him all my secrets but the frightened ones that ask, that might have asked, for the biggest kind of forgiveness— You don't understand. I tried to control myself. I'm sorry but I did try. I tried—

(BETH rips the broom from his hands.)

BETH: No. Sir. You didn't. Try.

(She brushes the pile of shells across the floor.)

MAN: I did *try*. Every day—

BETH: *Try?*... *Try* and tell that "poor me" story to someone who gives a shit. You will not get my forgiveness or peace or compassion. You made your bed. You made those choices, you did those things, that ruined my sisters. And me. You *did* those things, *to* us. You earned that disgust. You get nothing from me but contempt and good-bye.

(BETH gives him back the broom.
She walks off stage.
End.)

In This House
Scene Four
By John Walch

Kismet

The small house on fire. A cloud of smoke. A COOK (played by the actor who plays ROBERT) appears wearing an apron and holding the hood to a BBQ grill. The COOK places the hood over the house on fire. The sound of sizzling meat. The COOK lifts up the hood from the BBQ grill. A cloud of smoke and KATHY and BILL appear somewhere else on the stage standing beside a table with a checked tablecloth.

BILL: Smells good, I'm hungry.

KATHY: She's ten minutes late, how could she be—oh my God, she's changed her mind.

BILL: Honey, I'm sure she hasn't. Now, I'm gonna grab a menu from the counter.

KATHY: How can you think of food?

BILL: You'll feel better after a little brisket. …Kath, we can't wait forever.

KATHY: We've waited for three years already, we can wait ten minutes longer. Besides, how rude would it be if she walks in and we're covered with BBQ sauce?

BILL: We could get an appetizer.

KATHY: We could also get a Chinese baby, but we're not.

BILL: I still don't get what you have against the Chinese baby.

KATHY: It's not us, Bill. It's not me. I feel defective enough already; I don't need a constant reminder. I want—I need to at least be able to pretend that this baby is from me, us.

BILL: It will be.

KATHY: If she agrees. Don't blow this Bill, please.

BILL: Here comes the blame again—

KATHY: I'm not blaming, it's just the reality, because of your record—

BILL: You make it sound like I did hard time; I was twenty years old doing what every stupid college kid does.

KATHY: But you got caught. And now private adoption—this girl—is our best shot, but she has to like us. So forget about food, sit down, and hold my hand lovingly!

(Beat.)

BILL: You brought the pictures?

KATHY: Yes, Bill, but I'm not sure we should show them. Especially the nursery, what if she sees how adorable it is and changes her mind like that last girl, I can't go through that again. And the girl before her met ten couples—Oh my God, what if that's why she's late? 'Cause she's having tea or tapas with some other couple and she's just loving it—them—and has already made up her mind and we've lost this baby. Why did I suggest BBQ! That was so stupid, I'm such an idiot.

BILL: Kathy, relax. This one's different, I got a good feeling.

(Beat.)

KATHY: I want this so much, Bill.

BILL: I know you do, we both do.

(COOK raises the hood of the BBQ. A cloud of smoke. KAYLA appears, seven months pregnant. She sits at the table with BILL and KATHY and flips through a stack of photos.)

KAYLA: *(Looking at a picture.)* —It's a beautiful house. I told your wife that over the phone the other day—

BILL: Did she tell you we renovated it ourselves?

KATHY: Bill….

BILL: She's interested, right Kayla?

KATHY: She's not interested, Bill, right Kayla?

KAYLA: Well… I just. The, um, my ex— Robert. The father. He's a carpenter. That's what he does—restores things. Kind of ironic, when you think about it.

(KAYLA continues to look at the pictures.)

BILL: Well don't you worry, we did it all ourselves. No Roberts came in our house. Took us seven years and a lot of mistakes, but we didn't want anybody telling us where to put a window, or what type of tile to use in the bathroom, we wanted to take responsibility for every…

(KATHY shoots him a look, he falls silent. KAYLA is absorbed in a particular picture. Pause.)

KATHY: Bill, why don't you get us something to eat?

BILL: Right, yeah, I'm starving. Kayla, what can I get you?

KAYLA: Oh, maybe just some coleslaw.

BILL: Come on, you're eating for two. If you can't make up your mind, try the three-meat sampler.

KAYLA: I'm, uh, actually vegetarian, so the slaw will be fine.

KATHY: You know, the slaw actually sounds good for me too. *(To KAYLA.)* We hardly ever eat meat. *(To BILL.)* And Bill, you could stand to cut back. How about the vegetarian sampler?

BILL: But it's BBQ—

KAYLA: No, you should— I didn't mean— You should get what you want.

KATHY: And slaw is what I want. I love slaw and our child will be eating a lot of slaw, not all this junk.

KAYLA: It's okay, I don't mind— I mean, I don't want you thinking that I want you to raise, um, her, the same way I would. Sure, it'd be great if I knew she never ate fast food or anything processed—

KATHY: Believe me, bologna is something she will only know as an abstract concept, right Bill?

BILL: Right... what am I ordering?

KAYLA: Order what you always order. I want you to be yourselves.

BILL: I like the sound of that. Anything to drink with your slaw, Kayla?

KAYLA: Sure, I'll have a beer. ... Kidding. I'm just kidding. Water with lemon is fine.

BILL: Sense of humor, I like it. Kathy?

KATHY: Of course I like it! I like everything.

BILL: I meant, to drink?

KATHY: Oh...

(COOK raises the hood on the BBQ grill. A cloud of smoke. BILL disappears. KAYLA loses herself in the picture again. Pause.)

KATHY: If you don't like anything in there, we can change it: the curtains, the crib, the rocking chair—

KAYLA: No, no, it's . . . perfect. But hard.

KATHY: Kayla, I'm sorry, we should have taken that one out. We, Bill, thought you might want to see where—maybe—she might sleep, grow up— I'm sorry, we should have waited to show you the nursery, if this... progressed.

KAYLA: No, I'm... happy? ...It's super-cute. I can't believe you did all this.

KATHY: Well, we—we've had a lot of time and when you're waiting it's good to have something concrete to throw yourself into... hanging wallpaper, amazingly therapeutic. Bill was more from the "build it and they will come" school, but for me, it was a refuge.

(Beat.)

I lost one myself. A girl. She didn't have a heart. Can you believe that? This little girl growing inside me, but she didn't have a heart.

(Beat.)

Then all the troubles and tests began and—I don't know why I'm telling you all this—but not long after that we started on this room and thinking about well… meeting someone like you.

KAYLA: I'm glad you did.

KATHY: Really?

KAYLA: Yeah, I thought this was going to be such a nightmare process. How would I know who to pick? But my roommate told me I'd feel it if it's a good fit. And she was totally right. I feel it. Kismet.

KATHY: Kismet, what a great way of putting it.

KAYLA: Be a cool name too. Kismet. Kismet Anna-Achak-Nuttah-Numees-Nadie-Alsoonse-Hurit-Hausis Thomas.

KATHY: We had narrowed it down to Claire and Nicole, but I'm sure Bill would be open to—

KAYLA: No, it's cool. That's yours to decide, but Bill was good with the middle name?

KATHY: Oh… sure. You know he seems like a meat and potatoes man now, but he's actually quite open-minded. It's not a problem.

KAYLA: That's great. Great.

(Beat. KAYLA looks at picture again.)

Um, Kathy, could I ask for one more thing? I mean, besides the name?

KATHY: Of course, Kayla, whatever you need.

KAYLA: Could I… have this picture? I swear, it's the *last* thing I'll ask for, and I mean the *last*. You know what I mean?

KATHY: You're talking about contact?

KAYLA: Yeah, contact. I don't want any.

KATHY: But? The whole reason to do an open adoption is so you can see—

KAYLA: Look, I know, but I need to set this down so I can go on, and if I am constantly thinking about… I've thought a lot about this and I know what the books say, recommend, but it's not for me, you know? I don't want to see her.

(COOK raises the hood on the BBQ grill. A cloud of smoke. The sound of a baby crying. When the smoke clears the COOK is gone and in his place is the perfect house as we first saw it and a girl we haven't seen before [played by the actress who plays LYNNE]. Although we don't know it yet, this is CLAIRE ANNA. KAYLA and KATHY remain.)

CLAIRE: The books tell you different things. Some say you should, others (the older ones mostly) advise that unless there's a "dire" emergency, you shouldn't ever try to see her…

KAYLA: I *can't* see her… my baby.

CLAIRE: …My birth mother.

KAYLA: I mean I can barely even look at this picture, but I *can* look at it, because she's not in it. But if she were, I just— I would just keep wanting her back, and I can't live like that.

CLAIRE: By "dire" I'm guessing they mean something life and death like needing a bone-marrow transplant or a kidney, and not just years of wondering if I look like her, or imagining if she's happy, or if she likes the color red like me, but that's the way books are—open for interpretation.

(CLAIRE stoops to the small house and pulls a piece of red fabric from it. As she pulls, years pass, and she grows up. Lights begin to fall on KATHY and KAYLA.)

KAYLA: I just want her to be happy, and I see this picture and I can *imagine* her happy, which makes me happy and that's why I had to do it this way. But I can't see her. This picture lets me imagine, and that's all I ever want. No contact. Promise.

KATHY: I promise.

KAYLA: You think I'm heartless?

KATHY: Actually… I was thinking how alike we are. Kismet.

KAYLA: Kismet.

(The lights fade completely out on KAYLA and KATHY. They exit. CLAIRE finishes pulling the red fabric from the house and puts it around her neck as if she was getting ready to go out.)

CLAIRE: My parents tell me different things too. Dad says:

(CLAIRE removes the roof of the house; BILL's voice comes from it.)

BILL: *(Voice from the house.)* I'd be happy to help, Claire, when you feel ready to contact her.

CLAIRE: When Mom hears that, she politely reminds me to remember to take the knife out of her own heart after I've made contact. She also says:

KATHY: *(Voice from the house.)* That girl—

CLAIRE : —That's the only way she ever refers to her: *that girl.*

KATHY: *(Voice from the house.) That girl* wanted no contact. *That girl* made me promise over coleslaw that there'd be no contact!

CLAIRE: Coleslaw? What does coleslaw have to do with it? Me? Then Dad shouts back:

BILL: *(Voice from the house.)* She also made us promise that we would name her Anna-Numchuck-Nutcase, and you broke that promise! It's my turn to break a promise!

(She places the roof back on the house. The voices become muffled, indistinct. Lights fade except for a spotlight on the tiny house.)

CLAIRE: I am in my room, door closed, hearing it through the floorboards and the walls. They argue on and on, year after year about who said what, who was right, wrong. And then they argue about the name, exactly what it was, something Indian, they can never remember. But I listen, listen to them try…

(The voices inside the house fade as the light on the house fades, until all is dark, silent, and the house sleeps again.
End.)

END OF PLAY